THE FORCES IN AMERICAN ECONOMIC GROWTH
SERIES

Under the General Editorship of Alfred D. Chandler, Jr.

Slavery and the Southern Economy

Slavery and the Southern Economy

Sources and Readings

COMPILED AND EDITED BY

Harold D. Woodman

UNIVERSITY OF MISSOURI

Harcourt, Brace & World, Inc.

NEW YORK · CHICAGO · BURLINGAME

In Memory of My Mother

Library of Congress Catalog Card Number: 66–18864

THE FORCES IN AMERICAN ECONOMIC GROWTH SERIES

THE *Forces in American Economic Growth* series *provides a documentary record of the building of the American economy. Each book in the series concentrates on the economic force or forces that generated the most compelling pressure for change at key junctures in American history. In each volume the men responsible for change speak for themselves. By presenting such a record the editors hope to enhance the reader's sense of economic reality, his awareness of underlying historic currents, and his ability to investigate and interpret business and economic change and growth.*

The series attempts to achieve this goal by providing illustration and by permitting analysis. The documents presented are intended to show how new patterns of economic action occurred and how American entrepreneurs, managers, engineers, financiers, business analysts, workers, and labor-union leaders carried on their various activities at different periods of history. The record provides more than mere illustration. The documents have been collected and presented in a way to encourage analysis and interpretation. They raise questions of why and what as well as how. Why did new ways come when they did and in the way they did? What stimulated and what hindered change? What was the role of personality in producing innovation and bringing economic growth?

The series, in short, supplies the record, the source materials, that a reader can use to form his own judgment about the nature of economic and historical change. It will allow him to be his own historian and his own interpreter of the changing American business and economic scene.

ALFRED D. CHANDLER, JR.

CONTENTS

A GENERAL INTRODUCTION TO THE READINGS   1

STATISTICAL TABLES   13

PART I

Slavery and the Planter

INTRODUCTION   21

THE READINGS   25

1] Standard of Living of the Planter Class   25
    a] The Southern Yankee: Successful Businessman (D. R. Hundley, *Social Relations in Our Southern States,* 1860)   25
    b] The Wealthy Rice Planter: Unpretentious Gentleman (Solon Robinson, "Rice Estate of Gov. Aiken, of S.C.," 1852)   27
    c] The Small-Scale Planter: Shabby Middle Class (Frederick Law Olmsted, *A Journey in the Back Country,* 1860)   29

2] Comparative Advantages and Disadvantages in the Employment of Slave Labor   30
    a] Competitive Advantages of Negro Slavery Under the Plantation System (Lewis Cecil Gray, *History of Agriculture in the Southern United States to 1860,* 1933)   30
    b] Disadvantages of an Overcapitalized and Inelastic Labor Force (Ulrich B. Phillips, "The Economic Cost of Slaveholding in the Cotton Belt," 1905)   35

3] Measurement of Income from Planting with Slave Labor   45
    a] High Production Costs Absorb Profits (Charles Sackett Sydnor, *Slavery in Mississippi,* 1933)   45
    b] Multiplicity of Income Increases Profits (Thomas P. Govan, "Was Plantation Slavery Profitable?" 1942)   51
    c] Planters' Profits Equal Returns from Other Forms of Investment (Alfred H. Conrad and John R. Meyer, "The Economics of Slavery in the Ante Bellum South," 1958)   66

4] Future Prospects for Production by Slave Labor 97
  a] Limited Supply of Land to Stifle Slavery (Charles W. Rams-
    dell, "The Natural Limits of Slavery Expansion," 1929) 97
  b] Ample Supply of Land Available for Slavery's Expansion
    (Lewis Cecil Gray, *History of Agriculture in the Southern
    United States to 1860*, 1933) 106

PART II

Slavery and the Nonslaveholder

INTRODUCTION 113

THE READINGS 116

1] Planter-Farmer Competition 116
  a] Farmer Unable to Compete with Slaveowning Planter (Lewis
    Cecil Gray, *History of Agriculture in the Southern United
    States to 1860*, 1933) 116
  b] Opportunities Available for Ambitious and Efficient Farmer
    (Robert R. Russel, "The Effects of Slavery Upon Nonslave-
    holders in the Ante-Bellum South," 1941) 117

2] The Yeomen 127
  a] Prosperous Middle-Class Majority (Frank L. and Harriet C.
    Owsley, "The Economic Basis of Society in the Late Ante-
    Bellum South," 1940) 127
  b] Victims of the Slave System (Fabian Linden, "Economic
    Democracy in the Slave South: An Appraisal of Some Recent
    Views," 1946) 143

3] The Poor Whites 155
  a] Hereditary Misfits (D. R. Hundley, *Social Relations in Our
    Southern States*, 1860) 155
  b] Unfortunates Trapped by Environment (Frederick Law
    Olmsted, *A Journey in the Back Country*, 1860) 157

PART III

Slavery and the Slave

INTRODUCTION   165

THE READINGS   167

1] Slavery as a Civilizing Agency   167
   a] Trains Barbarians (Albert Taylor Bledsoe, "Liberty and
      Slavery: or, Slavery in the Light of Moral and Political
      Philosophy," 1860)   167
   b] Educates Backward Workers (Ulrich B. Phillips, *American
      Negro Slavery*, 1918)   169

2] Slavery as a Demoralizing and Brutalizing Force   170
   a] Limits Adequate Training (Frederick Law Olmsted, *A
      Journey in the Back Country*, 1860)   170
   b] Crushes Independent Intellectual Development (Frederick
      Douglass, *Life and Times of Frederick Douglass*, 1882)   171

PART IV

Slavery and Economic Development

INTRODUCTION   179

THE READINGS   182

1] Irrelevance of Slavery to Southern Development   182
   a] Problems of an Agricultural Economy (Robert R. Russel,
      "The General Effects of Slavery upon Southern Economic
      Progress," 1938)   182
   b] Neglect of Commerce and Manufacturing (J. D. B. De Bow,
      The Industrial Resources of the Southern and Western States,
      1852)   194

2] Economic Advantage of Slavery: A Source of National Wealth
   (David Christy, *Cotton Is King*, 1860)   196

3] Economic Disadvantages of Slavery
   a] Stifles Progress (Hinton Rowan Helper, *The Impending Crisis
      of the South: How to Meet It*, 1857)   200

b] Creates an Ignorant and Inefficient Labor Force (J. E. Cairnes, *The Slave Power: Its Character, Career and Probable Designs: Being an Attempt to Explain the Real Issues Involved in the American Contest,* 1863)   206

c] Discourages the Development of Manufacturing (Fabian Linden, "Repercussions of Manufacturing in the Ante-Bellum South," 1940)   215

d] Retards the Development of a Home Market (Eugene D. Genovese, "The Significance of the Slave Plantation for Southern Economic Development," 1962)   223

PART V

Legacy of Slavery:
The Economy Since the Civil War

INTRODUCTION   237

THE READINGS   239

1] Need for Plantation Organization (Ulrich B. Phillips, "The Economics of the Plantation," 1903)   239

2] Comparative Economic Development of the West and the South (Douglas F. Dowd, "A Comparative Analysis of Economic Development in the American West and South," 1956)   243

3] Stultifying Effects of Tradition (William H. Nicholls, *Southern Tradition and Regional Progress,* 1960)   255

CONCLUSION   259

SUGGESTED READINGS   260

A GENERAL INTRODUCTION
TO THE READINGS

A CHRONICLER of the early years of the Jamestown settlement in Virginia noted the sharp contrast between English and Spanish fortunes in the New World. How lucky the Spanish were "to happen in those parts where were infinite numbers of people, whoe had manured the ground with that providence that it afforded victuall at all times," and who, even more fortunately, "had the use of gold and silver." Here was a fabulous fortune, easily available to the Spaniard by "spoil and pillage" of the Indians, and not requiring "the labours of [his] owne hands."

No such treasure awaited the English settlers: "We chanced in a land even as God made it." A scattered and backward Indian population, "ignorant of the knowledge of gold, or silver, or any commodities," offered no opportunities for pillage or even for trade. Yet this account, written in 1612, was not pessimistic. The English ventures could be successful if colonies were permanently established and if the settlers learned to "bring to perfection the commodities of the countrie."

In 1612, there was little in the settlers' experiences to support such optimism. Few had survived the "starving time" of the previous years. Virginians still faced the elemental task of survival, and talk of prosperity and wealth probably seemed unreal. But the sanguine expectations of the chronicler did prove to be accurate. The English settlers soon discovered that they had found a treasure in the New World—not gold, but something which would prove far more valuable—fertile land and tobacco, a crop which found a ready market in Europe.

Land could mean wealth to those who would exploit it and export a cash crop, but the abundance of land meant its easy accessibility to almost everyone. The resulting labor shortage in the midst of economic opportunity led to an ironic contradiction in the American economy. On the one hand, labor commanded a premium and the result was the beginnings of the freest, most independent, as well as the highest paid, working class the world had ever known. On the other hand, these very same conditions encouraged the creation of servile labor systems: first indentured servitude and then slavery.

Bound servants and slaves were used throughout the English colonies in America, but the greatest numbers were concentrated in the South. Thus the shortage of labor in the colonies also helped to create sectional differences which time served to widen. By the nineteenth century, slavery had become the South's peculiar institution.

The Development of Colonial Slavery

When John Rolfe reported the arrival in 1619 of "a Dutch man of warre that sold us twenty negars," he was recording the purchase of indentured servants; at least this is how the English colonists—if not the Dutch sellers—seemed to have viewed these first Negroes in Virginia. Within a few decades, however, sharp distinctions began to be made between Negro and white servants imported into the colony. Gradually, the Negro servant emerged as a slave. Limited terms of service became lifetime servitude; the offspring of Negro servants became lifetime servants.

While Negroes in Virginia were being transformed from indentured servants into slaves, their numbers increased. By the end of the seventeenth century, the 28,000 Negroes—most of them slaves—who lived in the southern colonies were already a more important source of labor than the indentured whites. Ownership of Negro slaves seemed to have many obvious advantages in this place of high wages and relatively cheap land. Indentured servants had to be replaced after their service of five to ten years was over; the lifetime service of the slave provided a more stable work force. Moreover, white servants often ran away before their term of service had expired; the Negro slave, set apart by race, could not escape by melting into the population in a distant community. The number of Negro slaves increased rapidly in the eighteenth century. By 1780, more than half a million slaves lived in the United States, 90 percent of them in the South.

Slavery appeared to have solved the problem of a labor shortage on the colonial tobacco, rice, and indigo plantations, but there were other economic woes which plagued the southern planter. Soaring tobacco production drove prices down and many planters found themselves deeply in debt to their London merchants. Few planters traced their difficulties to slavery. They blamed the London merchants for depressing tobacco prices and inflating the cost of English exports, often adding that the merchants could exploit them only because the navigation laws drove out foreign competition. The refusal of the English to accept colonial schemes for crop reduction and issues of paper money to relieve the distress of tobacco growers was another often heard complaint.

When planters did have doubts about slavery they questioned it on social, rather than on economic, grounds. Many voiced the fear that the growing numbers of an alien race posed a social danger to the whites; those living in areas where there were large numbers of slaves were apprehensive of possible revolt. Only a few questioned the profitability of the slave system.

Some of the colonial opponents of slavery questioned its moral and ethical justification, an attitude which became especially articulate during the period of revolutionary ferment. For many patriots, support of slavery in the face of colonial demands for liberty and equality seemed gross hypocrisy. Wrote Abigail Adams to her husband in 1774, "It has always appeared a most iniquitous scheme to me to fight ourselves for what we are daily robbing and plundering from those who have as good a right to freedom as we have."

Thomas Jefferson, who was well aware of the tobacco planters' economic problems and who had the opportunity to observe the operation of the slave system first-hand, did not connect the two but based his opposition to slavery on moral grounds. In his draft of the Declaration of Independence he accused the king of waging "cruel war against human nature itself" for supporting the slave trade, a crime compounded by his "suppressing every legislative attempt to prohibit or to restrain this execrable commerce."

Jefferson's attack was deleted from the Declaration to propitiate delegates from both North and South. New Englanders remembered that merchants from their colonies had long been active in the slave trade. Southerners were reluctant to accept an attack on a trade in which they had, as buyers, participated, nor could they fail to see the logic of permitting its inclusion: success in the revolution would remove all restraints on closing the slave trade; indeed, it might open the way to the emancipation of the slaves.

Successful revolution did not solve the South's economic difficulties. On the contrary, problems seemed to have worsened. The tobacco market was glutted; prices were low, and there seemed little prospect of an improvement. Rice could be grown only in a few places, thereby limiting any significant expansion, and indigo production became unprofitable when British bounties on the commodity were withdrawn. In addition, a postwar deflation depressed prices, including those of slaves.

Planters with heavy investments in slaves, faced with low prices, a glutted market, and land which had lost much of its fertility, began to wonder if slavery had lost its economic value. Said George Washington in 1794, "Were it not then, that I am principled ag[ains]t selling negroes, as you would do cattle in the market, I would not, in twelve months from this date, be possessed of one, as a slave. I shall be happily mistaken, if they are not found to be a very troublesome species of property 'ere many years pass over our heads."

Washington reflected the opinions of some of the older tobacco planters who were attempting to turn from tobacco to general farming in an effort to resurrect their exhausted lands and find more profitable production. In his *Notes on the State of Virginia* (written, 1782), Thomas Jefferson recorded that wheat was beginning to replace tobacco as the main crop in his native state, and that he expected the process to continue. Virginians could not compete with tobacco growers on the "fresh and fertile lands" in the "western country on the Mississippi" and in the "midlands of Georgia," he explained, and were abandoning the growing of tobacco, "a culture productive of infinite wretchedness."

Yet, as they gave up tobacco, Virginia planters became aware of a new problem. General farming required less labor, and many farmers found their old slave force an economic burden. If, like Washington, the Virginia planters were reluctant to sell their slaves and break up families, they found themselves faced with the burden of supporting unproductive labor. Moreover, if the trend toward general farming continued, the problem of a surplus labor force would become worse. Many concluded that they would be better off if the slaves were freed, most adding that the free Negroes should be colonized because an alien race could not be absorbed into the white population.

But such attitudes did not prevail. In 1786, Jefferson noted that even in Virginia, where "the disposition to emancipate them is strongest," the majority opposed the ending of slavery. Emancipation in Maryland and North Carolina had even less support, and in South Carolina and Georgia there was "not the smallest symptom" of the sentiment. Jefferson was well aware of the reason: fresh tobacco lands were being opened to production. After the Revolution, tobacco exports from Georgia and South Carolina rose sharply, and the crop was grown in increasing amounts in the North Carolina back country. Moreover, periodic improvements in prices because of drought, speculation, or other causes would bring some of the older lands back into tobacco production. Given these circumstances, suggestions for the emancipation and colonization of the region's labor force were not favorably received.

Even if the majority of the planters were not ready to give up slavery, it seemed clear that the future of the institution was bleak. The "fresh and fertile lands" described by Jefferson might continue to support profitable tobacco planting with slave labor, but it was obvious that the tobacco market was limited, and a significant expansion of the slave system appeared unlikely.

Yet, even as Jefferson and Washington wrote, changes were already occurring which would revitalize the system of slavery in the South.

The Rise of the Cotton Kingdom

A remarkable series of inventions was working a revolutionary change in the British textile industry. The process had begun as early as 1733 when the weaver-mechanic John Kay accelerated the entire weaving process by perfecting the flying shuttle. Faster, more efficient weaving required greater quantities of thread and consequently stimulated a search for spinning devices to replace the slow and cumbersome spinning wheel. The first step in this direction was the spinning jenny, devised by James Hargreaves in the 1760's, which allowed a single workman to spin at first four, and later as many as eighty or one hundred threads at once.

At first the new techniques were limited by their reliance on human motive power, but in 1769, Richard Arkwright patented his water frame, thereby introducing the principle of power spinning. A decade later,

Samuel Crompton added a new improvement in spinning by combining features of both the jenny and the water frame; the resulting "crossbreed" became known as the mule. By 1790, Watt's steam engine was being used to run the mules. Edmund Cartwright, in the meantime (1785), had introduced his power loom, which eventually allowed mechanical power to be used in weaving.

These innovations in the textile industry led to an unprecedented increase in the demand for raw cotton. English imports jumped from an average of about one million pounds during the first half of the eighteenth century to about 56,000,000 pounds in 1800. Gradually the demand began to outstrip the traditional sources of English supply—the West Indies, the Isle of Bourbon, the Levant, and Brazil—and prices edged upward. Rising prices would soon lure southerners into cotton planting.

Cotton had been grown in the southern colonies since the founding of Jamestown, but it had never become a cash crop during the colonial period. Until the last quarter of the eighteenth century, the English demand had never been sufficient to induce commercial cotton growing. The Revolutionary War prevented Americans from feeling the initial effects of the spiraling English demand, but with the declaration of peace in 1783, southerners began to recognize the opportunities in cotton growing. Planters on the coast of South Carolina and Georgia and on the islands just off the coast found that the long-staple, black-seed cotton that grew so well on their lands was superior to that grown in the West Indies and brought a high price on the English market. With the profits from rice and indigo planting low, planters needed no urging to turn to the new and profitable cash crop, sea-island cotton.

A new cash crop had been found, but its value was limited to the few planters who had land along the coast. Long-staple cotton simply would not grow on lands removed even a short distance from the coast. To be sure, cotton was not unknown in the inland areas; some two or three million pounds were grown annually in the South Carolina and Georgia back country in the early 1790's. But this cotton was a short-staple variety. Its seeds were green, and they stuck to the staple with such tenacity that they had to be picked out, one by one, by hand. Even the prevailing high cotton prices could not pay for this laborious work, and short-staple cotton had little commercial value, its use confined to home manufacture.

Repeated efforts to grow the long-staple variety on interior lands were unsuccessful, as were efforts to cross the two varieties in hopes of producing an inland variety with seeds more easily removed. Then an enterprising Yankee visiting on a Georgia plantation solved the problem. In 1793, Eli Whitney perfected a working model of his cotton gin. Suddenly the growing of short-staple cotton became commercially feasible.

It would be difficult to overestimate the effects of this relatively simple technological innovation. Now the new cash crop, for which there seemed to be an inexhaustible demand, could be grown in the upland areas and in the fertile lands to the west. Cotton prices were high and the supply of good land appeared unlimited. An added benefit arose from Eli Whitney's failure to secure his invention, which meant there would be no monopoly prices for the essential gin.

Farmers who had been growing cotton for home use now expanded their production, and newcomers flocked into the upland regions of South Carolina and Georgia. The two million pounds grown in these states in the early 1790's jumped to about thirty million pounds in 1801; ten years later production had doubled. By 1815, a cotton kingdom had been established in central South Carolina and east central Georgia.

The new kingdom was not to be confined to the East. New lands in south central Alabama and on the rich Mississippi delta in northern Louisiana, Mississippi, Arkansas, and Tennessee soon yielded huge crops of cotton. By 1860, more than 4,500,000 bales, each averaging over 450 pounds, were produced in the United States. By then, too, the center of the cotton kingdom had shifted to the west. While Georgia and South Carolina still produced sizable crops, more than half the nation's cotton was grown in Mississippi, Alabama, and Louisiana; Texas and Arkansas were also heavy cotton producers.

Cotton spurred the rapid settlement of the vast southwestern area of the United States. The population of the South rose from less than two million in 1790 to more than eleven million in 1860. The Mississippi Territory had only 7,600 residents according to the census of 1800; by 1860 the population had jumped to 791,305. Alabama experienced an even more spectacular growth—from 1,250 in the territory in 1800 to 964,201 in 1860.

The entire country was affected by these changes in the South. Farmers moving into the Ohio Valley found a growing market for their food crops, since southern planters, eager to devote their entire energies to cotton growing, preferred to buy, rather than raise, the food they needed. The Mississippi River became a highway carrying northern foodstuffs to the expanding cotton kingdom, and the movement of population into the old Northwest proceeded rapidly. In the northeastern areas of the nation where it was increasingly difficult to compete in agricultural production with the rich lands opening in the West, people turned to shipping, insurance, and financial services and found many of their best customers in the cotton South. When the Northeast, in the 1830's and 1840's, turned also to manufacturing, the South became an important market for its goods, while the expansion of the textile industry in New England opened a new market there for the South's chief staple.

Southern cotton quickly became the nation's main export. Douglass C. North has calculated that as early as 1816–20, cotton comprised 39 percent of the total value of American exports. By the late 1830's, cotton's share of our total exports had climbed to 63 percent. In the last two decades before the Civil War, when American textile manufacturers were consuming about one quarter of the crop, cotton still accounted for half the nation's exports, despite the growing volume of exports from the agricultural West and the manufacturing East. Cotton, then, more than any other American product, helped pay for imports of manufactured goods and directly or indirectly induced the flow of foreign capital into the country.[1]

The Revival of Slavery

Thus, the growth of the cotton kingdom provided an immense stimulus to American economic development before the Civil War. At the same time, however, it revived the flagging institution of slavery. It is one of the ironies of American history that industrial progress, first in Britain and then in the United States, would help to perpetuate an anachronistic, servile labor system in a growing, expanding new nation which had been born under the slogan of securing life, liberty, and the pursuit of happiness for its people.

Although cotton could be grown by a small farmer with little investment except long hours of hard labor under the sun,[2] it was well suited to slave labor. Cultivation and picking kept a labor force busy most of the year. Late in the winter the ground had to be prepared for the planting in early spring. Throughout the summer there was steady work thinning the plants and chopping out the grass which perpetually threatened to choke the cotton. Late in August the bolls began to burst, announcing the start of a picking season that continued well into the winter. As picking progressed, the cotton had to be ginned, weighed, pressed into bales, wrapped in bagging, and then tied in preparation for its trip to market. After this work was completed, only a short period remained to repair fences, clean out ditches, cut firewood, and carry out other chores before preparations began for the planting of the next year's crop. Thus there was little time when slaves—who, unlike free workers, had to be supported whether they were working or not—were idle.

Cotton production also allowed for the close supervision slave labor required. In both hoeing and picking, the slaves could be moved across the fields in gangs, and, because cotton plants were low and did not hide the workers, a single man could supervise the labor of many.

The growing English demand, the availability of fertile lands, and the

---

[1] For a more detailed treatment of the effects of cotton on the growth of the national economy, see Stuart Bruchey, *Cotton and the Growth of the American Economy: 1790–1860* (New York: Harcourt, Brace & World, 1966), also in the Forces in American Economic Growth series.

[2] This was not true of two other southern staple crops. Rice could be grown only on land which could be flooded. Such land was expensive, as was the mechanical apparatus needed to control the water. Sugar production required a large investment in machinery. Thus, while many small farmers grew cotton (and tobacco), rice and sugar were grown only by the larger planters.

suitability of slavery to cotton production meant that as cotton moved west so, too, did slavery. Many planters in the eastern areas took their slaves and moved to new lands in the West. Mrs. Susan Dabney Smedes recalls her father's decision:

> About the year 1835 a great many Virginians were induced to remove with their families to the far South. For several reasons Thomas [Dabney] began to consider the expediency of moving to the then new country. He was considered one of the most successful wheat and tobacco farmers in his part of the State. But the expensive style of living in Gloucester began to be a source of serious anxiety. He knew that with a young and growing family to educate and provide for the difficulty would be greater each year. He felt also the increasing difficulty of giving to his negroes the amount of nourishing food that he considered necessary for laboring people. In view of these facts, he made up his mind that he must leave his home in Virginia for a new one in the cotton-planting States.[3]

After a trip through Alabama, Louisiana, and Mississippi in search of suitable lands, Dabney found an area to his liking in Mississippi and "succeeded in purchasing four thousand acres from half a dozen small farmers."

Those who remained in the East found the West a growing market for their surplus slaves. Travelers often commented on the traffic. "We saw to-day, the common sight of companies of slaves travelling westwards," noted the English visitor Harriet Martineau. Thomas Dew, the Virginia proslavery advocate, wrote of his "efforts to obtain some thing like an accurate account of the number of negroes every year carried out of Virginia to the South and Southwest," and concluded that "upwards of 6,000 are yearly exported to other States. Virginia is, in fact, a *negro* raising State for other States; she produces enough for her own supply and six thousand for sale."

What had seemed to planters such as George Washington to have been a dying institution took on renewed vigor as the West was opened to cotton production. Georgia, with fewer than 30,000 slaves in 1790, had more than 460,000 in 1860; the slave population of both Alabama and Mississippi grew to over 435,000 during the same period; and in Louisiana, cotton growing (in the north) and sugar planting (in the south) induced a tenfold increase in the slave population between 1810 and 1860. Even in the older, eastern areas, the slave population grew, albeit at a slower rate. Tobacco in Virginia and North Carolina and cotton and rice in South Carolina supported a growing slave population. Furthermore, agricultural reformers such as Edmund Ruffin argued that exhausted lands could be renewed through crop rotation and by careful use of fertilizers. Many planters in the East were convinced and used slave labor to grow

[3] Susan Dabney Smedes, *Memorials of a Southern Planter* (Baltimore: Cushings, Bailey, 1887), p. 42.

grain crops on what had seemed to be useless lands. Moreover, the danger of a surplus of slaves, which had worried Virginia planters in the 1780's and 1790's, was no longer a matter of concern; planters in the West eagerly snatched up any slaves offered them.

The cotton kingdom—along with the lesser kingdoms of tobacco, rice, and sugar—became a slave kingdom as well. The rest of the country was ridding itself of slavery (the census lists only eighteen slaves in the Northeast in 1860) or refusing to adopt the institution (only Missouri of the north central states had a sizable number of slaves in 1860; Kansas and Nebraska had proslavery adherents, but the slaves themselves were not risked in the uncertain political climate of these territories). But in the South, slavery fastened itself securely to the economy. By 1810, the 657,000 slaves of 1790 had passed the million mark; by 1840, there were almost 2,500,000 slaves in the South; and in 1860, over 3,838,000 slaves lived in the region. At this time, slaves comprised over 50 percent of the population of Mississippi and South Carolina, over 45 percent of the population of Alabama and Louisiana, and almost 44 percent of the inhabitants of Georgia. For the South as a whole (that is, all the slave states including Missouri), about one out of three inhabitants was a slave, and in the lower South almost 45 percent of the people were slaves.

These slaves were not distributed evenly over the countryside but were concentrated in certain areas within each slave state. Where the land was most fertile and most conducive to the production of the South's staple crops, the ratio of slave to free population was high. Slavery, as David Donald has put it, "occupied the best of the South." Much—but not all—of the best land was worked by slaves, and the great bulk of the South's money crops was produced by slave labor.

The Economics of Slavery

With slavery so important to the southern economy, it should not be surprising that planters and others began to defend it as necessary and beneficial to the section. What many had regarded at one time as a necessary evil (necessary primarily as a means of race control rather than as a labor system), began to be considered as a positive good. This attitude reflected both the economic significance of slavery in the southern economy and a defensive attitude on the part of southerners faced with the criticisms of abolitionists and free-soilers in the North. The proslavery argument became a widespread, almost official doctrine in the slave states. Abolitionist and antislavery sentiments, which had always been given a hearing if not widespread support, were systematically squelched by law, social pressures, and often violence. By the early 1830's, antislavery societies had disappeared. Southerners who favored abolition, for the most part, held their peace or spoke from the relative safety of the North.

Matching the proslavery argument in the South was the flood of anti-slavery material which poured from the abolitionist presses in the North and, to a lesser degree, in Europe. Travelers added to the literature of controversy. Few who visited the South failed to record their impressions of slavery and to express warm feelings, sometimes sympathetic and sometimes antagonistic, about the South's peculiar institution.

The discussion ranged widely. Slavery was attacked on moral and theological grounds, for both sides found what they considered ample biblical support for their arguments. The law, the constitution, and historical precedent were all scrutinized carefully. Sometimes the antagonists considered the question of the economics of slavery, and in so doing they raised a problem which has vexed historians and economists to this day: Was slavery profitable?

Modern scholars seem to be no closer to agreement on the profitability of slavery than were those who argued the question before the Civil War. In part, disagreement persists in this problem, as in many other historical problems, from a paucity of information and from the possibility of different interpretations of the available information.

Planters generally kept few records. Many of those that were kept have been lost. Even when rather full records have been found, they fail to yield the conclusive evidence which would end controversy. Tax legislation, which requires businessmen to keep full records showing various sources of income and which demands a careful accounting of expenses, is, of course, of recent vintage. Ante-bellum planters were not required to distinguish, in their records, between personal services rendered by slaves as house servants or valets (a form of income) and work in the fields (a business expense). Depreciation allowances were not set by law, and business-minded planters (probably the minority) had only to reckon depreciation by rule of thumb, an evaluation seldom found in records. The death of a slave was obviously regarded as a loss, the extent of which was usually calculated on the basis of his replacement value. But the death of a field hand would be a business loss while that of a favored house servant would be a personal loss. The distinction is vital to a modern accountant, but it had little meaning for a planter.

The difficulty in solving the problem of slavery's profitability, however, goes deeper than the lack of full records. A more fundamental problem arises over definitions. Often those who debate the question and come to opposite conclusions are really debating different questions. Basic to any consideration of the question "Was slavery profitable?" is another: "For whom was slavery profitable?" For the slaveowner? For the slave? For the nonslaveholder? For the South? For the entire country? Unless the problem is very carefully defined in these terms, conflicting conclusions may not be contradictory at all, but may simply be answers to very different questions. It is entirely conceivable—and some have argued—that slavery was profitable to the slaveowner, harmful to the slave, irrelevant to the nonslaveholder, detrimental to the South, and very beneficial to the economic development of the entire country. With such a configuration, the broader question "Was slavery profitable?" becomes meaningless by itself.

Asking the specific question "For whom was slavery profitable?" is not simply breaking a large question into its component parts. Rather, a number of new inquiries of a very different order are being made. When a writer deals with profits to the slaveholder, he is dealing with slavery as a business enterprise. He is concerned with the rate of return on a given investment, in this case the net return accruing to the planter using slave labor to grow cotton or one of the other southern money crops. When a writer deals with slavery's effects on the slave, he is treating slavery in its psychological and sociological, rather than in its business, aspects. He wants to know how slavery affected the slave as a workman and as a human being. Consideration of the question of the effect on the nonslaveholder is another aspect of slavery as a psychological and sociological system, in this case in relation to the majority of whites who had no direct financial stake in it. This aspect of the question also is concerned with business competition, the problem of whether or not it was an economic disadvantage for the nonslaveholder to be forced into competition with slave labor. Finally, if a writer emphasizes the effect of slavery on the South or on the nation as a whole, he is viewing slavery as an economic system. His major concern is with problems of economic growth and development.

Obviously the various questions are not unrelated. A system which induces economic stagnation, for example, might have very deleterious effects on the population in terms of education, income, standard of living, medical care, and the like. On the other hand, the nature of the relationship among the various questions may not be as obvious as it might appear. An underdeveloped area might, under certain circumstances, provide an ample living for millions of self-sufficient farmers.

Thus, problems of the profitability of slavery are not easily solved, as the experience of over one hundred years of dispute has made clear. The purpose of the readings which follow is to introduce the reader to the debate in the words of the debaters themselves.

STATISTICAL TABLES

TABLE 1. NEGRO POPULATION IN U.S., FOR REGIONS: 1790–1860

YEAR	NORTHEAST [a]		NORTH CENTRAL [b]		SOUTH [c]	
	TOTAL	SLAVE	TOTAL	SLAVE [d]	TOTAL	SLAVE
1790	67,424	40,354	—	—	689,784	657,327
1800	83,066	36,370	635	135	918,336	857,097
1810	102,237	27,081	6,934	3,304	1,268,637	1,160,977
1820	110,724	18,001	18,260	11,329	1,642,672	1,508,692
1830	125,214	2,780	41,543	25,879	2,161,885	1,980,384
1840	142,324	765	89,347	58,604	2,641,977	2,427,986
1850	149,762	236	135,607	87,422	3,352,198	3,116,629
1860	156,001	18	184,239	114,948	4,097,111	3,838,765

[a] Maine, New Hampshire, Vermont, Massachusetts, Rhode Island, Connecticut, New York, New Jersey, Pennsylvania.
[b] Ohio, Indiana, Illinois, Michigan, Wisconsin, Minnesota, Iowa, Missouri, North Dakota, South Dakota, Nebraska, Kansas.
[c] Delaware, Maryland, District of Columbia, Virginia, North Carolina, South Carolina, Georgia, Florida, Kentucky, Tennessee, Alabama, Mississippi, Arkansas, Louisiana, Texas.
[d] Virtually all the slaves in the north central region were living in Missouri, which was admitted to the Union as a slave state in 1820.

TABLE 2. SLAVE POPULATION, FOR SELECTED SOUTHERN STATES: 1790–1860

STATE	1790	1800	1810	1820	1830	1840	1850	1860
Virginia	292,627	345,796	392,516	425,148	469,757	448,987	472,528	490,865
South Carolina	107,094	146,151	196,365	258,475	315,401	327,038	384,984	402,406
North Carolina	100,783	133,296	168,824	204,917	245,601	245,817	288,548	331,059
Georgia	29,264	59,406	105,218	149,656	217,531	280,944	381,682	462,198
Mississippi	—	3,489	17,088	32,814	65,659	195,211	309,878	436,631
Alabama	—	—	—	41,879	117,549	253,532	342,844	435,080
Louisiana	—	—	34,660	69,064	109,588	168,452	244,809	331,726

TABLE 3. SLAVES AND SLAVEHOLDERS, BY STATES: 1860

NUMBER OF SLAVEHOLDERS AND SLAVES

STATES	1 SLAVE	2 SLAVES	3 SLAVES	4 SLAVES	5 SLAVES	6 SLAVES	7 SLAVES	8 SLAVES	9 SLAVES	10 AND UNDER 15	15 AND UNDER 20
Alabama	5,607	3,663	2,805	2,329	1,986	1,729	1,411	1,227	1,036	3,742	2,164
Arkansas	281	173	117	88	69	70	50	52	41	99	43
Delaware	237	114	74	51	34	19	15	10	8	17	8
Florida	863	568	437	365	285	270	225	186	169	627	349
Georgia	6,713	4,355	3,482	2,984	2,543	2,213	1,889	1,647	1,415	4,707	2,823
Kansas	2	—	—	—	—	—	—	—	—	—	—
Kentucky	9,306	5,430	4,009	3,281	2,694	2,293	1,951	1,582	1,273	3,691	1,580
Louisiana	4,092	2,573	2,034	1,536	1,310	1,103	858	771	609	2,065	1,157
Maryland	4,119	1,952	1,279	1,023	815	666	523	446	380	1,173	545
Mississippi	4,856	3,201	2,503	2,129	1,809	1,585	1,303	1,149	1,024	3,432	2,057
Missouri	6,893	3,754	2,773	2,243	1,686	1,384	1,130	877	640	1,734	666
North Carolina	6,440	4,017	3,068	2,546	2,245	1,887	1,619	1,470	1,228	4,044	2,029
South Carolina	3,763	2,533	1,990	1,731	1,541	1,366	1,207	1,095	973	3,334	1,876
Tennessee	7,820	4,738	3,609	3,012	2,536	2,066	1,783	1,565	1,260	3,779	1,744
Texas	4,593	2,874	2,093	1,782	1,439	1,125	928	791	667	2,237	1,186
Virginia	11,085	5,989	4,474	3,807	3,233	2,824	2,393	1,984	1,788	5,686	3,088
Total, States	76,670	45,934	34,747	28,907	24,225	20,600	17,235	14,852	12,511	40,367	21,315
TERRITORIES											
District of Columbia	654	225	112	72	53	31	24	12	11	20	7
Nebraska	1	4	—	—	—	1	1	—	—	—	—
Utah	8	2	—	—	—	—	—	—	—	1	—
Total, Territories	663	231	112	72	53	32	25	12	11	21	7
Total, States and Territories	77,333	46,165	34,859	28,979	24,278	20,632	17,260	14,864	12,522	40,388	21,322

STATES	NUMBER OF SLAVEHOLDERS AND SLAVES										AGGREGATE HOLDERS OF SLAVES	TOTAL NO. OF SLAVES
	20 AND UNDER 30	30 AND UNDER 40	40 AND UNDER 50	50 AND UNDER 70	70 AND UNDER 100	100 AND UNDER 200	200 AND UNDER 300	300 AND UNDER 500	500 AND UNDER 1,000	1,000 AND OVER		
Alabama	2,323	1,253	768	791	550	312	24	10	—	—	33,730	435,080
Arkansas	35	13	8	6	4	—	—	—	—	—	1,149	111,115
Delaware	—	—	—	—	—	—	—	—	—	—	587	1,798
Florida	333	171	99	116	42	45	2	—	—	—	5,152	61,745
Georgia	2,910	1,400	739	729	373	181	23	7	1	—	41,084	462,198
Kansas	—	—	—	—	—	—	—	—	—	—	2	2
Kentucky	1,093	296	96	51	12	6	1	—	—	—	38,645	225,483
Louisiana	1,241	695	413	560	469	460	63	20	4	—	22,033	331,726
Maryland	487	179	81	75	24	15	—	1	—	—	13,783	87,189
Mississippi	2,322	1,143	755	814	545	279	28	8	1	—	30,943	436,631
Missouri	349	120	33	26	8	4	—	—	—	—	24,320	114,931
North Carolina	1,977	870	474	423	188	118	11	4	—	—	34,658	331,059
South Carolina	1,984	1,083	579	710	487	363	56	22	7	1	26,701	402,406
Tennessee	1,623	643	284	219	116	40	6	1	—	—	36,844	275,719
Texas	1,095	491	241	194	88	52	2	—	—	—	21,878	182,566
Virginia	3,017	1,291	609	503	243	105	8	1	—	—	52,128	490,865
Total, States	20,789	9,648	5,179	5,217	3,149	1,980	224	74	13	1	383,637	3,950,513
TERRITORIES												
District of Columbia	7	—	—	1	—	—	—	—	—	—	1,229	3,185
Nebraska	—	—	—	—	—	—	—	—	—	—	6	15
Utah	—	—	—	—	—	—	—	—	—	—	12	29
Total, Territories	7	—	—	1	—	—	—	—	—	—	1,247	3,229
Total, States and Territories	20,796	9,648	5,179	5,218	3,149	1,980	224	74	13	1	384,884	a 3,953,742

a Exclusive of 18 colored apprentices for life (in the State of New Jersey), by the act to abolish slavery, passed April 18, 1846.

TABLE 4. U.S. COTTON PRODUCTION, EXPORTS, AND PRICES: 1790–1860

| | SUPPLY, CONSUMPTION, EXPORTS (SURPLUS STOCKS AND PRICES) | | | | | PRICES (MIDDLING UPLAND) PER POUND | | | | | |
| | | | | | | IN NEW YORK | | | IN LIVERPOOL | | |
YEAR	CROPS (BALES)	CONSUMPTION (BALES)	EXPORTS (BALES)	STOCKS a (CLOSE OF YEAR) (BALES)	NET WEIGHT OF BALES (POUNDS)	LOWEST (CENTS)	HIGHEST (CENTS)	AVERAGE (CENTS)	LOWEST (PENCE)	HIGHEST (PENCE)	AVERAGE (PENCE)
1790–91	8,889	No data	889	No data	225	—	—	26	13	30	—
1791–92	13,333	do	635	do	225	—	—	29	20	30	—
1792–93	22,222	do	2,222	do	225	—	—	32	13	22	—
1793–94	35,556	do	7,407	do	225	—	—	33	12	18	—
1794–95	35,556	do	27,822	do	225	—	—	36½	15	27	—
1795–96	44,444	do	27,141	do	225	—	—	36½	12	29	—
1796–97	48,889	do	16,837	do	225	—	—	34	12	37	—
1797–98	66,667	do	41,600	do	225	—	—	39	22	45	—
1798–99	88,889	do	42,366	do	225	—	—	44	17	60	—
1799–00	155,556	35,556	79,066	do	225	—	—	28	16	36	—
1800–01	210,526	39,474	91,716	No data	228	—	—	44	17	38	18
1801–02	241,228	No data	120,619	do	228	—	—	19	12	38	16
1802–03	252,101	do	158,454	do	238	—	—	19	8	15	12½
1803–04	240,741	do	129,756	do	270	—	—	20	10	18	14
1804–05	281,128	44,177	154,101	do	249	—	—	23	14	19	16½
1805–06	347,826	No data	155,032	do	230	—	—	22	12	15	18¼
1806–07	285,714	do	228,362	do	280	—	—	21½	10	14	14½
1807–08	271,739	do	38,516	do	276	—	—	19	9	30	22
1808–09	366,071	do	227,635	do	224	—	—	16	10	18	20
1809–10	340,000	64,000	373,046	do	250	—	—	16	10	19	15½
1810–11	269,360	57,239	208,950	No data	297	—	—	15½	—	12½	—
1811–12	304,878	No data	117,428	do	246	—	—	10½	—	16¾	—
1812–13	304,878	do	77,683	do	246	—	—	12½	—	23	—
1813–14	284,553	do	72,069	do	246	—	—	15½	—	29½	—
1814–15	363,636	90,000	301,814	do	275	—	—	21	—	20¾	—
1815–16	457,565	No data	302,388	do	271	—	—	29	—	18¼	—
1816–17	460,993	do	303,721	do	282	—	—	26	—	20⅛	—
1817–18	448,029	do	331,438	do	279	—	—	34	—	20	—
1818–19	596,429	do	314,275	do	280	—	—	24	—	13½	—
1819–20	606,061	do	484,319	do	264	—	—	17	—	11½	—

1820–21	647,482	No data	449,257	No data	278	11	20	14.32	7	9¼	8.14
1821–22	742,049	do	511,219	do	283	10	18	14.32	5¾	7¾	6.95
1822–23	620,805	do	582,964	do	298	9	17	11.40	6¼	8½	7.21
1823–24	762,411	do	504,857	do	282	11½	18	14.65	7	9	7.66
1824–25	891,608	do	616,958	do	286	12	30	18.59	7	16¾	11.62
1825–26	1,121,667	do	655,562	do	312	9	17½	12.19	5½	6¾	5.85
1826–27	957,281	149,516	854,000	do	331	8¾	11½	9.29	4⅞	6⅞	5.79
1827–28	720,593	120,593	600,000	40,000	335	8¼	13	10.32	5	6⅜	5.84
1828–29	870,415	118,853	740,000	30,000	341	8	11½	9.88	5	6⅛	5.32
1829–30	976,845	126,512	839,000	35,000	339	8	12½	10.04	6	6⅞	6.44
1830–31	1,038,847	182,142	773,000	119,000	341	7½	13¼	9.71	5⅛	6	5.38
1831–32	987,477	173,800	892,000	41,600	360	7	12	9.38	5¼	7	6.22
1832–33	1,070,438	194,412	867,000	48,200	350	9½	17	12.32	6¾	10⅜	7.87
1833–34	1,205,394	196,413	1,028,000	29,600	363	9½	18	12.90	7½	9½	8.10
1834–35	1,254,328	216,888	1,023,000	41,600	367	12½	20	17.45	7⅞	10½	9.13
1835–36	1,360,725	236,733	1,116,000	43,300	373	12½	20	16.50	7¾	10	8.79
1836–37	1,423,930	222,540	1,169,000	75,800	379	7½	20	13.25	5	8	6.09
1837–38	1,801,497	246,063	1,575,000	40,300	379	7¼	14	10.14	5¾	7½	6.28
1838–39	1,360,532	267,018	1,074,000	52,250	384	9½	17	13.36	6¼	8¾	7.19
1839–40	2,177,835	295,193	1,876,000	58,442	383	6	13½	8.92	5⅛	6½	5.42
1840–41	1,634,954	297,288	1,313,500	72,470	394	7	11½	9.50	5¼	6⅝	5.73
1841–42	1,683,574	267,850	1,465,500	31,807	397	5	10½	7.85	4⅝	5⅜	4.86
1842–43	2,378,875	325,129	2,010,000	94,486	409	6⅛	8½	7.25	3⅞	5	4.37
1843–44	2,030,409	346,750	1,629,500	159,772	412	5¾	9½	7.73	3⅞	5¾	4.71
1844–45	2,394,503	389,000	2,083,700	98,420	415	5	6¾	5.63	3	4⅜	3.92
1845–46	2,100,537	422,600	1,666,700	107,122	411	7	9½	7.87	4	7	4.80
1846–47	1,778,651	428,000	1,241,200	214,837	431	8½	13¾	11.21	4⅜	7⅞	6.03
1847–48	2,439,786	616,044	1,858,000	171,468	417	6	13	8.03	3	4⅞	3.93
1848–49	2,866,938	642,485	2,228,000	154,753	436	5⅞	10⅝	7.55	4	6⅜	4.09
1849–50	2,333,718	613,498	1,590,200	167,930	429	10	13⅞	12.34	5⅞	7⅞	7.10
1850–51	2,454,442	485,614	1,988,710	128,304	416	8¾	15	12.14	4½	7⅝	5.51
1851–52	3,126,310	689,603	2,443,646	91,176	428	8½	11⅜	9.50	4⅝	5¾	5.05
1852–53	3,416,214	803,725	2,528,400	135,643	438	9¾	11¾	11.02	5⅜	6½	5.54
1853–54	3,074,979	737,236	2,319,148	135,603	430	10	11¾	10.97	4 13/16	6	5.31
1854–55	2,982,634	706,417	2,244,209	143,336	434	8½	13	10.39	4⅞	6⅜	5.60
1855–56	3,655,557	777,739	2,954,606	64,171	420	9	11⅝	10.30	5⅜	6⅞	6.22
1856–57	3,093,737	819,936	2,252,657	49,258	444	11⅝	15¾	13.51	5½	9⅛	7.73
1857–58	3,257,339	595,562	2,590,455	102,926	442	8⅞	15¾	12.23	6 13/16	7⅜	6.91
1858–59	4,018,914	927,651	3,021,403	149,237	447	11	13⅜	12.08	6	7⅛	6.68
1859–60	4,861,292	978,043	3,774,173	227,708	461	10½	11¾	11	5½	7⅛	5.97

[a] Port stocks.

SOURCES

TABLE 1. U.S. Bureau of the Census, *Historical Statistics of the United States* (Washington, D.C.: U.S. Government Printing Office, 1960), pp. 11–12.

TABLE 2. U.S. Bureau of the Census, *Negro Population, 1790–1915* (Washington, D.C.: U.S. Government Printing Office, 1918), p. 57.

TABLE 3. U.S. Bureau of the Census, *Agriculture of the United States in 1860* (Washington, D.C.: U.S. Government Printing Office, 1864), p. 247.

TABLE 4. James L. Watkins, *King Cotton* (New York: James L. Watkins & Sons, 1908), pp. 29–31.

PART I
Slavery and the Planter

INTRODUCTION

❰ At first glance, the answer to the question "Was slavery a profitable business enterprise?" may appear to be self-evident. Slavery must have been profitable, it could be argued, otherwise planters would not have continued to invest their money in it. Indeed, they *could* not, in the long run, continue to invest in a system in which they regularly lost money. Certainly planters were aware of investment opportunities and profit margins in other businesses. It would seem that they would quickly have foregone a losing enterprise in favor of profitable investment. Hence, the very persistence of the institution would appear to be adequate evidence of its profitability.

As reasonable as this argument may appear, there is ample evidence that by itself it is inadequate to solve the question of slavery's profitability. In the first place, slavery was more than a business enterprise. Only one completely unfamiliar with the literature of the ante-bellum period or an ardent and mechanical economic determinist could fail to appreciate that the peculiar institution was a part of an agrarian mode of living. It was associated with a way of life and was not simply a business investment. The ownership of slaves brought social status and often political power. Men who were successful as merchants and storekeepers bought plantations and became slave owners, thereby diverting some—or, all—of their resources to slave owning. The desire for maximum profits is insufficient to explain this attitude.

Moreover, a business enterprise might be unprofitable in a comparative sense and still not be destroyed by losses. Thus, a planter's return on his investment might continually be lower than the possible return from other forms of investment or less than the going rate of interest—and in this sense, unprofitable—without his going bankrupt. Other, nonmonetary inducements might serve to sustain an investment in a comparatively unprofitable enterprise. Indeed, even if nonmonetary inducements were not present, the relatively short-term duration of the ante-bellum period might have the same effect. A single generation, or, in the older areas, two generations, would span the entire period. Tradition and inertia, combined with periodic good years, would be more than sufficient to perpetuate a comparatively unprofitable enterprise under these circumstances.

The profitability of slavery as a business enterprise, then, cannot be maintained on a priori grounds. Answers must come only through an investigation of the operation of the institution itself. Here, the lack of full records poses serious methodological problems. It is the purpose of the following readings to introduce the reader to the nature of these problems and the ways in which they have been solved by various writers.

The readings in the first section approach the problem indirectly, via the standard of living of the planter class. The three authors represented were all contemporaries; all purport to record what they had seen themselves. Daniel Robinson Hundley was an Alabama lawyer. Trained at Harvard and the University of Virginia, he traveled extensively in the northern states. His book, *Social Relations in Our Southern States* (1860), presents a complex view of southern society. Ecstatic in his praise of the "gentleman," and a warm admirer of the yeoman, Hundley is often bitterly critical of other groups in his section. In the selection presented here, he looks with distaste at what he calls the "Southern Yankee," who has the businessman's attitude toward planting in that profits stand above all in his calculations. Hundley's sympathies are clearly with the gentleman, but he does grant the Yankee the distinction of bringing energy, along with his boorish greed, to the planting business. Planting is profitable, he argues, if one is willing to be a Southern Yankee. He implies that the gentleman's responsibilities, social and intellectual, might stand in the way of good profits.

These social and intellectual bars to high profits are made explicit in the second selection, the description of Governor Aiken's rice estate in South Carolina. This sketch was written by Solon Robinson, an Indiana advocate of agricultural reform who traveled widely in the agricultural regions of the United States and published his observations in the New York *Tribune,* the *American Agriculturalist,* and other journals. Profits are low and living conditions modest on the vast estate he describes; other, nonmonetary considerations obviously come first.

The third selection was written by the most famous of the many travelers in the ante-bellum South, Frederick Law Olmsted. The son of a prosperous Hartford merchant, Olmsted was educated at Yale and for a time ran a farm on Staten Island. In 1852, he was commissioned by the New York *Times* to tour the South and report on conditions he observed. He eventually made three separate trips south, reporting his findings in newspaper articles as he went along and finally publishing four books on his adventures. Although he was antagonistic toward slavery, Olmsted's observations were generally accurate and objective. In this selection, he records his impressions of the living standards of the smaller planter as inferior to those of a northern farmer with a similar investment.

The readings in the second, third, and fourth sections are attempts by modern scholars to assess the profitability of slavery as a business enterprise. Their approaches to the problem vary sharply, as do their methods. In the second section, historians Lewis Cecil Gray and Ulrich B. Phillips consider the relative advantages and disadvantages of the use of slave labor as compared with free labor. Gray, whose monumental, two-volume *History of Agriculture in the Southern United States to 1860* remains today, more than three decades after its publication, the basic work in the field, finds that slave labor had a definite competitive advantage over free labor in the South. Phillips arrives at very different conclusions. A pioneer historian of American Negro slavery, Phillips' researches led him to believe that the initial economic advantages of slavery were lost because of the great expense involved in the capitalization of the labor force.

In the third section, several modern day scholars attempt to judge profitability by actually measuring the income accruing to planters who used slave labor. These writers attempt to build some form of economic model of the slave plantation. The first selection is taken from the study *Slavery in Mississippi* by a historian of the South, Charles S. Sydnor. Sydnor's conclusions, like those of a number of other state studies published during the 1920's and 1930's,[1] tended to support the findings of Phillips. On the basis of contemporary records, Sydnor calculated the costs of production and the income on a typical Mississippi plantation, concluding that profits were low. Only by spending the interest and other hidden charges (interest on capital invested in slaves, depreciation of slave property, land, and equipment) and by not calculating their own wages as supervisors of the business, could planters seem to make a profit. This view is sharply criticized by Thomas P. Govan, an economic historian and biographer of Nicholas Biddle. Govan contends that Sydnor and others erred in their conclusions because they failed to consider all possible sources of profit in making their calculations (services received from household slaves, food and other provisions grown on the plantation and used by the owner, and the increase in the value of land and slaves) and because they considered interest on investment as an expense when in reality it should be considered part of profits. When these adjustments in bookkeeping methods are made, Govan concludes, slave ownership emerges as a highly profitable business.

In the third selection, two Harvard economists approach the question from a very different angle. Their purpose, declare Alfred H. Conrad and John R. Meyer, is to take the argument over profitability out of the realm of accounting and, instead, to measure profitability according to economic concepts. To this end, they construct an economic model of a southern cotton plantation for the years 1830 to 1860 and then compute the return on investment using a Keynesian capital-value formula. Returns vary according to the quality of the land, but for most planters, Conrad and Meyer conclude, production with slave labor was a profitable business.

Still another approach to the question of the profitability of slavery as a business enterprise is presented in the fourth section. Historians Charles W. Ramsdell and Lewis Cecil Gray consider the probable future of slavery as a business enterprise had not the Civil War intervened to end the system. Ramsdell finds that slavery could not have expanded; indeed, it had reached the limits of its expansion even before the Civil War and was already doomed to eventual extinction. Gray comes to an opposite conclusion, arguing that there was ample room for the expansion of slavery on the eve of the Civil War.

In evaluating the arguments presented by the various authors, one group of questions the reader should consider concerns semantics. What exactly does each author mean by *profitable?* Is he concerned merely with income accruing to planters using slave labor? Or does he base his conclusions on a comparison of the rate of return received by planters on their investments with the rate earned by investors in northern enterprises? Or does he attempt to compare income from slave labor with that which might have been earned had free labor been used in the South? Should profits be considered only in an economic sense? Is it legitimate to include nonmonetary factors in considering profitability?

[1] Rosser Howard Taylor, *Slaveholding in North Carolina* (Chapel Hill: University of North Carolina Press, 1926); Ralph Betts Flanders, *Plantation Slavery in Georgia* (Chapel Hill: University of North Carolina Press, 1933); Charles S. Davis, *The Cotton Kingdom in Alabama* (Montgomery: Alabama State Department of Archives and History, 1939).

Another set of questions concerns method. How typical is the evidence used by each author to prove his point? What methods does the author use to fill gaps in his knowledge? What are each author's theoretical assumptions—either implicit or explicit? What evidence is given to support these assumptions?

THE READINGS

1] Standard of Living of the Planter Class

a] THE SOUTHERN YANKEE: SUCCESSFUL BUSINESSMAN

. . . AT THE present time, the Southern Yankee is quite an institution in the South. Although he has sprung up in the last fifty years, he has thriven faster than Jonah's gourd, has waxed fat exceedingly, and already elevates his horn amazingly high in the land. He flourishes like a green bay-tree in every Southern State. Whether this has been owing to the influence and example of his Northern brother, or to the sudden wealth bestowed upon the South by the invention of the cotton-gin and the purchase of Louisiana, or to some other undefined and indefinable cause, we are not prepared to say. We simply record the fact, as in duty bound to do, and leave to more inquisitive minds the labor of tracing out the cause.

.   .   .   .

Like his Northern brother, the Southern Yankee is deterred by no obstacle whatever from his tireless pursuit of riches. In the tobacco-fields of Virginia, in the rice-fields of Carolina, in the cotton-fields of Alabama, or among the sugar-canes of Louisiana, when a farmer or planter, he is in all things similar and equally bent on the accumulation of the sordid pelf: and the crack of his whip is heard early, and the crack of the same is heard late, and the weary backs of his bondmen and his bondwomen are bowed to the ground with over-tasking and over-toil, and yet his heart is still unsatisfied; for he grasps after more and more, and cries to the fainting slave: "Another pound of money, dog, or I take a pound of flesh!" And the lash is never staid, save by one single consideration only—*will it pay?* Will it pay to press the poor African beyond what he can endure, and thereby shorten his life, or is it better to drive him just so far as his health and continued usefulness will justify? this is the great and the only question with every Southern Yankee: Conscience? *Basta!* he knows no such a thing as conscience: he cares only to get gain, and get it he will, and let conscience go to the dogs. Religion? Kiss your grandmother! Go talk to the women and the parsons about religion: a man who has uncounted treasures visible and tangible, will not be such a fool as to give them up for those which can be neither seen nor felt, and the enjoyment of which is postponed to the Hereafter. Humanity? The devil! what care I for your humanity? Don't I see every body else trying to cheat every body, and to get the

FROM D[aniel] R[obinson] Hundley, *Social Relations in Our Southern States* (New York: Henry B. Price, 1860), pp. 131–35, 156–57.

upper hand; and shall I remain such a milksop as to let every body get ahead of me? So he reasons; and he acts accordingly. . . .

The farming class of Southern Yankees abounds more in the Gulf States, than in those which border on the Free States. This is owing to the greater richness of the soil in the former States, as well as to the greater profitableness of cotton-raising or sugar-planting as compared to the production of tobacco, wheat, or hemp. Besides, in the extreme South, the Southern Yankee puts himself to very little expense about any sort of improvements on his plantation, and his gin-house not unfrequently costs twice as much as his mansion. Sometimes, indeed, he lives in a log-cabin similar to those furnished his negroes, and even when he possesses a better and more pretentious dwelling, he rarely keeps it painted, but lets it rot down over his head, being too penurious to spend the money necessary to keep it in repairs. Usually there is only a "worm fence" of rails around his yard, in which pigs, poultry, cows, sheep, horses, and the like are allowed to roam at will; and his stables, barns, negro cabins, and other out-houses, are, in most cases, not more than a stone's throw from his own domicil. Under such circumstances, is it at all wonderful that the Southern Yankee is fully as restless as the Yankees of the North—always on the move, or ready to sell out at any time if settled? Home to be loved must be made attractive, but he who is so wedded to filthy lucre as to despise all ornament that costs money, is not capable of entertaining in his selfish and narrow bosom so refining a passion as the love of home, or the love of any thing else, indeed, that is pure and beautiful. . . .

In regard, however, to the dwellings, or log cabins rather, of those persons who have just moved into any of the new States of the South-west, the reader will please observe, that there is a great difference between the man who lives in a log cabin from necessity and because nothing better is to be had, and the individual who does so from choice, and because he is too penurious to own a better dwelling. For you will find in many a log cabin in all the South-western States as perfect gentlemen—gentlemen of the first breeding and education—as in most of the mansions on Fifth Avenue.

. . . .

Having said so many hard things about the Southern Yankee, perhaps we had better now say a good word in his favor; for he is not altogether without redeeming qualities. Although swallowed up completely in selfishness, which prevents his ever undertaking any object or enterprise unless well assured beforehand that it "will pay," he is still of very great advantage to the community at large, and in most cases is a useful citizen. The Northern Yankee proper (for all New England men even are not Yankees, by great odds) has been the main instrument in advancing the North to her present proud position, as a great manufacturing, inventive, and commercial community. So, on the other hand, the Southern Yankee, aided by the thrifty Middle Classes, has contributed no little to the present unprecedented prosperity of the Slave States: for, aside from his own labors and industry, he has also stimulated the Southern Gentleman to activity and enterprise. Certainly there is a vast difference between the motives which have instigated the two, the latter being influenced by public spirit and patriotic pride, while the former has only sought to make money and to advance his private interests; yet the result of their labors has been the same. Thus the worn-out lands of Virginia and the Carolinas, which ten years ago went a-begging at five dollars per acre, by judicious culture and scientific manuring have been so improved that they now readily command from twenty to fifty dollars per acre. So, also, the vast savannas and heavily-timbered forests of the Gulf and South-western States, have been brought under cultivation, until the lands on which fifty years ago stood one grand and primeval forest, now produce annually more than two hundred millions of dollars' worth of *surplus* agricultural products. In the achievement of these wonderful results, the Southern Yankee has played no mean part; but he has ever been foremost among the pioneers, clearing up the "new grounds," and draining the swamps, preparatory to introducing the virgin soil to the close embraces of "de shovel and de hoe." Neither has he been backward in assisting the South to build her great lines of railway, most of which are profitable investments; and the Southern Yankee troubles himself about nothing else, if satisfied that the investment will prove pecuniarily profitable.

.   .   .   .

b] THE WEALTHY RICE PLANTER: UNPRETENTIOUS GENTLEMAN

. . . WE CANNOT refrain from introducing, from the American Agriculturist, the sketch of a visit, by Solon Robinson, Esq., to Jehossee Island, the magnificent rice estate of Ex-Governor Aiken, of South Carolina. We have ourselves frequently passed this plantation, between Savannah and Charleston, and know that it is one of the most perfect in the world.

. . . There are 1,500 acres of rice lands, divided into convenient compartments for flooding, by substantial banks, and all laid off in beds, between ditches three feet deep and only thirty-five feet apart. Part of the land was tide-water marsh, and part of it timber swamp. Besides this, Gov. Aiken cultivates 500 acres in corn, oats, and potatoes; the balance is gardens, yards, lawns, and in woods, pasture and unreclaimed swamp.

.   .   .   .

The average annual sales of the place do not vary materially from $25,000, and the average annual expenses not far from $10,000, of which sum $2,000 is paid the overseer, who is the only white man upon the place, besides the owner, who is always absent during the sickly months of summer. All the

FROM Solon Robinson, "Rice Estate of Gov. Aiken, of S.C.," as reprinted in J. D. B. De Bow, *The Industrial Resources of the Southern and Western States* (New Orleans: De Bow's Review, 1852), II, 424–26.

engineers, millers, smiths, carpenters and sailors, are black. A vessel, belonging to the island, goes twice a week to Charleston and carries a cargo of one hundred casks. The last crop was 1,500 casks; the year before, 1,800, and all provisions and grain required made upon the place. Last year, there was not more than half a supply of provisions.

.   .   .   .

The number of negroes upon the place is just about 700, occupying 84 double frame houses, each containing two tenements of three rooms to a family, besides the cockloft. Each tenement has its separate door and window, and a good brick fireplace, and nearly all have a garden paled in. There are two common hospitals and a "lying-in hospital," and a very neat, commodious church, which is well filled, every Sabbath, with an orderly, pious congregation, and service performed by a respectable Methodist clergyman, who also performs the baptismal, communion, marriage and burial rites.

There is a small stock of cattle, hogs and sheep, kept upon the place for meat, which are only allowed to come upon the fields in winter, under charge of keepers. The buildings are all of wood, but generally plain, substantial and good. There is a pretty good supply of tools, carts, boats, &c., and the land is estimated to be worth $100 an acre, for the rice land,

which would be,	$150,000
The 500 acres upland, $25 per acre,	12,500
The negroes, at $300 each,	210,000
Stock, tools and other property, say,	7,500
	$380,000

which will show rather a low rate of interest, made from sales of crops, notwithstanding the amount of sales look so large.

Now, the owner of all this property lives in a very humble cottage, embowered in dense shrubbery and making no show, and is, in fact, as a dwelling for a gentleman of wealth, far inferior, in point of elegance and convenience, to any negro house upon the place, for the use and comfort of that class of people.

He and his family are as plain and unostentatious, in their manners, as the house they live in; but they possess, in a most eminent degree, that true politeness and hospitality that will win upon your heart and make you feel at home in their humble cot, in such a manner that you will enjoy a visit there better than in a palace.

Nearly all the land has been reclaimed, and the buildings, except the house, erected new, within the twenty years that Governor Aiken has owned the island. I fully believe that he is more concerned to make his people comfortable and happy, than he is to make money.

c] THE SMALL-SCALE PLANTER: SHABBY MIDDLE CLASS

CONTINUING THE horseback journey commenced in the rich cotton-bearing soils which border the Mississippi river, I turned eastward, not far above Natchez, and pursued an indirect route towards Tuscaloosa in Alabama. The country grew less fertile, and the plantations smaller. . . . The more common sort of plantations and the common middle-class planter, can hardly be seen by a tourist in any other way than that I now pursued, traveling in the interior, away from the rivers and the ordinary lines of communication, and independently of public conveyances; there is consequently less general knowledge of them, I apprehend, than of any other portion of the population of the South, yet of the class properly termed "the planters" they constitute probably nine tenths.

The majority of the interior plantations which came under my observation belong to resident planters, and are from four hundred to one thousand acres in extent, the average being perhaps six hundred acres. The number of negroes on each varies from ten to forty, more frequently being between twenty and thirty. Where there are fewer than ten negroes, the owners are frequently seen holding a plow among them; where there are over twenty, a white overseer is usually employed, the owner perhaps directing, but seldom personally superintending, the field labor.

The characteristics of this latter class of cotton-planters vary much. I shall, I think, be generally rightly understood if I say that the majority of them possess more dignity of bearing and manner, that they give a stranger an impression of greater "respectability" than the middle class of farmers at the North and in England, while they have less general information and less active and inquiring minds. The class of farmers in New England and New York, with whom I compare them, have rarely received any education beyond that of the public schools, which, in the last generation, afforded a very meager modicum of instruction. The planters of whom I speak, I judge to have usually spent a short time at boarding-schools or institutions of a somewhat superior order to the common, or "primary" schools of the country—but their acquisition of knowledge subsequently to their school-days by newspapers and books, and by conversation, has been very small.

It is frequently the case, however, that the planter has started as a poor, and entirely self-dependent young man, the basis of whose present fortune consisted of his savings from the wages earned by him as overseer—these are commonly as illiterate as the very poorest of our northern agricultural laborers. Yet again there are those who, beginning in the same way, have acquired, while so employed, not only a capital with which to purchase

FROM Frederick Law Olmsted, *A Journey in the Back Country* (New York: Mason Brothers, 1860), pp. 158–62.

land and slaves, but a valuable stock of experience and practical information, and somewhat of gentlemanly bearing from intercourse with their employers. In respect to the enjoyment of material comforts, and the exercise
of taste in the arrangement of their houses and grounds, the condition of
these planters, while it is superior to that of the Texans, is far below that
of northern farmers of one quarter their wealth. But an acquaintance
with their style of living can only be obtained from details, and these I
shall again give by extracts from my journal, showing how I chanced to
be entertained night after night, premising that I took no little pains to
select the most comfortable quarters in the neighborhood which I reached
at the close of the day. To avoid repetition, I will merely say with regard
to diet, that bacon, corn-bread and coffee invariably appeared at every
meal; but, besides this, either at breakfast or supper, a fried fowl, "biscuit"
of wheat flour, with butter were added—the biscuit invariably made heavy,
doughy and indigestible with shortening (fat), and brought to table in
relays, to be eaten as hot as possible with melting butter. Molasses usually,
honey frequently, and, as a rare exception, potatoes and green peas were
added to the board. Whiskey was seldom offered me, and only once any
other beverage except the abominable preparation which passes for coffee.

.   .   .   .

2] Comparative Advantages and Disadvantages in the Employment of Slave Labor

a] COMPETITIVE ADVANTAGES OF NEGRO SLAVERY UNDER THE PLANTATION SYSTEM

THE TENDENCY for slave labor to displace free labor where conditions
were favorable to producing and marketing the staples raises the
question as to what economic characteristics gave slavery an advantage
over rival systems of labor. . . . The consideration of this question need
not involve either the ethical aspects of slavery or its general social and
economic advantages and disadvantages from the standpoint of national
or sectional welfare.

.   .   .   .

The essential question is not whether the South would have been better
off if its entire population had been made up of white laborers of western
European origin working under the wages system; but whether the South
could have employed the African Negro, after he was brought to this
country, in any more effective manner; and more than this, why the Negro

FROM Lewis Cecil Gray, *History of Agriculture in the Southern United States to 1860*
(Washington, D.C.: Carnegie Institution of Washington, 1933), I, 462, 470–71, 473–75,
478–80.

slave, in spite of the alleged inferiority of slavery as a method of stimulating exertion, was able to displace the economy of free small farmers.

For one thing, considering the characteristic immediacy of the primitive Negro, it is probable that the rewards and punishments of the plantation system were more powerful stimuli than the rewards of industry would have been for him under a system of free labor. By no means were all slaves sullen, wretched, and driven cattle, working only under the lash. On the smaller plantations, especially, they felt an interest in the affairs of the plantation, and their advice was not infrequently asked by the master. In many cases they took pride in the master's wealth and prosperity, tacitly accepting the position of inferiority and subordination—a position that probably caused them little sorrow.

Slavery as an industrial system possessed certain positive advantages even as compared with the system of wage labor. From the standpoint of the employer, slavery provided a stable labor supply. Barring ordinary accidents and sickness, the laborer's services were always available—an important advantage in large-scale farming. There was possibly a certain degree of economic inelasticity in the supply of labor, particularly at harvest time, when there was little surplus labor except children, and slave labor flowed less readily than free labor to the type of employment promising greatest economic opportunity, due partly to lack of diversity in the Negro's economic experience, partly to the difficulties in transferring the capital values of the slave's labor. As compared with serfdom, however, slavery possessed the manifest advantage that the laborer could be moved to the point of greatest productive advantage, while the serf was bound to a particular manor. It was found practicable to employ slave women in field labor, as well as men, while throughout America custom did not ordinarily sanction the employment of white women in the fields. Furthermore, it was practicable to use child labor from a comparatively early age in such activities as worming and suckering tobacco and picking cotton. Slavery involved no problem of unemployment, and the system bred no lockouts, blacklists, and strikes.

.   .   .   .

The actual basis of the competitive power of Negro slavery was greatly obscured by capitalization, for the prospective series of annual incomes from the ownership of a slave were capitalized on the same principle as a terminable annuity or any other terminable use-bearer. In the case of the slave the process of capitalization involved more obscurity than for bonds or other contractually predetermined income, for it was necessary to anticipate future earnings. As compared with land, the valuation of the slave involved the uncertainties of loss by sudden death or incapacity for labor through disability. Although the actuarial risk presumably was discounted in the purchase price of slaves, the possibility of loss by death was a considerable element in the risks of the individual planter. The risk was greater for small than for large planters, and this fact, accentuated by the rising prices of slaves, appears to have been one of the reasons for the concentration of slave ownership that occurred just before the Civil

War. In the last two decades before the Civil War insurance companies were beginning to insure the lives of slaves, but it is doubtful if there was a widespread tendency for planters to avail themselves of this form of protection.

About the period of the Revolutionary War slaves were reported to be capitalized at 4 to 6 times the average annual hire. In 1791 Jefferson estimated the ratio at 5 to 1. In Missouri, just before the Civil War, the rates of hire by the year averaged about 14 per cent of capital values in the case of male slaves and about 6 per cent for female slaves.

As already noted, the question of the relative competitive advantages of slave labor and of free labor was confused from time to time by a tendency to assume that the interest and replacement fund calculated at a certain rate on the capital value of the slave was an extra cost which the employer of free labor did not have to assume, representing therefore a special and notable disadvantage in the case of slave labor. Such an assumption, however, was the reflection of incorrect economic analysis. When capitalization was accurately effected, the series of successive incomes as they became available actually were equivalent to interest and replacement; for interest and replacement would have been allowed for in the relatively low value that the owner paid for the services of the slave, capitalized on a terminable basis. In short, the process of capitalization obscures the fact that the so-called interest on investment and the replacement fund constitute actually the surplus over cost of maintenance appropriable from the ownership of the slave.

. . . .

An understanding of the reasons for the competitive superiority of slave labor as compared with free labor in regions favorable to the commercial production of staples rests on a comparatively simple basis. In the New World, with its abundance of fertile land, labor, when employed with a reasonable degree of efficiency, could produce a volume of physical goods larger than the bare requisites of its subsistence from birth to death. The owner of the slave had legally appropriated his services for life, and therefore was in a position to appropriate the surplus above the requisites of subsistence. Of course, land, equipment, and supervision were necessary to employ this labor productively, but these requisites exist also in the employment of free labor. The physical surplus might disappear for a time on account of crop failure and price fluctuations might also cause the value surplus to vanish for short periods, but normally there was both a physical and a value surplus for the full lifetime of the slave, which was appropriable by reason of the institution of slavery.

It was this appropriable surplus that gave slave labor under plantation organization an irresistible ability to displace free labor, whether hired or engaged in production on family-sized farms. Substantially, the minimum level of competition in the case of slave labor was bare subsistence. The planter was able, if necessary, to produce at price levels that left little more than the expense of maintaining the slave. White labor could bid no lower. As a matter of fact, however, the basis of competition rarely reached so low a level. There were extensive areas of fertile land where white labor could find an outlet for its energies without coming into acute competition with slave labor. Where free white labor did come into direct competition with slave labor in the South there resulted the process of geographical segregation already pointed out. The possession of areas suitable to the marketing of products was of vital importance to the owner of slaves, for otherwise he could enjoy the surplus product of their labor only in the form of a food surplus, which it was impossible to consume, or in an excess of personal services. In competition for the locations favorable to commercial agriculture the planter was able, if necessary, to pay a portion of the annual value of the slave or its capitalized equivalent as a premium to outbid free labor in the acquisition of land.

.   .   .   .

The competitive superiority that enabled slave labor to triumph over free labor under conditions favorable to commercial cultivation of the staples was dependent upon and facilitated by the plantation system of organization. Although the system was originally developed as a means of organizing colonial expansion, after the introduction of Negro slaves it became economically and socially essential—a necessity sufficiently demonstrated by the chaos that resulted from emancipation in the West Indies and in the South, and by the reestablishment of the system after the Civil War.

Certain characteristics of slavery itself and of Southern agriculture, previously mentioned, were favorable to large-scale organization. The labor supply was stable and under absolute control. Southern staples are all-year crops, furnishing a maximum continuity of employment. The periods of peak demand for labor involve processes in which women and children can be employed. No complex machinery is requisite, and the processes of cultivation are comparatively simple, and therefore capable of being standardized and reduced to routine.

Since the organization of labor under intelligent supervision was an essential requirement for industrial efficiency, it was desirable to economize expense of supervision by employing as many slaves under a single management as was consistent with adequate oversight and control, the most economical number varying in accordance with kind of staple crop and character of land. The relatively smaller risk of loss from death of slaves on the large plantation was an important advantage of large-scale production. There was economy in fixed costs incurred for machinery required for preparing crops for market, particularly sugar. In Louisiana, it was observed, the equipment for a plantation capable of producing 600 hogsheads required but little more outlay than was necessary for a capacity of 300. The expense of a rice mill was so great that only large planters could afford one, although the influence of this condition was reduced by the existence of toll mills and by the practice of exporting rough rice. For cotton and tobacco the influence of such fixed costs was of less importance.

The large planter enjoyed other advantages incident to large organization: superior facility for obtaining credit, ability to purchase in large quantities on favorable terms to secure the best land, supplies and equipment, and the advantages derived from superior intelligence and influential connections. Olmsted observed that on the large plantations in the Southwest the land was unusually well cultivated. Of some of the plantations along the Mississippi, Red, and Brazos rivers he asserted:

> The soil was a perfect garden mould, well drained and guarded by levees against the floods; it was admirably tilled; I have seen but few Northern farms so well tilled; the labourers were, to large degree, tall, slender, sinewy, young men, who worked from dawn to dusk, not with spirit, but with steadiness and constancy. They had good tools; their rations of bacon and corn were brought to them in the field, and eaten with efficient dispatch between the cotton plants. They had the best sort of gins and presses, so situated that from them cotton bales could be rolled in five minutes to steam-boats, bound direct to the ports on the gulf. They were superintended by skillful and vigilant overseers. These plantations were all large, so large as to yet contain much fresh land, ready to be worked as soon as the cultivated fields gave out in fertility.

The large planters obtained not only "the best land on which to apply their labor," but also "the best brute force, the best tools, and the best machinery for ginning and pressing, all superintended by the best class of overseers." The cotton was "shipped at the best season, perhaps all at once, on a boat or by trains expressly engaged at the lowest rates of freight." Because of the size of the shipment it received the best attention, not only by the transport agencies, but also by the commission merchants.

Comparing the large planters in Texas with the small German farmers who were endeavoring to raise cotton, Olmsted declared:

> It would not surprise me to learn that the cultivation of cotton by the German settlers in Texas had not, after all, been as profitable as its cultivation by the planters employing slaves in the vicinity. I should attribute the superior profits of the planter, if any there be, however, not to the fitness of the climate for negro labor, and its unfitness for white labor, but to the fact that his expenses for fencing, on account of his larger fields and larger estate, are several hundred per cent less than those of the farmer; to the fact that his expenses for tillage, having mules and plows and other instruments to use at the opportune moment, are less than those of the farmer, who, in many cases, cannot afford to own a single team; to the fact that he has, from experience, a better knowledge of the most successful method of cultivation; to the fact that he has a gin and a press of his own in the midst of his cotton fields, to which he can carry his wool at one transfer from the picking; by which he can put it in order for market expeditiously, and at an expense much below that falling upon the farmer, who must first store his wool, then send it to the planter's gin and press and have it prepared at the planter's convenience, paying, perhaps, exorbitantly therefor; and, finally, to the fact that the planter deals directly with the exporter.

Olmsted saw clearly that these advantages of large-scale organization were having the result of hastening the concentration of slave ownership—especially in the Southwest. The large planters, with their favorable advantages for production and marketing, made handsome profits under prices for cotton prevailing in the sixth decade. Many of them were thrifty, and reinvested a large part of their gains in more land and slaves. Their superior credit made it possible to be always in the market for slaves, while their superior facilities for production enabled them to offer prices that the small interior planter could not afford to pay. In the sixth decade, therefore, the prices of slaves were being determined largely by the net product of their labor when employed under most favorable circumstances: that is, on the best land, with the best equipment, and under large-scale organization.

b] DISADVANTAGES OF AN OVERCAPITALIZED AND INELASTIC LABOR FORCE

WHETHER NEGRO slavery was an advantage in the early colonies and whether it became a burden in the later period, and, if so, how the change occurred, and why the people did not relieve themselves of the incubus—these are a few of the fundamental problems to which the student must address himself. The present essay, based on a study of slave prices, deals with the general economic conditions of slaveholding, and shows the great transformation caused by the opening of the cotton belt and the closing of the African slave trade.

Negro slavery was established in the South, as elsewhere, because the white people were seeking their own welfare and comfort. It was maintained for the same economic reason, and also because it was thought to be essential for safety. As soon as the negroes were on hand in large numbers, the problem was to keep their savage instincts from breaking forth, and to utilize them in civilized industry. The plantation system solved the problem of organization, while the discipline and control obtained through the institution of slavery were considered necessary to preserve the peace and to secure the welfare of both races. Private gain and public safety were secured for the time being; but in the long run, as we shall see, these ends were attained at the expense of private and public wealth and of progress.

This peculiar labor system failed to gain strength in the North, because there was there no work which negro slaves could perform with notable profit to their masters. In certain parts of the South the system flourished because the work required was simple, the returns were large, and the shortcomings of negro slave labor were partially offset by the ease with which it could be organized.

Once developed, the system was of course maintained so long as it appeared profitable to any important part of the community. Wherever the immediate profits from slave labor were found to be large, the number

FROM Ulrich B. Phillips, "The Economic Cost of Slaveholding in the Cotton Belt," *Political Science Quarterly*, XX (June, 1905), 257, 259–75.

of slaves tended to increase, not only through the birth of children, but by importations. Thus the staple-producing areas became "black belts," where most of the labor was done by slaves. With large amounts of capital invested in slaves, the system would be maintained even in times of depression, when the plantations were running at something of a loss; for, just as in a factory, the capital was fixed, and operations could not be stopped without a still greater loss. When property in slaves had become important, the conservative element in politics became devoted, as a rule, to the preservation of this vested interest. The very force of inertia tended to maintain the established system, and a convulsion or crisis of some sort was necessary for its disestablishment in any region.

As a matter of fact it was only in special industries, and only in times of special prosperity, that negro slave labor was of such decided profit as to escape condemnation for its inherent disadvantages. But at certain periods in Virginia and in the lower South, the conditions were unusual: all labor was profitable; hired labor was not to be had so long as land was free; indentured white servants were in various ways unsatisfactory, and negro slaves were therefore found to be of decided profit to their masters. The price of Africans in colonial times was so low that, when crops and prices were good, the labor of those imported repaid their original cost in a few years, and the planters felt a constant temptation to increase their holdings of land and of slaves in the hope of still greater profits.

Thus in Virginia there was a vicious circle: planters bought fresh lands and more slaves to make more tobacco, and with the profits from tobacco they bought more land and slaves to make more tobacco with which to buy yet more land and slaves. The situation in the lower South was similar to that in Virginia, with rice and indigo, or sugar, or in latter times cotton, substituted for tobacco. In either case the process involved a heavy export of wealth in the acquisition of every new laborer. The Yankee skipper had a corresponding circle of his own: he carried rum to Guinea to exchange for slaves, slaves to the plantation colonies to exchange for molasses, molasses to New England to exchange for more rum, and this rum again to Guinea to exchange for more slaves. The difference was that the Yankee made a genuine profit on every exchange and thriftily laid up his savings, while the southern planter, as a rule, invested all his profits in a fictitious form of wealth and never accumulated a surplus for any other sort of investment.

From an economic point of view the American system of slavery was a system of firmly controlling the unintelligent negro laborers, and of capitalizing the prospective value of the labor of each workman for the whole of his life. An essential feature of that system was the practice of buying and selling the control over the slave's labor, and one of the indexes to the economic situation at any time may be found in the quotations of slave prices.

The slave trade had no particular local home or "exchange," but it extended throughout all the slaveholding districts of America. Though the number and frequency of slave sales was relatively small, the traffic when once developed had many of the features of modern stock or produce markets. It cannot be forgotten, of course, that the slave trade involved questions of humanity and social organization as well as the mere money problem; but from the financial point of view the slave traffic constituted simply an extensive commodity market, where the article dealt in was life-time labor. As in any other market, the operations in the slave trade were controlled by economic laws or tendencies. There were bull influences and bear influences, and occasional speculative campaigns. And when at times the supply was subjected to monopoly control, the prices tended to go wild and disturb the general system of finance in the whole region.

In the general slave market there was constant competititon among those wishing to sell, and among those wishing to buy. The volume of the colonial slave trade and the rate of slave prices tended to fluctuate to some extent with the tides of prosperity in the respective staple-producing areas; but during the colonial period the plantations in the different regions were of such varied interests, producing tobacco, rice, indigo, cotton, sugar and coffee, that depression in one of these industries was usually offset, so far as concerned the slave-trader, by high profits in another. Barbadoes was the information station. The slave ships touched there and gathered news of where their "ebony" was to be sold the highest. The Royal African Company had the best system of intelligence, and about 1770 and 1780 it sold its cargoes at a fairly uniform price of £18 to £22 per head, while the independent traders appear to have obtained from £15 to £25, according to the chances of the market. American-born slaves, when sold, brought higher prices than fresh Africans, because their training in plantation labor and domestic service rendered them more valuable. The prices of the home-raised slaves varied considerably, but so long as the African trade was kept open, the price of field hands of all sorts was kept reasonably near to the price of the savage African imports.

In the very early period the sellers in the slave market were more eager than the buyers, and the prices ranged nearly as low as the cost of purchasing slaves in Africa and transporting them to America; but great prosperity in all the different groups of plantations at the same period soon greatly increased the demand, and the ships in the traffic proving too few, prices rapidly advanced. After this, however, there came a decline in tobacco profits; then the war of revolt from Great Britain depressed all the staple industries simultaneously, and following that the American production of indigo was ruined by foreign competition. Thus in 1790–95 slave prices reached the bottom of a twenty years' decline.

The developments following Whitney's invention of the cotton gin revolutionized the situation. Slave prices entered upon a steady advance, which was quickened by the prohibition of the African trade in 1808. They were then held stationary by the restrictions upon commerce, and were thrown backward by the outbreak of war in 1812. But with the peace of Ghent the results of the new cotton industry and of the cessation of African imports became strikingly manifest. The inland fields of the lower South proved to be peculiarly adapted for the production of cotton. The simplicity of the work and the even distribution of the tasks through the seasons made negro slave labor peculiarly available. With the increasing demand of the world for cotton, there was built up in the South perhaps the greatest staple monopoly the world had ever seen. The result was an enormous demand for slaves in the cotton belt. American ports, however, were now closed to the foreign slave trade. The number of slaves available in America was now fixed, the rate of increase was limited, and the old "tobacco South" had a monopoly of the only supply which could meet the demand of the new "cotton South."

Till 1815 "colonial" conditions prevailed, and the market for slave labor was relatively quiet and steady. In 1815 began the "ante-bellum" régime, in which the whole economy of the South was governed by the apparently capricious play of the compound monopoly of cotton and slave labor. The price of cotton was governed by the American output and its relation to the European demand. And the price of slaves was governed by the profits in cotton and the relation of the labor demand to the monopolized labor supply.

For an understanding of slaveholding economics, a careful study of the history of slave prices is essential. Prior to the middle of the eighteenth century, the scarcity of data, the changing value of gold, the multiplicity of coinage systems and the use of paper money with irregular depreciations unfortunately present so many obstacles that any effort to determine the fluctuation of slave prices would be of very doubtful success. For the following periods the study is feasible, although under the best of existing circumstances slave prices are hard to collect and hard to compare. The proportion of the slave population on the market at any time was very much smaller than the student of prices could wish for the purpose of his study; and many of the sales which were made are not to be found in the records. The market classification of the slaves was flexible and irregular; and, except in Louisiana, most of the documents in the public archives do not indicate the classification. To make thoroughly accurate comparison of slave prices at different times and places, we should need to know, among other things, the sex, age, strength and nativity of the slaves; the purity or mixture of blood of the negroes, mulattoes, quadroons, mestizoes, etc.; and their special training or lack of it. For such statistical purposes, however, the records have many shortcomings. In many cases they state simply that the slave Matt or Congo or Martha, belonging to the estate of William Jones, deceased, was sold on the date given to Thomas Smith, for, say, $300, on twelve months' credit. Such an item indicates the sex and states the price, but gives little else. In other instances the slaves are classed as infants, boys, men (or fellows) and old men; girls, wenches and old women. Whole families were often sold as a lot, with no individual quotations given. Women were hardly ever sold separate from their young children. In the dearth of separate sale quotations, any study of the prices of female slaves would have to be based chiefly upon appraisal values, which of course were much less accurate than actual market prices.

The sales made by the professional slave traders were generally recorded each in a bill of sale; but in most of the localities these were not transcribed into the formal books of record, and the originals have mostly disappeared.

The majority of the sales of which records are to be found were those of the slaves in the estates of deceased persons. These sales were at auction; and except in abnormal cases, which may often be distinguished, they may be taken as fairly representative of slave prices for the time and place.

There was always a great difference between the values of individual slaves. When the average price of negroes ranged about $500, prime field hands brought, say, $1,000, and skilled artisans still more. At that rate, an infant would be valued at about $100, a boy of twelve years and a man of fifty at about $500 each, and a prime wench for field work at $800 or $900.

The most feasible comparison of prices is that of prime field hands, who may be defined as well-grown, able-bodied fellows, with average training and between eighteen and thirty years of age. To find the current price of prime field hands in lists where no classification is given, we take the average of the highest ordinary prices. We ignore any scattering extreme quotations, as applying probably to specially valuable artisans, overseers or domestic servants, and not to field hands. Where ages are given, we take the average of the prices paid for grown fellows too young to have received special training. We leave aside, on the other hand, the exceptionally low quotations as being due to infirmities which exclude the slave from the prime grade. The professional slave traders in the domestic traffic dealt mostly in "likely young fellows and wenches." In the quotations of the sales by these traders, when no details are recorded, we may assume that the average, except for children, will range just a little below the current rate for prime field hands.

In view of all the hindrances, the production of a perfectly accurate table of prices cannot be hoped for, even from the exercise of the utmost care and discrimination. The table which follows is simply an approximation of averages made in a careful study of several thousand quotations in the state of Georgia.[1]

The parallel quotations of cotton prices[2] afford a basis for the study of slave-labor capitalization. In examining these quotations it will be noticed that during many brief periods the prices of slaves and cotton rose and fell somewhat in harmony; but that in the whole period under review the price of cotton underwent a heavy net decline, while slave prices had an extremely strong upward movement. The change which took place in the relative slave and cotton prices was really astonishing. In 1800 a prime field hand was worth in the market about 1500 pounds of ginned cotton; in 1809, about 3000 pounds; in 1818, about 3500; in 1826, about 5400; in 1837, about 10,000; in 1845, about 12,000; in 1860, 15,000 to 18,000. In his

[1] The sources used for this tabulation are the documents in the Georgia state archives and the records of Baldwin, Oglethorpe, Clarke and Troup counties, all lying in the Georgia cotton belt, together with bills of sale in private hands, travelers' accounts, and articles in the newspapers of the period. Instances of sudden rise or fall in slave prices and sales of large and noted estates were often reported in the local press, with comments. There is no printed collection of any large number of slave-price quotations.

[2] The cotton price averages are made from the tables given by E. J. Donnell in his *Chronological and Statistical History of Cotton*, New York, 1872, with the aid of the summaries published by G. L. Watkins, *Production and Price of Cotton for One Hundred Years*, U.S. Department of Agriculture, Washington, 1895.

SLAVE AND COTTON PRICES IN GEORGIA

YEAR	AVERAGE PRICE OF PRIME FIELD HANDS	ECONOMIC SITUATION AND THE CHIEF DETERMINANT FACTORS	AVERAGE N.Y. PRICE OF UPLAND COTTON	YEARS
1755	£55			
1773	60			
1776–1783	—	War and depression in industry and commerce		
1784	70	Peace and returning prosperity		
1792	$300	Depression due to Great Britain's attitude toward American commerce		
1793	—	Cotton gin invented		
1800 [a]	450		30 cents	1795–1805
1808	—	African slave trade prohibited		
1809	600	Embargo moderates rise in prices	19 cents	1805–1810
1813	450	War with Great Britain	12 cents	1813
1818	1000	Inflation	29 cents	1816–1818
1819	—	Financial crisis	16 cents	1819
1821	700	Recovery from panic	14 cents	1821
1826	800	Moderate prosperity	15 cents	1824–1827
1827	—	Depression		
1828	700		10 cents	1827–1828
1835	900	Flush times	17½ cents	1835
1837	1300	Inflation—crash	13½ cents	1837
1839	1000	Cotton crisis	13½ cents	1839
1840	700	Cotton crisis; acute distress	9 cents	1840
1844	600	Depression	7½ cents	1844
1845	—	Severe depression	5½ cents	1845
1848	900	Recovery in cotton prices Texas demand for slaves	9½ cents	1847–1848
1851	1050	Prosperity	12 cents	1851
1853	1200	Expansion of cotton industry and simultaneous rise in tobacco prices [c]	11 cents	1850–1860
1859	1650			
1860 [b]	1800			

[a] The quotations down to this point are lowland quotations. There were very few slaves in the uplands before 1800.

[b] In the later fifties there were numerous local flurries in slave valuations. In central Georgia prime negroes brought $2,000 in 1860, while in western Georgia and central Alabama the prices appear not to have run much above $1,500. For prices in the other parts of the South in that decade, see G. W. Weston, Who are and who may be slaves in the United States, a pamphlet published in 1856. See also Brackett, The Negro in Maryland; Ingle, Southern Sidelights; Hammond, The Cotton Industry, and De Bow's Review, vol. xxvi, p. 647.

[c] The rise in tobacco prices and the revival of prosperity in Virginia in this decade tended to diminish the volume of the slave trade and contributed to raising slave prices. Cf. W. H. Collins, The Domestic Slave Trade in the Southern States, N.Y., 1904, p. 57.

capacity for work, a prime negro in 1800 was worth nearly or quite as much as a similar slave in 1860; and a pound of cotton in 1860 was not essentially different from a pound of cotton in 1800. But our table shows that within that epoch of three-score years there was an advance of some 1000 or 1200 per cent in the price of slaves as measured in cotton.

The decline in the price of cotton was due in some measure to a lessening of cost, through improvements in cultivating, ginning and marketing. The advance in slave prices was due in part to the increasing intelligence and ability of the negroes and to improvements in the system of directing their work on the plantations, and also in part to the decline in the value of money. But the ten-fold or twelve-fold multiplication of the price of slaves, when quoted in terms of the product of their labor, was too great to be explained except by reference to the severe competition of the planters in selling cotton and in buying slaves. Their system of capitalized labor was out of place in the modern competitive world, and burdened with that system all the competition of the cotton planters was bound to be of a cut-throat nature. In other words, when capital and labor were combined, as in the American slaveholding system, there was an irresistible tendency to overvalue and overcapitalize slave labor, and to carry it to the point where the financial equilibrium was unsafe, and any crisis threatened complete bankruptcy.

Aside from the expense of food, clothing and shelter, the cost of slave labor for any given period of time was made up of several elements:

(1) Interest upon the capital invested in the slave.

(2) Economic insurance against (a) his death, (b) his illness or accidental injury, and (c) his flight from service. Of course insurance policies were seldom taken out to cover these risks, but the cost of insurance against them must be reckoned in the cost of slave labor for any given period.

(3) The diminishing value of every mature slave by reason of increasing age. Because of the "wear and tear" of his years and his diminishing prospect of life and usefulness, the average slave of fifty-five years of age would be worth only half as much as one of twenty-five years, and after fifty-five the valuation decreased still more rapidly. In computing the cost of any group of slaves it will be necessary to set over against this depreciation the value of the children born; but, on the other hand, the cost by groups would be increased by the need of supporting the disabled negroes who were not in the working gangs.

(4) Taxation assessed upon the capitalized value of the slaves. In the slaveholding region as a whole, in the later ante-bellum period, the total assessed value of slave property was at least as great as that of all the other sorts of property combined.

The rate of slave hire would furnish a good index of the current price of slave labor year by year, if sufficient quotations on a stable basis could be obtained. But on account of the special needs or wishes of the parties to the individual bargains, there were such opportunities for higgling the rate in individual cases that the current rate is very elusive. The following averages, computed from a limited number of quotations for the hire of men slaves in middle Georgia, are illustrative: In 1800, $100 per year; in

1816, $110; in 1818, $140; in 1833, $140; in 1836, $155; in 1841, $140; in 1860, $150. These were in most cases the years of maximum quotations in the respective periods. The local fluctuations in short periods were often very pronounced; but in the long run the rate followed a gradual upward movement.

The relation between the price of slaves and the rate of their hire should theoretically have borne, in quiet periods, a definite relation to the rate of interest upon capital; but the truth is that in the matter of slave prices there was, through the whole period after the closing of the African trade, a tendency to "frenzied finance" in the cotton belt. Slave prices were largely controlled by speculation, while slave hire was regulated more largely by the current rate of wages for labor in general. The whole subject of these relations is one for which authentic data are perhaps too scanty to permit of thorough analysis.

Negro slave labor was expensive, not so much because it was unwilling as because it was overcapitalized and inelastic. The negro of himself, by reason of his inherited inaptitude, was inefficient as a self-directing laborer in civilized industry. The whole system of civilized life was novel and artificial to him; and to make him play a valuable part in it, strict guidance and supervision were essential. Without the plantation system, the mass of the negroes would have been an unbearable burden in America; and except in slavery they could never have been utilized, in the beginning, for plantation work. The negro had no love of work for work's sake; and he had little appreciation of future goods when set over against present exemption from toil. That is to say, he lacked the economic motive without which voluntary civilized industry is impossible. It is a mistake to apply the general philosophy of slavery to the American situation without very serious modification. A slave among the Greeks or Romans was generally a relatively civilized person, whose voluntary labor would have been far more productive than his labor under compulsion. But the negro slave was a negro first, last and always, and a slave incidentally. Mr. Cairnes and others make a great mistake when they attribute his inefficiency and expensiveness altogether to the one incident of regulation. Regulation actually remedied in large degree the disadvantages of using negro labor, though it failed to make it as cheap, in most employments, as free white labor would have been. The cotton planter found the negro already a part of the situation. To render him useful, firm regulation was necessary. The forcible control of the negro was in the beginning a necessity, and was not of itself a burden at any time.

In American slaveholding, however, the capitalization of labor-value and the sale and purchase of labor-control were permanent features; and when the supply was "cornered" it was unavoidable that the price should be bid up to the point of overvaluation.[3] And this brings us to the main economic disadvantage of the system.

[3] In the periods of high slave prices employers found that slave labor was too expensive to be used with profit except in plantation industry under the most favorable circumstances. Striking proof of this is to be seen in the eager employment, wherever they could be had, of Irish and German immigrants for canal and railway building, ditching and

In employing free labor, wages are paid from time to time as the work is done, and the employer can count upon receiving from the products of that labor an income which will enable him to continue to pay its wages in the future, while his working capital is left free for other uses. He may invest a portion of his capital in lands and buildings, and use most of the remainder as circulating capital for special purposes, retaining only a small percentage as a reserve fund. But to secure a working force of slaves, the ante-bellum planter had to invest all the capital that he owned or could borrow in the purchase of slaves and lands; for the larger his plantation was, within certain limits, the more economies he could introduce. The temptation was very strong for him to trim down to the lowest possible limit the fund for supplies and reserve. The slaveholding system thus absorbed the planter's earnings; and for such absorption it had unlimited capacity, for the greater the profits of the planters the more slaves they wanted and the higher the slave prices mounted. Individual profits, as fast as made, went into the purchase of labor, and not into modern implements or land improvements. Circulating capital was at once converted into fixed capital; while for their annual supplies of food, implements and luxuries the planters continued to rely upon their credit with the local merchants, and the local merchants to rely upon their credit with northern merchants and bankers.

Thus there was a never-ending private loss through the continual payment of interest and the enhancement of prices; and, further, there was a continuous public loss by the draining of wealth out of the cotton belt by the slave trade. With the stopping of the African slave trade, the drain of wealth from the lower South was not checked at all, but merely diverted from England and New England to the upper tier of southern states; and there it did little but demoralize industry and postpone to a later generation the agricultural revival.

The capitalization of labor lessened its elasticity and its versatility; it tended to fix labor rigidly in one line of employment. There was little or no floating labor in the plantation districts; and the planter was obliged to plan in detail a whole year's work before the year began. If he should plant a larger acreage than his "force" could cultivate and harvest, a part of the crop would have to be abandoned, unless by chance some free negro or stray Irishman could be found for the odd job. As an illustration of the financial hardships which might befall the slaveholder, it may be noted that in 1839 William Lowndes Yancey happened to lose his whole force of slaves through poisoning in the midst of the working season. The disaster involved his absolute ruin as a planter, and forced him to seek some other opening which did not require the possession of capital.

In the operations of cotton production, where fluctuating and highly uncertain returns demanded the greatest flexibility, the slaveholding system was rigid. When by overproduction the price of cotton was depressed, it could be raised again only by curtailing the output in the American cotton belt, which had the monopoly. But the planter, owning cotton lands and

---

any other labor which might prove injurious to a negro's health and strength. Slaves were growing too dear to be used. . . .

slaves trained in the cotton field alone, found it hard to devote his fields with success to other crops or to sell or lease his negroes to any one else, for no one else wanted them for any other purpose than cotton production. In fact, the proportion of the southern resources devoted to cotton production tended always to increase. To diminish the cotton output required the most heroic efforts. As a rule, the chances of heavy gains from cotton planting outweighed those of loss, in the popular estimation; and the strong and constant tendency was to spoil the market by over-supply.

There were uncertain returns in cotton raising, and great risks in slave-owning. The crop might be heavy or light in any year, according to the acreage and the weather, and prices might be away up or away down. A prime slave might be killed by a rattlesnake or crippled in a log-rolling or hanged for murder or spirited away by the underground railroad. All these uncertainties fostered extravagance and speculation.

In the cotton belt inflation and depression followed each other in rapid succession; but the times of prosperity brought less real advantage and periods of depression caused greater hardship in the slaveholding South than in any normally organized community. For by the capitalizing of labor, profits were generally absorbed through the purchasing of additional slaves at higher prices, while in time of need the cotton-planter found it impossible to realize upon his investment because his neighbors were involved in the same difficulties which embarrassed him, and when he would sell they could not buy.

When after the peace in 1815 the system of industry and finance of the ante-bellum South had fully developed itself, the South and its leaders were seized in the grip of social and economic forces which were rendered irresistible by the imperious laws of monopoly. The cotton-planters controlled the South, and for some decades they dominated the policy of the federal government; but the cotton-planters themselves were hurried hither and thither by their two inanimate but arbitrary masters, cotton and slavery.

Cotton and slavery were peculiar to the South, and their requirements were often in conflict with the interests and ideas prevailing in the other parts of the United States. As that conflict of interests and sentiments was accentuated, it became apparent that the South was in a congressional minority, likely to be overridden at any time by a northern majority. Ruin was threatening the vested interests and the social order in the South; and the force of circumstances drove the southern politicians into the policy of resistance. To the leaders in the South, with their ever-present view of the possibility of negro uprisings, the regulations of slavery seemed essential for safety and prosperity. And when they found themselves about to become powerless to check any legislation hostile to the established order in the South, they adopted the policy of secession, seeking, as they saw it, the lesser of the evils confronting them.

Because they were blinded by the abolition agitation in the North and other historical developments which we cannot here discuss, most of the later generation of ante-bellum planters could not see that slaveholding was essentially burdensome. But that which was partly hidden from their vision is clear to us to-day. In the great system of southern industry and commerce, working with seeming smoothness, the negro laborers were inefficient in spite of discipline, and slavery was an obstacle to all progress. The system may be likened to an engine, with slavery as its great fly-wheel —a fly-wheel indispensable for safe running at first, perhaps, but later rendered less useful by improvements in the machinery, and finally becoming a burden instead of a benefit. Yet it was retained, because it was still considered essential in securing the adjustment and regular working of the complex mechanism. This great rigid wheel of slavery was so awkward and burdensome that it absorbed the momentum and retarded the movement of the whole machine without rendering any service of great value. The capitalization of labor and the export of earnings in exchange for more workmen, always of a low degree of efficiency, together with the extreme lack of versatility, deprived the South of the natural advantage which the cotton monopoly should have given. To be rid of the capitalization of labor as a part of the slaveholding system was a great requisite for the material progress of the South.

3] Measurement of Income from Planting with Slave Labor

a] HIGH PRODUCTION COSTS ABSORB PROFITS

. . . .

THE BARE fact that Mississippi imported tremendous numbers of slaves is perhaps sufficient proof that her citizens wanted slaves, believing that ownership of them would bring wealth. It was certainly the current belief that slave-owners were rich. Olmsted was told that the plantations adjacent to the road entering Natchez from the south were owned by men worth without exception from a hundred thousand to ten million dollars. Ingraham thought that as a class Southern planters were perhaps wealthier than any other class of men in America. He declared that in the southwestern part of Mississippi annual incomes of twenty thousand dollars were common and that several individuals received from forty to fifty thousand dollars a year. This is his description of the way these great estates were amassed:

> The southern farmer can make from fifteen to thirty per cent. by his farm. He works on his plantation a certain number of slaves, say thirty, which are to him what the sinewy arms of the Yankee farmer are to himself. Each slave ought to average from seven to eight bales of cotton during the season, especially on the new lands. An acre will generally average from one to two bales. Each bale averages four hundred pounds, at from twelve to fifteen cents a pound. This may not be an exact estimate, but it is not far from the true one. Deducting two thousand and five hundred dollars for the expenses of

FROM Charles Sackett Sydnor, *Slavery in Mississippi* (New York: D. Appleton-Century Co., 1933), pp. 194–202.

the plantation, there will remain the net income of eleven thousand dollars. Now suppose this plantation and slaves to have been purchased on a credit, paying at the rate of six hundred dollars apiece for his negroes the planter would be able to pay for nearly two-thirds of them the first year. The second year, he would pay for the remainder, and purchase ten or twelve more; and the third year, if he obtained his plantation on a credit of that length of time, he would pay for that also, and commence his fourth year with a valuable plantation, and thirty-five or forty slaves, all his own property, with an increased income for the ensuing year of some thousands of dollars. Henceforward, if prudent, he will rank as an opulent planter.

Undoubtedly there were some planters in Mississippi who equaled or bettered the estimates of Ingraham. Consider the following figures taken from the federal census of 1860. In Issaquena County there were 5,193 slaves between ten and seventy years old. (Including infants and aged, the total was 7,244 slaves. There were only 587 white persons in the county.) These negroes produced 41,170 bales of cotton of an average weight of about 400 pounds. Without deducting cooks, house-servants, blacksmiths, carpenters, and others who did little field work, this was an average of eight bales for every negro over ten and under seventy. Valuing cotton at eleven cents a pound, the owners received about $350 per negro.

Most planters, even in their best years, did not equal such high profits as these. The following records better represent the earnings of normal Mississippi plantations. In 1851, on the Bowles plantation in Lafayette County, approximately twenty-three working hands produced 122 bales, an average of about 5.5 bales of 400 pounds each to the hand. In 1858, fifteen hands on the Wheeless plantation in Yazoo County produced eighty-seven bales, or slightly over 5.8 bales each. During the three years 1857, 1858, and 1859, an average of twenty-four hands on the McArn plantation in Jefferson County produced an average crop of six bales to the hand. These plantations were in different cotton-producing sections of the State. The first two were under the management of overseers; the third may have been. In each case, the largest number of negroes who picked cotton on any day was taken as the number of hands on that estate. House-servants, infants, the aged, and others who did not pick cotton were not included.

On the basis of these and other figures, let us investigate the profitableness of raising cotton by slave labor in the 1850's on a plantation of fifty slaves.

The chief source of income would be from cotton. Probably thirty of the fifty negroes worked in the field. If these produced 5¾ bales each, there would be a total of 158 bales which, at ten cents a pound, would be worth   [$6,320] [1]

The expenses of the plantation would be as follows: 50 negroes at $600 each (in the late 'fifties the price was higher) represented an investment of $30,000. Calculating interest at 6 per cent, this amounted to   1,800

At least an equal amount should be added for depreciation in slave property by accidents, deaths, old age, etc.   1,800

[1] [Figure omitted in original—H.D.W.]

As the average hand worked about twelve acres, 600 acres would be ample for pastures and woodland as well as fields. Allowing $10 an acre, the investment in land at 6 per cent interest involved a yearly carriage charge of   360
and it ordinarily depreciated at the rate of at least 3 per cent a year in value   180
Annual hire of an overseer, at least   300
Purchases from New Orleans or elsewhere of negro clothing, miscellaneous plantation supplies, etc.   1,000
Without including various miscellaneous expenditures, such as the purchase of corn and pork, of which few plantations produced enough, the total of the expenses and interest charges was $5,440

On the basis of these calculations, the planter received $880 profit, though he was, of course, free to spend the interest on his investment in negroes and land, and this was the item that caused the profits from Mississippi plantations to appear high. The $880 might be considered the wages of the planter for managing the enterprise.

If anything, the above statement is too optimistic. P. R. Leigh, a very intelligent planter, managed forty-nine slaves. From his detailed accounts it appears that the net profit of his plantation from July, 1851, to June, 1852, was $2,194.81. It is evident that he but slightly exceeded 6 per cent interest on his investment with no allowance for such items as depreciation and his own wages as director of the enterprise.

In 1834, a year of prosperity and good prices, the Polk plantation was established in Yalobusha County. Eight hundred acres of land were purchased at $10 an acre, though only 271 acres were cleared five years later and 566 acres by 1851. Thirty-seven slaves valued at $16,000 were placed on the land. Considering the amount of cleared land and the value of the negroes, it is probable that there were less than twenty hands in the lot. The total investment was close to $25,000. In 1860, the plantation was sold for $30,000, though some of the slaves had been otherwise disposed of. In 1851, if we may judge by the amount of land in cultivation, there must have been considerably more slaves than in either 1834 or 1861.

During the nine years from 1849 through 1857, the average net proceeds from the cotton crop was about $5,375. This was the total receipts from cotton less the various costs of marketing it: fire and river insurance, shippers' charges, freight, charges for storage and weighing, and commission on sale.

While $5,375 was the average annual net receipt from cotton, this was not the net profit from the plantation. The overseer was paid from $350 to $550 a year. Plantation supplies must have cost at least $500 a year, besides the expenses of recapturing fugitive slaves, costs of medicines and medical attention, and the other miscellaneous needs of a plantation. This left an average annual income of less than $4,500 from property that sold for $30,000 after some of the slaves had been disposed of. Making allowance for the aging of the negroes, the return was by no means princely even though the commission merchant several times stated that the price of the Polk cotton bettered the general market price because of its mark.

Captain Isaac Ross died in 1836, leaving property worth $150,000, in addition to 165 negroes. The latter must have been worth $100,000. The estimated annual income of his estate was $20,000, which was 8 per cent of the investment. This was in 1836, when cotton sold for sixteen cents a pound.

Such figures as these explain why few cotton planters were able to follow Ingraham's optimistic plan of buying negroes and land on credit and paying for them in three years. While many tried, few succeeded. More stayed in debt, with crops mortgaged several years in advance, finally getting ahead with a good crop or in lean years losing part or all of their negroes. Even though successful, the planter was constantly tempted to enlarge his fields and increase his slave force on credit. Sheriffs' and trustees' sales, adverse balances on the books of New Orleans merchants, and debts to slave-traders were all evidence that cotton plantations were not sure roads to wealth.

On the other hand, it must be remembered that the planter's life had attractions and obligations that kept many from deserting it, even though their investments showed an inadequate return. The plantation supplied its owner with many of the necessities of life, and the planter often had numerous house and yard servants to give a pleasurable distinction and dignity to his mode of life as well as to relieve him and his family from physical labor.

Cotton, however, was not the only source of profit. A planter who barely made expenses by the sale of cotton might find his estate yearly increasing in value by the rearing of young negroes. With a good price for cotton in 1836, Isaac Ross was making $20,000 a year with 165 slaves. With the drop in the price of cotton, he would probably not have made expenses in 1848. However, his slaves had increased without a single purchase to 235. Though Ross was not a speculator, for by his will he freed his negroes and returned them to Africa, their value had greatly increased in twelve years. Without planning to sell a single negro, and without speculating on a rising market, the planter who gave reasonable attention to the care of negro children would have good reason to believe that he was building a valuable estate for his own children. But all were not so wise. Especially in the regions of large and productive plantations, many slave-owners, according to M. W. Philips, drove the negroes too hard in making large cotton crops and thereby diminished the normal natural increase of their slaves. As that Mississippian wrote, they "killed the goose for the golden egg," instead of having due regard for both sources of profit—cotton and negroes.

Large plantations probably yielded a larger return in proportion to the investment than small farms. One overseer could superintend fifty negroes almost as well as five, and negroes on large plantations could be trained for more specialized tasks. Olmsted, who did not believe slavery was profitable in most sections of the South, made the following judicious generalizations concerning Mississippi:

It is quite plain, notwithstanding all the drawbacks attending the employment of forced labor, and notwithstanding the high price of slaves, that slave labor is employed profitably by the large planters in Mississippi, and in certain other parts of the South, in the culture of cotton. . . .

Nor do I think myself warranted in denying that the production of cotton per acre on many Mississippi plantations may not be as large as it can be economically made with land as low and slaves as high in price as is at present the case.

In brief, many Mississippi planters prospered in spite of slavery because cotton was profitable and land cheap.

The average free laborer seldom receives in exchange for his work more than food, clothing, shelter, and medical attention for himself and his family, with a guarantee against unemployment and a modest old-age pension. The planter paid these directly to his slave. In addition he paid from $500 to $1,800 to a slave-trader. What did he receive in return for the latter? He secured a perpetual contract to the slave's labor which guaranteed him a steady labor supply undisturbed by capricious turnover or wholesale strikes. He also gained the right to use force, if necessary, to extort from the negro work which in most cases amounted to no more than a fair amount a day. However, as the planter was not vexed by having his laborers work one day and loaf the next, the slave probably did considerably more in a year, though little more in a day, than free-negro farm hands of the present time.

The plantation of thirty working hands represented an investment for land and negroes of about $40,000. With free labor, this should not have exceeded $10,000. Slave labor greatly increased the capital investment and, therefore, the interest charges. On the venture was imposed the necessity of supporting an investment which added nothing to the productivity of the soil or to the betterment of the farm equipment. It is most improbable that the efficiency of the working force was increased enough to justify the enlarged investment of capital.

The Mississippi planter made more money as a slaveholder than he would have done by his own labors. It is probable that his income would have been even larger with free labor. Had neither slave nor free labor been available, the soil would have been conserved better for later generations; but as it was, profits were reinvested in slaves. This accelerated the transformation of rich soil into cotton and poor land. The larger the profits from cotton, the more numerous were the purchases of slaves and "after that, it was more negroes to work more land to the end of the chapter." From an economic standpoint, it is very questionable whether slaves were a good investment year in and year out even in Mississippi. But whether the profits were large or small, they were invested mostly in negroes and the total, by 1860, was enormous. At $800 apiece, the 436,691 slaves in Mississippi, in 1860, were worth $349,344,800. According to the federal census of that year, the total cash value of all farm land, unimproved as well as improved, of farming implements and of all live-stock in the State was $241,478,571.

It is impossible to say without qualification whether the conversion of this share of the capital of the State into negro slaves was economically sound. Much of this capital, it must be remembered, had been created by the labor of these slaves; on the other hand, immigrant white farmers would have come eventually to till the soil. Viewed in the light of subsequent history, the question resolves itself chiefly into this: Would Mississippi be in better or worse condition to-day, if its negro population were replaced by whites? On the other hand, if one cares to speculate on the soundness of Mississippi's large investment in slaves had slavery continued for a much longer period than it did, the answer would depend on whether the price of slaves held up. Since a fall in price of two dollars a slave would cause a drop of nearly a million dollars in the capital value of the slaves in the State, the profitableness of the institution depended largely on the price of slaves.

Considering the prices of cotton, land, and negroes, there were three periods when Mississippi planters prospered. Immediately before 1820 little cotton was being produced but those who raised it must have reaped very large profits. The per cent of profit was not quite so large in the middle 'thirties, but much more cotton was sold. In spite of higher prices for slaves and lower prices for cotton, better varieties of the latter allowed cheaper production and large profits remained. In the third period, the late 'fifties, cotton brought only a fair price and slaves were very high. The margin of profit was therefore small. However, the increased price of slaves was not felt by those who already had them and not many were imported during this period. The average planter, while making a little better profit from cotton, also found that his stock of slaves was more valuable than formerly. To have both income and investment increase was encouraging, even though the ratio of income to investment did not improve. Finally, in this last period cotton crops were large.

Considering the three periods of prosperity, the price of cotton was lower in each peak than in the previous one; the cost of slaves was higher; and the crop of cotton was larger.

It is easy to understand why the defense of slavery proved popular in the well-nigh statewide prosperity of the 'thirties. Why did the veneration of slavery continue during the depression from 1837 until 1855? Considering the price of slaves and of cotton, it was impossible for a planter to make large profits and many of them lost heavily. Neither does the moderate prosperity of the late 'fifties seem to have been sufficient to justify renewed confidence in the economic soundness of slavery. By 1860 Mississippi had nearly as many slaves as it needed. With the natural increase in slave population the price must have declined unless a market for the surplus could be found. Texas for a time could buy from Mississippi as Mississippi had for years bought from Virginia, but when Texas and the rest of the new Southwest were supplied, slave prices would fall unless more territory suited to slave labor could be discovered. As there was little probability of finding this within the Union, economics demanded that the slave-owner be an expansionist, for without a market slave prices must soon have declined.

b] MULTIPLICITY OF INCOME INCREASES PROFITS

THE DEBATE over the profitableness of slavery has been going on, in one form or another, for almost one hundred and fifty years. It is, perhaps, too late for a definitive settlement of the question because of the destruction of so much of the evidence, but there can be an attempt at a reconciliation of the conflicting conclusions of the various students who have written about it.

The argument, too frequently, has been concerned with the question of whether or not slave labor was as profitable as free? Or, could a planter who made money with slaves have made more if he had employed free workers? These are interesting questions for speculation, but hardly more, because materials for a comparison do not exist. An experiment to test their truth or falsity probably could not have been made in the ante-bellum South where slavery appears to have been not so much an economic system as a social order to permit two unlike peoples to live together. At least it does not seem to have been tried. Comparisons between free labor farms in the North and West and slave plantations of the South are of little value because of the widely varying climatic conditions, the nature of the crops, and other circumstances. Similarly profits of a plantation before and after emancipation could hardly be compared because of the vastly different conditions in the two periods.

But if the question is narrowed to the particular one of whether the planters of the Old South were making money from their operations, there is still no agreement to be found among the writers on southern agriculture. Ulrich B. Phillips concluded that by the close of the 1850's it was "fairly certain that no slaveholders but those few whose plantations lay in the most advantageous parts of the cotton and sugar districts and whose managerial ability was exceptionally great were earning anything beyond what would cover their maintenance and carrying charges." Lewis C. Gray, expressly denying Phillips's conclusion, wrote, "Far from being a decrepit institution, the economic motives for the continuance of slavery from the standpoint of the employer were never so strong as in the years just preceding the Civil War."

The same contradictions are to be found among ante-bellum observers. Solon Robinson, the noted agricultural reformer, published a report of his observations at the plantation of Colonel L. M. Williams of Society Hill, South Carolina. The profits of the plantation, according to this statement, were very low. But the editor of the Columbia *South Carolinian,* in complete disagreement, took the same figures and proved that the profits were very large.

Robinson, in his statement, valued the plantation's 4,200 acres (2,700 of which were in cultivation) at $63,000 or $15 per acre; 254 slaves at $88,900

FROM Thomas P. Govan, "Was Plantation Slavery Profitable?" *Journal of Southern History*, VIII (November, 1942), 513–35. Copyright 1942 by the Southern Historical Association. Reprinted by permission of the Managing Editor.

or $350 each; and other assets including livestock, plantation tools, and equipment at $8,502; making a total of $160,402. Expenses amounted to $17,894.48 and included the following: interest at 7 per cent on the investment in land, slaves, and livestock (but not on the investment in tools and equipment), totaling $11,103; taxes on slaves and land; medical care; wages of three overseers; average expenditures for iron, tools, and equipment (the equivalent of depreciation); shoes, hats, and clothing; molasses, tobacco, and salt; and freight, commission, and other costs of selling and shipping cotton. The plantation produced 331,136 pounds of cotton. Its income from other sources amounted to $2,430, so that the average cost of a pound of cotton was 4.07 cents. Had this cotton sold at 6 cents, Robinson concluded, the profits would have been $1,973.68, at 7 cents, $5,385.04, which was about what it brought, being a little more than 3 per cent.

The editor of the *South Carolinian,* however, completely rejected Robinson's conclusions. First he protested against the uniform valuation of all land at $15 per acre when 1,500 acres were not in cultivation. The plantation did not need more than 750 acres of unimproved land for wood lot, grazing, etc., so that the remaining 750 acres were not, according to the writer, a legitimate part of the plantation. This reduced the real capital by $11,250 to $150,152. "But," continued the editor:

the most glaring inconsistency which our agricultural tourist exhibits in calculating the profits of a business investment, is in adding the item of interest upon capital as expense. A person investing money in any enterprise is justly considered to be doing a fair business if he makes a small percentage over interest and expenses; and the statement which Mr. Robinson furnishes of Col. Williams's plantation, only proves that our fellow-citizen makes about 12½ per cent. on his capital, and that too with the price of cotton placed as low as six cents *in Charleston*—for freight and commission are included in the table of "expenses."
. . . we deny the principle of adding interest on capital, as part of the expenses, when the object is to find out the profits upon that capital. . . . Mr. Robinson calculates interest upon the cost of the stock of the plantation, which is obviously fallacious and deceptive, where its natural increase must amount to more than the interest. . . . He omits to add to the income of the plantation the natural increase of the labor employed thereon—an item which is always prominent in the planter's calculation, and which would unquestionably amount to 5 or 6 per cent. per annum upon their original cost. And . . . he has certainly neglected the increased value arising from the yearly improvement of a well cultivated plantation. . . . The result then, according to our views, will be as follows [table on p. 53].
These profits amount to over *thirteen per cent. per annum* over all expenses— the *Charleston* price of cotton being only put down at 6 cents. Suppose the crop averaged eight cents in Charleston, as it would do at the present time, the profits would be $26,614.40, or nearly 18 per cent.

Thus, two contemporary observers, using essentially the same figures, arrive at quite different results. One said profit for the year was only $1,973.68, while the other was equally certain that it was $20,001.68. Paradoxically, both were essentially correct, because each meant something different when he wrote of profit. "Perhaps no term or concept in economic

CAPITAL INVESTED, $150,152.00

INCOME OF THE FARM

331,136 lbs. cotton, at 6 cents	$19,868.16
Bacon and other provisions	2,430.00
Increase of negroes, say 5 per cent., set down as capital $89,000	4,495.00
	26,793.16
The annual expenses of the farm, as itemized by Mr. Robinson, a full estimate, including freight and commission,	6,791.48
Net profit of capital invested	$20,001.68

discussion is used with a more bewildering variety of well established meanings than profit," Frank H. Knight, a modern economist, has stated.

Solon Robinson, probably following the definition of Jean-Baptiste Say, the French nineteenth-century economist, apparently considered profit as mere wages of management. Almost all classical economists "recognized at least three elements in the income of the capitalist entrepreneur: one a payment for the bare use of the capital (equal to the interest rate); a second element representing payment for the entrepreneur's activities as manager; and a third connected in a rather vague way with the carrying of the risks or hazards of the enterprise." Most of them, however, continued to apply the term profit to the combination of the three elements of the proprietor's income. But Say insisted "on a separation between profit and interest and the treatment of profit as a species of wage."

The editor of the *South Carolinian,* however, was not writing of economic profit. He was writing as an ordinary businessman or farmer according to the most generally accepted definition of profit, that of accounting. To him, the entire net income of the proprietor, after the deduction of all expenses, including depreciation and loss of value of assets, was profit.

Unfortunately, Robinson does not seem to have completely realized the meaning of his profit figure. He acted upon the definition of profit as wages of management, deducting interest upon investment as a cost of doing business, but he then assumed that there was a relation between the profit figure and the planter's investment. Actually there was no connection between the two. And when Robinson said that if the cotton were sold at seven cents, the profit would be $5,385.04, or about 3 per cent on the investment, he was merely saying that Colonel Williams' wages for managing the plantation were the equivalent of a 3 per cent return on his capital. The total income of Colonel Williams from the plantation during the year, by Robinson's statement, was $16,488.04, a 7 per cent return on his investment, or $11,103, plus $5,385.04, wages for management.

If this deduction or charge for "interest on investment" had been called "profit on investment," which would be equally accurate, Robinson's statement would not have been so completely misinterpreted by one modern student, who, in his rewriting of it, said, "The cash expenditures totalled

$17,879.48, and included the following: interest on capital at 7 per cent."
This interest, it must be repeated, was not an expenditure of the planter,
but was part of his income.

Most of the modern historians who deny the profitableness of slavery
seem to confuse profit, as defined by Say and those who follow him, with
the ordinary conception of profit used by businessmen and farmers. None
of these historians, so far as can be ascertained from their studies, have
used the rather elaborate financial statistics in the census of 1850 and 1860;
or, at least, they have made no attempt to reconcile the conflict between
their low estimates of profit from plantation operation and the overwhelming indication of a large increase of wealth in the South between 1850 and
1860.

Selected figures [1] for thirteen of the slave states, excluding rather arbi-
trarily Missouri and Delaware, show this increase very clearly:

	1850	1860
Number of farms	508,680	665,417
Total improved acres in farms	51,451,040	67,478,629
Average improved acres in farms	101.15	101.41
Total unimproved acres in farms	118,612,338	156,996,549
Average unimproved acres per farm	233.32	235.94
Average size of farms	334.47	337.35
Total cash value of farms	$1,035,544,075.	$2,288,179,125.
Average cash value of farms	$2,035.75	$3,438.71
True value of real and personal property	$2,809,875,462.	$6,245,129,163.
True value of real and personal property per capita—whites and free Negroes	$490.49	$878.08
Total number of slaveholders	326,054	358,728
Total number of slaves	3,110,652	3,833,782
Average number of slaves per slaveholder	9.54	10.69

Many objections to these figures can be raised. They were collected by
the marshals of the various districts and many of them may be inaccurate.
Some of these figures lump slaveholders and nonslaveholders together, while
others combine rural and urban wealth without distinction. Nevertheless,
they are the most complete and accurate now available. Fortunately, however, the manuscript returns of individuals for 1850 and 1860 have in many
instances been preserved. From these Dr. Herbert Weaver has studied the
individual fortunes of five hundred persons engaged in agriculture in Jefferson and Jones counties, Mississippi. Two hundred and three of these men

[1] Compiled from: James D. B. De Bow, *Statistical View of the United States . . . Being
a Compendium of the Seventh Census* (Washington, 1854), 82, 95, 169; *The Seventh
Census of the United States, 1850* (Washington, 1853), xxxiii; *The Eighth Census of the
United States, 1860*, 4 vols. (Washington, 1864–1866) II, *Agriculture* (1864), vii, 222,
247–48; Joseph C. D. Kennedy, *Preliminary Report on the Eighth Census, 1860* (Washington, 1862), 195.

were nonslaveholders, and the remainder slaveholders, in 1850. In reporting the results of his investigation, he stated:

> The only items checked were number of slaves, amount of improved and unimproved land owned, and the value of farms. By thus tracing individuals through a ten year period, the great prosperity enjoyed by all groups was established beyond all doubt. In practically every case there was an increase in every column. Slaveholdings, if they were slaveholders, showed a decided upward trend, and numerous nonslaveholders were found to own slaves in 1860. . . . Landholding increased . . . , but . . . it seems that the value of the land increased more than the acreage. A part of this was certainly due to a general increase in valuation of land, but the increase was too great to be attributed entirely to that fact. A great part of the increase in value represented increased acreage and improvements. Landholdings increased by about fifty per cent throughout the state, but the value of farms increased more than three fold.

These figures from the census reports and the manuscript returns do not prove that slavery on southern plantations was profitable in its last decade but they do indicate this conclusion strongly enough to place the burden of proof upon those who deny that planters were making profits. Ulrich B. Phillips did not present any direct evidence on this problem but merely stated his own belief that slavery probably was not profitable in the late 1850's. He did not bear this out by citing figures based upon the actual experience of plantation owners, or upon contemporary estimates in newspapers or periodicals. Apparently his principal interest was not in the profits of the plantation owner but in comparing the cost of slave and free labor.

The most complete and comprehensive attempt to estimate the profits of plantation slavery is to be found in *Slavery in Mississippi* (1933) by Charles S. Sydnor. In this he has prepared a profit and loss statement, based on average figures from a large number of plantations, which indicates a very small rate of return for plantation owners and advances Professor Sydnor's doubt of the profitableness of slavery. This statement, however, is open to so many objections and questions that a detailed and critical analysis seems appropriate. In his statement, Professor Sydnor said:

> The chief source of income would be from cotton. Probably thirty of the fifty negroes worked in the field. If those produced 5¾ bales each, there would be a total of 158 bales which, at ten cents a pound, would be worth $6,320.00
>
> The expenses of the plantation would be as follows: 50 negroes at $600 each (in the late 'fifties the price was higher) represented an investment of $30,000. Calculating interest at 6 per cent, this amounted to $1,800.00
> At least an equal amount should be added for depreciation in slave property by accidents, deaths, old age, etc.   1,800.00
> As the average hand worked about twelve acres, 600 acres would be ample for pastures and woodland as well as fields. Allowing $10 per acre, the investment in land at 6 per cent interest involved a yearly carriage charge of   360.00

and it ordinarily depreciated at the rate of at least three per cent a year in value	180.00
Annual hire of an overseer, at least	300.00
Purchases from New Orleans or elsewhere of negro clothing, miscellaneous plantation supplies, etc.	1,000.00
Without including various miscellaneous expenditures, such as the purchase of corn and pork, of which few plantations produced enough, the total of the expenses and interest charges was	$5,440.00
Profit of the planter	880.00

From these figures Louis Hacker, in the *Triumph of American Capitalism* (1940), drew the conclusion that the hypothetical planter made only 2 per cent on his invested capital. By the same reasoning a man who lent money at 5 per cent would show a loss of 1 per cent because of the deduction of 6 per cent interest on investment.

Professor Sydnor, himself, understood that "interest on investment" was not an actual expense of the planter, because, as he said, the planter "was, of course, free to spend the interest on his investment in negroes and land, and this was the item that caused the profits from Mississippi plantations to appear high." He also stated that "the $880 might be considered the wages of the planter for managing the enterprise," but he never recognized that, according to many economists and the generally accepted definition of accountants and businessmen, profit is a combination of this interest on investment and wages for management.

Other objections must be made to the statement. In the chapter "Profitableness of Slavery," Professor Sydnor wrote, "Cotton, however, was not the only source of profit. A planter who barely made expenses by the sale of cotton might find his estate yearly increasing in value by the rearing of young negroes." This certainly seems true because there was a steady natural increase in the slave population during the entire ante-bellum period. In addition, the price of slaves tended generally upward except in years of financial crisis. Nevertheless, in his own estimate of plantation income, Professor Sydnor did not take this increase in value into account. Instead he deducted, as an expense, $1,800 "for depreciation in slave property by accidents, deaths, old age, etc." It hardly seems correct to consider a working force which not only reproduced itself but increased in number, skill, and price, as a source of expense to the planter.

Similarly the expense figure of depreciation of land seems difficult to justify. At 3 per cent a year the land would be almost valueless after thirty-three years. But Mississippi land is still growing cotton. Unquestionably almost every crop takes something out of the land. But with equal certainty it can be said that the yearly work of the slaves, preparing the soil, ditching the fields, and clearing additional acres, aided fertility and increased value. This sometimes necessitated a cash expenditure for fertilizer or equipment, which would be a just charge to plantation expense; but it seems impossible now, with our limited and inadequate knowledge, to be certain whether there was a net gain or loss in value of land from the yearly plantation activity.

Professor Sydnor's estimate of the value of the planter's investment in land and slaves may also be questioned, because he seems to have assumed that the value of an asset is its market value at the particular moment. Prices, however, are the result of so many complex and unascertainable factors that they rarely can be taken as the equivalent of actual value. It is only under ideal circumstances that classical economists accept price as equal to value, and most other economists look on price as one of the evidences of value, not its exact expression.

Neither can the accountant accept this, because it would mean that assets fluctuate in value annually, which would introduce into the profit and loss statement a variable figure unrelated to the activities of the particular enterprise. A profit or loss (the equivalent of an increase or decrease in value of an asset) is usually not considered by an accountant until it has been realized. Prices rise and fall for various reasons, and if these "paper" profits or losses from the unrealized increase or decrease of the market price of an asset were accepted as real, the actual profit or loss from operations during the accounting period would be obscured. For this reason an accountant usually values an asset at its cost, less depreciation, and not at its current market price.

Most of the land and slaves in the South did not change hands after 1849 and consequently the market price in the 1850's had little or nothing to do with their cost. Certainly a majority of the slaves had been reared by their owners, and their capital value as an asset was the cost of their rearing. There is no exact statistical information concerning the cost of rearing the slave, but it hardly could have amounted to Professor Sydnor's figure of $600, which was based on market price in the early 1850's. This arbitrary capitalization of all slaves at the current market price introduces another element of uncertainty into the statement—again because of the deduction of "interest on investment." For if investment increases each year, with the rise in the price of slaves, the deduction from profit of "interest on investment" is also larger. Consequently the planter shows a decrease instead of an increase in profit from the raised capital value of his assets.

This "interest on investment," some economists say, is a cost of doing business, to others it is a part of profit; and there is also disagreement about how it is to be figured and what rate is to be charged. Some define it as the current rate of return. If it is, no entrepreneur, according to theory, could be expected to make more without attracting competitive capital into the same enterprise. It is also a virtually impossible task to ascertain the current rate of return during this period. Others say it is the current rate of interest on borrowed money. But this figure fluctuated widely with various individuals and sections of the South, and the information upon which to base an average is lacking. Still others insist that it is the so-called "pure" interest rate, the one yielded by the safest investment, but this would be more difficult to ascertain than either of the others. Phillips recommended that such a charge be made in figuring the cost of slave labor, but he made no estimate as to what the rate should be. Sydnor who used 6 per cent and Robinson who used 7 per cent are alike in that they gave no reasons for their respective choices.

This difficulty in arriving at a satisfactory figure is one of the reasons why the financial accountant makes no use of interest on investment.[2] Another is the technical impossibility of handling a deduction from profit that is neither an expenditure nor the decrease in value of an asset. But the chief argument against its use, is that it gives no information. It is merely the separation of the proprietor's income into two parts, interest upon investment, and profit above that interest. This is of little or no importance to the owner or the accountant, and of interest only to the economist who, in reality, is forced to guess as to the proper apportionment between the two.

If these objections to Professor Sydnor's statement are valid, the hypothetical planter seems to be somewhat better off. The results from his operations would be something like this:

Income from cotton		$6,320.00
Expenses:		
Annual hire of overseer	$ 300.00	
Plantation supplies	1,000.00	1,300.00
Gross profit		5,020.00

This is the total of the money income and expenditure, though it was stated that no provision had been made for "miscellaneous expenditures such as the purchase of corn and pork, of which few plantations produced enough," and no consideration has been given to the various selling and transportation charges such as freight, insurance, packing costs, and factor's commissions.

It is not, however, a complete statement of the financial condition of the plantation, but it is almost all that can be known with any certainty. If the increase or decrease in value of assets is taken into consideration, so many approximations have to be used that the resulting figures are virtually without meaning. Each acre of land would have to be valued separately; its original cost ascertained; the loss of fertility from the year's crop, the

---

[2] There is a serious debate among cost accountants as to whether interest on investment has a proper place in that limited and specialized field of accounting. Some argue, as does Ulrich B. Phillips in his analysis of the cost of slave labor, "that the provision of capital is a necessary expense of a business just as is rent, insurance, or wages, and that it should be treated in the same manner as these expenses." But the majority seem to believe that the return on capital is not an expense but a profit, and the business world is accustomed so to consider it. As a result, to treat interest on investment as a cost of operation would produce financial statements which are misleading. William B. Lawrence, *Cost Accounting* (New York, 1925), 312–13; Roy B. Kester, *Advanced Accounting* (New York, 1933), 515–17; Phillips, "Economic Cost of Slaveholding," 268–69. Some cost accountants insist that interest on investment should be included "in order to determine what would be a fair profit in a given case," or "to determine whether it is better to manufacture or to buy goods in the open market, and whether it is better policy to manufacture by means of expensive machinery and other equipment or by manual labor." But even these suggest a technical arrangement whereby interest on investment is charged as a manufacturing expense to get manufacturing cost, but is then removed from the books before the net profit is arrived at, so that interest on investment is not shown in the financial statement at all. Jerome Lee Nicholson and John F. D. Rohrback, *Cost Accounting* (New York, 1919), 139–40; Kester, *Advanced Accounting*, 140.

increase in fertility from the year's work, and expenditures for fertilizer and equipment, would have to be balanced against each other; and the resulting figure be shown as income or expense, as the case might be. Obviously this could not be done with any degree of accuracy. Each slave would then have to be valued on the basis of his cost—the cost of rearing him to work age if born on the plantation, or his original purchase price— his physical condition, age, experience, and special training; and a balance struck as to his increase or decrease in value during the particular year. The totals of these increases or decreases in value would have to be added to or taken away from another figure which would show the net gain or loss from births and deaths of slaves. Only in this way could an accurate figure for a particular plantation be ascertained.

Most of this, however, is hypothetical, and cannot be ascertained from surviving records. It was seldom taken into consideration by the planters themselves who usually were content with the simplest records and figured profits or losses on the basis of cash income and expenditure. They, like the modern accountant, businessman, and farmer, considered their entire net income as profit, and made no attempt to divide it, according to classical theory, into interest on investment, wages of management, and compensation for risk.

If attention is turned to the actual results of plantation operations as they are to be found in some surviving account books and papers, and in reports of contemporary newspapers and periodicals, no consistent pattern of profits is to be found. Cotton, rice, and tobacco, the staples of the South, were such speculative crops that there were wide variations in profit from plantation to plantation, and from year to year. For instance, in 1846–1847 on an Alabama plantation owned jointly by Mrs. R. Brown and Franklin H. Elmore, working 108 slaves and having an estimated value of $70,000, the profits from the sale of 199 bales of cotton were $7,352.40, or 10.5 per cent, with no direct superintendence by either of the proprietors. On the other hand, Farish Carter, one of the most successful Georgia planters, in 1851 made profits of $1,530 on a plantation valued at $150,000. This was a return of only 1¼ per cent on his investment. In neither of these statements was credit taken or deduction made for the increase or decrease in value of slaves, the depreciation or appreciation of land, or any other intangible item.

Published estimates of the cost of growing cotton and of profits of plantations must be accepted with caution, particularly in the late 1840's and 1850's. During these years the merchants of Liverpool and the manufacturers of Manchester were protesting against the American monopoly of cotton production. The Cotton Supply Association was organized in Manchester with the openly avowed purpose of breaking the American domination of cotton supply by encouraging its growth in the colonies of the empire. Southern cotton growers and merchants, frightened by the possibility of increased competition, attempted to prove that the price of cotton was too low rather than too high, and that the profits from cotton planting had been grossly overstated.

One of these, who acknowledged his purpose, estimated that the gross profits from raising cotton on a well-equipped plantation with 100 slaves and valued at $100,000 would amount only to $1,750 with cotton selling at five cents a pound. But this, according to the writer, did not include anything "for the support of the planter . . . nor . . . to meet those contingent and incidental losses and costs . . . as the loss of servants from epidemics, the loss of *whole teams* from diseases, the frequent accidents to gins and houses from fire, losses from overflows, breaking of levees, &c." Another, writing in the *Soil of the South,* also said that the profits of cotton planting were overestimated, but was forced to admit that "there are more fortunes made at planting than at any other business." His explanation of the paradox was that it was "attributable not to the supposed fact that there is more money made at the business than any other, but because planters are, as a class, more economical, and live more at home than any other." He estimated that the average cost of raising 2,000 pounds of ginned cotton was $160.16, or slightly over 8 cents a pound, but included, as part of cost, 7 per cent profit on the investment in slaves, land, and mules, or $105.76.

One of the longest and most detailed records of a plantation which has been preserved is that of Hopeton on the Altamaha River in Glynn County, Georgia. This plantation was established before the War of 1812 by John Couper, a Scotsman, and remained in his possession until January 1, 1827. In a letter summarizing the results under his ownership, he said:

> You know I commenced planting without capital. Of course had to go in debt and 8 per cent compound interest I found to be the real perpetual motion. Though tolerable successful sometimes, yet I had sad reverses—Embargo, non-intercourse & War—interfered with my prospects, whilst interest progressed— My loss of 60 prime effective negroes—carried off by the Enemy—lessened my annual income full $15,000—to supply their places *in part* I bt. 120 slaves for which I paid an average of 450$. Crops were not favorable. In the year 1824— I had *matured* a crop of 600 Bales cotton—which would have produced $90,000 —This was lost in 12 hours by hurricane. In 1825 I again nearly lost my crop by caterpillar. Cotton then sunk in price, without any prospect of improvement. Lands were reduced to ⅓ of their value. Slaves to 250 or 200. In short I saw no hope of paying my debts and retaining my property—& tho not pushed—I thought best during my life to meet the storm. So to make a long story short— Mr. Hamilton being my principal creditor—on his agreeing to pay what other debts I owed—I surrendered to him all my property, debt, and dues of every description in a lump without valuation—except my lands on St. Simons and one hundred slaves—So on the 1st day of January 1827 I was thrown on the world without a dollar to support my people and family—Am glad to get off so well. Even though at a reasonable valuation the property I surrendered, was more than sufficient to pay my debts, yet had it been brought to a forced sale, it might have done less. I am satisfied and relieved from much anxiety. By this event neither my standing in society—nor my mode of living have suffered any change.

This reads as a confession of failure, but though John Couper suffered many grievous misfortunes, he had, by his own statement, begun planting without capital, and ended, after paying all his debts, with a plantation and 100 slaves, worth from fifty to a hundred thousand dollars. He had also, with a large family, lived in luxurious surroundings during most of the period, which is certainly no slight return from a lifetime devoted to planting.

John Couper had turned Hopeton over to his principal creditor, James Hamilton, a Scots merchant, and Hamilton in turn sold half of the plantation and 380 slaves to James H. Couper, son of John, for $137,000 to be paid over a period of fifteen years at 6 per cent interest. Couper was to have the entire management for which he was to receive $2,000 per year, the run of the plantation, and half the profits. This arrangement continued until January 1, 1841, when Couper, to clear himself of debt, turned back his interest in the plantation to the Hamilton estate. After this, until 1852, Couper continued to manage the plantation for the estate. During the entire period of his management of the plantation from 1827 to 1852, he kept elaborate records of all phases of plantation operations including detailed financial information concerning receipts and expenditures.

From these records it is possible to establish year by year the cost value of the investment in the plantation, the gross and net sales, expenditures, and net profit. As the rate of profit varied widely from year to year it has seemed clearer to present the results in tabular form.

YEAR	CAPITAL	GROSS SALES	NET SALES	EXPENSES	PROFIT	RATE OF PROFIT
1827	$274,000.00	—	$ 4,367.19½	$12,239.56¼	$ 7,871.76¾ [a]	
1828	294,895.22	—	15,043.50	6,924.93	8,118.57	2.7%
1829	298,014.40	—	11,707.08	9,021.95	2,685.13	.9
1830	298,014.40	—	15,235.55	12,730.26	2,505.29	.8
1831	298,046.40	—	22,482.34	16,949.10	5,533.24	1.85
1832	300,126.65	—	17,030.23	10,910.86	6,119.37	2
1833	302,617.07	—	22,016.37	10,937.07	11,079.30	3.6
1834	302,617.07	—	20,609.24	9,918.72	10,690.52	3.5
1835	302,617.07	—	26,897.48	11,857.64	15,039.84	4.9
1836	302,617.07	—	31,977.27	8,452.16	23,525.11	7.7
1837	302,617.07	—	45,970.72	9,868.87	36,101.85	11.9
1838	302,617.07	—	35,889.13	12,939.44	22,949.69	7.2
1839	302,617.07	$38,484.06	36,199.90	10,022.71	26,177.19	8
1840	302,617.07	26,476.34	24,228.01	11,276.11	12,951.90	4.2

[a] Deficit.

The profits during these years were not large except in the years when the income from crops was supplemented by the hire of slaves to work on the Brunswick Canal. But the figures alone do not give the complete story.

As soon as James Couper took over the management of the plantation he began an experiment in sugar raising which turned out unsuccessfully. This not only caused an expenditure of $22,443.82 for machinery in the first six years but also diverted a part of the labor force from other crops. This was not a foolish or reckless experiment, because sugar planters, under not unsimilar conditions in Louisiana, were making great fortunes, but it, apparently, was chiefly responsible for the low profits in the first few years.

As the plantation was turned back to the established crops, rice and sea-island cotton, the rate of profit began to increase to a more satisfactory figure. The statement of plantation expenses also appears to contain a substantial amount—the exact figure cannot be ascertained—for the personal and household expenses of Couper and his family. It is to be remembered that as part of his compensation for management he had the use of house servants, horses, and boats, as well as produce for his table from his plantation. This was no inconsiderable item if the report of Sir Charles Lyell was correct. He visited the plantation in 1845 when conditions were probably the same as between 1827 and 1840. He described the separate villa maintained for Couper and his family on nearby St. Simon's Island, the library containing "Audubon's Birds, Michaud's Forest Trees, and other costly works on natural history," and then added:

> Much has been said in praise of the hospitality of the southern planter, but they alone who have traveled in the southern states can appreciate the perfect ease and politeness with which a stranger is made to feel himself at home. Horses, carriages, boats, servants, are all at his disposal. Even his little comforts are thought of, and everything is done as heartily and naturally as if no obligations were conferred. . . .
>
> The landed proprietors here visit each other in the style of English country gentlemen, sometimes dining out with their families and returning at night, or, if the distance be great, remaining to sleep and coming home the next morning. A considerable part of their food is derived from the produce of the land; but, as the houses are usually distant from large towns, they keep large stores of groceries and of clothing, as is the custom in country houses in some parts of Scotland.

These were real profits and must be considered, even if it is not possible to set a figure for them. At the same time the plantation was increasing, not decreasing, in value. No charge for depreciation on lands, or slaves, or other capital assets, was placed on Couper's books. He had not even written off as loss the cost of the unsuccessful experiment in sugar, but there was no need to. The year by year increase in value of the plantation more than offset these losses.

When Couper turned back his half interest in the plantation to the Hamilton estate on January 1, 1841, three commissioners were appointed by the Superior Court of Glynn County. These commissioners estimated the value of the plantation to be $381,425, or an increase over original cost and additional investment of $78,807.93. This represented a net gain in value of 26 per cent in fourteen years. This estimate, apparently, was too high for Couper and the trustees of the estate, and the actual transfer of title was made at a book value of $342,481.88. The increase in value was $39,864.81, or 13 per cent.

During the twelve years from 1840 to 1852 the plantation was owned by the Hamilton estate but managed by Couper, at a salary of $5,000 a year for ten years and $6,000 a year for two. The same arrangement in regard to household expenses that had been true during the first period appears also to have been in effect during the second and must be remembered in connection with the actual figures of profits. The 1840's were probably the worst decade, economically, in the agricultural history of the ante-bellum South, but the results of Couper's management, after deduction of his and the overseers' salaries, were as follows:

YEAR	CAPITAL	GROSS SALES	NET SALES	EXPENSES	PROFIT	RATE OF PROFIT
1841	$347,481.88	$30,470.58	$27,974.83	$16,821.98	$11,152.85	3.2%
1842	344,681.88	18,905.86	17,232.27	15,752.97	1,479.30	.43
1843	344,681.88	23,392.47	20,770.26	13,240.05	7,530.21	2.2
1844	344,181.88	30,411.03	27,699.58	17,259.71	10,439.87	3
1845	344,181.88	26,370.14	24,436.28	13,120.11	11,316.17	3.3
1846	344,181.88	41,161.97	37,602.85	13,685.68	23,917.17	6.9
1847	343,617.56	29,893.75	27,335.05	14,914.55	12,420.50	3.6
1848	343,617.56	30,807.12	27,810.52	16,397.00	11,413.52	3.3
1849	340,017.56	36,988.17	33,280.75	15,341.87	17,938.88	5.3
1850	342,017.56	35,795.48	32,571.73	16,583.30	15,988.43	4.7
1851	349,474.60	29,587.54	26,603.62	17,627.43	8,976.19	2.6
1852	349,474.60	39,761.40	35,268.04	17,938.93	17,329.11	5

The changes in capital from year to year were the result principally of purchases and sales of land and slaves. Land to the value of $8,789.58 was purchased, while $2,057.56 was received from sales of land, during the twenty-six years. In the same period seven additional slaves were bought and twenty sold. The land evidently had increased in fertility because the crops were larger and produced more income in the later years than in the earlier. The slave record for the plantation has not been located. But Sir Charles Lyell gave indirect evidence of an increase in the number of slaves when he wrote that in 1845 there were 500 at Hopeton, or an increase of 120 from the original 380.

Another plantation for which an extensive record has been preserved is Gowrie, owned by Louis Manigault and located on the Savannah River. The sole money crop was rice. The original value of the plantation was $40,000, and on it were 220 acres of cleared ground, 80 acres uncleared, a fine rice mill, and 50 slaves. The plantation was gradually increased in size until finally it had 638 acres in cultivation, and from time to time additional slaves were purchased. The average value of the plantation during the first six years was approximately $42,115. Net proceeds of the crops of these years were $43,750, total expenses were $12,000, which made the average profit $5,095 a year or 12 per cent on the investment.

There is a gap of sixteen years in the records; then for six years there is a detailed account of all receipts and expenditures. Manigault's investment, through the purchase of additional land and slaves, had increased to approximately $80,000 by 1857. The gross sales of rice for the six years from 1855 to 1861 were $103,739.55. Selling costs for the same period were $22,964.73, making net sales $80,774.82. Plantation expenses totaled $22,135.84, leaving as total net profits for six years, $58,638.98, or an average annual profit of $9,766.49. This amounted to a 12.2 per cent return upon the capital invested in the plantation.

The profits from Gowrie were much higher than those from Hopeton. This may be accounted for in part by the difference in the years which the records cover, but probably more because Manigault did not make his home on the plantation, and no household expenses are included in the statement of plantation expenditures. It is certain, however, that Manigault did not consider these last six years to be extraordinarily successful ones. On the contrary he believed them to be particularly difficult.

The plantation had suffered epidemics of cholera in 1852 and 1854 in which twenty slaves, including "many of our *very best* hands," had died. There had been a destructive freshet in 1852, and a hurricane on September 8, 1854, both of which not only injured the standing crops but also strewed the entire plantation with loose rice "to the vast injury" of succeeding crops. Manigault's experienced overseer died in December, 1855, and it was not until April 8, 1859, that another capable man was employed. The overseers in the interim neglected the plantation and the slaves, and it took a year for the new overseer to repair injuries done by his predecessors.

This was satisfactory to the owner, who, in writing his report of operations during 1859–1860, said:

> Mr. Capers has not made a large crop but he says it was much on a/c of the bad condition in which he found the plantation, & I believe him, I am satisfied thus far with him, feeling that he has had no chance. We have bought two new Mules this winter, working in all six mules. During the past winter Mr. Capers has done much work. He has cut a new Canal through two squares, on the upper portion of the plantation, which I think will be of service. We have for the first time used the double horse ploughs, turning the lands much deeper than previously.

In spite of all these difficulties and neglect the land evidently had not deteriorated. The average production for the six years from 1833 to 1838 was 374 barrels of clean rice, while during the six years from 1855 to 1861 the crop averaged 843 barrels. There was, as said above, an increase in acreage devoted to rice from 220 to 638, or 190 per cent, but there was also an increase in production from a low of 220 barrels in 1833 to a high of 995 barrels in 1856, or 397 per cent.

The plantation lost thirty-eight slaves in three cholera epidemics in 1834, 1852, and 1854, which forced Manigault to purchase forty-six slaves, between 1833 and 1861, in addition to the original fifty. This makes a total of ninety-six slaves brought to or purchased for the plantation; but there still were ninety-seven slaves on the plantation in 1857, the last year in which there is a record of the number of slaves. Consequently, it is not correct to charge any of this additional investment in slaves to expense. All that happened was that the natural increase in number and value was wiped out by the epidemics and the plantation neither made nor lost money on its working force.

A third plantation for which there is record of capital, expense, and profits, is that of James H. Hammond of South Carolina, also on the Savannah River. Early in the 1850's Hammond offered his plantation, which he valued at $163,750, for sale. The plantation according to this offer consisted of the following:

1.	150 Negroes who shall constitute 80 task or effective hands and only 2 to 3 non-effective	$80,000.00
2.	6300 acres . . . excluding . . . the Silverton Residence & tract of 280 acres & on the other side the Marsh & 1000 or 1500 acres as it may be, but including about 3000 acres of cleared land in good order—650 of it drained land—all except about 100 acres well marled, with mills, landing, etc. @$12 per acre	75,600.00
3.	6000 bushels corn—60,000 pds. fodder	3,500.00
4.	30 mules & horse under 12 years mostly under 9 years	3,000.00
5.	5 fair Plantation Waggons. 3 ox carts. 4 Horse carts. 30 sets of gears. 60 ploughs, etc.	1,000.00
6.	100 head of hogs @ 1.50 & 40 head Cattle all ½ to Ayreshire with full blood bull and 10 oxen @ 10.00	650.00
		$163,750.00

The detailed records of income and expenditure on Hammond's plantation do not appear to have been preserved but there is a memorandum in his papers which gives exact information for the five-year period from 1849 to 1853. During these years the total income from the sale of cotton, corn, rice, and fodder was $81,088.83. Plantation expenses amounted to $27,019.37, leaving a profit of $54,069.46, or an average annual profit of $10,813.89. Accepting his offer of sale as the total value of his investment, though its original cost to him probably was much less, Hammond had an average net annual return of 6.66 per cent.

Unlike most planters, Hammond kept a separate record of his family expenses apart from the plantation records. In the same five years these expenses amounted to $31,913.55, which, if deducted from profits, gives him an annual net income over all expenses, business and personal, of $4,431.18, or 2.7 per cent.

There seems to be no more justification for a depreciation charge against land or slaves on this plantation than there was at Gowrie or Hopeton, because, at least in Hammond's opinion, the plantation was gaining, not losing value. In 1859 he again wrote out an offer of sale, but this time he asked $175,000 and included only 140 Negroes comprising 70 full hands, 5,500 acres of land, fewer horses, mules, cattle, and pigs, and less corn and fodder.

The records of these three plantations have been presented, not because they are considered to be typical of the plantation system, but merely because, through accident, they have been preserved in more detail than most others. Each was larger than the average plantation in the South, and all three were located in the older part of the South, where, incidentally, by common report, profits were lower than in the newer districts. They do indicate, however, that year after year, during periods of financial crisis or prosperity, some plantations were making profits in the ordinary business sense of the term, and were increasing, not decreasing in value.

The evidence from these plantations, together with the overwhelming evidence of increase in wealth found in the census reports and in Herbert Weaver's study of the individual returns in two counties of Mississippi, all seem to point in a single direction. And that is to the tentative conclusion that the students who have stated that slavery was profitable are more nearly correct than those who deny its profitableness.

c] PLANTERS' PROFITS EQUAL RETURNS FROM OTHER FORMS OF INVESTMENT

I. OBJECTIVES AND METHODS

THE OUTSTANDING economic characteristics of southern agriculture before the Civil War were a high degree of specialization and virtually exclusive reliance on a slave labor force. The large-scale, commercial dependence upon slave labor was to distinguish the ante bellum South not only from other regions in its own time but from all regions at all other times in American agricultural history. Because of this unique historical status, ante bellum southern agriculture has been a subject for special historical attention. Above all else, attention has been focused upon the proposition that, even without external intervention, slavery would have toppled of its own weight. This allegation has its source in the assertions of slave inefficiency to be found in the writings of men who lived with slavery: American or English liberals like G. M. Weston, H. R. Helper, or J. E. Cairnes and southern slaveowners who, in a religious, self-righteous age, could find every motive for the protection of the slave system except that it was personally profitable. The argument is to be found most strongly stated in the work of later southern historians, especially C. W. Ramsdell and U. B. Phillips, who take the position that the Civil War, far from being an irrepressible conflict, was an unnecessary blood bath. They argue that slavery had reached its natural limits and that it was cumbersome and inefficient and, probably within less than a generation, would have destroyed itself. To the question why emancipation was not resorted to, they reply that slavery was for the southerners an important (and evidently expensive) duty, part of their "unending task of race discipline." On the other side, Lewis Gray and Kenneth Stampp have strongly contested this view, contending that southern plantation agriculture was at least as remunerative an economic activity as most other business enterprises in the young republic.

The evidence employed in this debate has been provided by the few, usually fragmentary, accounting records that have come down to us from

FROM Alfred H. Conrad and John R. Meyer, "The Economics of Slavery in the Ante Bellum South," *Journal of Political Economy*, LXVI (April, 1958), 95–122. Reprinted by permission of The University of Chicago Press. © 1958 by The University of Chicago Press.

early plantation activities. The opposing parties have arranged and rearranged the data in accordance with various standard and sometimes imaginary accounting conventions. Indeed, the debate over the value of the different constituent pieces of information reconstructs in embryo much of the historical development of American accounting practices. For example, virtually all the accounting valuation problems have been discussed with relation to the slave question, including the role and meaning of depreciation, the nature and accountability of interest charges, and the validity of distinctions between profits and payments of managerial wages. But, despite the fact that the problem is ostensibly one in economic history, no attempt has ever been made to measure the profitability of slavery according to the economic (as opposed to accounting) concept of profitability. This paper is an attempt to fill this void.

Thus this paper is devoted to establishing methodological as well as historical points. Specifically, we shall attempt to measure the profitability of southern slave operations in terms of modern capital theory. In doing so, we shall illustrate the ways in which economic theory might be used in ordering and organizing historical facts. An additional methodological point is also made evident by this exercise, namely, how the very simple statistical concepts of range and central tendency as applied to frequency distributions of data can be employed in interpreting or moderating inferences from historical facts.

In executing these tasks, we must ask first what it is we are talking about and, second, whether we can say anything that can be proved or disproved. For example, we must ask what the slave economy was. Was it cotton culture? Was it cotton and sugar and tobacco? Was it all of ante bellum southern agriculture? In answering, we shall define slavery in terms of two production functions. One function relates inputs of Negro slaves (and the materials required to maintain the slaves) to the production of the southern staple crops, particularly cotton. The second function describes the production of the intermediate good, slave labor—slave-breeding, to use an emotionally charged term which has colored, even determined, most of the conclusions about this problem.

What do we mean by "efficiency"? Essentially, we shall mean a comparison of the return from the use of this form of capital—Negro slaves—with the returns being earned on other capital assets at the time. Thus we mean to consider whether the slave system was being dragged down of its own weight; whether the allocation of resources was impaired by the rigidity of capitalized labor supply; whether southern capital was misused or indeed drawn away to the North; and, finally, whether slavery must inevitably have declined from an inability of the slave force to reproduce itself.

The hypothesis that slavery was an efficient, maintainable form of economic organization is not a new one, of course. Nor are we, by one hundred years, at least, among the first to conclude that Negro slavery was profitable in the ante bellum South. What we do feel to be novel, however, is our approach. Postulating that American Negro slavery was characterized by two production functions, we argue that an efficient system developed in which those regions best suited to the production of cotton (and the other important staples) specialized in agricultural production, while the less productive land continued to produce slaves, exporting the increase to the staple-crop areas. It is this structure that we are examining.

We propose to test the hypothesis by putting appropriate values on the variables in the production functions and computing the rate of return over cost, the stream of income over the lifetime of the slave. This rate of return, the marginal efficiency of slave capital, must, in turn, be shown to be at least equal to the rate of interest currently available in the American capital markets. It is further necessary to show that appropriate markets existed to make this regional specialization possible and that slavery did not necessarily imply the disappearance or misallocation of capital. Evidence on the ability of the slave force to maintain itself numerically will be had as a corollary result. For these purposes it is necessary to obtain data on slave prices and cotton prices, the average output of male field hands and field wenches, the life-expectancy of Negroes born in slavery, the cost of maintaining slaves during infancy and other nonproductive periods, and, finally, the net reproduction rate and the demographic composition of the slave population in the breeding and using areas.

Looked upon simply as a staple-commodity agriculture, the southern system must appear to have been burdened—possibly even to have been on the verge of collapse—under the weight of areas of inefficient, unprofitable farming. We submit that this view is in error and that the error arises from the failure to recognize that an agricultural system dependent upon slavery can be defined operationally only in terms of the production function for both the final good—in our case, cotton—and the production function for the intermediate good—Negro slaves. Considered operationally, in terms of a neoclassical two-region, two-commodity trade system, it must be seen that a slave system produces labor as an intermediate good. The profitability of the system cannot be decided without considering the system's ability to produce chattel labor efficiently.

There are also non-historical reasons for taking up once again the economics of ante bellum southern slavery. A detailed re-evaluation of the profits of plantation slavery in the American South might help us evaluate the possibilities, first, that the near-slavery existing today in many highly agricultural, underindustrialized lands is an institution that can be expected to disappear automatically or, second, that dislodging it will require substantial governmental pressure or interference. These are, of course, often key policy questions in former colonial countries that are just beginning to develop modern industrial economies.

The possible relevance of the American experience in this connection increases, moreover, as the underlying economic motivations of a slave system are analyzed and established. This happens primarily because, once these motives are recognized, it becomes possible better to understand and predict the political structures that will accompany slavery. In other words, the interrelationships between certain economic and political goals of slavery can be better understood once the underlying economic factors are understood.

II. THE ECONOMIC RETURNS ON SLAVEHOLDING

FROM THE standpoint of the entrepreneur making an investment in slaves, the basic problems involved in determining profitability are analytically the same as those met in determining the returns from any other kind of capital investment. The acquisition of a slave represented the tying-up of capital in what has appropriately been called a roundabout method of production. Like the purchase of any capital, a slave purchase was made in the anticipation of gaining higher returns than are available from less time-consuming or capital-using methods. This model is particularly applicable in the present case, because slave investments, like the forests or wine cellars of classic capital theory, produced a natural increase with the passage of time.

Investment returns are properly computed by using the capital-value formula, $y = x_t/(1 + r)^t$, where y is the cost of the investment, x_t is realized return t years hence, and r is the internal rate of return[1] or what Keynes called the marginal efficiency of capital. When returns are realized over a number of years, the total earnings of the capital can be found by simple summation in this formula. The criterion for a profitable investment is that the marginal efficiency exceeds the interest rate (in the Keynesian terminology). From this statement of the problem, it is obvious that the following information is needed to determine the profitability of slaveholding from the slaveholder's point of view: (a) the longevity of slaves; (b) the costs of slaves and any necessary accompanying capital investments; (c) the interest rate; and (d) the annual returns from slave productive activities, defined to include both field labor and procreation. We shall consider each of these in turn and then put the pieces together to determine the approximate profitability of slave investments.

A. The Longevity of Slaves

Slave longevity corresponds, of course, to the period for which a slave investment was made. We shall limit attention here to the purchase of twenty-year-old Negroes in the immediate pre-Civil War era, and we shall deal only with the typical or median life-expectancy for this group. These limits greatly simplify the problem and still include the vast majority of relevant cases.

There is a scarcity of good longevity data for the period, but it is known that in 1850 Negroes lived just about as long as whites in the two states for which acceptable data are available. The available figures are given in Table 1. There is doubt about the quality of these estimates because they show Negroes in New England expecting a longer life than whites. This is not the case today, nor was it the case in 1900, when the first good data

---

[1] Computation of rate of return in this way is preferable to the usual recording of net profit rates on total plantation investment in slaves, land, and durable equipment, because of the reproductive character and the limited durability of slave investments. Clearly, the same characteristics do not apply to non-depreciable investments in land. A non-depreciable investment in agricultural land is, however, quite rare.

TABLE 1. EXPECTATION OF LIFE AT BIRTH IN YEARS FOR WHITE AND COLORED MALES, UNITED STATES, 1850

STATE	WHITE	COLORED
Massachusetts	38.3	39.75
Maryland	41.8	38.47
Louisiana	—	28.89

SOURCE: Reported in L. I. Dublin, A. J. Latka, and M. Spiegelman, *Length of Life* (New York: Ronald Press Co., 1949), p. 54, where the source is given as the L. W. Meech table based on the records of the 1850 Census and first published in J. C. G. Kennedy, *The Seventh Census—Report of the Superintendent of the Census, Dec. 1, 1852* (Washington, D.C., 1853), p. 13. The Maryland colored data are for slaves only; the Louisiana, for slaves and free together.

became available. Also, Negroes would appear in this table to have had a longer life-expectancy in 1850 than they had fifty years later. Although surprising, this may be perfectly correct. Negroes could have received better care under slavery, because plantation owners had an economic interest in keeping Negroes alive. Furthermore, the Negro in the period after emancipation generally lacked the means to participate equally in the new medical advances, in contrast to his position of roughly equal medical care in the period before 1860.

Life-expectation at birth does not tell us much, of course, about the expectation of a twenty-year-old man. Actually, there are no data on Negro life-expectancy at different age levels in the prewar period except for some imperfect estimates made by Sydnor for Mississippi slaves. Using the average reported age at death of those over the age of twenty who died in 1850, he estimated a life-expectancy of twenty-two years for a twenty-year-old Mississippi slave. This figure is probably low for two reasons. First, the estimating procedure tells more about life-expectancy in the years preceding 1850 than after, unless we make the dubious assumption that there was no advance in medical and dietary knowledge around the middle of the century. Second, estimates from deaths reported at the end of ten-year intervals and averaged back over the decade would tend to underestimate life-spans at the younger ages. Doubts about the quality of the Sydnor data are borne out by consideration of the Massachusetts life-expectancy of 40.1 years for twenty-year-old males, white and Negro, in 1850. Looking back at the data in Table 1, there is no reason to expect twenty-year-old Massachusetts Negroes to have a lower life-expectancy than Massachusetts whites, though both clearly lived longer than southern Negroes of the period. Taking all these factors into account, an estimate of thirty to thirty-five years of life-expectancy seems most plausible for twenty-year-old Negroes working as prime cotton hands on southern plantations in the period 1830–50, and a thirty-year life-expectancy will generally be used in the succeeding calculations.

B. The Cost of the Capital Investment

The capital investment in plantation operations included investment both in slaves and in the land and equipment on which the slaves worked.

The price of slaves fluctuated widely, being subject to the waves of speculation in cotton. Furthermore, the price depended, among other things, upon
the age, sex, disposition, degree of training, and condition of the slave.
In order to hold these variables roughly constant, we shall confine our
present analysis to eighteen- to twenty-year-old prime field hands and
wenches. Some summary data on slave prices were compiled by U. B.
Phillips on the basis of available market quotations, bills of transactions,
and reports of sales in most of the important slave markets of Georgia. His
estimates of the best averages for several years between 1828 and 1860 are
presented in Table 2. On the basis of these data it would appear that

TABLE 2. ESTIMATED AVERAGE SLAVE PRICES IN GEORGIA, SELECTED YEARS, 1828–60

YEAR	AVERAGE PRICE OF PRIME FIELD HANDS
1828	$ 700
1835	900
1837	1,300
1839	1,000
1840	700
1844	600
1848	900
1851	1,050
1853	1,200
1859	1,650
1860	1,800

SOURCE: U. B. Phillips, "The Economic Cost of Slaveholding in the Cotton Belt," *Political Science Quarterly*, XX, No. 2 (1905), 267.

both the median and the mean price for prime field hands were in the
range of from $900 to $950 in the period 1830–50. Because of the substantial
price increases in the last ante bellum decade, these averages would run
substantially higher for the entire slave period after 1830; specifically, about
$1,100–$1,200. Since the prices of field wenches usually averaged about
$100–$150 less than those of hands, they were probably in the range of
from $800 to $850 in the years 1830–50 and between $900 and $1,100 for
the entire period 1830–60. . . .

As for the non-slave capital, by far the most important was the investment
in land. Since the land values varied widely, depending on the quality of
the soil and the type of agriculture pursued, experimental control on our
calculations requires that attention be confined to cotton culture. The
range in cotton-land prices in the period 1830–50 is fairly well bracketed
by the $6 per acre paid for poor upland pine land in Alabama and the
$35–$40 per acre paid for cleared Mississippi alluvium. Such a range even
encompasses the costs of new lands in the Southwest. Although such land

was obtained for nominal original cost, the usual costs of clearing, draining, and otherwise preparing it, plus the transportation of slaves and supplies, would amount to something in the range of $20–$30 per acre. There was also variation in the number of acres needed per hand. Counting garden land and woodlots, as well as productive fields, the usual number of acres per field hand was between 15 and 35, the exact figure depending primarily on the quality of the land. This meant an original land investment per hand of somewhere between $90 and $1,400, with $180–$600 encompassing the vast majority of instances.

The price per acre was, of course, related to the durability of the land, which immediately introduces a further dimension into the capital cost problem. Cotton lands lasted between ten and forty years, depending upon original quality and fertilization. In the land-rich, labor-scarce economy of the nineteenth-century United States, fertilization was a rare practice. Furthermore, planters clearly had the choice between operating less capital intensively on low-durability land or more capital intensively on high-durability land. For example, poor Alabama pine land might be expected to last ten years and require 30–35 acres per hand; this meant that $180–$210 had to be reinvested every ten years to utilize the slave force properly. Assuming thirty-year slave longevity and an 8 per cent interest rate, the present value of the land investment for one slave's lifetime was $302–$350 for an upland-pine operation. On the alluvium, by contrast, the land would typically outlast the slave in usefulness; assuming, though, that both lasted the same number of years and that 16 acres of cleared and 10 of uncleared land (at $10 per acre) were used per hand, a total land investment of $660 per hand is indicated. This difference in value of the land investment was presumably a function of different yields. At any rate, the typical case was probably halfway between these two, involving a land investment of about $450 per hand.

Similar problems arise in estimating the investment in plows, gins, wagons, cabins, and miscellaneous implements. Such investments ran about $25 per hand in original outlay and had to be renewed every fifteen years. This gives a total present value in such items (again on the assumption of thirty-year slave longevity and 8 per cent interest) of about $33. A small investment was required in work horses and oxen, but in this case the stock was likely to be self-replenishing, reducing the costs to interest on the investment at most. Putting all these capital costs together indicates that $1,400–$1,450 was a fair approximation of the typical or average total investment per male slave in terms of present values. The range ran from $1,250 to $1,650.

C. The Interest Rate

Determining the relevant rate of interest—the rate with which the cotton-slave returns must be compared—is perhaps empirically the easiest and conceptually the most difficult of the tasks in computing the economic returns on slave investments. While there is a relative abundance of data on interest rates in this period, none corresponds exactly to the desired rate. In a strict conceptual sense, the relevant rate of interest is that which plantation owners or other investors in southern agriculture could have earned on their money in other pursuits if slavery had gone out of existence. This is difficult to arrive at on the basis of historical evidence, since it assumes circumstances contrary to the facts. The closest substitute would be earnings on other investments that were *least* dependent upon cotton and southern agriculture. Given the importance of cotton in the American economy prior to the Civil War and the general interdependence of economic systems, even in so primitive an economy as that of the United States in the first half of the nineteenth century, it is difficult to find any conceptually correct figures. The figures that follow are offered in complete recognition of their fallability on this count, yet they are probably as good as are available.

In the contemporary chronicles it is obvious that southerners and northerners alike considered 6–8 per cent a reasonable rate of return and a reasonable asking price for loans. Figures in this range are repeated over and over again and must be given some significance. This is all the more true because these figures are consistent with reported rates charged on prime commercial paper and other debt instruments in the principal money markets before 1860. The prime commercial rates charged in New York and Boston in the period 1830–65, shown in Table 3, illustrate this point.

TABLE 3. AVERAGE ANNUAL INTEREST RATES ON PRIME COMMERCIAL PAPER
FROM 1831 TO 1860

	NEW YORK [a]	BOSTON [b]		NEW YORK [a]	BOSTON [b]
1831	5.1	6.5	1849	10.0	12.0
1832	5.3	6.5	1850	8.0	7.5
1833	6.9	6.0	1851	9.7	7.0
1834	14.6	14.5	1852	6.6	6.0
1835	7.0	5.0	1853	10.2	10.7
1836	18.4	20.3	1854	10.4	12.0
1837	14.1	6.0	1855	8.9	7.0
1838	9.0	7.0	1856	8.9	10.0
1839	13.2	9.0	1857	12.9	9.0
1840	7.8	6.0	1858	5.0	4.5
1841	6.9	6.0	1859	6.8	7.0
1842	8.1	7.8	1860	7.0	6.0
1843	4.5	3.0	1861	6.5	—
1844	4.9	5.0	1862	5.8	—
1845	6.0	6.0	1863	5.0	—
1846	8.3	8.0	1864	6.0	—
1847	9.6	6.0	1865	7.6	—
1848	15.1	15.0			

SOURCES: *New York data:* Federal Reserve Bank of New York, *Monthly Review,* March 1, 1921, p. 3. The figures are also reproduced in A. O. Greef, *The Commercial Paper House in the United States* (Cambridge, Mass.: Harvard University Press, 1938), p. 79. *Boston data:* Joseph G. Martin, *One Hundred Years' History of the Boston Stock and Money Markets* (Boston: The Author, 1898), pp. 52–53.
  [a] Two-name sixty–ninety-day paper.
  [b] "First class three to six months, bankable paper." The rate reported is either one sustained for a major portion of the year or an arithmetic average.

Similarly, the rates on New York Stock Exchange call loans, New England municipal issues, and rail debentures, shown in Table 4, fall for the most part within, or below, this same 6–8 per cent range. While the average annual rates fluctuated widely in the years between 1830 and 1850 and the distribution of rates is skewed, the central tendency was clearly close to the 6–8 per cent range. Specifically, the New York average was 9.2 per cent, the median was 8.0, and the mode was between 6.0 and 7.0 per cent. Because of the skew, the median rate of 8 per cent is probably the best measure of central tendency for the present analysis.

The interest rates for the Civil War years, although they lie somewhat outside the time period of this investigation, may be conceptually the most pertinent figures in Tables 3 and 4. The Civil War represents as good an approximation as is achievable of a controlled experiment to determine investment returns in the North under complete divorce from the plantation economy. The difficulty is, of course, that too many other structural changes took place concomitantly with the withdrawal of the southern cotton economy: above all else, the Lincoln administration adopted the very essence of Keynesian expansionary fiscal policies. It simultaneously ran a large deficit budget and closed the economy with high tariffs and buy-American clauses in government contracts. On the supply side of the money market, the war meant that the southern withdrawal was consummated without any flow of capital out of slavery and into other ventures. Consequently, returns on northern investments unquestionably remained higher than they would have if southern cotton had been withdrawn without offsetting government action and with a flow of southern capital into northern money markets. On the other hand, there might have been compensatory government action even without the war, and the loss of southern funds was at least partially offset by the loss of southern opportunities. The 6–7 per cent average returns in the period 1860–65 can be viewed as indicative of at least what could be achieved in the United States in the absence of cotton investment opportunities.

The realization on short-term, high-quality commercial paper might normally be expected to be below the realization on longer-term investments of the type represented by ownership of a cotton plantation. However, in the period 1840–60 banking practices were rather lax and potentially or actually inflationary, as indicated by the recurrent financial panics of the time. Such unstable financial conditions may have given equity a premium that it might otherwise not have enjoyed. Furthermore, the existence of well-established slave and real estate markets made most plantation investments highly negotiable, thereby reducing the time commitment in such investments. There are some reports available on the realizable returns on longer-term investments; for example, Table 4 presents the rates at which some municipal and railroad development bonds were floated in the prewar period. In addition, Davis reports returns of 16.76 per cent on total capital stock in the 1844–48 period and 5.75 per cent in the 1848–53 period for nine of the larger and more prosperous Massachusetts textile firms.

From these many disparate sources it seems safe to estimate that a

TABLE 4. YIELDS ON VARIOUS ECONOMIC ACTIVITIES, 1857–65

YEAR	NEW ENGLAND MUNICIPAL BOND YIELDS (JANUARY INDEX NUMBERS)	CALL MONEY RATES AT THE NEW YORK STOCK EXCHANGE (ARITHMETIC AVERAGE OF MONTHS)	RAILROAD BOND YIELDS (JANUARY AVERAGE FOR ALL RAILROADS)
1857	5.2	9.3	8.1
1858	5.3	4.2	8.7
1859	4.8	5.4	7.4
1860	4.8	6.0	7.5
1861	4.9	5.8	7.4
1862	5.2	5.2	7.5
1863	4.4	6.2	5.6
1864	4.7	6.6	6.0
1865	5.2	6.2	6.2

SOURCE: Frederick R. Macaulay, *The Movements of Interest Rates, Bond Yields and Stock Prices in the United States since 1856* (New York: National Bureau of Economic Research, 1938), pp. A172–A173 and A34–A38.

wholesale withdrawal of capital from slave operations in southern agriculture would not have depressed marginal investment returns in the prewar United States economy much below 4.5–5 per cent. Similarly, it seems safe to conclude that the withdrawn capital could not have expected to earn returns much in excess of 8 per cent. Between these high and low estimates, a return of 6 per cent seems the most probable and, therefore, appropriate for comparison in our model.

D. Annual Returns

The appropriate return figure to enter in the capital equation is the net return on current account, or the difference between gross sales and all out-of-pocket expenses. The expense deduction is limited to out-of-pocket expenses, because all the book charges that complicate the usual accounting procedures are taken into account in the process of constructing the capital cost estimate.

Estimates of plantation expenses have been taken primarily from three excellent, exhaustive records of the available material: J. L. Watkins' *The Cost of Cotton Production,* Lewis C. Gray's *History of Agriculture in the Southern United States to 1860,* and Kenneth Stampp's *The Peculiar Institution.*[2] A reasonably thorough check of these secondary sources against

[2] These three secondary sources carefully and consistently record the estimates available from three basic types of primary material. Gray's *History of Agriculture in the Southern United States to 1860* (Washington, D.C., 1933). esp. pp. 529–67, covers the cost estimates intermittently reported in the principal agricultural and business journals read by the planters and traders: *DeBow's Review, Farmers' Register, Farmer and Planter,*

some primary sources and against one another for consistency indicates that these surveys have been reliably and accurately made. A digest of the estimates is presented in Table 5. The total figure of $20–$21 annual

TABLE 5. TYPICAL ANNUAL OUT-OF-POCKET COSTS OF MAINTAINING AND WORKING PRIME FIELD HANDS ON SOUTHERN PLANTATIONS IN THE PERIOD 1840–60

A. Food and clothing	
(1) Out-of-pocket costs where most food was produced on plantation and most clothing was hand-sewn	$ 2.50–$ 3.46
(2) Cash costs if purchased	25.00– 40.00
(3) Out-of-pocket costs where some ready-made clothing and meat, fish, and other food "delicacies" were purchased	7.00– 10.00
B. Medical care	1.50– 2.00
C. Taxes	0.39– 1.20
D. Supervision	5.00– 15.00
Total, based on means of the estimates above and option (3) under A	20.00– 21.00

PRINCIPAL SOURCES: J. L. Watkins, *The Cost of Cotton Production* (United States Department of Agriculture, Division of Statistics, Miscellaneous Series, Bull. 16 [Washington, D.C.: Government Printing Office, 1899]); Lewis C. Gray, *History of Agriculture in the Southern United States to 1860* (Washington, D.C.: Carnegie Institution, 1933), pp. 529–67; Kenneth Stampp, *The Peculiar Institution* (New York: A. A. Knopf, Inc., 1956), chaps. vi, vii, and ix.

out-of-pocket slave maintenance costs will be used in subsequent calculations. These costs are to be subtracted from the annual gross return figures on slave activities.

For a male field hand the returns considered will be limited to the sales of products realized from his field labor; in the case of a female hand, an addition must be made for the returns realized on the labor and sale of her children. Because of these basic differences in the production functions for the two sexes, they will be treated separately.

For the male field hand, limited to the returns on his field labor, the gross proceeds will depend on the price of cotton and the quantity of his annual output. The output, in turn, will be crucially dependent on the quality of the land on which the slave was employed and, to a much lesser degree, upon the quality and amount of capital goods with which he was equipped. The figures in Table 6 illustrate the possible variation in productivity per hand. These estimates agree with frequent statements in contemporary journals that in the typical case a prime field hand could be expected to raise from 3.5 to 4 bales per year. The maximum seems to have been 7–8 bales on the best lands, and 2–3 bales was the minimum on the poorest land.

Southern Planter, Southern Agriculturist, and *Hunt's Merchants' Magazine.* Watkins' *The Cost of Cotton Production* (U.S. Department of Agriculture, Miscellaneous Series, Bull. 16 [Washington, D.C., 1899]) includes the estimates recorded in the Patent Office and the Commissioner of Patents' *Annual Reports,* especially for the years 1844, 1849, 1850, 1852, 1854, and 1855. Stampp's *The Peculiar Institution* (New York, 1956), esp. chaps. vi, vii, and ix, reports the estimates available from diaries and individual plantation records still in existence.

TABLE 6. REPORTED YIELDS PER PRIME FIELD HAND

LOCATION	YEAR	BALES PER HAND	SOURCE
South Carolina coastal	1849	4⅓	Watkins
Mississippi (De Soto County)	1849	4	Watkins
Unidentified	1844	7	Watkins
Alabama (Cherokee County)	1855	4	Watkins
Mississippi (Vicksburg area)	1855	8	Watkins
New Southwest land	1850's	5	Gray, p. 912
South Carolina upland	1852	3	Gray, p. 912
Texas	1859	10	Stampp, p. 408
Arkansas River	1859	7	Stampp, p. 408

The relevant price of cotton for valuing these yields is the net price realized at the farm (in order that price and cost data be comparable). This means that export prices at the major ports must be adjusted downward by the amount of freight, insurance, storage, drayage, and factor's commission charges that were properly chargeable to the planter. Gray estimates that these costs generally ran between $2.50 and $4 per bale. Somewhat more detailed information is presented by Watkins, whose findings are summarized in Table 7. The Gray and Watkins findings are fully compatible, and a marketing cost of from 0.7 to 0.8 cent per pound appears to be properly deductible from the export price in determining the price f.o.b. farm.

The export price itself fluctuated widely over the period. As can be seen

TABLE 7. COTTON MARKETING COSTS PER BALE CHARGEABLE TO PLANTERS IN 1840

	AT MOBILE	AT CHARLESTON
Freight in	$1.50[a]	$1.25[b]
Drayage	0.125	0.13
Weighing	0.125	0.06
Storage (1 month)	0.20	0.24
Insurance (1 month)	[c]	0.25
Factor's commission (2–2.5 per cent)	0.80	0.60–1.61
Total per bale	$2.75	$3.03[d]
Total cents per pound [e]	0.69	0.76[d]

SOURCE: Watkins, *op. cit.*, pp. 38, 39.
  [a] By river.
  [b] From Columbia.
  [c] Not reported. Note that the higher (Charleston) figures have been used in the profit computations to follow.
  [d] Assuming $1.10 factor's commission.
  [e] Four hundred pounds to a bale.

TABLE 8. WEIGHTED YEARLY AVERAGE PRICES OF SHORT-STAPLE COTTON (USUALLY LOUISIANA OR MISSISSIPPI MIDDLING OR SECOND GRADE) AT NEW ORLEANS FOR THE CROP YEARS 1830–60

YEAR	PRICE	YEAR	PRICE	YEAR	PRICE
1830	8.4	1840	9.1	1850	11.7
1831	9.0	1841	7.8	1851	7.4
1832	10.0	1842	5.7	1852	9.1
1833	11.2	1843	7.5	1853	8.8
1834	15.5	1844	5.5	1854	8.4
1835	15.2	1845	6.8	1855	9.1
1836	13.3	1846	9.9	1856	12.4
1837	9.0	1847	7.0	1857	11.2
1838	12.4	1848	5.8	1858	11.5
1839	7.9	1849	10.8	1859	10.8
				1860	11.1
Decade average price	11.2		7.6		11.2

SOURCE: Gray, *op. cit.*, Table 41, pp. 1027–29.

from Table 8, New Orleans cotton prices averaged almost 50 per cent higher in the thirties and fifties than they did in the depressed forties. Even in the forties, however, the export price level was sufficient to insure an average net farm price of not much less than 6.5 cents. Since prices at any given port were usually equal to the Liverpool price minus ocean shipping rates, the New York and Mobile prices were generally somewhat higher. Taking all this into consideration, 7–8 cents seems a realistic and conservative estimate of the average realized farm price for the whole period.

Finally, the price, productivity, and capital cost estimates must be combined in order to compute the actual profitability of investments in male slave labor for cotton production. Capital costs must be included in the computations, since the present value of the capital outlay will depend, as was previously shown, upon the rate of return. In lieu of a single computation, several cases involving different capital outlays, yields per hand, and realized farm prices have been constructed; the results are given in Table 9.[3] Cases 1, 2, and 3 are the most typical; cases 4, 5, and 6 represent the situation on somewhat better land. These first six cases, with returns ranging between 4½ and 8 per cent, encompass the majority of

[3] No allowance has been made in these computations for the expenses of maintaining slaves in their dotage. This would not appear to be a serious omission. Generally speaking, slaves were considered to be virtually fully productive in field labor until their fifty-fifth birthdays—which corresponds to the average life-expectancy on the purchase of a twenty-year-old slave. Furthermore, the direct out-of-pocket costs of simply maintaining a slave were only $10–$15, figures considerably below productive value in field work. Given the possibility of specialized use of older labor in such occupations as garden-tending, nursery operations, and supervision, it seems doubtful if many slaves lived long enough to be economic drains on current account.

ante bellum cotton plantation operations. Cases 7, 8, and 9 represent the minimum of profitability or what might be expected on poor upland pine country or the worked-out lands of the eastern seaboard. By contrast, cases 10, 11, and 12 show the upper range of profitability which was realized on the best lands of the new Southwest, the Mississippi alluvium, and the better South Carolina and Alabama plantations.[4]

The calculations in Table 9 represent an estimate of potential returns for the relatively simple production function of prime field hands. With

TABLE 9. REALIZED RETURNS ON PRIME FIELD HANDS UNDER
VARIOUS HYPOTHESIZED CONDITIONS

CASE	PRESENT VALUE OF CAPITAL OUTLAY PER HAND	YIELD PER HAND (BALES)	AVERAGE NET FARM PRICE (CENTS)	APPROXIMATE RETURN (PER CENT)
1	$1,350–$1,400	3¾	7	4.5
2	$1,350–$1,400	3¾	8	5.2
3	$1,350–$1,400	3¾	9	6.5
4	$1,600	4½	7	5.0
5	$1,600	4½	8	7.0
6	$1,600	4½	9	8.0
7	$1,250–$1,300	3	7	2.2
8	$1,250–$1,300	3	8	3.9
9	$1,250–$1,300	3	9	5.4
10	$1,700	7	7	10.0
11	$1,700	7	8	12.0
12	$1,700	7	9	13.0

the female hand or prime field wench the situation becomes much more complex: in addition to her productivity, the productivity of her children and the returns realized on their sale must be considered. Similarly, the extra cost of maintaining the children and the maternity and nursery costs associated with their birth must also be counted.

To make the calculations in this rather complex situation manageable, the following assumptions will be made:

1. Each prime field wench produced five to ten marketable children during her lifetime. (The computations for the ten-child or upper-limit case are shown in Table 10, while those for the lower limit of five children are shown in Table 11.) Furthermore, we assume that successful pregnancies were spaced two years apart. It must be recognized that these figures represent assumptions more about what was achievable than about

[4] A purist might ask how different returns can be realized in what is ostensibly the same type of economic activity in a relatively competitive industry. The question overlooks the fact that it took a much larger initial outlay to attain productive situations like those in cases 10–12. This is all the more true, since the capital outlay in these cases would be concentrated at the start of the undertaking, while in cases 7–9 some of the outlay would be delayed ten or fifteen years until the land wore out.

TABLE 10. ANNUAL RETURNS ON A PRIME FIELD WENCH INVESTMENT (WORKING ON LAND WHICH YIELDED 3.75 BALES PER PRIME MALE FIELD HAND, ASSUMING A 7.5-CENT NET FARM PRICE FOR COTTON AND TEN "SALABLE" CHILDREN BORN TO EVERY WENCH)

YEAR FROM PURCHASE DATE	PERSONAL FIELD RETURNS	CHILD FIELD RETURNS	CHILD SALE RETURNS	PERSONAL UPKEEP	CHILD UPKEEP	NET RETURNS
1	$56	—	—	$20	—	$ 36
2	40	—	—	20	$ 50	−30
3	56	—	—	20	10	26
4	40	—	—	20	60	−40
5	56	—	—	20	20	16
6	40	—	—	20	70	−50
7	56	—	—	20	30	6
8	40	$ 3.75	—	20	80	−56.25
9	56	7.50	—	20	45	−1.50
10	40	15.00	—	20	95	−50.00
11	56	22.50	—	20	60	−1.50
12	40	37.50	—	20	110	−52.50
13	56	52.50	—	20	75	13.50
14	40	75.00	—	20	130	−35.00
15	56	97.50	—	20	95	47.50
16	40	127.50	—	20	150	−2.50
17	56	157.50	—	20	115	78.50
18	40	195.00	—	20	165	55.00
19	56	232.50	—	20	130	134.30
20	40	195.00	$875	20	170	920.00
21	56	232.50	—	20	130	138.50
22	56	195.00	875	20	120	986.00
23	56	232.50	—	20	120	148.50
24	56	195.00	875	20	110	996.00
25	56	232.50	—	20	110	158.00
26	56	195.00	875	20	100	1,006.00
27	56	232.50	—	20	100	168.00
28	56	187.50	875	20	90	1,008.50
29	56	225.00	—	20	90	171.00
30	56	180.00	875	20	80	1,011.00
31	—	210.00	—	—	80	130.00
32	—	157.50	875	—	60	972.50
33	—	180.00	—	—	60	120.00
34	—	120.00	875	—	40	955.00
35	—	135.00	—	—	40	95.00
36	—	67.50	875	—	20	922.50
37	—	75.00	—	—	20	55.00
38	—	—	875	—	—	875.00

TABLE 11. ANNUAL RETURNS ON A PRIME FIELD WENCH INVESTMENT (WORKING ON LAND WHICH YIELDED 3.75 BALES PER PRIME MALE FIELD HAND, ASSUMING A 7.5-CENT NET FARM PRICE FOR COTTON AND FIVE "SALABLE" CHILDREN BORN TO EVERY WENCH)

YEAR FROM PURCHASE DATE	PERSONAL FIELD RETURNS	CHILD FIELD RETURNS	CHILD SALE RETURNS	PERSONAL UPKEEP	CHILD UPKEEP	NET RETURNS
1	$56	—	—	$20	—	$ 36
2	40	—	—	20	$50	−30
3	56	—	—	20	10	26
4	40	—	—	20	60	−40
5	56	—	—	20	20	16
6	40	—	—	20	70	−50
7	56	—	—	20	30	6
8	40	$ 3.75	—	20	80	−56.25
9	56	7.50	—	20	45	−1.50
10	40	15.00	—	20	95	−50.00
11	56	22.50	—	20	60	−1.50
12	56	37.50	—	20	60	13.50
13	56	52.50	—	20	65	23.50
14	56	75.00	—	20	65	46.00
15	56	97.50	—	20	75	58.50
16	56	127.50	—	20	75	88.50
17	56	157.50	—	20	85	108.50
18	56	191.25	—	20	85	142.25
19	56	225.00	—	20	90	171.00
20	56	180.00	$875	20	75	1,016.00
21	56	210.00	—	20	75	171.00
22	56	157.50	875	20	60	1,008.50
23	56	180.00	—	20	60	156.00
24	56	120.00	875	20	40	991.00
25	56	135.00	—	20	40	131.00
26	56	67.50	875	20	20	958.50
27	56	75.00	—	20	20	91.00
28	56	—	875	20	—	911.00
29	56	—	—	20	—	36.00
30	56	—	—	20	—	36.00

actual happenings. Slave infant mortality data are too poor to permit inferences about the latter.

2. The prime field wench was one-half to two-thirds as productive as a prime field hand when she was actually at work in the field. This estimate is based on the fact that, when prime field hands and wenches were hired out, the hiring rate on the latter was usually one-half to two-thirds the hiring rate on the former. Thus, it is assumed that the market hiring rate

reflects the relative productivity of the two sexes. In addition, adjustments must be made for the time lost by the female during pregnancy and post-natal period. It is assumed here that three months' productive field time was lost for each successful pregnancy; the entire deduction has been made in the year in which the successful birth took place, despite the fact that it would probably be more realistic to assume that one month and a half was lost on each unsuccessful as well as each successful pregnancy. This allowance for "lost time" is probably too generous, since the only births that really cost any important productive field time were those occurring during the peak agriculture seasons, planting and picking time.

3. The wench's children began to be productive in field labor at age six, with the males becoming self-sustaining by age nine (that is, they then earned the adult maintenance charge of $20 per year), while females became self-sustaining by age thirteen. This can be represented by letting the male productivity go up $5 every year between ages six and nine and letting female productivity increase by $2.50 for every year between the ages of six and thirteen. These rates are in keeping with the previously stated principle that females were roughly half as productive in field labor as males. After reaching a self-sustaining status at these ages, it is further assumed that their productivity continued to rise linearly until the children reached their full adult productivity at age eighteen; thus, male productivity is assumed to rise $10 per year between ages nine and eighteen and the female productivity $5 per year between ages thirteen and eighteen.

4. The typical wench had as many male as female children. For purposes of computation, the productivity, sales price, and other data for the two sexes have been averaged. For example, the final sales price of a typical child is assumed to be $875, halfway between the average price of $825 for prime field wenches and the average price of $925 for prime field hands.

5. Nursery costs were about $50 per successful pregnancy.

Using these assumptions, hypothetical annual returns for a typical prime field wench can be determined; such calculations are shown in Tables 10 and 11. In constructing these tables, it was assumed that the prime field wench and her children worked on land that returned 3.75 bales of cotton per year for every prime male hand employed; that is, the land is of approximately average fertility. Also, a 7.5 cent net farm price for cotton has been used. The first successful pregnancy has been assumed to occur in the second year after the prime field wench is purchased; further successful pregnancies occur at regular two-year intervals. The children were sold at age eighteen, and the annual maintenance cost per child was assessed at the rate of $10 per year for one—six-year-olds, $15 per year for seven—twelve-year-olds and $20 per year, the full adult maintenance cost, for those age thirteen and over. The maternity costs have been included in the annual charge for the children's upkeep; similarly, the $16 decline every other year for the first few years in the wench's own field returns represents the allowance for time lost because of pregnancy. Rates of return were computed on the streams of net returns shown in the far right-hand columns of the tables on the assumption that the total investment in the prime field wench, land, and equipment amounts to $1,200–$1,300, figures which would appear to be very good averages. A rate of return of 8.1 per cent was thus obtained for the mother bearing ten children and a return of 7.1 per cent for the mother with five children.

These figures are, of course, somewhat higher than those calculated for the prime field hands. A proper working of the market mechanism would suggest that the attainable returns on the two sexes should be approximately equal. That is, the price differential between males and females should be such that the rate of return on the two types of investment turns out to be roughly equal in the typical or average case. The question therefore arises why a somewhat higher estimated return is obtained for the female.

Several answers can be made to this question. First, the difference between the estimated returns for the two sexes may arise because it probably took a somewhat higher return on the females to attract capital investment into that type of productive activity. Slave-breeding and slave-trading were not generally considered to be high or noble types of activity for a southern gentleman. Indeed, many plantation owners would stoop to all sorts of subterfuge to disguise the fact that they were engaging in any part of the slave trade or breeding operations. Second, the investment in the female was a longer-term affair; from Tables 10 and 11 it is apparent that the bulk of the returns on a female were realized twenty or more years after the investment was made, when the children had grown to marketable ages. To the extent that more distant developments are more uncertain, investments in female slaves could be expected to demand a higher return. Finally, the over-all average price of prime field wenches quoted from Phillips may be too low for proved "childbearers"; . . . a female who had proved herself fertile was worth more than a female who had yet to bear her first child.

But these qualifications do not change the principal conclusion that slavery was apparently about as remunerative as alternative employments to which slave capital might have been put. Large or excessive returns were clearly limited to a few fortunate planters, but apparently none suffered excessively either. This general sharing in the prosperity was more or less guaranteed, moreover, if proper market mechanisms existed so that slaves could be bred and reared on the poorest of land and then be sold to those owning the best. Slavery in the immediate ante bellum years was, therefore, an economically viable institution in virtually all areas of the South as long as slaves could be expeditiously and economically transferred from one sector to another.

III. REPRODUCTION, ALLOCATION, AND SLAVE MARKETS

I T THUS remains to be determined whether an efficient supply mechanism—efficient in both its generative and its allocative functions—existed in the ante bellum South. That the slave force might reproduce itself was not sufficient; there must also have been a capital market capable of getting the labor to the areas where production was expanding if slavery was to be profitable. It will be useful to introduce the secondary propositions by stating several arguments which together form the orthodox opposition to the present hypothesis. The arguments follow, in every case accompanied by a citation as a talisman against any possible charge that we are setting up straw men.[5] (i) slaves are notoriously inefficient and unwilling workers; (ii) slave property, unlike wage labor, must be supported in the years before and after the slave is economically productive; (iii) slaveholding absorbed plantation earnings; (iv) slave economies are constantly threatened by decline because they cannot in general maintain the number of slaves; and (v) capitalization of the labor force inhibits the efficient allocation of labor.

The first and second of these arguments are implicitly tested in the computation of the rate of return on slave capital. We are not concerned with efficiency per se, however that might be measured, or with the efficiency of slaves as opposed to free white laborers. The more sophisticated version of this efficiency argument—that slave ineptness forced the planters to use a particularly wasteful form of agriculture—is probably untestable because of the difficulties of identification where impetus or motives are being considered. It might be suggested as a partial answer, however, that extensive farming was not peculiarly a characteristic of slave agriculture or even of plantation cotton culture. It was common to all North American colonial agriculture and, as late as the end of the nineteenth century, was reputed to be characteristic of farming in the Northwest wheat lands. It is, generally, a salient feature of agriculture where labor is scarce relative to land. But, insofar as slaves were inefficient, the inefficiency must be reflected in the returns computed in our model. Similarly, the costs of maintaining slaves in infancy and dotage are accounted for in our cost of production.

The third argument—that the South lost from the payment of interest and the constant enhancement of prices (and, therefore, overcapitalization of the labor force)—rests in part upon two misapprehensions, attributable to U. B. Phillips: (1) that capitalization involves a net loss through the payment of interest and (2) that slaves were, somehow, a fictitious form of wealth. We have already shown that slave capital earned returns at least equal to those earned by other contemporary forms of capital. For the overcapitalization part of the argument, it remains to be shown that slave prices did not run away from cotton values.

The last two of the assertions state the negative of our principal secondary hypothesis, which is that an efficient market system existed for the supply of slaves to the rapidly growing cotton industry of the Southwest from the exhausted land of the Old South. It will be shown below that the slave population, in all but the Louisiana sugar area, more than reproduced itself. It will be further shown that the border states were not

[5] (i) J. E. Cairnes, *The Slave Power* (New York: Follett Foster & Co., 1863), pp. 44–50; F. L. Olmsted, *The Cotton Kingdom* (New York: Mason Bros., 1861), pp. 100–110 (1953 ed.; New York: A. A. Knopf); W. A. Lewis, *Theory of Economic Growth* (Homewood, Ill.: Richard D. Irwin, Inc., 1955), pp. 107–8; (ii) U. B. Phillips, *Life and Labor in the Old South* (Boston: Little, Brown & Co., 1935), pp. 174–75; (iii) U. B. Phillips, "The Economic Cost of Slaveholding in the Cotton-Belt," *Political Science Quarterly*, XX (1905), 257–75; (iv) Lewis, *op. cit.*, pp. 111–13; (v) J. S. Duesenberry, "Some Aspects of the Theory of Economic Development," *Explorations in Entrepreneurial History*, III (1950), 9. This is, of course, intended only as a list of examples, chosen in the hope that they are particularly well stated.

being depleted to provide for western needs but that only the natural increase was being exported. Finally, avoiding the emotion-wracked testimony of the time, we will attempt to demonstrate the existence of regional specialization and an efficient market by comparing the demographic composition of the cotton and border states and by examining the price behavior in the market for Negro slaves.

A. The Reproduction of the Slave Labor Force

The history of slavery is full of examples of slave economies which could not reproduce their population and collapsed because of a failure of supply. Frequently, as in the Roman case, the supply was dependent upon a steady flow of military prisoners. The Augustan peace and the stabilization of the borders of the empire are credited with the decline of Roman slavery for this reason. Similarly, the labor supply in the Caribbean sugar islands could be maintained only by importation. It is generally argued that slavery disappeared from Jamaica because of the inability of the slave population to reproduce itself once the slave trade had been closed and not because of abolition in 1834.

By contrast, the ante bellum cotton-slave economy of the southern states managed to maintain and allocate its labor supply by a system of regional specialization which produced slaves on the worn-out land of the Old South and the border states for export to the high-yield cotton land of the Mississippi and Red River valleys. For the whole nation the Negro rate of increase in the six decades before the Civil War was only slightly below the rate for the white population; for most of the period, the slave rate was very much above that for free Negroes. In the South the disparity between Negro and white rates of increase is in favor of the Negro rate; considering the relative rates of immigration of whites and Negroes after the first decade of the nineteenth century, the discrepancy in natural increase is even more striking. The evidence in Table 12 does not admit

TABLE 12. PERCENTAGE DECENNIAL INCREASE IN WHITE AND NEGRO POPULATION, 1790–1860

CENSUS YEAR	INCREASE DURING PRECEDING TEN YEARS		NEGRO		
	TOTAL	WHITE	TOTAL	SLAVE	FREE
1800	35.1	35.8	32.3	28.1	82.2
1810	36.4	36.1	37.5	33.1	71.9
1820	33.1	34.2	28.6	29.1	25.3
1830	33.5	33.9	31.4	30.6	36.8
1840	32.7	34.7	23.4	23.8	20.9
1850	35.9	37.7	26.6	28.8	12.5
1860	35.6	37.7	22.1	23.4	12.3

SOURCE: Bureau of the Census, *Negro Population in the United States, 1790–1915* (Washington, D.C., 1918), Tables 2 (chap. ii) and 1 (chap. v) and pp. 25 and 53. The sharp declines in the rate of increase for slaves in the decades ending in 1840 and 1860 probably reflect the generation cycle following the increase in importations, mostly of mature Negroes, in the years just prior to 1808.

of any doubt that the slave population was capable of producing a steady supply of labor for the plantation economy.

B. Slave Markets and Allocation

The more important issue, however, is whether or not the slave force could be allocated efficiently. The natural rate of increase was more than sufficient in the Old South to meet the needs of agriculture in the region, but in the West it was less than sufficient to meet the demands for increased cotton production. By direct export and by the migration of planters with their work forces, the eastern areas supplied the needs of the Southwest. In every decade before the Civil War, the increase of slaves in the cotton states was much above and in the Atlantic and border states much below the rate of increase for the whole slave population. Indeed, in the decades ending in 1840 and 1860, the net rate of population increase in the Old South was only slightly above the level sufficient to maintain the population at a constant level, 4.5 per cent and 7.1 per cent (see Table 13). From 1790

TABLE 13. PERCENTAGE RATE OF POPULATION INCREASE, BY RACE, IN THE COTTON AND BORDER STATES, 1790–1860

DECADE ENDING	COTTON STATES [a]		BORDER STATES [b]	
	WHITE	NEGRO	WHITE	NEGRO
1800	42.9	47.4	27.9	24.4
1810	37.5	61.3	23.5	23.4
1820	38.8	48.0	19.5	15.5
1830	40.0	46.8	19.0	14.0
1840	31.3	37.6	21.1	4.5
1850	34.1	35.6	34.5	11.0
1860	27.6	29.0	39.2	7.1

SOURCE: Ernst von Halle, *Baumwollproduktion und Pflanzungswirtschaft in den Nordamerikanischen Sudstaaten* (Leipzig, 1897), p. 132. His sources were Tucker, *Progress of the United States* (to 1840), *Census of Population* (1850 and after), and H. Gannett, *Statistics of the Negroes in the United States.*
[a] North Carolina, South Carolina, Georgia, Florida, Alabama, Mississippi, Louisiana, Texas, Arkansas, and Tennessee.
[b] Delaware, Maryland, District of Columbia, Virginia, West Virginia, Kentucky, and Missouri.

to 1850 the increase of slaves in the Atlantic states was just 2 per cent per annum, while in the Gulf states (including Florida), Arkansas, and Tennessee the rate was 18 per cent per annum. A rough but probably conservative estimate of the export from the selling states between 1820 and 1860 is given by W. H. Collins. Taking the difference between the average natural increase and the actual rate in the selling states, Collins arrived at the following estimates: [6]

[6] W. H. Collins, *The Domestic Slave Trade of the Southern States* (New York, 1904), chap. iii. In the first decade the selling states include Virginia, Maryland, Delaware, North Carolina, Kentucky, and the District of Columbia; the buying states are assumed to be South Carolina, Georgia, Alabama, Mississippi, Tennessee, and Missouri. In 1830, Florida, and in 1850, Texas were added to the buying group. Tennessee, Missouri, and North Carolina are very uncertain assignments, since these states were far from homoge-

1820–30	124,000
1830–40	265,000
1840–50	146,000
1850–60	207,000

Collins estimated that at least three-fifths of the removals from the border states were due to emigration to the Southwest rather than to export. While this has little bearing upon the issue of allocative efficiency, it does have significance for the corollary assertion that the slaveowners of the border states, consciously or unconsciously, were engaged in a specialized breeding operation, producing chattel labor for the growing Southwest. In 1836 the *Virginia Times* estimated that, "of the number of slaves exported [from Virginia], not more than one-third have been sold, the others being carried by their masters, who have removed." Ruffin supposed that the annual sale in 1859 "already exceed in number all the increase in slaves in Virginia by procreation." Bancroft goes beyond these estimates and states that "in the 'fifties, when the extreme prejudice against the interstate traders had abated and their inadequate supplies were eagerly purchased, fully 70 per cent of the slaves removed from the Atlantic and the border slave states to the Southwest were taken after purchase or with a view to sale, that is, were the objects of slave-trading." Whatever the accuracy of these several estimates, which range from two-fifths to four-fifths of total exports of slaves from the border and the Atlantic states, it is clear that sales of slaves provided an important capital gain for the exporting states. There is ample documentary evidence that planters in the Old South were aware of this, that some welcomed it and depended upon it, and that others were fearful of its effect upon the agriculture of the area and upon the tenability of slavery. Some spoke frankly about Virginia as a "breeding state," though the reply to such allegations was generally an indignant denial. Whether systematically bred or not, the natural increase of the slave force was an important, probably the most important, product of the more exhausted soil of the Old South.

The existence of such specialization is evident in the demographic composition of the cotton and breeding areas and in the price behavior in the markets for slaves. Table 14 demonstrates that the selling states contained, in 1850 and 1860, a greater proportion of children under fifteen years and a substantially greater proportion of slaves above the age of fifty than did the buying states. While the disproportions are not great enough to characterize the selling states as a great nursery, the age composition is in the direction which our hypothesis would lead one to expect. The relationship between the prices of men and women in the slave market, when compared with the ratio of hiring rates for male and female field hands, gives an even stronger indication that the superior usefulness of females of breeding age was economically recognized. The relative hiring rates

neous slave-marketing areas; some parts imported, while other parts exported, during the period (cf. Halle, *op. cit.*, pp. 282 ff., and Fredric Bancroft, *Slave Trading in the Old South* [Baltimore: J. H. Furst, 1931], chap. xviii, for similar estimates, consistent with those given by Collins).

TABLE 14. SLAVE POPULATION BY AGE (PER CENT)

AGE (YEARS)	1860				1850		
	TOTAL	SELLING STATES [a]	BUYING STATES [b]	TOTAL	SELLING STATES [a]	BUYING STATES [b]
Under 15	44.8	45.6	43.8	44.9	45.6	44.3
15–19	11.4	11.5	11.4	11.1	11.3	11.0
20–29	17.6	16.5	18.9	18.0	17.0	18.9
30–39	11.7	10.7	11.8	11.3	10.5	12.1
20–49	36.4	34.4	38.1	36.4	34.6	38.1
50 and over	7.5	8.5	6.7	7.5	8.5	6.6

SOURCE: J. C. G. Kennedy, *Population of the United States in 1860* (Washington, D.C., 1864), "Classified Population," Tables No. 1, by state; J. D. B. DeBow, *Statistical View of the United States, . . . Being a Compendium of the Seventh Census* (Washington, D.C., 1854), Part II, Table LXXXII, pp. 89–90.
[a] Virginia, Maryland, Delaware, South Carolina, Missouri, Kentucky, District of Columbia.
[b] Georgia, Alabama, Mississippi, Florida, Texas, Louisiana.
NOTE.—The exclusion of Tennessee and North Carolina is explained in n. 6. Missouri was included with the selling group because of its apparent net selling position in this period.

for men and women in 1860, shown in Table 15, can be taken as a measure of their relative values in the field.[7]

To compare to these rates, we have purchase prices of male and female slaves, in the same markets, in 1859 and 1860. The purchase prices should reflect the relative usefulness of the sexes for field work. More than this,

TABLE 15. ANNUAL HIRING RATES FOR MALE AND FEMALE SLAVES (INCLUDING RATIONS AND CLOTHING), BY STATES, 1860

STATE	MEN	WOMEN	RATIO (MEN : WOMEN)
Virginia	$105	$ 46	2.28
North Carolina	110	49	2.25
South Carolina	103	55	1.87
Georgia	124	75	1.65
Florida	139	80	1.74
Alabama	138	89	1.55
Mississippi	166	100	1.66
Louisiana	171	120	1.43
Texas	166	109	1.52
Arkansas	170	108	1.57
Tennessee	121	63	1.92

[7] The rates are quoted in Hammond, *op. cit.*, p. 90, from *Report of the Commissioner of Agriculture, 1866* (Washington, D.C., 1867), p. 416. Three Virginia newspaper quotations in G. M. Weston, *Who Are and Who May Be Slaves in the United States* (undated pamphlet), give ratios ranging between 2 and 2.5, supporting Hammond's estimate. There is a possible overestimate in these ratios, if they are to be used to infer relative usefulness in the field, since some allowance was probably made for time lost for delivery by pregnant females. No evidence has been found on this point, however.

TABLE 16. SELECTED PRICES OF MALE AND FEMALE SLAVES, 1859 AND 1860

STATE (YEAR)	AGE	CONDITION	MALE PRICE	FEMALE PRICE	RATIO
Virginia (1859)	17–20	Best	$1,350–$1,425	$1,275–$1,325	1.07
South Carolina	—	Prime	$1,325	—	
	—	Wench	—	$1,283	1.03
South Carolina (1859)	—	Field hand	$1,555	—	
	—	Girl	—	$1,705	.91
Georgia	21	Best field hand	$1,900	—	
	17	(9 mo. inf.)	—	[$2,150]	.88
Georgia (1859)	—	Prime, young	$1,300	—	
	—	Cotton hand, houseservant	—	$1,250	1.04
Alabama (1859)	19	—	$1,635	—	
	18, 18, 8	—	—	$1,193	1.37
Mississippi	—	No. 1 field hand	$1,625	$1,450	1.12
Texas	21, 15	—	$2,015	$1,635	1.23
Texas (1859)	17, 14	—	$1,527	$1,403	1.09

however, if there is any additional value to slave women—for breeding purposes, presumably—there should be a premium in the form of a narrower price differential than is found in the hiring rates. . . . Whenever possible, 1860 is used; wherever necessary, 1859. Table 16 includes age designations and, when available, a description of the grade or class represented in the average price.[8] This evidence is a striking confirmation of the validity of the model. In every case but one, the purchase-price differential is narrower than the hiring-rate differential. The price structure clearly reflects the added value of females due to their ability to generate capital gains. It is especially interesting in this regard to note that the price ratios in Virginia and South Carolina, the two breeding states represented in the list, show practically no differential. This evidence clearly shows that the Old South recognized in the market the value of its function as the slave-breeding area for the cotton-raising West.

C. The "Overcapitalization" of the Labor Force

The aspect of slave economics that causes the most confusion and outright error is that which relates to the capitalization, and, in the ante bellum southern case, the presumed overcapitalization, of slave labor. Phillips speaks of an "irresistible tendency to overvalue and overcapitalize" and argues that slaveholding had an unlimited capacity for absorbing the planters' earnings through the continual payment of interest and the en-

8 With one exception—the South Carolina, 1860, comparison—the pairings are taken from single sales. In addition, the pairings are made, as far as possible, with slaves of apparently comparable quality. The Virginia and Mississippi quotations are from average-price listings and are probably most useful for present purposes.

hancement of prices. For the Cotton Belt this was presumably aggregated into a continuous public drain of wealth, first, to England and New England and, later, to the upper South. Moreover, a series of writers from Max Weber down to the most recent theorists of economic growth have argued that capitalization tends to rigidify the pattern of employment. "Free labor is necessary to make free transfers of labor possible. A production organization cannot be very flexible if it has to engage in the purchase or sale of slaves every time it changes its output." But this is really a question of how good the market is; no one, after all, claims that manufacturing is made suicidally inflexible by the fact that expanding sectors must buy the capitalized future earnings of machinery. There are three issues to be distinguished in this argument: first, the alleged tendency toward overcapitalization; second, the inflexibility of chattel labor and the difficulty of allocating it, geographically and industrially; and, third, the loss of wealth.

First, was the southerner his own victim in an endless speculative inflation of slave prices? The assertion of an irresistible tendency to overvalue and overcapitalize must mean that he was so trapped, if it means anything. Phillips answered the question by comparing the price of cotton with the price of prime field hands, year by year. He found, or believed he found, a permanent movement toward overcapitalization inherent in American slaveholding. But speculative overexpansion is capable of reversal: from the inflation of 1837 to the bottom of the depression in 1845, slave prices fell as sharply as cotton prices. If the rise from that lower turning point is a demonstration of speculative mania, it was a mania solidly based on the increase in the value of the crop per hand, owing to the concentration of production in more fertile areas, the greater efficiency of the American-born slaves, lowered transportation costs, and the development of new high-yield varieties of cotton from the fourth decade of the century on. Finally, the choice of the initial period in Phillips' analysis exaggerates the decline in cotton prices relative to the price of slaves: at the turn of the century the demand for cotton was increasing rapidly, supporting remarkably high prices, while the unrestricted African slave trade kept domestic slave prices well below the level that might be expected in view of the level of profits. Table 17 and Chart 1 demonstrate the relationship among slave prices, cotton prices, and the value of cotton output per slave (of field work age, ten to fifty-four). Several things become clear in this comparison. To begin, the relationship between slave and cotton prices is significant for Phillips' purposes only if there is no increase in productivity. While he is struck by the fact that slave prices rise more rapidly than cotton prices in the long upswing starting in the early 1840's, it is equally striking to observe that (New Orleans) slave prices rose about one and one-half times between the low point in 1843–45 to 1860, while values of cotton production per hand rose more than three times from the low in 1842. This was recognized in the *New Orleans Daily Crescent* in 1860, as follows:

> Nor do we agree with our contemporaries who argue that a speculative demand is the unsubstantial basis of the advance in the price of slaves. . . . It

TABLE 17. VALUE OF COTTON PRODUCTION AND SLAVE POPULATION, 1802–60, NEW ORLEANS PRICES

YEAR	CROP (THOU-SANDS OF POUNDS)	AVER-AGE PRICE (CENTS PER POUND)	VALUE (THOU-SANDS)	NO. OF SLAVES AGED 10–54 YEARS a	CROP VALUE PER SLAVE	PRICE OF PRIME FIELD HAND	CROP VALUE PER HAND PER DOLLAR SLAVE PRICE
1802	55,000	0.147	$ 8,085	550,708	$ 14.68	$ 600	.02
1803	60,000	.150	9,000	568,932	15.82	600	.03
1804	65,000	.196	12,740	587,157	21.70	600	.04
1805	70,000	.233	16,310	605,381	26.94	600	.05
1806	80,000	.218	17,440	623,606	27.97	600	.05
1807	80,000	.164	13,120	641,831	20.44	600	.03
1808	75,000	.136	10,200	660,055	15.45	640	.02
1809	82,000	.136	11,152	678,280	16.44	780	.02
1810	85,000	.147	12,495	696,505	17.94	900	.02
1811	80,000	.089	7,120	717,376	9.93	860	.01
1813	75,000	.155	11,625	759,118	15.31	600	.03
1814	70,000	.169	11,830	779,989	15.17	650	.02
1815	100,000	.273	27,300	800,860	34.09	765	.05
1816	124,000	.254	31,496	821,731	38.33	880	.04
1817	130,000	.298	38,740	842,602	45.98	1,000	.05
1818	125,000	.215	26,875	863,473	31.12	1,050	.03
1819	167,000	.143	23,881	884,344	27.00	1,100	.03
1820	160,000	.152	24,320	905,215	26.88	970	.03
1821	180,000	.174	31,320	933,517	33.55	810	.04
1822	210,000	.115	24,150	961,818	25.11	700	.04
1823	185,000	.145	26,825	990,120	27.04	670	.04
1824	215,000	.179	38,485	1,018,421	37.99	700	.05
1825	255,000	.119	30,345	1,046,723	28.99	800	.04
1826	350,000	.093	32,550	1,075,024	30.28	840	.04
1827	316,900	.097	30,739	1,103,326	27.86	770	.04
1828	241,399	.098	23,657	1,131,627	20.91	770	.03
1829	296,812	.089	26,416	1,159,929	22.77	770	.03
1830	331,150	.084	27,817	1,208,034	23.03	810	.03
1831	354,247	.090	31,882	1,247,489	25.56	860	.03
1832	355,492	.100	35,549	1,275,061	27.88	900	.03
1833	374,653	.112	41,961	1,302,633	32.21	960	.03
1834	437,558	.155	67,821	1,330,206	50.99	1,000	.05
1835	460,338	.152	69,971	1,357,778	51.53	1,150	.05
1836	507,550	.133	67,504	1,385,350	46.79	1,250	.04
1837	539,669	.090	48,510	1,412,923	34.38	1,300	.03
1838	682,767	.124	84,663	1,440,495	58.77	1,220	.05
1839	501,708	.079	39,635	1,468,067	27.00	1,240	.02
1840	834,111	.091	75,904	1,507,779	50.34	1,020	.05
1841	644,172	.078	50,245	1,568,022	32.04	870	.04
1842	668,379	.057	38,098	1,611,269	23.65	750	.03
1843	972,960	.075	72,972	1,654,516	44.11	700	.06
1844	836,529	.055	46,009	1,697,762	27.10	700	.04
1845	993,719	.068	67,573	1,741,009	38.81	700	.06

TABLE 17. VALUE OF COTTON PRODUCTION AND SLAVE POPULATION, 1802–60, NEW ORLEANS PRICES (*Cont.*)

YEAR	CROP (THOUSANDS OF POUNDS)	AVERAGE PRICE (CENTS PER POUND)	VALUE (THOUSANDS)	NO. OF SLAVES AGED 10–54 YEARS [a]	CROP VALUE PER SLAVE	PRICE OF PRIME FIELD HAND	CROP VALUE PER HAND PER DOLLAR SLAVE PRICE
1846	863,321	.099	85,469	1,784,256	47.90	750	.06
1847	766,599	.070	53,662	1,827,503	29.36	850	.04
1848	1,017,391	.058	59,009	1,870,750	31.54	950	.03
1849	1,249,985	.108	134,998	1,913,996	70.53	1,030	.07
1850	1,001,165	.117	117,136	1,979,059	59.19	1,100	.05
1851	1,021,048	.074	75,558	2,034,482	37.14	1,150	.03
1852	1,338,061	.091	121,764	2,080,554	58.53	1,200	.05
1853	1,496,302	.088	131,675	2,126,626	61.92	1,250	.05
1854	1,322,241	.084	111,068	2,172,698	51.12	1,310	.04
1855	1,294,463	.091	117,796	2,218,770	53.09	1,350	.04
1856	1,535,334	.124	190,381	2,264,843	84.06	1,420	.06
1857	1,373,619	.112	153,845	2,310,915	66.57	1,490	.05
1858	1,439,744	.115	165,571	2,356,988	70.25	1,580	.04
1859	1,796,455	.108	194,017	2,403,060	80.74	1,690	.05
1860	2,241,056	.111	$248,757	2,460,648	$101.09	$1,800	.06

SOURCE: *Crops:* Computed from the data on number of bales and average weight of bales in James L. Watkins, *Production and Price of Cotton for One Hundred Years* (U.S. Department of Agriculture, Miscellaneous Series, Bull. 9 [Washington, D.C., 1895]). *Price:* Gray, *op. cit.* Table 41: "Weighted Yearly Averages and Monthly Prices in Cents per Pound of Short-Staple Cotton at New Orleans for the Crop Years 1802–1860." *Slaves:* Bureau of the Census, *Negro Population in the United States, 1790–1915*, "Slave and Free Colored Population at Each Census by Sections and Southern Divisions: 1790–1860," p. 55, and "Negro Population in Years Specified, Classified by Sex and Age Periods; 1830–1910," p. 166. *Slave prices:* Estimated visually from the chart "Approximate Prices of Prime Field Hands in Hundreds of Dollars per Head: . . . at New Orleans . . . ," in U. B. Phillips, *Life and Labor in the Old South* (Boston, 1935), p. 177.

[a] To estimate the slave population in the intercensal years, the increase over each decade was divided into equal parts and assigned to each year in the decade. The proportion of Negroes in the field-work age brackets (between the ages of ten and fifty-four) was .641 in 1860, .635 in 1850, .621 in 1840, and .610 in 1830. The census-year proportions at the beginning and end of each decade were averaged for use in the intervening years. For the years before 1830, an estimate of .60 was used. There is no implication that we have measured the number of field hands, but it should be noted that the range .60–.65 brackets several contemporary estimates of the proportion of the slave population employed in cotton agriculture (see, e.g., P. A. Morse, "Southern Slavery and the Cotton Trade," *De Bow's Review*, XXIII [1857], 475–82).

is our impression that the great demand for slaves in the Southwest will keep up the prices as it caused their advance in the first place, and that the rates are not a cent above the real value of the laborer who is to be engaged in tilling the fertile lands of a section of the country which yields the planter nearly double the crop that the fields of the Atlantic States do.

Futhermore, it would appear that slave prices fluctuate less than do cotton prices. This and the less clear-cut lag of the slave prices make it difficult to accept the image of unwary planters helplessly exposing themselves in a market dominated by speculators. It would make more sense to argue simply that the rising trend of slave prices coupled with a growing slave population is in and of itself strong evidence of the profitability of slavery.

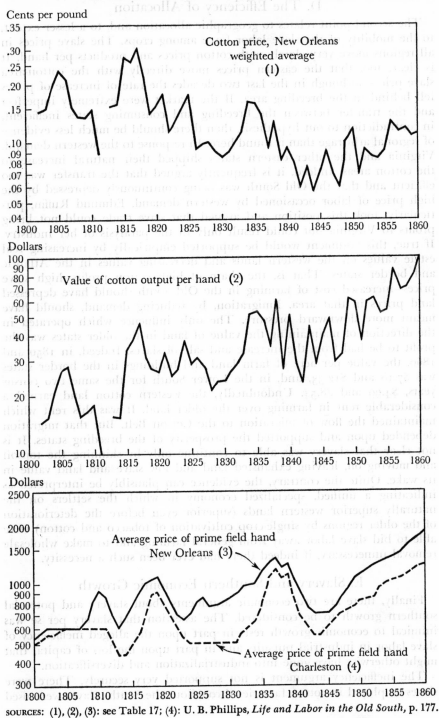

CHART I. SLAVE POPULATION AND PRICES AND THE VALUE
OF COTTON PRODUCTION, 1802–60 (RATIO SCALES)

Cents per pound

Cotton price, New Orleans
weighted average
(1)

.35
.30
.25
.20
.15
.10
.09
.08
.07
.06
.05
.04

1800 1805 1810 1815 1820 1825 1830 1835 1840 1845 1850 1855 1860

Dollars

Value of cotton output per hand (2)

100
90
80
70
60
50
40
30
20
10

1800 1805 1810 1815 1820 1825 1830 1835 1840 1845 1850 1855 1860

Dollars

Average price of prime field hand
New Orleans (3)

Average price of prime field hand
Charleston (4)

2500
2000
1500
1000
900
800
700
600
500
400
300

1800 1805 1810 1815 1820 1825 1830 1835 1840 1845 1850 1855 1860

SOURCES: (1), (2), (3): see Table 17; (4): U. B. Phillips, *Life and Labor in the Old South*, p. 177.

D. The Efficiency of Allocation

The second point relates to geographic allocation and, to a lesser extent, to the mobility of the slave labor force among crops. The slave prices in all regions move very closely with cotton prices and products per hand. It is clear, too, that the eastern prices move directly with the cotton-area slave prices, although in the last two decades the rate of increase of prices fell behind in the breeding area. If the market were extremely imperfect and the transfer between the breeding and consuming states inefficient, in contradiction to our hypothesis, then there should be much less evidence of regional arbitrage than is found here. In response to the western demand, Virginia and the other eastern states shipped their natural increase to the cotton areas. Indeed, it is frequently argued that the transfer was too efficient and that the Old South was being continuously depressed by the high price of labor occasioned by western demand. Edmund Ruffin, particularly, took this position and argued that slave trade could not bring profits to Virginia but could result only in the paralysis of her industry. If true, this argument would be supported empirically by increasing real estate values on the western lands and decreasing values in the Atlantic and border states. That is, the chain of high cotton profits—high slave prices—increased cost of farming in the Old South should have depressed land prices in that area. Emigration, by reducing demand, should have meant more downward pressure. The only influence which operated in the direction of maintaining the value of land in the older states was the profit to be had from the increase and sale of slaves. Indeed, in 1850 and 1860, the value per acre of farm land and buildings in the border states was $7.18 and $12.33, and, in the Lower South for the same two census years, $4.99 and $8.54. Undoubtedly, the western cotton land earned a considerable rent in farming over the older land. It was this rent which maintained the flow of migration to the Cotton Belt. But that migration depended upon and supported the prosperity of the breeding states. It is not clear that slavery was able to continue only by skinning the topsoil and moving on, leaving exhausted land and low slave and land value in its wake. Quite the contrary, the evidence can plausibly be interpreted as indicating a unified, specialized economy in which the settlers on the naturally superior western lands (superior even before the deterioration of the older regions by single-crop cultivation of tobacco and cotton) were able to bid slave labor away from general farming and to make wholesale removal unnecessary, if indeed there had ever been such a necessity.

E. Slavery and Southern Economic Growth

Finally, there are two economic arguments about slavery and potential southern growth to be considered. The assertion that slavery per se was inimical to economic growth rests in part upon the alleged inefficiency of slave labor in industrial pursuits and in part upon the loss of capital that might otherwise have gone into industrialization and diversification.

The inefficiency argument is not supported very securely. There were slaves employed in cotton factories throughout the South. Slaves were used in the coal mines and in the North Carolina lumbering operations. In the ironworks at Richmond and on the Cumberland River, slaves comprised a majority of the labor force. Southern railroads were largely built by southern slaves. Crop diversification, or the failure to achieve diversification, appears to have been a problem of entrepreneurship rather than of the difficulties of training slaves. In the face of the demand for cotton and the profits to be had from specializing in this single crop, it is hardly difficult to explain the single-minded concentration of the planter.

In what ways was slavery allegedly responsible for the drain of capital from the South? The lack of diversification, to the extent of a failure even to provide basic supplies, made necessary the import of much food and virtually all manufactured articles from the North. But half of this assertion, the argument that laid the responsibility for the single-crop culture upon slavery, has been found questionable already.

The major avenues by which wealth is said to have been drained from the cotton states were the excessive use of credit (through dependence upon factors' services) and the "absorption" of capital in slaves. The dependence upon advances was, in effect, a dependence upon the New York or London money market and was, therefore, an impediment to the accumulation of capital in the South. Good crop years bring the temptation to expand production; bad years do not bring any release from the factors. But resort to factoring is characteristic of speculative, commercial agriculture, whether or not the labor force is organized in slavery. It is also frequently argued that slavery gave southern planters a taste for extravagant, wasteful display, causing the notorious lack of thrift and the relative lack of economic development, compared to that experienced in the North and West. This is a doubtful inference, at best. Slavery did not make the Cavalier any more than slavery invented speculation in cotton. However, insofar as successful slave management required military posture and discipline, the southerner's expensive image of himself as a *grand seigneur* was encouraged. It is beyond the scope of this paper to offer hypotheses about the reasons for the relative degrees of entrepreneurship in Charleston and Boston; in this context it is sufficient to state that slavery per se does not seem to have been responsible for the excessive reliance upon factoring and external sources of credit.

There remains only the absorption of capital in slaves to set the responsibility for lack of growth in the South upon the peculiar institution. Earnings that might have gone out of the South to bring in investment goods were fixed in the form of chattel labor. For the early years, during the external slave trade, there is some plausibility to this argument, though it is difficult to see how the capitalization of an income stream, excellent by contemporary standards, can be said to count as a loss of wealth. In the later years there was, except to the extent that northern or English bankers drew off the interest, a redistribution of wealth only within the slave states: from the cotton lands back to the less profitable field agriculture of the older section. And, to the extent that the old planting aristocracy used the profits to maintain the real or fancied magnificence of the preceding century, capital was absorbed. Slavery made this possible, so long as the natural increase could be shipped off. But, as Russel pointed out, slavery also made the profits in the cotton fields and the resultant demand for eastern hands. We are left with the conclusion that, except insofar as it made speculation in cotton possible on a grander scale than would otherwise have been the case and thereby weakened whatever pressure there might have been for diversification, capitalization of the labor force did not of itself operate against southern development.

IV. CONCLUSION

IN SUM, it seems doubtful that the South was forced by bad statesmanship into an unnecessary war to protect a system which must soon have disappeared because it was economically unsound. This is a romantic hypothesis which will not stand against the facts.

On the basis of the computation of the returns to capital in our model of the ante bellum southern economy and the demonstration of the efficiency of the regional specialization, the following conclusions are offered:

1. Slavery was profitable to the whole South, the continuing demand for labor in the Cotton Belt insuring returns to the breeding operation on the less productive land in the seaboard and border states. The breeding returns were necessary, however, to make the plantation operations on the poorer lands as profitable as alternative contemporary economic activities in the United States. The failure of southern agriculture on these poorer lands in the post bellum period is probably attributable, in the main, to the loss of these capital gains on breeding and not, as is so often suggested, to either the relative inefficiency of the tenant system that replaced the plantations or the soil damage resulting from war operations. These factors were unquestionably contributing elements to the difficulties of post bellum southern agriculture, but they were of relatively small quantitive importance compared with the elimination of slave-breeding returns.

2. There was nothing necessarily self-destructive about the profits of the slave economy. Neither the overcapitalization argument nor the assertion that slavery must have collapsed because the slaves would not reproduce themselves is tenable. Slave prices did not outpace productivity, and the regional slave price structure would imply a workable transfer mechanism rather than the contrary.

3. Continued expansion of slave territory was both possible and, to some extent, necessary. The maintenance of profits in the Old South depended upon the expansion, extensive or intensive, of slave agriculture into the Southwest. This is sufficient to explain the interest of the Old South in secession and does away with the necessity to fall back upon arguments of statesmanship or quixotism to explain the willingness to fight for the peculiar institution.

4. The available productive surplus from slavery might have been used for economic development or, as in totalitarian regimes in this century, for militarism. In spite of this good omen for development, southern investment and industrialization lagged. It is hard to explain this except on the

social ground that entrepreneurship could not take root in the South or
on the economic ground that the South did not really own the system but
merely operated it. Furthermore, the American experience clearly suggests
that slavery is not, from the strict economic standpoint, a deterrent to
industrial development and that its elimination may take more than the
workings of "inexorable economic forces." Although profitability cannot
be offered as a sufficient guaranty of the continuity of southern slavery, the
converse argument that slavery must have destroyed itself can no longer
rest upon allegations of unprofitability or upon assumptions about the
impossibility of maintaining and allocating a slave labor force. To the
extent, moreover, that profitability is a necessary condition for the continuation of a private business institution in a free-enterprise society, slavery
was not untenable in the ante bellum American South. Indeed, economic
forces often may work toward the continuation of a slave system, so that
the elimination of slavery may depend upon the adoption of harsh political
measures. Certainly that was the American experience.

4] Future Prospects for Production by Slave Labor

a] LIMITED SUPPLY OF LAND TO STIFLE SLAVERY

THE CAUSES of the expansion of slavery westward from the South
Atlantic Coast are now well understood. The industrial revolution
and the opening of world markets had continually increased the consumption and demand for raw cotton, while the abundance of fertile and
cheap cotton lands in the Gulf States had steadily lured cotton farmers
and planters westward. Where large-scale production was possible, the
enormous demand for a steady supply of labor had made the use of slaves
inevitable, for a sufficient supply of free labor was unprocurable on the
frontier. Within one generation, the cotton-growing slave belt had swept
across the Gulf region from eastern Georgia to Texas. A parallel movement
had carried slaves, though in smaller ratio to whites, into the tobacco and
hemp fields of Kentucky, Tennessee, and Missouri. The most powerful
factor in the westward movement of slavery was cotton, for the land
available for other staples—sugar, hemp, tobacco—was limited, while slave
labor was not usually profitable in growing grain. This expansion of the
institution was in response to economic stimuli; it had been inspired by
no political program nor by any ulterior political purpose. It requires
but little acquaintance with the strongly individualistic and unregimented

FROM Charles W. Ramsdell, "The Natural Limits of Slavery Expansion," *Mississippi
Valley Historical Review,* XVI (September, 1929), 153–62, 166–71.

society of that day to see that it would have been extremely difficult, if not impossible, to carry out such an extensive program; nor is there any evidence that such a program existed. There was incentive enough in the desire of the individual slaveowner for the greater profits which he expected in the new lands. The movement would go on as far as suitable cotton lands were to be found or as long as there was a reasonable expectation of profit from slave labor, provided, of course, that no political barrier was encountered.

The astonishing rapidity of the advance of the southern frontier prior to 1840 had alarmed the opponents of slavery, who feared that the institution would extend indefinitely into the West. But by 1849–50, when the contest over the principle of the Wilmot Proviso was at its height, the western limits of the cotton-growing region were already approximated; and by the time the new Republican party was formed to check the further expansion of slavery, the westward march of the cotton plantation was evidently slowing down. The northern frontier of cotton production west of the Mississippi had already been established at about the northern line of Arkansas. Only a negligible amount of the staple was being grown in Missouri. West of Arkansas a little cotton was cultivated by the slave-holding, civilized Indians; but until the Indian territory should be opened generally to white settlement—a development of which there was no immediate prospect—it could not become a slaveholding region of any importance. The only possibility of a further westward extension of the cotton belt was in Texas. In that state alone was the frontier line of cotton and slavery still advancing.

In considering the possibilities of the further extension of slavery, then, it is necessary to examine the situation in Texas in the eighteen-fifties. Though slaves had been introduced into Texas by some of Stephen F. Austin's colonists, they were not brought in large numbers until after annexation. Before the Texas Revolution, the attitude of the Mexican government and the difficulty of marketing the products of slave labor had checked their introduction; while during the period of the Republic, the uncertainty as to the future of the country, the heavy tariff laid upon Texas cotton by the United States, which in the absence of a direct trade with Europe was virtually the only market for Texas cotton, and the low price of cotton after 1839, had been sufficient in general to restrain the cotton planter from emigrating to the new country. Annexation to the United States and the successful termination of the war with Mexico removed most of these impediments. Thereafter there was no tariff to pay; slave property was safe; land agents offered an abundance of cheap rich lands near enough to the coast and to navigable rivers to permit ready exportation; and the price of cotton was again at a profitable figure. Planters with their slaves poured into the new state in increasing numbers. They settled along the northeastern border, where they had an outlet by way of the Red River, or in the east and southeast along the rivers which flowed into the Gulf. But these rivers were not navigable very far from the coast, and the planter who went far into the interior found difficulty in getting his cotton to market. He must either wait upon a rise in the river and depend upon occasional small steamers or the risky method of floating his crop down on rafts; or he must haul it during the wet winter season along nearly impassable pioneer roads and across unbridged streams to Houston or Shreveport, or some other far-off market. The larger his crop, the more time, difficulty, and expense of getting it to market.

Obviously, there was a geographic limit beyond which, under such conditions, the growth of large crops of cotton was unprofitable. Therefore, in the early fifties, the cotton plantations tended to cluster in the river counties in the eastern and southern parts of the state. While the small farmers and stockmen pushed steadily out into the central section of Texas, driving the Indians before them, the cotton plantations and the mass of the slaves lagged far behind. The up-country settlers grew their little crops of grain on some of the finest cotton lands of the world; and they sold their surplus to immigrants and to army posts. Few negroes were to be found on these upland farms, both because the prices demanded for slaves were too high for the farmers to buy them, and because the seasonal character of labor in grain growing rendered the use of slaves unprofitable. Though negro mechanics were in demand and were hired at high wages, the field hand had to be employed fairly steadily throughout the year if his labor was to show a profit. Negroes were even less useful in handling range stock than in farming and were rarely used for that purpose.

Therefore, the extension of the cotton plantation into the interior of Texas had to wait upon the development of a cheaper and more efficient means of transportation. As all attempts to improve the navigation of the shallow, snag-filled rivers failed, it became more and more evident that the only solution of the problem of the interior planter lay in the building of railroads. Throughout the eighteen-fifties, and indeed for two decades after the war, there was a feverish demand for railroads in all parts of the state. The newspapers of the period were full of projects and promises, and scores of railroad companies were organized or promoted. But capital was lacking and the roads were slow in building. Not a single railroad had reached the fertile black-land belt of central Texas by 1860. There can hardly be any question that the cotton plantations with their working forces of slaves would have followed the railroads westward until they reached the black-land prairies of central Texas or the semi-arid plains which cover the western half of the state. But would they have followed on into the prairies and the plains?

It is important to recall that eastern Texas, like the older South Atlantic and Gulf cotton region, is a wooded country, where the essential problem of enclosing fields was easily solved by the rail fence. But in the black-land prairies there was no fencing material, except for a little wood along the creeks; and during the fifties the small fields of the farmers were along these streams. The prairies, generally, were not enclosed and put under the plow until after the introduction of barbed wire in the late seventies. Unless the planter had resorted to the expense of shipping rails from eastern Texas, there was no way in which he could have made more use of the prairie lands than the small farmers did. Here, then, in the central black-land prairies, was a temporary barrier to the westward movement of the slave plantation. Beyond it was another barrier that would have been permanently impassable.

Running north and south, just west of the black-land belt, and almost in the geographical center of the state, is a hilly, wooded strip of varying width known as the East and West Cross Timbers, which is prolonged to the south and southwest by the Edwards Plateau. West of the Cross Timbers begins the semi-arid plain which rises to the high, flat table-land of the Staked Plains, or Llano Estacado, in the extreme west and northwest. Except for a few small cattle ranches, there were almost no settlements in this plains country before 1860; and despite the heavy immigration into Texas after the Civil War, it was not until the eighties that farmers began to penetrate this section.

The history of the agricultural development of the Texas plains region since 1880 affords abundant evidence that it would never have become suitable for plantation slave labor. Let us turn, for a moment, to this later period. The Texas and Pacific Railroad, completed by 1882 and followed by the building of other roads into and across the plains, afforded transportation; and the introduction of barbed wire solved the fencing problem. State and railroad lands were offered the settlers at low prices. Farmers began moving into the eastern plains about 1880, but they were driven back again and again by droughts. It took more than twenty years of experimentation and adaptation with windmills, dry-farming, and new drought-resisting feed crops for the cotton farmer to conquer the plains. There is little reason to believe that the conquest could have been effected earlier; there is even less basis for belief that the region would ever have been filled with plantations and slaves. For reasons which will be advanced later, it is likely that the institution of slavery would have declined toward extinction in the Old South before the cotton conquest of the plains could have been accomplished, even had there been no Civil War. But if the institution had remained in full vigor elsewhere, it would have been almost impossible to establish the plantation system in this semi-arid section where, in the experimental period, complete losses of crops were so frequent. With so much of his capital tied up in unremunerative laborers whom he must feed and clothe, it is hard to see how any planter could have stayed in that country. Moreover, in the later period the use of improved machinery, especially adapted to the plains, would have made slave labor unnecessary and unbearably expensive. The character of the soil and the infrequency of rainfall have enabled the western cotton farmer, since 1900, with the use of this improved machinery to cultivate a far larger acreage in cotton, and other crops as well, than was possible in the older South or in eastern Texas. The result has been the appearance of a high peak in the demand for labor in western Texas in the cotton-picking season. This has called for transient or seasonal labor as in the grain fields—a situation that could not be met by the plantation system of slave labor. During the last twenty-five years this section has become populous and prosperous; but the beginning of its success as a cotton-growing region came fifty years after the Republican party was organized to stop the westward advance of the "cotton barons" and their slaves. It may or may not have any significance that the negro has moved but little farther west in Texas than he was in 1860—he is still a rarity in the plains country—although it may be presumed that his labor has been cheaper in freedom than under slavery.

But let us look for a moment at the southwestern border of Texas. In 1860 slavery had stopped more than one hundred and fifty miles short of the Rio Grande. One obvious explanation of this fact is that the slaveowner feared to get too close to the boundary lest his bondmen escape into Mexico. There is no doubt that this fear existed, and that slaves occasionally made their way into that country. But it is worth noting that very little cotton was grown then or is yet grown on that border of Texas, except in the lower valley around Brownsville and along the coast about Corpus Christi. Other crops have proved better adapted to the soil and climate and have paid better. More significant still is the fact that very few negroes are found there today, for Mexican labor is cheaper than negro labor now, as it was in the eighteen-fifties. During the decade before secession, Mexican labor was used exclusively south of the Nueces River. After emancipation there was still no movement of negroes into the region where Mexican labor was employed. The disturbances which began in Mexico in 1910 have sent floods of Mexicans across the Rio Grande to labor in the fruit and truck farms of the valley and the cotton fields of south Texas. An interesting result is that the Mexican has steadily pushed the negro out of south Texas and to a considerable degree out of south-central Texas. Wherever the two have come into competition either on the farms or as day laborers in the towns, the Mexican has won. This would seem to show that there was little chance for the institution of African slavery to make headway in the direction of Mexico.

There was another situation which checked the extension of slavery into southwestern Texas. A large area of the most fertile lands had been settled by German immigrants, who had begun coming into that district in the late eighteen-forties. Not only were the Germans opposed to slavery; they were too poor to purchase slaves. They needed labor, as all pioneers do; but their needs were met by the steady inflow of new German immigrants, whose habit it was to hire themselves out until they were able to buy small farms for themselves. The system of agriculture of these industrious and frugal people had no place for the African, whether slave or free. Even today one sees few negroes among the original and typical German settlements. In 1860, east and southeast of San Antonio, these Germans formed a barrier across the front of the slaveholders.

By the provisions of the Compromise of 1850, New Mexico, Utah, and the other territories acquired from Mexico were legally open to slavery. In view of well-known facts, it may hardly seem worth while to discuss the question whether slavery would ever have taken possession of that vast region; but perhaps some of those facts should be set down. The real western frontier of the cotton belt is still in Texas; for though cotton is grown in small quantities in New Mexico, Arizona, and California, in none of these states is the entire yield equal to that of certain single counties in Texas. In none is negro labor used to any appreciable extent, if at all. In New Mexico and Arizona, Mexican labor is cheaper than negro labor, as has been the case ever since the acquisition of the region from Mexico. It was well understood by sensible men, North and South, in 1850 that soil, climate, and native labor would form a perpetual bar to slavery in the vast territory then called New Mexico. Possibly southern California could have sustained slavery, but California had already decided that question for itself, and there was no remote probability that the decision would ever be reversed. As to New Mexico, the census of 1860, ten years after the territory had been thrown open to slavery, showed not a single slave; and this was true, also, of both Colorado and Nevada. Utah, alone of all these territories, was credited with any slaves at all. Surely these results for the ten years when, it is alleged, the slave power was doing its utmost to extend its system into the West, ought to have confuted those who had called down frenzied curses upon the head of Daniel Webster for his Seventh-of-March speech.

At the very time when slavery was reaching its natural and impassable frontiers in Texas, there arose the fateful excitement over the Kansas-Nebraska Bill, or rather over the clause which abrogated the Missouri Compromise and left the determination of the status of slavery in the two territories to their own settlers. Every student of American history knows of the explosion produced in the North by the "Appeal of the Independent Democrats in Congress to the People of the United States," written and circulated by Senator Chase and other members of Congress. This fulmination predicted that the passage of the bill would result in debarring free home-seeking immigrants and laborers from a vast region larger, excluding California, than all the free states, and in converting it into a dreary waste filled with plantations and slaves. It was a remarkably skillful maneuver and it set the North, particularly the Northwest, on fire. But, in all candor, what of the truth of the prophecy? Can anyone who examines the matter objectively today say that there was any probability that slavery as an institution would ever have taken possession of either Kansas or Nebraska? Certainly cotton could not have been grown in either, for it was not grown in the adjacent part of Missouri. Hemp, and possibly tobacco, might have been grown in a limited portion of eastern Kansas along the Missouri and the lower Kansas rivers; and if no obstacle had been present, undoubtedly a few negroes would have been taken into eastern Kansas. But the infiltration of slaves would have been a slow process.

Apparently there was no expectation, even on the part of the pro-slavery men, that slavery would go into Nebraska. Only a small fraction of the territory was suited to any crops that could be grown with profit by slave labor, and by far the greater portion of Kansas—even of the eastern half that was available for immediate settlement—would have been occupied in a short time, as it was in fact, by a predominantly non-slaveholding and free-soil population. To say that the individual slaveowner would disregard his own economic interest and carry valuable property where it would entail loss merely for the sake of a doubtful political advantage seems a palpable absurdity. Indeed, competent students who have examined this subject have shown that the chief interest of the pro-slavery Missourians in seeking to control the organization of the territorial government was not so much in taking slaves into Kansas as in making sure that no free-soil territory should be organized on their border to endanger their property in western Missouri. They lost in the end, as they were bound to lose. The census of 1860 showed two slaves in Kansas and fifteen in Nebraska. In short, there is good reason to believe that had Douglas' bill passed Congress without protest, and had it been sustained by the people of the free states, slavery could not have taken permanent root in Kansas if the decision were left to the people of the territory itself.

.   .   .   .

The agitation for the re-opening of the African slave trade is an interesting episode. Its proponents were a small group of extremists, mostly Secessionists, whose ostensible object was to cheapen the cost of labor for the small farmer who was too poor to pay the high prices for slaves that prevailed in the fifties. Another argument for re-opening the trade was that cheaper slave labor would enable the institution to extend its frontiers into regions where it was too expensive under existing conditions. Finally, the proponents of the movement insisted that unless the cost of slaves declined, the northern tier of slave states would be drained of their negroes until they themselves became free states, thus imperiling the security of the cotton states. There is some reason to suspect that their leaders designed to stir up the anti-slavery element in the North to greater hostility and to renewed attacks in the hope that the South would be driven into secession, which was the ultimate goal of this faction. These agitators were never able to commit a single state to the project, for not only did the border states condemn it but the majority of the people of the Gulf states also. Even Robert Barnwell Rhett, who was at first inclined to support the program, turned against it because he saw that it was dividing the state-rights faction and weakening the cause of southern unity. This in itself seems highly significant of the southern attitude.

If the conclusions that have been set forth are sound, by 1860 the institution of slavery had virtually reached its natural frontiers in the west. Beyond Texas and Missouri the way was closed. There was no reasonable ground for expectation that new lands could be acquired south of the United States into which slaves might be taken. There was, in brief, no further place for it to go. In the cold facts of the situation, there was no longer any basis for excited sectional controversy over slavery extension; but the public mind had so long been concerned with the debate that it could not see that the issue had ceased to have validity. In the existing state of the popular mind, therefore, there was still abundant opportunity for the politician to work to his own ends, to play upon prejudice and passion and fear. Blind leaders of the blind! Sowers of the wind, not seeing how near was the approaching harvest of the whirlwind!

Perhaps this paper should end at this point; but it may be useful to push the inquiry a little farther. If slavery could gain no more political territory, would it be able to hold what it had? Were there not clear indica-

tions that its area would soon begin to contract? Were there not even some
evidences that a new set of conditions were arising within the South itself
which would disintegrate the institution? Here, it must be confessed, one
enters the field of speculation, which is always dangerous ground for the
historian. But there were certain factors in the situation which can be
clearly discerned, and it may serve some purpose to indicate them.

Reference has already been made to the increasingly high prices of slaves
in the southwestern states throughout the eighteen-fifties. This price-boom
was due in part to good prices for cotton; but though there had always
previously been a fairly close correlation between cotton and slave prices,
the peculiarity of this situation was that slave prices increased much faster
than cotton prices from 1850 to the end of 1860. Probably the explanation
lies in the abundance of cheap and fertile cotton lands that were available
for planting in Louisiana, Arkansas, and Texas. Cheap lands enabled the
planter to expand his plantation and to invest a relatively larger amount
of his capital in slaves, and the continued good prices for cotton encouraged this expansion. These good prices for slaves were felt all the way back
to the oldest slave states, where slave labor was less profitable, and had the
effect of drawing away planters and slaves from Maryland, Virginia, North
Carolina, Kentucky, and Missouri to the new Southwest. This movement,
to be sure, had been going on for several decades, but now the migration
from the old border states was causing alarm among the pro-slavery men.
Delaware was only nominally a slave state; Maryland's slave population was
diminishing steadily. The ratio of slaves to whites was declining year by
year in Virginia, Kentucky, and even in Missouri. The industrial revolution was reaching into these three states, and promised within less than
another generation to reduce the economic interest in planting and slaveholding, as already in Maryland, to very small proportions.

The pro-slavery leaders in Virginia and Maryland endeavored to arrest
this change by improving the condition of the planter. They renewed their
efforts for a direct trade with Europe, and further stimulated interest in
agricultural reforms. As already seen, the proponents of the revival of the
African slave trade argued that cheaper slave labor in the lower South was
necessary to prevent the border states from ultimately becoming free-soil.
Though agricultural reform made headway, the other remedies failed to
materialize; and the slow but constant transformation of the Atlantic border
region proceeded. The greatest impediments were in the reluctance of the
families of the old states, where slavery was strongly patriarchal, to part
with their family servants, and in the social prestige which attached to the
possession of an ample retinue of servants. It was evident, however, that
the exodus would go on until the lure of the Southwest lost its force.

As long as there was an abundance of cheap and fertile cotton lands, as
there was in Texas, and the prices of cotton remained good, there would
be a heavy demand for labor on the new plantations. As far as fresh lands
were concerned, this condition would last for some time, for the supply
of lands in Texas alone was enormous. But at the end of the decade, there
were unmistakable signs that a sharp decline in cotton prices and planting
profits was close at hand. The production of cotton had increased slowly,

with some fluctuations, from 1848 to 1857, and the price varied from about ten cents to over thirteen cents a pound on the New York market. But a rapid increase in production began in 1858 and the price declined. The crop of 1860 was twice that of 1850. Probably the increase in production was due in part to the rapid building of railroads throughout the South toward the end of the decade, which brought new lands within reach of markets and increased the cotton acreage; but part of the increase was due to the new fields in Texas. There was every indication of increased production and lower price levels for the future, even if large allowance be made for poor-crop years. There was small chance of reducing the acreage, for the cotton planter could not easily change to another crop. Had not the war intervened, there is every reason to believe that there would have been a continuous overproduction and very low prices throughout the sixties and seventies.

What would have happened then when the new lands of the Southwest had come into full production and the price of cotton had sunk to the point at which it could not be grown with profit on the millions of acres of poorer soils in the older sections? The replenishment of the soil would not have solved the problem for it would only have resulted in the production of more cotton. Even on the better lands the margin of profit would have declined.[1] Prices of slaves must have dropped then, even in the Southwest; importation from the border states would have fallen off; thousands of slaves would have become not only unprofitable but a heavy burden, the market for them gone. Those who are familiar with the history of cotton farming, cotton prices, and the depletion of the cotton lands since the Civil War will agree that this is no fanciful picture.

What would have been the effect of this upon the slaveowner's attitude toward emancipation? No preachments about the sacredness of the institution and of constitutional guarantees would have compensated him for the dwindling values of his lands and slaves and the increasing burden of his debts. It should not be forgotten that the final formulation and acceptance of the so-called "pro-slavery philosophy" belonged to a time when slaveowners, in general, were prosperous. With prosperity gone and slaves an increasingly unprofitable burden, year after year, can there be any doubt that thousands of slaveowners would have sought for some means of relief? How they might have solved the problem of getting out from under the burden without entire loss of the capital invested in their working force, it is hard to say; but that they would have changed their attitude toward the institution seems inevitable.

There was one difficulty about the problem of emancipation that has been little understood in the North, one that the Abolitionist refused to

---

[1] Improved farm machinery, which was already beginning to be introduced on the plantations, would certainly have lowered the cost of crop production; but it must have resulted both in an increase of acreage—thus further reducing prices by increasing the total yield—and the replacement of slave labor to some extent by machinery and the reduction by so much of the demand for and the value of slaves. In fact, there is strong reason to believe that the introduction of labor-saving agricultural machinery would have done much to destroy chattel slavery.

admit. It was the question of what to do with the freed negro. Could he take care of himself without becoming a public charge and a social danger? Would it not be necessary to get rid of the slave and the negro at the same time? But to get rid of the negro was manifestly impossible. Should he not then remain under some form of control both in his own interest and in the interest of the larger social order? There is some evidence that this problem was actually being worked out in those older states which had a large population of free negroes. In Virginia and Maryland, where the number of slaves on the plantation had been reduced in the interest of economy as improved farming machinery came into use, free negroes were coming to be relied upon when extra or seasonable labor was required. Though it is impossible to say how far this practice would have gone in substituting free-negro labor for slave labor, it would inevitably have accustomed increasing numbers of employers to the use of free negroes and have weakened by so much the economic interest in slavery. The cost of rearing a slave to the working age was considerable, and it is well within the probabilities that, in an era of over-stocked plantations and low cotton prices, the planter would have found that he was rearing slaves, as well as growing cotton, at a loss. New codes for the control of the free negroes might easily, in the course of time, have removed the greatest objection on the part of the nonslaveowners to emancipation.

In summary and conclusion: it seems evident that slavery had about reached its zenith by 1860 and must shortly have begun to decline, for the economic forces which had carried it into the region west of the Mississippi had about reached their maximum effectiveness. It could not go forward in any direction and it was losing ground along its northern border. A cumbersome and expensive system, it could show profits only as long as it could find plenty of rich land to cultivate and the world would take the product of its crude labor at a good price. It had reached its limits in both profits and lands. The free farmers in the North who dreaded its further spread had nothing to fear. Even those who wished it destroyed had only to wait a little while—perhaps a generation, probably less. It was summarily destroyed at a frightful cost to the whole country and one third of the nation was impoverished for forty years. One is tempted at this point to reflections upon what has long passed for statesmanship on both sides of that long dead issue. But I have not the heart to indulge them.

b] AMPLE SUPPLY OF LAND AVAILABLE FOR SLAVERY'S EXPANSION

HAD NO restrictions been placed on the slave trade the supply of slaves might ultimately have become so great that the value of their product would have barely exceeded the cost of maintaining slaves. This might have resulted either from the law of diminishing returns due to scarcity of

FROM Lewis Cecil Gray, *History of Agriculture in the Southern United States to 1860* (Washington, D. C.: Carnegie Institution of Washington, 1933), I, 475–78.

land, or to depression in the prices of products due to overproduction. In his *Political Economy of Slavery* Edmund Ruffin recognized the former possibility. Tucker concluded that slavery would tend to become economically moribund when the density of population reached 66 per square mile.

.   .   .   .

It is conceivable, of course, that the operation of the law of diminishing returns might be greatly postponed through development of industrialism. If this tendency had occurred it is probable that the emancipation of the slave would have resulted, because freedom would have provided conditions more favorable to initiative and the exercise of intelligence. Under such conditions, as some economists have recognized, the slave's productivity would have become so much greater, when allowed to shift for himself, that he could have paid his master the equivalent of his earnings as a slave and obtained enough above this to accumulate the means of purchasing his freedom.

The belief, however, that in 1860 slavery in the South was on the point of being "strangled for lack of room to expand" is a wholly mistaken interpretation of actual conditions. The plantation system was not seriously limited by scarcity of land. It had utilized only a small fraction of the available land area. The most fertile and easily available soils may have been occupied, but there was an extensive area remaining, a considerable part of which has been brought into cultivation since 1860. Before the Civil War railways were rapidly opening up new fertile areas to plantation agriculture. Far from being a decrepit institution, the economic motives for the continuance of slavery from the standpoint of the employer were never so strong as in the years just preceding the Civil War.

The argument that slavery was becoming unprofitable just before the Civil War has been presented by Professor U. B. Phillips from another standpoint. While recognizing clearly that the value of the slave was largely the result of a capitalization of net earnings, he argues that speculation had carried slave prices beyond the point at which slaves could be profitably employed except under the most favorable conditions. He points to the fact that cotton was very much lower in 1860 than it had been in the third and fourth decades, while the value of slaves was very much higher. It is easily possible, however, to derive a mistaken conclusion from this fact. Professor Phillips appears to defend the position that the movement toward overcapitalization was permanent, resulting in a steadily growing tendency for plantation agriculture to become unprofitable. Achille Loria also accepts and elaborates this interpretation. The present writer does not agree with this conclusion. Overexpansion of market prices of slaves, land, bonds, or other income-bearers in relation to net earnings, as a result of speculation, is at most only a temporary phenomenon. Expansion and contraction of slave prices occurred several times during the ante bellum period in relation to variations in the prices of the great Southern staple, cotton. Moreover, as compared with earlier periods, prices of cotton should be considered in relation to the fact that in the interval from 1794 to 1860 there was a considerable reduction in cost of producing cotton. It is not improbable, also, that slave prices in the earlier period had not completely risen to the point justified by the enormous profits that contemporary accounts describe; for slaves had not come to have the scarcity value later arising from restriction of the trade, whereas demand for cotton increased for a time very rapidly, giving rise to prices far in excess of even the high costs of production. There is no apparent reason why high market values of slaves should be a permanent cause for unprofitable plantation economy. Had such a condition prevailed for a considerable period, affecting the profits of a great majority of those who were actively demanding slaves, this demand must ultimately have declined, and with it the excessive values. It must be remembered, however, that the active demand which tended to enhance the prices of slaves came from those planters who were making large profits and who sought to expand their slaveholdings on the basis of these profits.

If competition had worked smoothly and slave labor had flowed readily to the points of most advantageous employment, as assumed in the Ricardian theory of rent, the rent-bearing land would have been the land of superior quality and location, and the return from the employment of slaves on such land would have tended to be the same as on the no-rent land, the rent merely measuring the difference in the gross product of an equal quantity of labor and equipment employed on the two grades of land.

In practice, however, the complete mobility assumed was not fulfilled. From time to time new areas were opened to settlement containing lands superior to those occupied in areas of earlier settlement, the natural inferiority of which was being steadily intensified by deterioration. While the value of these new lands rose rapidly on account of the inflow of population, yet immigration was not rapid enough to cause land values to absorb all the differential in productivity as compared with the poorer lands in the older regions of settlement. On account of the retardation in the bidding up of values of the better lands commensurate with their full superiority, labor tended to earn in the newer areas a return that was considerably higher than in the older regions, handicapped as they were by impairment of fertility.

The large differential in productivity stimulated the transfer of slave labor to the Southwest, either by sale or by migration. The compulsion came about through the fact that the newer regions were able to capitalize slave labor so high that in the regions of earlier settlement it could not earn interest at the market rate on these higher capital values. It was in this sense that the employment of slave labor in general farming was frequently unprofitable. In the same sense, it was unprofitable when employed in the production of cotton in some of the older cotton producing regions. It could not produce a surplus sufficiently large to pay interest on the high capital values made possible by competition of regions where slave labor was employed to better advantage. Nevertheless, slave labor of the older regions—probably even in colonial New England—was able to earn a surplus above cost of maintenance, and had it not been for the competition of the new lands of the West, it would have continued profitable in the older regions as long as it was possible to average something above cost of subsistence.

It was the fact that slavery tended to be profitable in new regions, while unprofitable in regions in the wake of expansion, that resulted so generally in the mistaken conclusions that slavery can thrive only on the basis of geographical expansion and a migratory economy, that slavery is adapted only to extensive agriculture, that it inevitably results in soil exhaustion, and that it cannot be profitable in general farming; none of which conclusions, . . . appears to be justified in the absolute sense in which it has been asserted.

It will be apparent also that the idea that the interest on the capital value of slaves was a necessary element in cost of production is true only in the sense that, being earned by one region or industry, it must be paid by other regions and industries in order to command the services of labor. In a general sense, however, this surplus was not a necessary charge. If the prices of all Southern products had fallen so low that it was impossible in any industry or region to earn more than a few dollars a year as the net return for slave labor, it would still have been advantageous to employ it.

PART II

Slavery
and the Nonslaveholder

INTRODUCTION

〖Most southerners owned no slaves, and of the group that did, only a tiny minority could be classified as wealthy planters. Moreover, the majority of the population was not part of the region's staple economy. A relatively small group of slaveowners raised the bulk of the cotton, sugar, tobacco, and rice.

For the nonslaveholders, as well as for the farmers who owned only a few slaves, the business aspects of slavery were largely irrelevant. These nonslaveholders were occupied primarily as self-sufficient farmers, raising corn and other crops. Because they had little or no investment in slave labor, the level of profits from such labor had little direct effect upon them.

It does not necessarily follow, however, that slavery as an economic system—as distinguished from a business enterprise—had no effect upon them. Such a conclusion is warranted only if it can be shown that their *position in the economy* was unrelated to the existence of slavery.

The problem of evaluating the effect of slavery on the nonslaveholder, then, resolves itself into two separate questions. What was the position of the nonslaveholder in southern society? (This question involves the standard of living of the nonslaveholder, the facilities available to him for health and education, his opportunities for economic and political advancement, and the like.) And, to what degree, if any, was this position determined or affected by slavery?

These questions have been hotly disputed since ante-bellum times. Before the Civil War, of course, the argument had strong political overtones. If slavery's opponents could prove that the system consigned the great majority of white southerners to a life of poverty and hardship, they would then have a damning indictment of the system. This was the main purpose of Hinton Rowen Helper's vitriolic book, *The Impending Crisis* (1857). Because of slavery, he found the "South stripped of every laurel, and sinking deeper and deeper in the depths of poverty and shame," while those who suffered, the nonslaveholders, stood by and did nothing. "Never were the poorer classes of a people, and those classes so largely in the majority. . . . so basely duped, so adroitly swindled, or so damnably outraged." [1]

Proslavery southerners, of course, denied the charge. Editor-journalist, J. D. B. De Bow, for example, maintained that all white southerners benefited from slavery. Merchants prospered because they handled the goods produced by slave labor, but the white worker in the South also benefited. He had status by virtue of being a white man; he was not forced to work in unhealthy shops as was his white brother in the North; and, most important of all, he had the oppor-

[1] (New York: A. B. Burdick, 1857), pp. 41, 44. A selection from Helper's book is reprinted in a somewhat different context in Part IV.

tunity of becoming a slaveholder and by so doing relieving himself and his wife of drudgery in the fields.[2]

The readings which follow present analyses of these questions. The first section deals specifically with the relations between the slaveholder and the nonslaveholder. Agricultural historian Lewis Cecil Gray argues that the small farmer was unable to compete with slave labor and was driven off the best land in the South. Robert R. Russel, an economic historian who has written extensively on the South, denies that free labor could not compete with slave labor; it could, he argues, and it did, at least in cotton and tobacco planting. Slavery provided opportunities for the more ambitious and efficient farmers; it did not foster lack of ambition and inefficiency.

In the early 1940's, a number of scholars, led by Frank L. Owsley of Vanderbilt University, began to publish studies which analyzed the role of the small farmer in the southern economy. In the second section, Frank and Harriet Owsley summarize some of their extensive research dealing with what they call the yeoman class in southern society, the vast majority of the population owning few or no slaves. They conclude, as did those who followed their lead,[3] that not only did this middle class enjoy eco-

nomic and social well-being in the South before the Civil War, but that its position improved rather than deteriorated over the years. All southern economic historians did not agree with the Owsleys, however. Fabian Linden, the author of the next selection, while accepting the existence of the yeoman class, subjects the Owsleys' analysis to close scrutiny and refutes each point in their argument.

In addition to planter and yeoman, the ante-bellum South contained another group, often derisively labeled "poor white trash." The problem of the possible relation between slavery and the poor whites is treated by two contemporaries in the third section. Daniel Robinson Hundley has the southern gentleman's scorn for this group, which he traces to the paupers, convicts, and other undesirables who came to America as indentured servants. In Hundley's eyes, heredity, not environment, becomes responsible for the poor white. A different point of view is presented in the next selection, Yankee traveler Frederick Law Olmsted's description of a night he spent with a poor white. The farmer, Olmsted notes, is industrious enough, but seems to be trapped by his environment. Unable to hire labor and too poor to buy slaves, he cannot grow enough cotton to earn a profit. As a result, he cannot break out of his poverty-stricken life. Olmsted suggests that the South would be better off with free labor, and the farmer agrees, but expresses his fear of a free Negro population.

Clearly, to this nonslaveholder slavery was much more than an economic system; it was also a means to control a potentially dangerous population. Does this attitude explain the support given to the slave system in the South by the majority of whites who had no economic interest in the system, and who, indeed, might have been victimized by it? Or

2 J. D. B. De Bow, "The Non-Slaveholders of the South," *The Interest in Slavery of the Southern Non-Slaveholder* (Charleston: Evans & Cogswell, 1860), pp. 3–12.

3 Herbert Weaver, *Mississippi Farmers, 1850–1860* (Nashville: Vanderbilt University Press, 1945); Harry L. Coles, "Some Notes on Slave Ownership and Land Ownership in Louisiana, 1850–1860," *Journal of Southern History*, IX (August, 1943), 381–93; Blanche Henry Clark, *The Tennessee Yeoman, 1840–1860* (Nashville: Vanderbilt University Press, 1942). For a more extensive study by Owsley, see his *Plain Folk of the Old South* (Baton Rouge: Louisiana State University Press, 1949).

did economic matters predominate in the nonslaveholder's mind? Did he support the system because of his hope that he might some day become a slaveholder himself? If so, what were his chances of achieving this goal? Did the slave system provide economic opportunities for the mass of nonslaveholders? Or did it so narrow opportunities that only a few could hope to gain any economic advantages from it? Were there any other economic opportunities, beyond production with slave labor, open to the southern white? Did slavery stand in the way of his realization of these opportunities?

THE READINGS

1] Planter-Farmer Competition

a] FARMER UNABLE TO COMPETE
WITH SLAVEOWNING PLANTER

IN THE general course of economic evolution a significant phenomenon was the tendency of slavery and the plantation system, under favorable conditions, to supplant other types of economy. This process was repeated over and over again. Where conditions favored commercial production of staples, the small farmers found themselves unable to resist the competitive power of slave labor organized under the plantation system. Gradually they were compelled either to become great planters—and many did not possess sufficient ability and command over capital to accomplish this—or to reëstablish a régime of rude self-sufficing economy in a region less favorable for commercial agriculture. As in the Roman dominion during the later Republican period, small farmers and free laborers of the South at first worked side by side with slaves in the fields; as the supply of slaves increased, they found themselves unable to compete with slave labor; and finally, they were forbidden to compete by rigid social laws under which labor was invidious and stamped with the brand of servility. From another standpoint, however, the tendency may be regarded as a process of geographic specialization whereby the plantation system triumphed in regions most suitable to production of staples, while the self-sufficing or intermediate types of economy developed and survived in regions geographically adapted to them, although unfavorable to a plantation economy.

These tendencies found expression in many regions. In the coastal plain of Virginia and Maryland . . . a number of plantations were early established as a result of systems of colonization and land policy. These existed, however, in the midst of a society composed largely of small freeholders—a class that multiplied rapidly as a result of the short terms of indentured servants. It is probable that from the close of the Company period to the later years of the seventeenth century the relative importance of the plantation system was declining. With the rapid introduction of slaves in the last two decades of the century the competitive influence of the plantation system was strengthened, and the small freeholders gradually excluded from the better lands. Even in eastern North Carolina, in spite of its commercial handicaps, the plantation system made considerable progress during the first half of the eighteenth century, displacing in part the earlier régime of backwoods farmers. The experience of Georgia under the Trustees is a

FROM Lewis Cecil Gray, *History of Agriculture in the Southern United States to 1860* (Washington, D. C.: Carnegie Institution of Washington, 1933), I, 444–45.

notable instance of the triumph of slave labor and the plantation system in spite of determined efforts to develop an economy of small landowning farmers. After the invention of Whitney's cotton gin this tendency, which Professor Bassett speaks of as the "process by which slavery always eats out all the life of a free yeomanry," was repeated in region after region. A similar tendency had earlier appeared in South Carolina and in Barbados, St. Christopher, and other West Indian islands.

b] Opportunities Available for Ambitious and Efficient Farmer

PERHAPS NO interpretation of the economic history of American Negro slavery is more generally accepted today than that the institution was detrimental to the nonslaveholding whites of the South. . . . It is the purpose of this article to attempt to show that the commonly accepted interpretation requires great qualification to bring it into accord with the truth.

In 1860 approximately one-fourth of the white families of the South were slaveholding and three-fourths nonslaveholding; and of the slaveholding families a great many had only one or two slaves each. In earlier years of the period, the proportion of slaveholders was slightly larger.

The slaves and slaveholders were very largely concentrated in belts—the so-called black belts—which coincided with the areas devoted to the growing of staples, chiefly cotton, tobacco, sugar, and rice. There were also many slaves in the cities and towns in or near the staple-growing areas. These had been marked out by climate, the character of the soil, and, not least, by accessibility to market. Cotton, for example, for climatic reasons could not be grown to advantage north of an irregular line crossing North Carolina, Tennessee, and Arkansas. South of this line cotton was grown on the better lands which lay within reasonable distances of navigable rivers or of railroads. Some of the best of the present-day cotton lands were not utilized for that crop as late as 1860, because they were too far from navigable rivers while railroads had not yet penetrated into their vicinity.

The great majority of the nonslaveholding whites lived outside the principal staple-growing districts in what is commonly called back, up, or hill country, or in mountainous regions. In these areas there were comparatively few slaves. The people were mostly small farmers and, because of lack of markets or inaccessibility to them, were engaged in a more or less self-sufficing agriculture with much household manufacturing.

It is difficult to see how people living in the back country could be injured by slavery in the black belts. Except possibly to a slight extent and in a most indirect way, it was not slavery which prevented them from producing staple crops for market; it was inaccessibility. Such markets as they had for their surplus bacon, lard, mules, whiskey, etc. were chiefly among the

FROM Robert R. Russel, "The Effects of Slavery upon Nonslaveholders in the Ante-Bellum South," *Agricultural History*, XV (April, 1941), 112–26.

planters or in the towns which served the staple-producing districts. Insofar as it was slavery which caused planters to concentrate on the growing of the great market crops while purchasing various supplies elsewhere, the institution created markets for back-country farmers and thus benefited them.

It is said that slavery had driven nonslaveholding whites out of the black belts and out of staple production and had thus worked them a great injury; that, had it not been for slavery, more of them would have lived in the staple-producing regions and raised the great market crops and would have had a higher standard of living on that account.

This time-honored indictment of the peculiar institution has such great plausibility that its validity has seldom been questioned. The black belts were a fact. Even nonslaveholding whites who lived in the staple-growing areas did not produce the staples in quantities proportionate to their numbers. Virtually all the sugar and rice and the bulk of the cotton and tobacco were produced by slave labor. In 1850, according to J. D. B. De Bow, there were about 800,000 slaves engaged in cotton growing and only about 100,000 whites, and there is no reason to doubt the essential accuracy of his estimate. Much the greater part of the cash farm income of the South was received by a comparatively small number of planters, all of whom employed slave labor, of course. In the cotton States in 1850, according to William E. Dodd, "A thousand families received over $50,000,000 a year, while all the remaining 666,000 families received only about $60,000,000." This may also be accepted as approximately accurate. Yet, in spite of such prima facie evidence, the contention that slavery drove nonslaveholding whites out of staple production and thus did them a great injury contains considerably less than a half truth. Both the extent to which slavery excluded nonslaveholding whites from commercialized agriculture and the extent of the injury caused by such exclusion have been greatly exaggerated.

It is recognized at the outset that the problem involves not only the question of the comparative effectiveness of Negro slave labor and free white labor, but also that of the efficiency of the plantation as compared with the small farm as a unit of agricultural organization. The plantations of the ante bellum South were operated with slave labor almost exclusively. Almost all white agricultural workers were employed on small farms; very few served as wage earners on plantations. Moreover, the plantation system could not have existed extensively in the ante bellum South without slave labor, for the simple reason that, where land was cheap and plentiful and it was easy to become an independent farmer, free whites would not work for low enough wages, in large enough numbers, and with a sufficient degree of regularity to permit large-scale farming. White indentured servitude, with which the earliest plantations had been started, was an impossibility in the ante bellum period. Therefore, any competitive advantages which the plantation may have possessed over the small farm as a unit of farm organization must be accredited to the institution of slavery.

In sugar and rice culture the plantation undoubtedly had great competitive advantages over the small farm. Sugar growers who owned sugar-making machinery had a great advantage over those who did not, and the machinery was so expensive that only large producers could afford it. The cost of building levees also was conducive to large-scale operations. The plantation had similar advantages over the small farm in rice growing. Since plantations would have been impossible without slavery, it is proper to conclude that slavery kept small farmers from growing sugar cane and rice or, at least and more probably, from growing other crops on lands which were actually devoted to sugar and rice.

In the growing of cotton and tobacco, however—and these staples employed about eight slaves to every one in sugar and rice—it is very doubtful that the plantation was superior to the small farm as a unit of agricultural production. The planter might buy supplies, sell his produce, and obtain credit—a very doubtful advantage—on somewhat better terms than the small farmer. Joseph C. Robert has described the marketing of tobacco in ante bellum Virginia in great detail. The buyers were very numerous, widely distributed, and quite competitive. The planter seems to have had little advantage over the small farmer in selling his product. In a newer community where marketing facilities were not so well developed, the advantage of the large-scale farmer in buying and selling may have been considerable. In a district where the large planters bought and sold through nonresident merchants or agents and the small farmers were too few and too poor to support competitive buyers and retail merchants adequately, the small farmers would receive considerably less than the planters for what they might sell and pay considerably more for what they might buy.

The planter was able to effect a division of labor among his hands that was not possible on a small farm, but the operations and the machinery required in farming in those days were too simple to permit any considerable advantage to be gained from that. In fact the division of labor on a large plantation tended to become fixed and, by its inflexibility, may have impaired rather than promoted efficiency. For example, there would have been a moral difficulty about sending a dignified coachman to the field to plow or "chop." A farm worker of a reasonable degree of competence probably increases his efficiency by making the frequent changes from one sort of common task to another which are necessary on the farm.

The slaveholder had no compunctions about putting female slaves in the field gangs. White women and girls of small-farm families also worked in the fields to a considerable extent. Frederick Law Olmsted reported: "I have, in fact, seen more white native American women at work in the hottest sunshine in a single month, and that near midsummer, in Mississippi and Alabama than in all my life in the Free States, not on account of an emergency, as in harvesting, either, but in the regular cultivation of cotton and of corn, chiefly of cotton." However, white farm women and girls certainly did not go into the fields as regularly as slave women and girls. The planter had an advantage here as far as production of field crops was concerned.

The cotton planter usually had his own gin and press while his small-farm neighbor had to pay toll. Whether the planter had a competitive advantage in his ownership depended upon the tolls paid by the farmer. The advantage may have been the other way. Other implements and tools used in cotton production and the implements and tools used in tobacco farming were too simple and cheap to give any advantage to the large-scale farmer in their use; it would be a poor farmer indeed who could not afford a plow and a mule.

These competitive advantages of the plantation over the farm, to the extent that they existed, were at least partially offset by certain disadvantages. The overhead expenses of the large planter were proportionally greater than those of the small farmer. The large planter had to hire an overseer or overseers and often had various other functionaries such as manager, foremen, drivers, and yard boy. The production and curing of tobacco required especially close supervision because care in handling greatly affected the quality, which was an important factor in determining price. The number of slaves which could be supervised efficiently by one overseer was, therefore, small. The planter himself, the mistress, and the sons and daughters did not ordinarily engage in physical labor, as did members of the small-farm family. The plantation house was often literally overrun with domestic servants.

If large-scale farming had possessed any considerable competitive advantages over small-scale farming in producing cotton and tobacco, there would not have been so many small farms and small plantations devoted to their production. Perhaps one-half the cotton was grown on farms where there were either no slaves at all or fewer than ten or a dozen. Such farms were too small to possess in any material degree the alleged advantages of large-scale production. Probably an even larger percentage of Southern tobacco was produced on small farms or small plantations.

.   .   .   .

Slave labor was efficient enough, if employed at tasks for which it was adapted, to produce for the masters, taking one year with another, an appropriable surplus over the cost of maintenance. However, the appropriable surplus of the individual slave was normally so small that a master could not enjoy a large income unless he had a large number of slaves. A farmer with a few slaves worked along with them and made a somewhat better living than his neighbor who had no slaves. A farmer with a larger number of slaves might escape physical toil and enjoy a still higher standard of living. Only the great planters could live in a liberal style. The evidence seems conclusive that planters with fewer than about fifteen slaves did not live well.

Except, then, in special cases like sugar and rice where much capital other than slaves was required for effective production, the much touted advantage of the plantation with slave labor over the small farm with white labor reduces to about this: The plantation could not produce more in proportion to land and equipment or to the number of hands employed; if large enough it could produce more goods and leisure for the white family. That, in all common sense, was why people acquired slaves and ran plantations. The small farm with reasonably good management and reasonable industry on the part of members of the farm family afforded at least as high a standard of living as the plantation afforded the planter family and the slaves averaged together.

Why, then, if Negro slave labor was not inherently superior to free white labor, and if the plantation possessed little, if any, competitive advantage over the small farm as a unit of agricultural organization, did nonslaveholding whites fail to produce a larger share of the cotton and tobacco? There were several reasons.

First and foremost come the major matters of enterprise and managerial ability. Nowadays, the more competent and industrious farmers in any community generally get the better land and larger acreages. In slavery days in the South, the better farmers got the more desirable lands, larger holdings, and also the slaves to work them and grew more cotton and tobacco. If a small farmer in the cotton or tobacco belt prospered by growing the staple of his region or otherwise, the natural and attractive thing to do was to buy land and slaves as he could. If he continued to thrive, he would eventually become a planter. Thus a small farmer would have been "driven out" by a planter. Of course the man who inherited land and slaves had a better chance of remaining in the planter class than one who had inherited nothing had of entering it. However, many a young man who inherited wealth in slavery days mismanaged his patrimony, lost it in whole or in part, and ended his days in "reduced" circumstances, while many a young man who started with neither land or slaves became a prosperous planter. Thomas J. Wertenbaker has shown that the planter class originated in this latter fashion in colonial times. Olmsted admitted that small farmers were not debarred from becoming planters in the ante bellum period. One suspects that most farmers who prospered did so not because they had come by land and slaves but because they attended to business and managed well, while most of those who failed did so because they took life too easy and managed badly. Credit has too often been given to slavery or the farm organization which rightfully belongs to the master.

Secondly, even in the staple-growing districts, the small farmers did not have as strong incentives to grow the staples for market as the planters had. They found it to their advantage to do a more general type of farming with more household manufacturing. In contrast, planters almost of necessity produced for the market. There would have been few planters if it had not been possible to grow market crops profitably on plantations. As a rule, a master will not employ a large labor force in a self-sufficing economy, because, after a certain volume of production has been reached, an additional application of labor can contribute but little to satisfy the wants of the farmer and his family but only to raise the standard of living of the laborers, something in which an employer is only mildly interested. In a self-sufficing economy in America a family with a considerable number of slaves would have enjoyed a rude plenty and have been freed from grinding toil but would have had the various cares and worries involved in slaveholding. A family without slaves would have enjoyed the same rude plenty, and, although it must have engaged in hard labor, would not have had the cares and worries of the slaveholding family. A planter in the ante bellum

South produced the various necessary and desirable articles for home consumption which could be produced cheaper on the plantation than they
could be bought in the market. However, the wants of the slaves were simple,
perforce, and easily satisfied, and the demand of the planter's family for
such articles was limited. These wants having been satisfied, the planter
sought to produce as large a salable surplus as possible in order that he
might command for his slaves certain things from outside the community
which might be necessary for their continued efficiency and for himself and
family the various articles of necessity, comfort, and luxury which could
not, or at least not advantageously, be produced on the plantation. The
small, nonslaveholding farmer, on the contrary, found it desirable to devote
a larger share of his labor to the production of the numerous articles for
consumption which could be produced advantageously at home, because,
in proportion to numbers, the farmer family consumed larger quantities of
such things than did the planter family and the slaves together.

The small farmer of the nineteenth century had a further reason for
carrying on more self-sufficing activities than the planter. This was the
feeling, already mentioned, that white women and girls, although allowed
to work at various household industries which were just as useful and productive as plowing and hoeing, nevertheless, should not be expected to
labor in the fields. The planter was under no moral pressure not to send
his female slaves into the fields.

The planter had a further reason to concentrate his efforts on the growing of cotton or other staples in the fact that Negro slave labor was relatively more efficient therein than in the production of the various other
things commonly produced on Southern farms in slavery days, for examples,
fruit, poultry, dairy products, bacon, lard, soap, candles, whiskey, coarse
textiles, clothing, and axe and hoe handles. The planter, on this account,
sometimes found it to his advantage to grow more cotton or tobacco and
buy other things. The small farmer and his family, on the other hand, could
produce the varied articles of the general farm more effectively than could
the slaves and, therefore, more often found it advantageous to produce
them at home instead of buying them at the store. The fact that in a given
community planters specialized more in producing the great Southern
staples while small farmers went in more for general farming does not of
itself prove that white labor was less efficient than slave labor in cotton
and tobacco, as has so often been assumed; it can just as well prove that
white labor was more efficient than slave labor in general farming.

.   .   .   .

Since planters had such strong incentives to produce staple crops for
market, they must remain where there was access to markets. Small farmers,
who did relatively more subsistence farming regardless of location, were
not under such pressure to remain in the commercialized farming districts.
Therefore, if planter neighbors made attractive offers for the land, the
farmers might find it to their advantage to sell and move to a more remote
region where land was cheaper but about as well adapted to their type of
farming.

The American people during the slavery period were already a race of land speculators. Large numbers moved to the frontier and submitted for the time to frontier living conditions with the hope that the "progress of the country" and especially the development of means of transportation would soon catch up with them and give their lands a value far in excess of the original cost. Masters with numerous slaves would not or could not be frontiersmen unless the frontier had natural facilities for transportation to market and could almost at once be reduced to cultivation. If they had debts, as most masters did, they were under strong economic compulsion to get cash incomes every year. It follows, therefore, that the proportion of small farmers in the commercialized-farming districts would tend to be reduced by this movement toward the frontier. If a few years later the planter followed the small farmer to the erstwhile frontier and bought up his farm, the farmer was not injured; at least he had done what he had hoped to do and could move on to a new frontier to repeat the process.

Once a given district became rather thickly settled with masters and slaves, small farmers moved out to get away from the "niggers" and live in a neighborhood where there were more of their own kind. Repelling them from good neighborhoods was probably the principal way in which slavery worked to the economic detriment of nonslaveholding whites. . . .

It is true, of course, that if slavery had never been established in the United States and, therefore, the plantation system had not developed extensively, the lands held by planters would have been held by small farmers who, in many instances no doubt, would have been the same persons who were planters. In that hypothetical case, being located near transportation facilities and finding prices, at least of cotton, somewhat higher than they actually were by reason of the smaller production which would have occurred, small farmers would have grown greater quantities of cotton and tobacco, but considerably less than actually were grown in the South by planters and farmers combined. In this sense, then, slavery may be said to have "driven" nonslaveholding farmers out of staple production and deprived them of an economic opportunity. This is far different from the usual implication, namely, that plantations produced a great quantity of cotton and tobacco very cheaply and thereby depressed prices so greatly that, while planters continued to make money, small white farmers could not make a living by growing the staples. Furthermore, even this concession requires qualification. It may well be that, if slavery had never been established in the South or, although established, had been abolished later, the direct benefits conferred upon small farmers by the absence or removal of competition from plantations and slaves would have been more than offset by the possible injury to the prosperity of the section as a whole.

The farmer folk of the South who received the most meager rewards were the "poor whites." Slavery has so often been blamed for the condition and even the existence of the poor whites that their relation to the institution seems to require special mention.

The poor whites were the ne'er-do-wells of the Southern countryside. They were poor, ignorant, shiftless, and almost utterly lacking in pride and the desire to improve their lot. They lived on the poorer lands interspersed among the plantations and better farms or in the pine barrens, sand hills, or other undesirable locations. In some cases they owned the land they occupied, in others they were merely squatters. They lived from hand to mouth. They farmed in a feeble sort of way, raising a little corn and garden truck and keeping a few hogs. Sometimes they raised a little cotton or tobacco. They hunted and fished a little. Some of them made corn whiskey and sold it to the planters and the slaves. They did odd jobs now and then for neighboring planters or farmers but shunned steady employment. They were often suspected of doing a lot of petty stealing from their more provident neighbors. Their most distinguishing characteristic was their lack of self-respect. Occasionally the terms "low whites" and "mean whites" were used to denote them.

The abolitionists were fond of denominating all the nonslaveholding whites of the Southern countryside as poor whites. This was a libel on the great majority of the small farmers of the section, who were reasonably industrious and self respecting and, in general, made a fairly comfortable living. There were, however, thousands of poor whites. William Gregg, a public-spirited cotton manufacturer of South Carolina, once estimated that one-third of the white population of his State belonged to that class. However accurate his estimate may have been, they were found in all the Southern States and the proportion was too high in all.

There seem to have been several causes for the development of the poor-white class. The poor quality of a large proportion of the indentured servants, so numerous in the South in colonial days, may explain it in part. The comparative ease of getting a living of a sort in a country where land, at least poor land, was so cheap, where corn, vegetables, and fruits grew without much care, where game, fish, and edible wild plants abounded, and where winters were short and mild, contributed to easy-going ways. Because of various historical factors, which will readily occur to anyone familiar with American colonial history, there had not been the feeling of community responsibility in the South that there had been in Puritan New England to insist that individuals conform to community standards of industry, thrift, and morality. Perhaps the principal cause was hookworm and repeated attacks of malaria, which sapped people's vitality and robbed them of hope and ambition, although it is not entirely clear whether people became poor whites because they had contracted hookworm or got hookworm because they were poor whites. The class of poor whites in all probability would have developed if slavery had never been introduced. There are poor whites now two generations after emancipation, and in spite of a greater density of population, better health services, more varied industry, public schools, and the many inducements to exertion offered by modern civilization. Similar classes, under different names, although perhaps not so great in numbers, are to be found in other parts of the country; and, for that matter, the same general type may be found in varying proportions in every country on the globe.

However, in at least two ways slavery seems to have contributed to the formation of the poor-white class of the South. Contrary to the usual rule, many of the poorer whites might have been better off as farm laborers under supervision than as independent farmers, but slavery retarded the development of a wage-earning class in the plantation districts. Originally planters had resorted to the use of bound servants because competent free laborers were scarce in a country where it was so easy for people of any competence at all to become independent farmers on land of their own. Once slavery was firmly established in a district, it in turn discouraged the development of a free-labor class. Planters preferred slaves to the poorer sort of whites. They also hesitated to attempt to use wage laborers instead of slaves, because, until a large wage-earning class should have developed, they could feel no assurance of being able to fill the vacancies that were certain to occur. Whites would not work in field gangs along with slaves under overseers. If it had not been for slavery, people with managerial ability might have made greater efforts to get the poor whites to work for wages or to rent the better lands and might have succeeded, as they did, in a measure, other things contributing, after the War for Southern Independence. By creating the black belts in ways described in preceding paragraphs, slavery created a social condition conducive to the development of such a class of poor whites. The more enterprising and intelligent of the small farmers either got out of the staple belts or graduated into the planter class leaving the less enterprising and less intelligent behind on poor lands which the planters could not use. Planters, having their own social life, took little interest in and felt little responsibility for their poor-white neighbors, except, perhaps, at election time. If the small-farmer population had remained larger, there might have been more churches, more schools, and a more wholesome community life in general, which would have given some stimulus, encouragement, and aid to the weaker and less fortunate members of society.

Slavery was certainly no more detrimental to nonslaveholding whites engaged in nonagricultural occupations than it was to small farmers. There seems to have been no dearth of employment in the Southern countryside for such white artisans as there were. It is true that planters often had slaves trained in various skilled crafts, and they often became excellent workmen. They were, indeed, frequently hired out by their masters to neighbors who needed their services. In general, however, the Negro artisans were not as competent as the white, and the latter were preferred. It was the scarcity of the white artisans which caused planters to resort to training slaves in the trades. This scarcity, in turn, was due to the strong inducement there was all through this period for people of good quality to get land and live on it.

In the cities and towns of the slaveholding States, white wage earners had to compete with free Negroes and with Negro slaves, who were either employed in their masters' businesses, hired out by their masters to other employers, or allowed to hire their own time. Such free Negroes and slaves worked at practically every sort of task. They had a monopoly of domestic service. Either because of its character, or because Negroes had so long predominated in it, or both, the whites had come to look upon such service as menial and degrading, and employers preferred the Negroes because they were more obsequious. In other occupations the whites and Negroes, sometimes of both sexes, worked side by side, usually, but not always, with some distinction in tasks in favor of the whites. For example, in the Tredegar Iron Works at Richmond, Virginia, each white master workman was given a Negro "assistant."

The white workers frequently resented the presence of the blacks, either because of race prejudice, or dislike of their competition, or both, and sought to have them excluded from the pursuits concerned. There was, for example, a strike of the white workers in the Tredegar works having this object, but it was unsuccessful, as were all other efforts to exclude Negroes. Employers could not afford to allow such a principle to be established, as white workers were not sufficiently numerous and permanent in most localities to permit reliance on them alone. The use of slaves, if they belonged to the owners of the business, gave the employers assurance that operations would not be interrupted or wages forced to too high levels by strikes and withdrawals; and, even if the slaves were hired from others, the assurance was nearly as great, for still there could be no strikes, and labor contracts were usually made for a year at a time.

In the skilled trades the white workingmen were more efficient and were, therefore, preferred. Negro competition was not keen. In unskilled and semiskilled labor the superiority of white workers to slaves was not so great, if, indeed any existed, but in general white workers had no difficulty in getting jobs, excepting, of course, that they sought none in domestic service. As the middle period wore on and the demand for labor in the cotton and sugar belts grew, there was a tendency for slave labor to be drawn from the towns to the farms, where white labor was not available, leaving places in towns open to the whites. This tendency was reinforced by the increasing difficulty of handling slaves amid urban surroundings and by the better adaptability, generally speaking, of slaves to agriculture than to urban occupations.

Nonslaveowning employers of labor in the cities had no particular disadvantage in competition with slaveowning employers as they would have had in the country, for they were able to hire either whites, slaves, free Negroes, or all three. In fact, railroad companies, manufacturing concerns, etc. usually found it necessary or desirable to start with hired labor, free or slave, because with hired labor it was not necessary to raise so much capital at the outset. Employers sometimes preferred to hire their hands also, because this permitted a selection more in accord with existing needs and enabled the employers to expand or contract their labor forces and more readily adjust production to the state of business.

In slavery days the cities and towns of the South, being neither numerous nor large, derived their support principally from plantation districts, where there were many slaves, rather than from small-farming regions, where there were few. It was chiefly the planters who bought, sold, borrowed, travelled, and sent their children to academies and colleges. It seems quite certain, therefore, that if it had not been for plantations and slavery, the cities and towns of the South would have been even fewer and smaller, resulting in even less opportunity for nonslaveholding whites.

· · · · · · · · · · · · · ·

In conclusion, Negro slavery was in some respects to the economic advantage of many of the nonslaveholding whites of the slaveholding regions; in others it was to their disadvantage. To many nonslaveholding whites it was a matter of economic indifference. It is impossible to strike a balance in which confidence can be placed. It is certain that the net injury, if there was any, has commonly been grossly exaggerated. The fact that nonslaveholding whites did not seek to destroy the institution as injurious to their economic interests may only show that their common sense operating upon a familiar matter was sounder than the economics of abolitionists theorizing at a distance or of some modern historians theorizing after a long lapse of time.

2] The Yeomen

a] PROSPEROUS MIDDLE-CLASS MAJORITY

THE PICTURE of the late ante-bellum South had become stereotyped by 1861. Northern and foreign, notably English, travelers had written a considerable body of literature dealing with the South during the period of the slavery controversy and, with few exceptions, these travelers and commentators were agreed that the rural population was divided into three social and economic classes: slaveholders, "poor whites," and Negroes. The slaveholders were somehow thought of in terms of great planters who lived like nabobs in white-columned mansions. They were the great monopolists of their day: they crowded everyone else off the good lands and even off the lands from which modest profits might be realized; they dominated politics, religion, and all phases of public life. The six or seven million nonslaveholders who composed the other portion of the free population of the South were thought of as "poor whites," who had been pushed off into the pine barrens and the sterile sand hills and mountains, where they lived in squalid log huts. They were illiterate, drunken outcasts for whom the social system of the slaveholders had no use, squatters upon the wornout lands of the planters or upon the government lands. Between the great unwashed and the slaveholders there was a chasm that could not be bridged, one that became greater with time. Everywhere the rich were getting richer and the poor were growing poorer.

George Weston, for example, wrote in 1856:

> The whites of the South not connected with the ownership or management of slaves, constituting not far from three-fourths of the whole number of whites, confined at least to the low wages of agricultural labor, and partly cut off even from this by the degradation of a companionship with black slaves, retire to the outskirts of civilization, where they lead a semi-savage life, sinking deeper and more hopelessly into barbarism with each succeeding gen-

FROM Frank L. and Harriet C. Owsley, "The Economic Basis of Society in the Late Ante-Bellum South," *Journal of Southern History*, VI (February, 1940), 24–45. Copyright 1940 by the Southern Historical Association.

eration. The slave owner takes at first all the best lands, and finally all the lands susceptible of regular cultivation; and the poor whites, thrown back upon the hills and upon the sterile soils—mere squatters without energy enough to acquire the title even to the cheap lands they occupy, without roads, and at length, without even a desire for education, become the miserable beings described to us.

The British writer, John E. Cairnes, expressed the opinion that "the constitution of a slave society . . . resolves itself into three classes, broadly distinguished from each other, and connected by no common interest—the slaves on whom devolves all the regular industry, the slave-holders who reap all its fruits, and an idle and lawless rabble who live dispersed over vast plains in a condition little removed from absolute barbarism." These mean whites are the natural growth of the slave system; "regular industry is only known to them as the vocation of slaves, and it is the one fate which above all others they desire to avoid." Frederick L. Olmsted was very decidedly of the opinion that the majority of the southern people were "poor whites" who lived in idleness because work was identified with slavery. Whatever is associated with the slave as having been peculiarly attached to his condition," he wrote, was regarded with disfavor. "For manual agricultural labor, therefore, the free man looking on, has a contempt, and for its necessity in himself, if such necessity exists, a pity quite beyond that of the man under whose observations it has been free from such an association of ideas."

While slavery and the plantation system have been in the process of re-examination in the light of the new types of source material first utilized by Ulrich B. Phillips—that is, plantation records, private letters, diaries, and other such sources—little systematic attempt has been made to study the manner of life of those millions, both small slaveholder and non-slaveholder, who fell outside the plantation economy, and to fit these into the general economic and social structure of the South. That is to say, the large planter has received all the attention while the society of the Old South as a whole has been neglected. This neglect to restudy southern life except as manifested in the large planter class is probably due to two causes: first, an almost complete lack of personal letters and farm records of the nonslaveholder, the small slaveholder, and even the small planter; second, an assumption that the European and northern travel literature produced amid the slavery controversy and most frequently part of it, was, notwithstanding this fact, both objective and otherwise competent reporting. The result of the failure to reassess the chief material upon which the conception of the Old South was based in ante-bellum times is that the current conception of the Old South is essentially the stereotype of 1861. That we should continue to know the old regime in the South through the eyes of those who traveled fast and saw only from an external point of view, and through the eyes of those who came with an unfriendly mission, must have seemed to all thoughtful students of southern history to be an act of faith out of keeping with scientific methods and historical criticism. Yet it has not been necessary to rely solely upon such sources for there has always existed a great body of objective historical material concerning not only the large planter class but also the entire white population from which a systematic and scientific study of the social and economic structure of the Old South could be made. This material consists of the county records and the court records of both state and Federal government. The county records are the most comprehensive and valuable, particularly if the unpublished Federal census reports are included. Long before the historian even suspected that the county records were the sources for social and economic history, the genealogists were systematically using and publishing this material in the older states. They correctly seized upon the will books, administration of estates, proceedings of orphans courts, minutes of the county courts, deed books, marriage records, tax books, and the unpublished Federal census returns as the most significant documents. Out of these, wills and administration of estates more than all other documents recreate the personal and family relationships in community life. It is this type of material, indeed, so personal and intimate in its nature, that goes far toward supplying a substitute for the private letters, diaries, farm records, and journals which, unlike the planter, the mass of people failed to preserve. For a statistical analysis of the population, the county tax lists and the unpublished Federal census returns furnish all the essential data.

Excerpts from wills illustrate the uses to which these documents may be put in recreating the life of those millions who have left few if any private and personal papers. Two nonslaveholders have been selected for this purpose since this class has left less personal, private documents than any others. The will of John Davidson of Dickson County, Tennessee, substantial farmer and owner of about three hundred acres of land, numerous horses and work stock, swine and cattle, is given in part:

> In the name of God, Amen. I John Davidson Sen'r being of sound mind but in a low state as to health do make and publish this as my last will and testament. First I desire that all my debts be paid as soon as possible out of the first money that comes into the hands of my beloved wife or my executor. Second, as to what property we have we in the bond of affection have laboured for it lovingly we have enjoyed it and now with a glad heart do I will and bequeath all that I may die possessed of whether it be lands, crops of any kind, household and kitchen furniture or fowls of all kinds . . . to my beloved wife during her natural life or widowhood for the support of herself and family.

Following this he made numerous parting gifts to his adult children who already seem to have been given a portion of their inheritance as was the custom. Thus, this plain man of the Old South in simple eloquence of biblical style bade farewell to his beloved family and all his earthly possessions without a word of regret or complaint. Here was a man of substance, of considerable education, who, together with his family, did not regard labor in the fields as degrading.

The will of Thomas Coy of Franklin County, Tennessee, bears the marks of tragedy. It was in the form of a personal letter to an intimate friend who had stood by Coy in need. One gets the impression that Coy was laboring under great mental stress brought on by what he considered an unjust accusation. His lack of literacy was made to seem even worse, perhaps, by this strain under which he labored. Coy was a man of some means. Excerpts from the will follow:

> Friend Willick you and wife have bin to friends to me through adversity as well as prosperity and will prove my thankfulness to you for it   it is no use to Raise my voice or to say a word in my defence   i am condemned by all for unfaithfulness of friendship   there was never any one more unjustly condemned to my best friends I leave my best respects   Except the Boon I offer you there is about Fifteen hundred Dollars   Give Ben Spyker my gun and watch   the remainder keep yourself   you will pay W Pryor for washing   let Dr Borrough have my tools   make it write with him   Dock does not owe me anything perhaps I owe him something   Keep all the rest yourself   O you must pardon me for this vast act   I cannot Buffet the waves any longer   God knows there is nobody tries harder to do right than I do tell Martha I still think of her till death   Martha you judged me wrong   But I forgive you only misunderstood my fairwell to all for I am not mad at nobody God knows it   Missis Spyker as a last token of my friendship for you except the small sum of five hundred Dollars from your unworthy friend Coy. I should have made you a much better present But I burnt it in a mistake a long with some letters and papers. Miss Spyker i am unjustly and ungreatfully [accused] i have not the strength of mind to [bear] it any longer. I am going to the Mountains there to wander the balance of my Days. I give Ben my watch Good Ben I bid you all goodby   I am mad at none of you   God knows it.

Poor Thomas Coy, who apparently had been falsely accused of unfaithfulness to his sweetheart, Martha, and who had been discarded by her had only a short time to wander in the mountains, for his will was soon probated as a sign of his death.

While such documents endow the plain people with souls and bodies, they do not make possible a systematic study of the general structure of southern society. We know from wills and deeds, administration of estates, and other court records of a personal nature that there was a large body of nonslaveholders and small slaveholders who possessed lands, livestock, farm produce, and money in sufficient quantities to enable them to live comfortably. From such documents it is possible to make a case study of the plain people of the Old South as Phillips and his followers have done for the large planter class. But from this type of material it would never be practicable to determine the proportions of the several social and economic groups. The county tax lists, however, furnish a fairly good basis for statistical, quantitative analyses for all classes. Unfortunately, most tax books for this early period have been destroyed; but where still in existence they are not comparable with unpublished Federal census reports for quantitative analysis of the population and its economic life. Beginning in 1850 there were six schedules made up by the census takers: Free Inhabitants, Slave Inhabitants, Mortality Statistics, Productions of Agriculture, Productions of Industry, and Social Statistics. For the study of the agricultural population, Schedules I, II, and IV, that is, Free Inhabitants, Slave Inhabitants, and Productions of Agriculture, respectively, are the basic documents. Indeed, the Productions of Agriculture is a veritable doomsday book. In making this study it has been used as a master chart upon which data from the other two schedules have been superimposed. The Agricultural Schedule gives the name of practically every farmer, the amount of improved and unimproved land that he used, a detailed account of his livestock and farm productions of the previous year, his home manufactures and slaughtered animals. This schedule, however, does not as a rule indicate whether a person owned or rented his land or worked it on shares, nor does it indicate whether or not he was a slaveowner. The ownership of land and the total value of one's real estate—as well as his personal property—can be determined by checking Schedule IV (Productions of Agriculture) against Schedule I (Free Inhabitants), while the ownership of slaves can be determined by checking Schedule IV against Schedule II (Slave Inhabitants). Eventually by making use of these three schedules in particular and others wherever desirable, almost complete data can be obtained concerning every individual family.

On the basis of this technique several southern states are being examined particularly for the late ante-bellum period, and final conclusions on many phases of society may now be reached. As a general proposition it can be said that at no time before 1860 was the rural white population of the South divided into two great social classes, slaveholders and nonslaveholders. Quite on the contrary, the population was divided into many economic and social categories ranging from destitute "poor whites" to immensely rich planters. Despite the complex social structure of the white population, the great mass of the farming population, whether slaveholding or nonslaveholding, were middle class people. Using a term common in colonial America and in England until the eighteenth century, it might be said that the bulk of the farming population of the South were yeomen. Numerous indices of well being applied to the population signify that the bulk of the white people of the South—the yeomanry—enjoyed with the planters a high degree of social and economic security. Despite the unkept appearance of the backwoodsman, the shabby aspect of much of even the best countryside, despite, indeed, the panoramic impression of decadence gained by the travelers from outside the region, the basic indices point to the conclusion that the bulk of the southern whites were not only economically secure, but that on the whole their position was, when considered over a period of years, constantly improving.

The state of Alabama has been selected for analysis and illustration since it seems to be typical of the Lower South; and the farming population will be used as the basis of analysis because Alabama was a rural state. Indeed, the entire South in 1860 was essentially rural, for even the towns were markets or places of residence for the well-to-do farmers and planters. One of the first indices of well-being in a farming population is the extent of landownership. Today, the black belt of Alabama and of the entire Lower South has 70 to 80 per cent landless farmers, a good portion of whom are whites. Before 1860 the reverse situation prevailed: landownership was widely diffused and was spreading rapidly. In analyzing the spread of landownership in Alabama before 1860—as well as examining the other indices of well-being—three regions have been selected as fairly typical of the state as a whole, namely, the piney woods, flats, and sand hills of South Alabama; the black belt stretching from east to west in a crescent across the state; and the piedmont lying above the black belt.[1]

First, let us examine the spread of landownership in the black belt. In Montgomery County 72 per cent of the farming population were land-owners in 1850 and 76 per cent in 1860.[2] Marengo County increased in landownership among its farm population from 75 per cent in 1850 to 87 per cent in 1860. Bibb County, only part of which lies in the black belt, showed a slight increase in the spread of landownership in the last ten years before the Civil War: in 1850, 69 per cent of those engaged in agriculture and in 1860, 70 per cent were landowners. Greene County in 1837, though still possessing large tracts of government land and a con-siderable squatter population, many of whom were large slaveholders, nevertheless had 53 per cent landowners. In 1844 landownership had increased to 60 per cent, in 1856 to 81 per cent, and by 1860 it had reached 82 per cent of the farm population.[3] In 1850 approximately 82 per cent of the farm population in Dallas County owned their land while in 1860, 84 per cent were landed proprietors.[4] Sixty-seven per cent of the agricultural population of Clarke County owned their farms in 1850 and 76 per cent in 1860. Monroe County had a 69 per cent ownership in 1850 but this had increased to 84 per cent by 1860. Perry County seems to have reached its maximum ownership of land in 1850, for in that year 84 per cent of the farm population were landowners while in 1860, 79 per cent fell in this category. The decrease in ownership was among the large slaveholders principally, for it will be seen presently that the percentage of landowners among the nonslaveholders steadily increased during this same period. Lowndes County experienced a similar shift in landownership. About 80 per cent owned their farms in 1850 while 77 per cent were landowners

[1] The Tennessee Valley region though examined in connection with this study is not included here because the Agricultural Schedule (IV) has been lost. The general property structure as seen in the other Schedules, however, appears to be about the same as that of the black belt both as to the spread of ownership and sizes of holdings.

[2] United States Census Reports, MSS., Schedule I, Free Inhabitants in the County of Montgomery, State of Alabama, 1850; Schedule II, Slave Inhabitants in the County of Montgomery, State of Alabama, 1850; Schedule IV, Productions of Agriculture in the County of Montgomery, State of Alabama, 1850; Schedule I, Free Inhabitants in the County of Montgomery, State of Alabama, 1860; Schedule II, Slave Inhabitants in the County of Montgomery, State of Alabama, 1860. All future references in this essay to the Federal Census will be to Schedules I, II, and IV for 1850, and to Schedules I and II for 1860. All the data with the exception of that for Greene and Dallas counties on which the analyses set forth in this paper are based were obtained from these above-named Schedules for each county under consideration. It will be unnecessary to repeat the citations. Schedules I and II are in the Census Office in Washington; Schedule IV, Productions of Agriculture for 1850, is in the Alabama State Department of Archives and History, Montgomery. Schedule IV for 1860 has been lost or destroyed.

[3] In addition to the unpublished census reports for Greene County discussed in n. 2 above, the Greene County Tax Books, 1837, 1844, and 1856 were used. The Tax Books are located in the Greene County courthouse, Eutaw, Alabama.

[4] These figures were compiled from both the census returns (as in n. 2) and the Tax Books of Dallas County for 1850. The Tax Books, Real Estate and Personal Property are located in the Alabama State Department of Archives and History.

in 1860. In this county a slight decrease had taken place among all classes of landowners. Despite the slight decline in Perry and Lowndes counties, the ownership of land in the black belt as a whole increased from an average of 74 per cent in 1850 to 80 per cent in 1860.

Three counties lying in the piedmont above the black belt have been selected as typical of this hilly country. These counties are Coosa, lying just above the black belt near the center of the state, Randolph, on the eastern border, rugged and isolated, and Fayette on the western border not unlike Randolph in its topography and soil. This large area typified by these counties has many fertile valleys and was generally productive in the period under discussion. Although the ground was uneven most of the soil was sandy loam and clay loam with a fine clay subsoil. The natural growth was oak, hickory, and pine, which is indicative of good soil. It will be recalled that much of this land had been in the hands of the Indians as late as 1836 and that the bulk of the Indian lands was still a part of the public domain as late as 1840. In 1850, 66 per cent of the agricultural population of Fayette County owned their farms but a decade later 82 per cent were landowners. Randolph County, completely across the state from Fayette as we have noted and a typically nonslaveholding region, had a 64 per cent landownership among its farmers in 1850 and 76 per cent ownership in 1860. Coosa County had a much larger slave population than Randolph or Fayette and represented a transitional belt between the plantation area and the up-country. It was not unlike such counties as Chambers, Talapoosa, and Tuscaloosa. In 1850, 75 per cent of the farmers of Coosa County owned their land but in 1860, 79 per cent were owners. The development in this piedmont region was strikingly similar to that of the black belt despite the continued existence of considerable tracts of public lands. Here ownership of land increased from 68 per cent in 1850 to 80 per cent in 1860, whereas in the black belt it had increased from 74 per cent to 80 per cent.

The pine land region of South Alabama presents an interesting situation. As late as 1855 this whole area was described as a forest one hundred miles square, most of which belonged to the Federal government. It was very sparsely settled and mostly by squatters, so it was said. This was a section of the pine timber belt frequently called the "pine barrens" (originally meaning pine hills and not barren soil as has been so often thought) which extended almost continuously from the coast of Texas to New Jersey; and it has been invariably selected as the home of the "poor whites." The Alabama pine barrens is typical of the whole piney woods area in the Lower South and in the Carolinas. The soil of this region in Alabama—as well as in the other states—varies greatly: a portion seems to be hardly more than sandbeds, penetrated quite frequently, however, with flat, shallow streams whose valleys are covered with alluvial deposits and are quite fertile; another portion has a sandy loam soil with clay subsoil and is fairly productive.

Three counties have been selected from this piney woods area, Covington, Coffee, and Washington (though portions of Washington are prairie and river lands) for the purpose of analysis. The ownership of land in this

area—despite the impression that most of it was government land and that
most of the population were squatters—was considerably diffused by 1850
and was rapidly increasing. In 1850, 46 per cent of the farming population
of Coffee County were landowners while the remaining 54 per cent were
chiefly squatters. In 1860 landownership had increased to 75 per cent of
the farming population. Landownership in Washington County increased
from 54 per cent in 1850 to 74 per cent in 1860. In Covington, poorest of
the lot, landownership increased from 40 per cent in 1850 to 68 per cent
in 1860.

The spread of landownership was always greater among slaveholders
than among nonslaveholders, but the gap between the two groups was
rapidly narrowing during the last ten years of the ante-bellum period.
Beginning with the pine belt we find that the ownership of land in
Coffee County increased from 41 per cent in 1850 to 72 per cent in
1860 among the nonslaveholders; while that of the slaveholders increased
from 68 per cent in 1850 to 91 per cent in 1860. This was a gain of 78
per cent for the nonslaveholders and about 32 per cent for the slaveholders
in the last decade before the Civil War. The nonslaveholders in Covington
County increased their ownership of land from 32 per cent in 1850 to
64 per cent in 1860—a gain of 100 per cent. The slaveholding farmers
increased their ownership of land from 78 per cent in 1850 to 92 per
cent in 1860, about 19 per cent. In Washington County the percentage of
landowners among the nonslaveholders increased from 36 per cent in 1850
to 67 per cent in 1860. This was a gain of 86 per cent. The slaveowners
increased their holdings from 75 per cent in 1850 to 84 per cent in 1860
which was not quite 6.5 per cent. Summing up, it may be said that landownership among the nonslaveholders of the piney woods region as
represented in these three sample counties increased about 87 per cent in
the ten years before the war while that of the slaveholders increased 19
per cent.

The piedmont region where the nonslaveholders made up 68 per cent
of the population in such counties as Coosa and 87 per cent in such
counties as Randolph shows, like the pine barrens, a much greater increase
in landownership for those who did not own slaves than for those who
did during the decade 1850–1860. In 1850, 67 per cent of the nonslaveholding farmers and 92 per cent of the slaveholding farmers of Coosa
were landowners; but in 1860 the ownership of land in these two groups
had increased to 73 per cent and 94 per cent respectively. Randolph
County, more rugged and having more public land and a larger squatter
population than Coosa, had a lower percentage of landownership in the
nonslaveholding group. In 1850, 60 per cent of the nonslaveholders and
96 per cent of the slaveholders had titles to their land. In 1860 landownership had increased to 73 per cent in the nonslaveholding class but had
decreased to 93 per cent among the slaveholders. Fayette County experienced a parallel development. About 58 per cent of the nonslaveholders
owned their farms in 1850 and 80 per cent in 1860. Nearly 94 per cent
of the slaveholding group of farmers were landed proprietors in 1850 and
96 per cent in 1860. The spread of landownership of the nonslaveholding

population had increased about 9 per cent in Coosa, 21 per cent in Randolph, and 38 per cent in Fayette. The increase in the slaveholding group had been about 2 per cent in Coosa and Fayette but in Randolph there had been a decrease of 3 per cent.

Such an increase in the distribution of landownership among the non-slaveholding population in the piedmont and piney woods regions where there were millions of acres of government lands [5] might have been anticipated. However, when both absolute and relative increase also takes place in the landownership of the nonslaveholder in the black belt it upsets the generalization that the rich were getting richer and the poor were getting poorer in the Cotton Kingdom. Sixty per cent of the nonslaveholders of Marengo County were landowners in 1850 and 80 per cent in 1860, an increase of 33 per cent. But the ownership of land among the slaveholding classes remained stationary at about 90 per cent during this time. In Greene County only 20 per cent of the nonslaveholders owned their farms in 1837, but in 1856, 75 per cent were landowners. This was an increase of 275 per cent in nineteen years. During this same time the ownership of land of the slaveholders increased from 68 per cent in 1837 to 86 per cent in 1856, a gain of 26 per cent in nineteen years.[6] The landownership of the nonslaveholders in Bibb County increased from 55 per cent of that class in 1850 to 60 per cent in 1860, an increase of 9 per cent. On the other hand, the percentage of slaveholders who held title to their land decreased from 95 per cent in 1850 to 92 per cent in 1860. Slightly over 47 per cent of the nonslaveholding farmers of Clarke County were landowners in 1850; but 67 per cent owned their land in 1860. This was a gain of 42 per cent. Of the slaveholders, 86 per cent were landed proprietors in 1850 and 91 per cent in 1860, a gain of not quite 6 per cent. Monroe County experienced a similar increase of landownership of both slaveholders and nonslaveholders in the period under discussion; but as in the other black belt counties already cited the greatest increase of ownership occurred among the nonslaveholders. Only 50 per cent of the nonslaveholders owned their land in 1850 but 75 per cent were owners in 1860, which represented a 50 per cent increase. Eighty-five per cent of the slaveholders owned their farms in 1850; but an additional 10 per cent became landowners during the following decade so that 94 per cent were proprietors in 1860. Perry County experienced some decline in the landownership of the slaveholders, but there was an increase of nonslaveholding landowners similar to that in Bibb County. As has been suggested, the nonslaveholding class was on the make even in this plantation county of black, rich prairie and clay loam lands. In

[5] The widespread distribution of landownership in the Lower South and the rapid increase of ownership were partly due to the existence of great tracts of public lands. In 1853 the Commissioner of the General Land Office reported that there were still 79,255,556 acres of government land in the five states of Alabama, Arkansas, Florida, Louisiana, and Mississippi. Of the 32,462,080 acres of land in Alabama, 15,049,693 acres at this date were Federal land. John Perkins, "The Public Lands and Land System of the United States," in *De Bow's Review*, XVII (1854), 140-71.

[6] See Greene County Tax Books, 1837, 1856, and n. 2 above, for the census material.

1850, 65 per cent of the nonslaveholding farmers in Perry County were landowners and in 1860, 69 per cent owned their farms, a rise of 6 per cent in ownership. Lowndes County experienced a slight decrease in the landownership of both slaveholders and nonslaveholders. The latter class declined from 63 per cent in 1850 to 58 per cent in 1860 while the former dropped from 90 per cent to 89 per cent in this period. Montgomery's slaveholding farmers and planters who owned land increased from 86 per cent in 1850 to 91 per cent in 1860; but the spread of landownership of the nonslaveholders decreased from 55 per cent to 50 per cent.

The pattern of increased distribution of landownership among the nonslaveholding classes was followed as we have noted in the pine barrens, the piedmont, and in all the counties of the black belt that were examined except Montgomery and Lowndes. The same trend of wider distribution of landownership was characteristic of the slaveholders—though to a less extent—in the piedmont and pine barrens. However, in several black belt counties the percentage of slaveholding landowners remained practically stationary and decreased slightly in Bibb, Perry, and Lowndes. It also decreased in Randolph in the piedmont.

The wide distribution of landownership is not sufficient in itself to measure potential well-being and security in an agricultural community. It must be determined whether landholdings are large enough and fertile enough to produce the basic necessities.

In analyzing the sizes of landholdings we will begin in the pine barrens and with the nonslaveholder. The structure of ownership among the nonslaveholding classes of the pine barrens was strikingly similar to that of the piedmont and of the black belt. The following tables [7] present a composite picture and a single county illustrative of the structure of landownership of the nonslaveholders:

PINE BARRENS AS A WHOLE		WASHINGTON COUNTY	
ACRES OWNED	PERCENTAGE OF NONSLAVEHOLDING LANDOWNERS	ACRES OWNED	PERCENTAGE OF NONSLAVEHOLDING LANDOWNERS
To 50	26.09	To 50	29.63
51–100	26.34	51–100	16.67
101–200	24.92	101–200	22.22
201–300	3.41	201–300	1.85
301–400	3.78	301–400	5.56
401–500	2.05	401–500	3.70
501–1000	1.94	501–1000	0.00
Not determined	11.47	1001–1500	1.85
		Not determined	18.52

[7] The date 1850 is used because Schedule IV that gives the sizes of holdings for 1860 is lost. See n. 2 above.

It will be observed that about 78 per cent of the nonslaveholding land-owners possessed up to 200 acres of land. However, when landholdings of undetermined sizes are distributed in the several categories it seems probable that those who owned up to 200 acres would be something above 80 per cent in the pine barrens. Washington County follows this composite picture of the pine barrens fairly well if one takes into account the amount of landholdings of undetermined sizes.

An analysis of landownership of the nonslaveholder in the piedmont is given in the following tables:

PIEDMONT AS A WHOLE		FAYETTE COUNTY	
ACRES OWNED	PERCENTAGE OF NONSLAVEHOLDING LANDOWNERS	ACRES OWNED	PERCENTAGE OF NONSLAVEHOLDING LANDOWNERS
To 50	24.22	To 50	23.69
51–100	25.42	51–100	27.87
101–200	26.60	101–200	29.27
201–300	5.49	201–300	8.71
301–400	4.71	301–400	2.44
401–500	.82	401–500	.70
501–1000	.82	501–1000	.70
Not determined	11.92	Not determined	6.62

The classification of the nonslaveholders in the piedmont was very nearly the same as that in the pine barrens, that is, 76 per cent owned up to 200 acres and there was a fairly large percentage of holdings whose sizes were not determined by the census taker. The distribution of this undetermined group would probably bring the class of land-owners who held up to 200 acres past 80 per cent of the total.

A division of the population in the black belt into slaveholders and nonslaveholders reveals the fact that the latter class constituted 44 per cent of the agricultural population in 1850. An analysis of the sizes of the landholdings of this large minority group indicates a pattern of ownership strikingly similar to that of the pine barrens and piedmont where the nonslaveholders were in an overwhelming majority. The follow-ing is a composite table of the landownership of the nonslaveholder in 1850. Perry County follows this composite picture very closely and will serve as a specific illustration of the structure of ownership of the non-slaveholder in this area. Just as in the pine barrens and the piedmont, practically 80 per cent of the nonslaveholding landowners of the black belt owned farms ranging up to 200 acres. In other words, something over three fourths of the nonslaveholding landowners of the three areas under examination owned up to 200 acres and a bit less than one fourth owned from 200 to 1,000 acres. A further analysis of the nonslaveholding farmers discloses the fact that roughly the three fourths who owned up to 200 acres

BLACK BELT AS A WHOLE		PERRY COUNTY	
ACRES OWNED	PERCENTAGE OF NONSLAVEHOLDING LANDOWNERS	ACRES OWNED	PERCENTAGE OF NONSLAVEHOLDING LANDOWNERS
To 50	24.29	To 50	27.93
51–100	23.90	51–100	23.79
101–200	29.66	101–200	28.97
201–300	8.70	201–300	7.59
301–400	4.77	301–400	4.14
401–500	2.72	401–500	1.38
501–1000	3.15	501–1000	2.07
Not determined	2.81	Not determined	4.13

cultivated about 50 acres of land or a three-horse farm. The fraction who owned above 200 acres cultivated from 50 to 200 acres of land, and usually employed hired labor which not infrequently embraced the slaves of some neighboring planter.

What of the sizes of the landholdings of the slaveowners? It is, perhaps, surprising to find that the majority of slaveowners even in the black belt of Alabama had farms that varied in size from a few to 500 acres, and that while the largest single group of nonslaveholders owned from 50 to 100 acres, the largest group of slaveholders owned from 100 to 200 acres of land. In other words, the majority of slaveholders even in the black belt were farmers rather than planters, who owned a few slaves and worked in the field with them. The chief difference between the slaveholder and nonslaveholder of this farmer class was that a much larger percentage of

PINE BARRENS AS A WHOLE		COFFEE COUNTY	
ACRES OWNED	PERCENTAGE OF SLAVEHOLDING LANDOWNERS	ACRES OWNED	PERCENTAGE OF SLAVEHOLDING LANDOWNERS
To 50	9.70	To 50	12.22
51–100	14.94	51–100	14.44
101–200	27.86	101–200	34.44
201–300	11.47	201–300	14.44
301–400	7.12	301–400	8.89
401–500	3.34	401–500	4.44
501–1000	15.27	501–1000	7.78
1001–1500	4.39	1001–1500	3.33
1501–2000	.93		
2000 up	1.96		
Not determined	3.37		

PIEDMONT AS A WHOLE		COOSA COUNTY	
ACRES OWNED	PERCENTAGE OF SLAVEHOLDING LANDOWNERS	ACRES OWNED	PERCENTAGE OF SLAVEHOLDING LANDOWNERS
To 50	3.63	To 50	3.70
51–100	12.51	51–100	8.80
101–200	27.37	101–200	28.70
201–300	15.77	201–300	9.72
301–400	15.77	301–400	22.22
401–500	4.75	401–500	3.94
501–1000	12.86	501–1000	13.19
1001–1500	1.32	1001–1500	1.85
1501–2000	.79	1501–2000	1.39
2000 up	.71	2000 up	.93
Not determined	4.52	Not determined	5.56

BLACK BELT AS A WHOLE		MARENGO COUNTY	
ACRES OWNED	PERCENTAGE OF SLAVEHOLDING LANDOWNERS	ACRES OWNED	PERCENTAGE OF SLAVEHOLDING LANDOWNERS
To 50	5.18	To 50	5.53
51–100	8.11	51–100	7.42
101–200	21.04	101–200	17.22
201–300	12.19	201–300	13.11
301–400	11.82	301–400	10.74
401–500	6.22	401–500	6.79
501–1000	20.29	501–1000	22.91
1001–1500	6.64	1001–1500	8.58
1501–2000	2.52	1501–2000	2.80
2000 up	3.11	2000 up	4.90
Not determined	2.88		

slaveholders than nonslaveholders owned from 200 to 500 acres. An analysis of the sizes of the farms and percentages of owners in each category for the pine barrens, piedmont, and black belt is presented in the [three tables above].

At this point it may be observed that the pattern of slaveownership and of landownership in the piedmont and pine belt were almost identical. About 80 per cent of the slaveholding population owned 10 or less slaves, and approximately 80 per cent of this same group owned 500 or less acres of land. In other words, as has been said, the bulk of the slaveholding part of the farm population were farmers rather than planters. In the black belt, while the pattern of land and slaveownership were similar they were not identical. In this region the majority of slaveholders were farmers, but only a bare majority: about 51 per cent owned 10 or fewer slaves (which classed them as farmers) and 500 or less acres of land. In the piedmont and pine barrens about 20 per cent of the slaveowners were planters and only a few of these owned over 30 slaves; but in the black belt 49 per cent were planters who owned from 11 slaves to several hundred, and from 500 to several thousand acres of land. However, most of the planter class in the black belt were merely well-to-do, not rich; for they owned less than 30 slaves and less than 1,000 acres of land. The large planter class constituted scarcely more than 12 per cent of the slaveholders in this region, and as might be expected they ranged from moderately wealthy to immensely rich. However, the small planters and the slaveholding and nonslaveholding farmers owned the larger portion of the landed wealth—perhaps 75 percent—in the black belt. In the other regions the nonslaveholders owned most of the property.

Thus far we have analyzed the spread of land among the farming population as a whole, which was found to be rapidly increasing during the last decade before the Civil War; next, landowners were divided into slaveholders and nonslaveholders and it was found that the ownership of land was widely diffused in both groups, but that the nonslaveholders were acquiring land more rapidly than the slaveholders. The third step was to analyze the sizes of farms and plantations of the slaveholders and nonslaveholders, from which analysis it was found that the great mass of slaveholders, like the nonslaveholders, were farmers and not planters. Finally, it was observed that the pattern of slaveownership and the pattern of landownership were virtually identical in the regions outside the plantation or black belt, and very similar in the black belt.

If, then, the majority of slaveholders were farmers and the majority of nonslaveholders were farmers who owned their lands, the stereotype of southern society of the late ante-bellum period, let us repeat, has no validity: society could not be divided into slaveholders and nonslaveholders, or, in other words, into "poor whites" and planters. If the several economic and social classes were graphically presented, the general appearance of the chart would be a gentle curve where small farmer, middle-sized farmer, large farmer, small planter, middle-sized planter, and large planter touched each other without any breaks.

By a certain arbitrariness, a very wealthy group at the top and a very poor group at the bottom of the economic structure may be segregated for examination. In the black belt the great planter class thus segregated was about 12 per cent of the slaveholding classes; but in the piedmont and pine barrens it hardly existed, for these regions could boast of only a small, moderately wealthy, planter class. As for determining the size of the "poor white" class certain elements have to be considered. The possession of a family-sized farm and sufficient livestock and tools to enable one to live comfortably would seem to eliminate 80 per cent of the white population of the piedmont and black belt and about 75 per cent in the piney woods from the "poor white" class in 1860. However, one fourth of the landless whites in the black belt were slaveholders, some of them large slaveholders. Many were obviously members of families with large landholdings, while others rented land. At any rate, such slaveholders could hardly be classed among the "poor whites" when they owned several thousand dollars worth of slaves, tools, and livestock, and often cultivated large farms or even plantations. The 15 per cent nonslaveholding group that had no land must be the source from which the "poor whites" can be isolated. On examination of the Agricultural Schedule for 1850, however, it is discovered that many of the farmers who did not own their land were renters who owned their tools, work stock, cows, swine, poultry, etc., and finally who, when judged from their agricultural productions, were as good farmers as their landed neighbors. But, one is finally able to reach a class of individuals in the black belt who possessed little or no livestock or poultry. They were not listed on the Agricultural Schedule because they possessed less than $100 worth of property and farm produce. This group made up hardly 5 per cent of the white population of the black belt.

In dealing with the piedmont and pine barrens it must be kept in mind that practically the entire population, despite their ownership of land, has been designated as "poor whites." No doubt the physical appearance of the great majority of these people was not pleasing to one from an urban civilization, or even to one from the black belt. There is no doubt that they "chawed" tobacco, that the women smoked their cob or clay pipes right along with the men and spat "amber" with the deadly accuracy of the long barrel squirrel rifle, into the fire, through the cracks between the logs, or into the eyes of an impertinent pig that insisted upon sticking his head into the door of the cabin. From an economic point of view, however, these people were not "poor whites." An examination of the Agricultural Schedule discloses the fact that the landowners and landless squatters were well supplied with the necessities of life. It discloses the fact that in both the pine barrens and the piedmont the raising of grain, fruits, and vegetables was far more important than the raising of cotton, and that finally, the chief business, the chief staple, was raising livestock.

An examination of the agricultural and livestock productions of Covington County in 1850 shows that, of the 332 heads of families who owned no land, 227 owned from one to five horses; 100 from one to eight work oxen; 244 from a single milch cow to 200. Over 200 of these squatters—for that is what they were—owned in addition to the milch cows as high as 200 other cattle. The ownership of swine was even more widespread. Two hundred and ninety-one of the 332 squatters in Covington possessed droves of swine ranging up to 200 head. The three most important food crops (garden, truck, and fruits were not usually reported) were corn, potatoes, and peas. One hundred and ninety of the squatters raised from 20 to 800 bushels of corn; about the same number raised from 10 to 500 bushels of sweet potatoes; and 102 raised from 1 to 90 bushels of peas. (Seventy-six of these squatters raised from 1 to 6 bales of cotton.)

An examination of the nonslaveholding and slaveholding landowners in the pine belt and piedmont reveals no great difference in either live-stock or agricultural productions. In the case of the landowner the value of the livestock in the pine barrens, and quite frequently in the piedmont, was greater than the land. The explanation of the existence of this grazing industry is that there were millions of acres of government lands, much of it open pine woods without undergrowth, covered almost the year around with wild peas, vetch, and a coarse grass, either wire grass or broomsedge. This open forest was free alike to all, which explains why the squatter was usually as well off as the landowner. Cattle and swine were shipped or driven to Montgomery, Mobile, or Pensacola, or driven back into the black belt and sold to the planters who, despite their effort at self-sufficiency, usually found themselves short of provisions.

While the slaveholding farmer and small planter dwelt on their land and usually worked with their slaves or sent their sons into the field, the rich slaveholding planter in Alabama (and the Lower South generally) more and more tended toward village or town life. The mansions of ante-bellum times were usually located in town or village at no great distance from the plantation. Today, if one wishes to see how the homes of the large planter of Alabama looked, he should get off the main thoroughfares and go to Eutaw, Greensboro, Lowndesboro, Selma, Hunts-ville, Demopolis, Marion, and Montgomery.[8]

Finally, it can be said in conclusion that while the great planter most frequently lived in village or town, and the farmers and small planters in the country, there was very little segregation of landholdings: the census returns and the tax lists show an intermingling of all economic classes. The hundred-acre farm would be sandwiched between two-thousand-acre plantations. Furthermore, there was no marked difference in the quality of the land held by the slaveholder and nonslaveholder in the black belt. When there was a difference in the land values, it could usually be attributed to the improvements, such as ditching, fencing, and the construction of more expensive buildings by slave labor. In the pied-mont and pine barrens the slaveholder would usually be settled on the bottom lands of the streams in small black belts; but here as in the black belt proper, nonslaveholders would be interspersed between planters.

There are a great many other matters such as education, religion, and political domination by the planter class that cannot be considered here because of lack of space. But, it is hoped that these matters may receive consideration at a future date. It can be stated, however, that planter monopoly in these realms as well as in the economic has been seriously overestimated.

---

[8] Location of residence can be determined from Schedule I of the census and from the Tax Books.

b] Victims of the Slave System

THE LIFE and affairs of the "common man" of the Old South are still an untold chapter in the broad and accumulating literature concerning that section's history. The reasons for this are many. Largely, they are entailed in the fact that the simple people, the submerged majority, remained, like those of other places and other times, for long periods, economically and socially inarticulate. While from the personal correspondences, the memoirs, the diaries, plantation books, periodicals, newspapers, official documents and other similar sources, there have been constructed at length the political vicissitudes and the romanticized myths of the old plutocracy, the classes of marginal economic status seem to have left small evidence of their fate.

In very recent years, however, a group of southern students, led by Dr. F. L. Owsley of Vanderbilt University, has recognized that a three-dimensional interpretation of the South required study "of those millions, both small slaveholder and nonslaveholder, who fell outside the plantation economy," and has emphasized the need "to fit these into the general economic and social structure of the South." For this purpose the unpublished Federal census manuscripts were found to be a rich depository. . . . The Vanderbilt historians . . . have harvested a full crop of propositions concerning the economic status of the plain people of the Old South.

Their findings have been formulated in a series of monographs which deal with the four slave states: Alabama, Louisiana, Mississippi and Tennessee. . . .

Briefly summarized, it is maintained by the Vanderbilt group that in ante-bellum Alabama, Louisiana, and Mississippi, there was "a very considerable" middle class and yeomanry; that ownership of land and slaves was well distributed; that large numbers of farmers, especially nonslaveholders, were able to buy their way into the owning class; that the small landowner ploughed soil which was comparable in quality to that cultivated by the large plantation holder; that during the fifties all economic levels in general and the lower income brackets in particular experienced a prosperous expansion; and finally, that the small farmer enjoyed a fairly "comfortable" standard of living. This picture, which in effect projects the ante-bellum South as a dynamic economic democracy, is noteworthily untraditional, and if valid demands a thorough revision of the more widely held notion that slavery was a closed, contracting system which wastefully barred large segments of the section's citizenry from participating constructively in the main currents of its economic and social life. It is the purpose of this paper therefore to appraise the Vanderbilt conclusions and since similar investigations covering other areas of the South are projected,

FROM Fabian Linden, "Economic Democracy in the Slave South: An Appraisal of Some Recent Views," *Journal of Negro History*, XXXI (April, 1946), 140–42, 147, 160–69, 172–75, 177–82, 184–89. First published by the Association for the Study of Negro Life and History, Inc.

to review the statistical methodology employed in the development of those conclusions.

.   .   .   .

That there was a substantial number of small and medium sized property holders in the slave South need hardly be argued. It is a fact widely accepted and readily established; its proof certainly does not require laborious processing of unorganized census manuscripts. A mere perusal of the published 1860 *Census of Agriculture* is sufficient. Within such numerically defined limits there was, to be sure, a "middle class" in the ante-bellum South. While perhaps it was somewhat less "considerable" than is contended, its place in the economic fabric is as unmistakable as the existence of the "poor white" element.

But a somewhat more inquisitive processing of census figures is mandatory. The economic status and significance of a class cannot be defined merely in terms of size but must also be described on the basis of the relative share of the wealth it claims. Palpably the proportion of total property owned by a class is not less relevant than its numerical size. Only by measuring the magnitude of productive potentials can the full impact which is exerted by a class on the economic life of a section, and, by inference, its importance in shaping or influencing sectional policy, be gauged. Hence, conclusions which rest solely on a breakdown of the number of farming families falling within the various classes, rests on partial data. As such it will almost invariably be unreliable and frequently deceptive. It is customary procedure in economic and sociological literature to indicate both the sizes of the various classes and the distribution of property among the classes. Such an analysis follows.

.   .   .   .

It is not possible to study land distribution in all the Alabama sample regions since the information in Dr. Owsley's article is limited. As in the Louisiana study, only percentages are shown. Published census returns might again be employed, but as already noted, those data camouflage many significant details. Through the judicious application of a number of relatives scattered through Dr. Owsley's pages we can, however, piece together an analysis of landownership for one of his three regions, i.e., the black belt.[1]

Table I once more affirms the traditional view that a small top elite of the southern plutocracy fenced off substantial proportions of fertile cash crop land. In 1850 two-thirds of all acres in the black belt were held by 17 per cent of the farming population and were part of plantations which

[1] The percentage distribution of landholders according to size of owning is indicated separately, by Dr. Owsley, for slaveholders and nonslaveholders. Since each series is an independent, closed unit (totaling 100 per cent) it was not possible to determine the aggregate landholdings of the various classes. For the black belt, however, the author has indicated that in 1850 about 74 per cent of all farming families were landowners, and that 56 per cent were slaveowners. These two additional facts applied to the frequency distributions made it possible to ascertain the landholdings of each economic strata, as shown in Table I.

TABLE I. DISTRIBUTION OF LAND AMONG SLAVEOWNERS AND NONSLAVEOWNERS
BY SIZE OF HOLDINGS

ALABAMA BLACK BELT,[a] 1850

	NON-HOLDERS		SLAVEHOLDERS		TOTAL	
ACRES HELD	FARMING FAMILIES	AGGREGATE HOLDINGS	FARMING FAMILIES	AGGREGATE HOLDINGS	FARMING FAMILIES	AGGREGATE HOLDINGS
None	19.5[b]	—	6.5[b]	—	26.0[b]	—
1–50	6.1	.5	2.6	.2	8.7	.7
51–100	6.0	1.5	4.1	1.0	10.1	2.5
101–200	7.5	3.8	10.8	5.5	18.3	9.3
201–300	2.2	1.9	6.2	5.3	8.4	7.2
301–400	1.2	1.4	6.0	7.2	7.2	8.6
401–500	.7	1.1	3.2	4.1	3.9	6.0
501–1,000	.8	2.0	10.3	26.4	11.1	28.4
1,001–2,000	—	—	4.7	22.3	4.7	22.3
Over 2,000	—	—	1.6	15.0	1.6	15.0
Total	44.0	12.2	56.0	87.8	100.0	100.0

[a] Includes following counties: Bibb, Clarke, Dallas, Greene, Lowndes, Marengo, Monroe, Montgomery, Perry.
[b] Dr. Owsley does not indicate the distribution of nonlandowning farmers between slaveowners and nonslaveowners for 1850. To make possible an effective statistical presentation of the available data, however, the ratio between those classes in 1850 was assumed to be the same as in 1860, for which year the author has shown the ratio. The error resulting from this procedure is probably negligible.

claimed over 500 acres. On the other end of the ladder farms of 100 acres or less covered roughly only 3 per cent of the land but were called to support approximately 19 per cent of all farm families. Non-slaveholders constituted 44 per cent of the farm population but only 12.2 per cent of the area's acreage fell to that group.

It should be mentioned that Dr. Owsley does show a passing concern for the proportional allocation of land among the various holding classes. Speaking of the black belt, he maintains that "the small planters and the slaveholding and nonslaveholding farmers owned the larger portion of the landed wealth—perhaps 75 per cent," and that the large planter class, involving about 12 per cent of all the slaveholders in the region, it is inferred, claimed only 25 per cent of the total acreage.

The breakdown shown in Table I suggests that farmers and small planters owned less than two-thirds of the landed wealth rather than three-quarters. Moreover, the large planter, defined by the author as owning over 1,000 acres, when measured against the entire farming population (which appears to be a somewhat more defensible base) shrinks from 12 per cent to 6.3 per cent. That class claimed well over one-third of the Delta lands.

The distribution data recorded by Dr. Owsley and Dr. Weaver also permit a somewhat more revealing statistical formulation of the ownership

Table II. Distribution of Land by Quartiles of Farm Population, Also Detail of Fourth Quartile: Selected Agricultural Areas, 1850, 1860

| | ALABAMA 1850 | | MISSISSIPPI 1860 | |
QUARTILES OF POPULATION	BLACK BELT	DELTA	NORTHEASTERN	PINE
Lowest	.0	1.0	.0	.2
Second	5.5	11.0	8.0	6.3
Third	18.5	25.5	19.0	19.0
Fourth	76.0	62.5	73.0	74.5
Detail of Fourth Quartile:				
Upper 5 per cent	33.0	24.5	33.5	39.0
Upper 3 per cent	24.5	18.0	26.0	32.5
Upper 1 per cent	10.0	8.0	10.0	15.0

pattern. Table II shows the aggregate landholdings of each quartile of the farm population for the sample regions of Mississippi and the black belt of Alabama. Also included is a detail of the top quartile. In developing this chart the distribution data . . . were plotted on a Lorenz curve. For the purpose of constructing the curve the two series of per cents for each region—farming families and aggregate holdings—were separately cumulated on a "less than" basis and the two values for each class interval were plotted as a point on a grid. The various points were linked and the per cents recorded in Table II ascertained from the resulting Lorenz curve.

While the frequency distributions discussed earlier, in which class intervals are in terms of size of holdings, makes possible an analysis of ownership within a reasonably homogeneous region it does not allow for meaningful comparisons of widely different areas. But by employing class intervals based on the ratio of total farm families, as in the quartile chart below, we are provided with a common denominator which enables comparisons of the ownership pattern in various and diverse regions. This makes it possible to evolve, within the limit of the sample, some general socio-economic principles concerning the class structure in the agricultural South.

The per cents shown in Table II sharply focus the fact that a very considerable proportion of the farm population, in the areas studied, owned an almost insignificant share of the land. In no instance—neither in the rich black belt of Alabama nor the less fertile pine barrens of Mississippi—did the lowest quartile of farming families own more than 1 per cent of the land. The lower 50 per cent of the farm population in the Mississippi Delta region claimed 12 per cent of the land while the same proportion of farmers owned only 5.5 per cent of the entire black belt acreage. The top quartile in every sample region, however, claimed roughly two-thirds to three-quarters of the landed wealth. Concentration was in fact even more pronounced than this suggests, for as little as 3 per cent of all farming families owned 32.5 per cent of the pine land and

26 per cent of the northeastern hill acres. In the Alabama black belt and in the Delta regions of Mississippi, the ratios were 24.5 per cent and 18 per cent, respectively.

But more illuminating than these details, is the striking similarity of the socio-economic pattern of ownership in all the regions studied. Although, as has been indicated earlier, land was concentrated by large plantations in the Alabama black belt while holdings were substantially smaller in the pine barrens of Mississippi, in every region studied, the coefficient of stratification tended to be constant. Even in such areas where there were few or none of the extensive slave estates this distribution pattern was distinct. The sociological significance of this fact is apparent. For the status, prestige, and influence of the farmer depended not so much on the absolute size of his acreage, but more on his rank within his immediate universe, on his place in the "pecking order" within the circumference of his own barnyard.

Thus it would appear that the proposition maintaining that property holdings in the ante-bellum South were "well distributed" or "widely diffused" has not been convincingly demonstrated. It arose from a dubious definition and evolved through a curious evolution. The initial premise that "there was a very considerable middle class" in the majority of regions studied has only very limited justification. From that questionable proposition the authors have drawn fallacious statistical inferences, invalidly bridging the specific and the general. Indisputably, a significant section of the ante-bellum population consisted of small and medium-sized property holders, but in the areas studied their relative numerical importance is somewhat less than the authors suggest, and their share of the section's operating income was considerably less than their numbers warranted. The large plantation holder, as is the orthodox view, controlled excessive proportions of the labor and land wealth.

Land distribution however is not an especially sensitive barometer of economic stratification. Numerous variables such as location, condition, age, crop grown and similar factors, tend to compromise the significance of class and country comparisons. It would be difficult for example, to make any quantitative generalizations concerning Louisiana land distribution in the sugar region as compared to the prairies. In the latter instance, land was employed largely for grazing and timber growing, both of which required comparatively large areas; sugar production, on the other hand, yielded considerably larger dollar returns by the acre. Similarly, even within a limited area, particularly when there is a wide divergence in quality, generalizations concerning aggregate class ownings must be qualified in consideration of the possibility that the superior quality land was held by large planters, and by inference, that less desirable plots fell to the small subsistence farmers. This point hardly requires detailed demonstration. It is sufficient to note simply that southern land is known to have sold for as little as twenty-five cents and for well above a hundred dollars an acre.

Thus for an analysis of the economic class structure of the ante-bellum South the distribution of slave property is certainly as fully an important measure as is acre ownership. To be concerned excessively or exclusively with the latter will result in conclusions less precise than available data permits. The advantages of slaveholdings as an economic indicator, on the other hand, consist exactly in the fact that there was a comparatively narrow differential between low and high end values. A study of hundreds of slave holdings indicated moreover that large and small plantations tended to be homogeneous as to the sex and age ratios of their slave forces.

Both Dr. Owsley and Dr. Weaver are aware that a difference in land values would minimize the usefulness of acre holdings as an economic index, and anticipate this limitation with the contention that "there was no marked difference in the quality of the land held by the slaveholder and non-slaveholder."

Now this constitutes a very original thesis; if valid it challenges some fundamental and long-standing concepts concerning the dynamics and evolution of the plantation economy. U. B. Phillips, for example, has attributed the origin and genesis of the slave system to a very considerable extent to the territorial expansion of the large slaveholder at the expense of the small. As the less fortunate farmer was forced by economic pressure to move further west, he maintains, their lots were bought up by the more prosperous slaveowners, which placed eventually "as a rule . . . the best acres" in the hands of the latter class. The mechanics of this process has been clearly and briefly summarized by Professor Phillips as follows:

> The tide of small farmers advancing toward the frontier in search of new opportunity was followed in many areas by a tide of planters who sought new openings where their capital might be employed more advantageously than in the older areas where the competition was more stringent. Districts which from the lack of the required qualities of soil or climate or of facilities of transportation were not available for the planters could be enjoyed by the farmers alone; but all others were entered by the planters sooner or later, and after more or less conflict were dominated by them.
>
> Some of the nonslaveholders moved away from the encroaching plantations and settled anew as yeoman farmers; others by thrift bought slaves and in time became planters; others simply held their own in spite of the disadvantage of competing with Negro labor in the same industry; while still others retrograded in the scale of life, drifted to the barren tracts, and lived from hand to mouth as anemic poor-whites. The planters, meanwhile, continued to encroach wherever they could upon the territory already occupied in part by the smaller industrial unit. The very nature of the plantation system caused this phenomenon.

L. C. Gray writing in more recent years, has accepted and carried forward Dr. Phillips' thesis of expansion. In some detail he has described the "competitive advantages" of the slave system and traces its aggressive thrusts into the most fertile soil area of the South. This "triumph of the plantation system over the small farm" is attributed in considerable measure to the ability of the planter to "outbid the farmer in the acquisition of land." Thus the Vanderbilt hypothesis, that there was no marked difference in the quality of land held by the small farmer and the larger planter, demands especially careful consideration. If this contention can be convincingly demonstrated consistency would require rejection of the more widely accepted Phillips-Gray encroachment-expansion thesis.

Let us first examine the arguments advanced by Dr. Owsley and Dr. Weaver in behalf of their position. Both offer as supporting evidence the fact that the order of listing in the pages of the census manuscript "often indicates that a small farmer lived in the midst of large plantations." From this it is inferred that small and large farms were adjacently located and hence claimed soil of comparable quality. This reasoning is palpably unconvincing.

For one thing farmers listed as "neighbors" in 1850 were quite often recorded pages apart in the schedule of the following census year, suggesting that the enumerators' canvass was certainly not sufficiently systematic to allow major historical generalizations. But even more relevant is the fact that the argument lacks convincing statistical presentation. That an occasional small farmer ploughed soil which was as good as, or even better than, his very wealthy neighbor's, is neither surprising nor significant. If the authors are to make their point they must show that small farmers and large planters bore the same numerical ratio to each other in the fertile land areas as they did in the total agricultural population. Only in that way would it be suggested that, on the average, the land of small farmers was comparable to that owned by large holders. As presented, however, no evidence is given even to indicate that the small holders were dispersed among the large more frequently than strands of poor quality land were dispersed among the more fertile. Indeed the relatively great number of small farmers (a fact which is consistently called to our attention by the Vanderbilt group) would require that the large be dispersed among the small rather than the argued reverse.

. . . .

Table III below, based on data in the original census manuscripts, shows the average dollar value per acre of farm land according to size of holdings. This was computed by dividing cash value of farm by total acres held.

TABLE III. CASH VALUE PER ACRE AND RATIO OF LAND IMPROVED: SELECTED COTTON AREAS,[a] 1860

NUMBER OF ACRES OWNED	PER CENT OF LAND IMPROVED	CASH VALUE PER FARM ACRE [b]
1–50	76.0	$ 7.20
51–100	46.4	7.87
101–200	42.6	8.38
201–300	42.8	10.80
301–500	49.1	13.63
501–1000	45.6	19.81
1001–2000	49.9	28.77
Over 2000	35.0	29.50

[a] Includes the following counties. Alabama: Barbour, Chambers, Coosa, Greene, Lowndes, Marengo, Perry, Wilcox; Mississippi: Calhoun, Hinds, Holmes, Issequena, Tallahatchie, Warren, Yazoo.
[b] This column was computed by dividing cash value of farm by total acreage owned.

Also indicated for each class is the percentage of total acres improved. Observations were taken from 15 random selected cotton counties located in Alabama and Mississippi. Approximately 300 holdings were studied.[2]

Clearly from this table the cash value per farm acre of large holdings was considerably greater than that of small. The trend is continuous, graduating upward as the size of farms grows larger. Although there is some variation among the classes in the ratio of total land improved it is so slight and of such nature as not to detract from the basic trend indicated in the column headed "cash value per farm acre." Two exceptions to this, however, are very small farms and large plantations. But the differences here tend to emphasize the steep differentials among acre values. Units of 50 or less acres had an average cash farm value per acre of $7.20, more than three quarters of the land being improved. In comparison, plantations consisting of more than 2,000 acres had an average acre value of $29.50, with only 35 per cent of their aggregate holdings improved.

To be sure this wide divergence in acre value is not attributable solely to differences in land quality; but it is very highly probable that fertility was a contributing factor, especially since the difference in per acre value between small and large units was so pronounced. Moreover it should be remembered that wealthy planters frequently built their expensive residences in urbanized areas, and that their holdings included a much higher ratio of unimproved acres as compared to small farms. The relative importance of land quality and land improvement as factors influencing average acre value cannot however be quantified.

Dr. Owsley anticipates the higher average acre value of large farms as compared to small, but rejects the implication that it is symptomatic of variation in land quality. "When there was a difference in the land values," he notes in connection with the black belt, "it could usually be attributed to the improvements, such as ditching, fencing, and the construction of more expensive buildings by slave labor." But here again we are in the realm of the nonquantified and the speculative. As Table III indicates, it is not a question of "when" there was variation in values, for clearly on the average this difference, especially between extreme classes, was overwhelming. Dr. Owsley is correct in attributing value variations to improvements, but no systematic evidence is offered to substantiate his claim that they constituted a sole factor, or concretely, that fertility was not an extremely important contributing cause.

Convincing verification of the Phillips-Gray thesis that in the South generally the most productive lands were property of the large plantation proprietors is readily found. It requires only the perusal of a topographic and a slave population map. The lines marking alluvial land areas tend to overlap systematically with the areas populated by large plantations. Throughout the South, with the exception of frontier sections, fertile land regions were big planter domain. To cite one instance among many, in the alluvial short staple river counties of southern Mississippi the median sized slaveholding was 70, while in the older upland cotton regions of

2 Census Report, MSS., Schedule IV, Agriculture, 1860.

Southwestern North Carolina it was only 17.[3] Even in spite of his comparable quality land thesis, Dr. Weaver notes that the state of Mississippi, "as a general rule, had more large farms in the areas where the soil was most fertile." Evidence attests to the fact that this was very probably a characteristic trend.

The Vanderbilt group not only argue that there was, on the eve of the Civil War, a very considerable yeomanry and middle class, owning slaves and substantial quantities of good land, but contend further that during the pre-war decade those classes enjoyed a singularly prosperous expansion. This latter position is projected in a series of propositions which maintain briefly, that numerous farmers acquired slaves and land during the fifties, that in fact land was acquired most rapidly by non-slaveholders, and that the small farmer owned sufficiently large lots to make possible "a fairly comfortable living." While all members of the group have not expressed each aspect of this configuration, all have played variations on the theme of an expanding and dynamic middle class and yeomanry. It may be that this general position is defensible but in every instance the statistics employed in its defense are ineffective.

.   .   .   .

The extent of property acquisition can in actual fact be measured with considerable accuracy through the use of aggregate sectional data. While, to be sure, there was movement in and out of the South, the volume was comparatively light and the effects of immigration and emigration would tend to cancel each other out, not only quantitatively but also qualitatively, for those leaving and those coming were on the average probably of similar economic status. A study of sectional figures fails to substantiate the contention that there was any appreciable extension of slaveownership during the fifties, but on the contrary, the increment in the number of new holders compares unfavorably with the emergence rate of new family units. In a decade in which the slave economy experienced a very considerable growth, some increase in the total number of slaveowners is to be expected. But while every facet of the economy was expanding with accelerated momentum the increase of ownership is unique in its slightness. During the fifties the increment in the number of white families in the entire South exceeded the growth in the number of slaveowners by over 25 per cent. Thus we must conclude that the propertied classes of the Old South constituted a relatively shrinking segment of the population.

.   .   .   .

It is also urged, and by all three authors, that landownership was rapidly increasing; and that "many" farmers who were without land in 1850 had purchased their way into the owning class during the decade. But again the procedure employed in attempting to support this position is un-

[3] The counties included are, in Mississippi: Wilkinson, Adams, Jefferson, Claiborne. In North Carolina: Mecklenburg, Union, Anson, Richmond, Rowan. Gray, *Agriculture*, I, 531-5.

acceptable. In its behalf it is demonstrated that the ratio of landowning farmers to total farming families was greater in 1860 than in 1850. Thus Dr. Owsley maintains, for example, that "non-slaveholders in Covington County increased their ownership of land from 32 per cent in 1850 to 64 per cent in 1860—a gain of 100 per cent." This technique, which is very extensively employed by both Dr. Owsley and Mr. Coles, serves as the basis for some very far reaching generalizations. As such it compels close examination.

Now palpably the evidence that a larger percentage of the 1860 farm population owned property than in 1850, does not necessarily establish the fact that there was an extension of ownership and most decidedly not an extension of a magnitude equal to the increment of the ownership co-efficient. The mere noting of variation in these proportions does not define the economic process responsible for such differences. Concretely, many factors may have contributed to a higher ownership ratio in 1860; among them being purchases by relatively prosperous planters who immigrated into the area studied, the emigration of non-property holders from those sections, the formal transformation of prosperous squatters to landowners, and, but not necessarily, the purchase of land by non-holders, as is suggested by Dr. Owsley and Mr. Coles. Undoubtedly, all these processes were part of the complex economic activity of the fifties. But the authors have failed to demonstrate the relative importance of each, or specifically, the extent to which acquisition was responsible for an increase in the coefficient.

The weakness of the method employed is effectively illustrated by the situation in Harrison County, Mississippi. Here in 1850 only 68 per cent of all farmers owned the land they tilled, but by the end of the decade the ratio had increased to 74 per cent. In Dr. Owsley's terms this would represent a 10 per cent "increase in the distribution of landownership" and another indication that the small farmer "was on the make." In actual fact he was on the move. The data reveal that in 1850 there were 166 farming families in that parish, of which 113 were landowners; but by 1860 the number of farming families had dropped to 102, of which only 83 were landholders. Thus while the method of comparing ownership coefficients would suggest to Dr. Owsley and Mr. Coles that "ownership was spreading rapidly" in Harrison County where the coefficient increased by about 10 per cent the absolute number of landowners actually decreased by over 25 per cent. Clearly then, while the coefficient may have a static value to the extent of defining the architecture of the economic hierarchy at a given point in time, it cannot be employed as a dynamic index in the sense of exposing the specific mechanics of change.

Not only was landownership spreading rapidly, according to Dr. Owsley, but remarkably the non-slaveholder was acquiring land at a more rapid pace than the slaveholder. Again the ownership coefficient technique is employed to establish this rather conspicuous generalization. It is demonstrated that while in Greene County, Alabama, only 20 per cent of the non-slaveowning class held land in 1837, nineteen years later, according to the county tax records, 75 per cent were property owners, "an increase of 275 per cent." But slaveholders during the same period acquired land apparently at the sluggish rate of only 26 per cent. From this it is suggested that farmers with neither slaves nor land were faring better than slaveholders who owned no land.

Here fallacy is compound. But we need not embark on a lengthy refutation. It is necessary merely to remember that, as has been previously demonstrated, an increase in the ownership coefficient is a symptom of many possible causes, but is not sufficient in itself to establish the fact that there was an actual extension of ownership. Nor are comparisons of percentages, as employed by Dr. Owsley, valid. The implausibility of his result—i.e. 275 per cent acquisition rate for slaveless farmers but only 26 per cent for slaveowners—is sufficient to suggest that not in broad economic trends but rather in arithmetic operation is an explanation to be found. Indeed, so unwieldy and deceptive is the statistical apparatus which is employed by Dr. Owsley that it has apparently misled its author. Thus while he asserts that "nonslaveholders were acquiring land more rapidly than the slaveholders" elsewhere in his article he makes the contradictory claim that the "spread of landownership was always greater among slaveholders than among nonslaveholders."

Finally and perhaps most important, all three authors suggest that in general the small ante-bellum farmer enjoyed economic "security and well-being." Substantiation appears to hinge on the question as to whether farms were "large enough and fertile enough to produce the basic necessities?" The point is well taken but essential to its solution are well defined standards. First, within the framework of southern society, what constituted "basic necessities" and "economic security," and once appropriate criteria are formulated, what was the minimum acreage necessary, separately defined for the various soil regions, to fulfill those criteria? No attempt is made to set up an applicable yardstick but nevertheless it is the implied conclusion of all three authors that the size and fertility of small holdings were adequate for a comfortable way of life. Thus it is claimed by Dr. Owsley that the "possession of a family-sized farm and sufficient livestock and tools to enable one to live comfortably would seem to eliminate 80 per cent of the white population of the piedmont and black belt and about 75 per cent in the piney woods from the 'poor white' class in 1860." What is the standard on which this measured generalization rests? Would, for example, the assets of James Fuller of Chamber County, Alabama, which consisted of a 20-acre farm valued at $200, two cows, six pigs, and implements worth $10 be considered sufficient to support "comfortably" a family of 10? In this connection it is perhaps necessary to recall that the working definition of "farmer" employed by Dr. Owsley and the other authors seems to have already eliminated about a quarter of the rural white population from consideration.

In summary then, the contention that there was a very considerable middle class and yeomanry in ante-bellum Alabama, Louisiana and Mississippi has, within the context of a broadened definition, only a minimum validity. Although these classes may have been substantial numerically they shared, in the areas studied, a relatively small proportion of the south's property, while conversely an almost negligible segment of the population owned a very significant portion of the productive lands and slave labor. Moreover, land quality was not constant, but rather large plantations claimed title to the more fertile areas, thus accentuating the already skewed property distribution chart, giving to the elevated stratum an even larger portion of the section's income than aggregate landownings alone indicate. Nor has the evidence presented validated the suggestion that southern class lines were fluid. On the contrary, the extension of ownership proceeded at a slower pace than did the emergence of new family units, making the property class increasingly restricted. Similarly the assertion that the very small farmer experienced an exceptional prosperity during the fifties has not been supported by an effective mobilization of facts. Unsubstantiated too is the claim that small farms were sufficiently large to permit a comfortable way of life. Objective criteria have not been developed which would make possible determination of this point. Finally, the data and conclusions presented by all three authors are, in some measure, both arbitrary and irrelevant. By definition, a significant segment of the rural population, consisting largely of those engaged in marginal occupations, was not considered in the various studies, and further the sample areas covered were found to be statistically unrepresentative of the states from which they were selected.

No one, of course, will protest the general thesis which is argued by the Vanderbilt group that "the old planter-poor-white stereotype of southern society" is an outmoded fiction. This was made apparent at the turn of the century in the early writings of U. B. Phillips, and in more recent years underscored by many students of the south, among them L. C. Gray, A. N. J. Den Hollander, R. B. Flanders, and R. W. Shugg. There was without question a large number of diverse economic classes, each subtly and gradually blending into the next upper level, running the social gamut from an Alabama clay eater to Jefferson Davis. It is the debunking of the "two class" fallacy that has now become the tedious cliché. And the excessive zeal sometimes displayed in the refutation tends to lay the groundwork for a new but no less spurious construction.

The Vanderbilt group, in its extensive and systematic utilization of the census manuscripts, has, however, made a contribution of considerable promise to the field of southern historiography. Those records, consisting of social and economic blueprints for literally hundreds of thousands of family units, spanning approximately the two generations prior to the Civil War, provide an almost limitless source from which may be evolved a comprehensive evaluation of the dynamics of slavery, not merely the Afro-American chapter, but slavery as an economic system. Nowhere before in the world history of labor bondage has there been left such a vast deposit of specific and detailed evidence. But to exploit the full historical potential, to distil a series of significant propositions from this wealth, it must be approached with sharpened statistical tools and with scientifically objective postulates.

Specific suggestions in this direction were made as early as 1908 by Joseph A. Hill in a talk entitled "The Historical Value of the Census Records," which was delivered at the Annual Convention of the American Historical Association. Calling attention to the availability of the census manuscripts, Mr. Hill made the following suggestions for investigation: a count of the number of slaveholders for the census years prior to 1850; frequency distributions of slaveowners by size of holdings for the same years; variations in the size of white families by nativity and occupation; and a number of other topics which are not directly related to the South. To these may be added, among others, the following suggested lines of inquiry which should be studied, in most instances, according to differences among the various economic classes, changes occurring during census periods, and to variation by agricultural areas: geographic and economic mobility; proportion of capital invested in land and in labor; per cent of total holding improved; number of work animals, and value of farm implements per improved acre; crop yield according to number of field hands; ratio of improved acres to field hands; utilization of slaves in nonagricultural occupations; age and sex composition of slave forces; trends in the direction of agricultural diversification and intensification; amount of livestock owned; size of farm unit and labor force making for optimum productive efficiency; curves of economic expansion and failure; siphoning of labor supply from worn to fertile areas through owner migration and slave purchases; age and sex of Negroes most frequently bought; correlation of "runaway" ratio with size and location of plantations; variations in mortality rates; economic status of the free Negro; age of family heads and number of dependents; economic position of urban, rural and foreign wage earners; the velocity of urbanization and ruralization; urban class stratification. And this cataloging might readily be extended. Answers to these problems would not only illuminate and quantify many unexplored facets of the slave labor system but would throw into proper juxtaposition its multiple economic currents and tensions, contradictory and reenforcing, and thus facilitate a more ramified interpretation of that "peculiar" social and political complex called the "Old South."

3] The Poor Whites

a] HEREDITARY MISFITS

. . . THE DENOUNCERS of the slaveholders . . . do not trouble themselves to inquire what are the natural causes of the existence in the South of a class of lazy vagabonds known as Poor Whites, or how great the number of these

FROM D[aniel] R[obinson] Hundley, *Social Relations in Our Southern States* (New York: Henry B. Price, 1860), 254–58.

may be, but rush madly and recklessly to the conclusion, that they form the bulk of the Southern masses, and are rendered the pitiable wretches they are by reason of the peculiar institution. Behold now, attentive and reflecting reader, how soon a plain unvarnished statement will render this whole subject intelligible.

As we took occasion to state in the first chapter, the early settlers of the South were not of equal fortune, or blessed alike with the same refinement and culture. We have already spoken of the Cavalier class, and their present descendants and representatives; of the past and present standing of the thrifty Middle Classes; of the Yeomanry and the useful position their off-spring yet occupy; and we would now like to know, what has become of those paupers and convicts whom Great Britain sent over to her faithful Colony of Virginia—of those indentured servants who were transported in great numbers from the mother country, or who followed their masters, the Cavaliers and Huguenots, when these bade adieu to the white cliffs of merry England and the purple-clad hills of La Belle France, to seek their fortunes in the New World? Sir William Berkeley, in 1670, in answer to interrogatories submitted to him by the Lords' Commissioners of Foreign Affairs, in which they inquire, "What number of English, Scotch, and Irish have for these seven years last past come yearly to plant and inhabit within your government; and also what *blacks* or *slaves* have been brought in within the same time?" answered: "Yearly there comes in of servants *about fifteen hundred;* most are English, few Scotch, and fewer Irish, and not above two or three ships of negroes in seven years." The servants here spoken of were indentured servants or paupers, who were sold pretty much like the Coolies are sold to the Cubans at the present time. They were considered as mere "goods, wares, and merchandise," to be sold publicly at places appointed by law. . . .

Now, does the reader fancy there is any thing in the nature of our soil and climate which would soon transmogrify such untutored, uncultivated, and servile creatures into freemen and gentlemen? Does he imagine that the glorious Declaration of Independence would alone suffice to put bread and meat into the mouths of paupers, or clothes upon their ragged backs? Is he so foolish as to believe that the overthrow of the Law of Primogeniture, the bestowal of the elective franchise, and the other levelling doctrines of Mr. Jefferson, would of themselves elevate to a position of thrift and intelligence, necessary to success in an honest competition with their more self-reliant fellows, those outcasts and paupers, picked up in the back slums and cellars of London, and transported at the public charge to Virginia, and there sold in the market-house to the highest bidder? If yea; then we must say, O candid reader, that you are a greater ninny than we supposed you were, be you sir or madam, miss or master.

For observe, if you please, the actual result has been far different. Just as the abolishment of the old feudal base tenures has been as yet productive of no perceptible advantages to the Old World peasants, so likewise the removal of the English paupers to the New World, to the enjoyment of all the immunities of freemen, and to a land of such cornucopian abundance that it may be said almost to flow with milk and honey, has as yet been productive of no material improvement in their condition as a class. An individual here and there may have become imbued with a more manly feeling than what he otherwise would have attained unto; but as a class, as a community, they remain in *statu quo*. Every where they are just alike, possess pretty much the same characteristics, the same vernacular, the same boorishness, and the same habits; although in different localities, they are known by different names. Thus, in the extreme South and South-west, they are usually called Squatters; in the Carolinas and Georgia Crackers or Sandhillers; in the Old Dominion, Rag Tag and Bob-tail; in Tennessee and some other States, People in the Barrens—but every where, Poor White Trash, a name said to have originated with the slaves, who look upon themselves as much better off than all "po' white folks" whatever.

To form any proper conception of the condition of the Poor White Trash, one should see them as they are. We do not remember ever to have seen in the New-England States a similar class; though, if what a citizen of Maine has told us be true, in portions of that State the Poor Whites are to be found in large numbers. In the State of New-York, however, in the rural districts, we will venture to assert that more of this class of paupers are to be met with than you will find in any single Southern State. For in examining the statistics of pauperism, as prepared by the Secretary of State for New-York, we learn that the number of her public paupers, permanent and temporary, is set down as 468,302—to support whom requires an annual outlay of one million and a half of dollars, which has to be raised by tax for the purpose. They are also found in Ohio, Pennsylvania, Indiana, and all the States of the North-west, though in most of these last they came originally from the South. But every where, North and South, in Maine or Texas, in Virginia or New-York, they are one and the same; and have undoubtedly had one and the same origin, namely, the poor-houses and prison-cells of Great Britain. Hence we again affirm, what we asserted only a moment ago, that there is a great deal more in *blood* than people in the United States are generally inclined to believe.

.   .   .   .

b] Unfortunates Trapped by Environment

A NIGHT WITH A "POOR WHITE"

. . . A PLANTER, at whose house I called after sunset, said it was not convenient for him to accommodate me, and I was obliged to ride till it was quite dark. The next house, at which I arrived, was one of the commonest sort of cabins. I had passed twenty like it during the day, and I thought I would take the opportunity to get an interior knowledge of them. The fact that a horse and wagon were kept, and that a considerable area of land in the rear of the cabin was planted with cotton, showed that

FROM Frederick Law Olmsted, *A Journey in the Back Country* (New York: Mason Brothers, 1860), pp. 197–204.

the family were by no means of the lowest class, yet, as they were not able even to hire a slave, they may be considered to represent very favorably, I believe, the condition of the poor whites of the plantation districts. The whites of the county, I observe, by the census, are three to one of the slaves; in the nearest adjoining county, the proportion is reversed; and within a few miles the soil was richer, and large plantations occurred.

It was raining, and nearly nine o'clock. The door of the cabin was open, and I rode up and conversed with the occupant as he stood within. He said that he was not in the habit of taking in travelers, and his wife was about sick, but if I was a mind to put up with common fare, he didn't care. Grateful, I dismounted and took the seat he had vacated by the fire, while he led away my horse to an open shed in the rear—his own horse ranging at large, when not in use, during the summer.

The house was all comprised in a single room, twenty-eight by twenty-five feet in area, and open to the roof above. There was a large fireplace at one end and a door on each side—no windows at all. Two bedsteads, a spinning-wheel, a packing-case, which served as a bureau, a cupboard, made of rough hewn slabs, two or three deer-skin seated chairs, a Connecticut clock, and a large poster of Jayne's patent medicines, constituted all the visible furniture either useful or ornamental in purpose. A little girl immediately, without having had any directions to do so, got a frying-pan and a chunk of bacon from the cupboard, and cutting slices from the latter, set it frying for my supper. The woman of the house sat sulkily in a chair tilted back and leaning against the logs, spitting occasionally at the fire, but took no notice of me, barely nodding when I saluted her. A baby lay crying on the floor. I quieted it and amused it with my watch till the little girl, having made "coffee" and put a piece of corn-bread on the table with the bacon, took charge of it.

I hoped the woman was not very ill.

"Got the headache right bad," she answered. "Have the headache a heap, I do. Knew I should have it to-night. Been cuttin' brush in the cotton this arternoon. Knew't would bring on my headache. Told him so when I begun."

As soon as I had finished my supper and fed Jude, the little girl put the fragments and the dishes in the cupboard, shoved the table into a corner, and dragged a quantity of quilts from one of the bedsteads, which she spread upon the floor, and presently crawled among them out of sight for the night. The woman picked up the child—which, though still a suckling, she said was twenty-two months old—and nursed it, retaking her old position. The man sat with me by the fire, his back towards her. The baby having fallen asleep was laid away somewhere, and the woman dragged off another lot of quilts from the beds, spreading them upon the floor. Then taking a deep tin-pan, she filled it with alternate layers of corn-cobs and hot embers from the fire. This she placed upon a large block, which was evidently used habitually for the purpose, in the center of the cabin. A furious smoke arose from it, and we soon began to cough. "Most *too* much smoke," observed the man. "Hope 't will drive out all the gnats, then," replied the woman. (There is a very minute flying insect here, the bite of which is excessively sharp.)

The woman suddenly dropped off her outer garment and stepped from the midst of its folds, in her petticoat; then, taking the baby from the place where she had deposited it, lay down and covered herself with the quilts upon the floor. The man told me that I could take the bed which remained on one of the bedsteads, and kicking off his shoes only, rolled himself into a blanket by the side of his wife. I ventured to take off my cravat and stockings, as well as my boots, but almost immediately put my stockings on again, drawing their tops over my pantaloons. The advantage of this arrangement was that, although my face, eyes, ears, neck, and hands, were immediately attacked, the vermin did not reach my legs for two or three hours. Just after the clock struck two, I distinctly heard the man and the woman, and the girl and the dog scratching, and the horse out in the shed stamping and gnawing himself. Soon afterward the man exclaimed, "Good God Almighty—mighty! mighty! mighty!" and jumping up, pulled off one of his stockings, shook it, scratched his foot vehemently, put on the stocking, and lay down again with a groan. The two doors were open, and through the logs and the openings in the roof, I saw the clouds divide, and the moon and stars reveal themselves. The woman, after having been nearly smothered by the smoke from the pan which she had originally placed close to her own pillow, rose and placed it on the sill of the windward door, where it burned feebly and smoked lustily, like an altar to the Lares, all night. Fortunately the cabin was so open that it gave us little annoyance, while it seemed to answer the purpose of keeping all flying insects at a distance.

When, on rising in the morning, I said that I would like to wash my face, water was given me for the purpose in an earthen pie-dish. Just as breakfast, which was of exactly the same materials as my supper, was ready, rain again began to fall, presently in such a smart shower as to put the fire out and compel us to move the table under the least leaky part of the roof.

At breakfast occurred the following conversation:

"Are there many niggers in New York?"

"Very few."

"How do you get your work done?"

"There are many Irish and German people constantly coming there who are glad to get work to do."

"Oh, and you have them for slaves?"

"They want money and are willing to work for it. A great many American-born work for wages, too."

"What do you have to pay?"

"Ten or twelve dollars a month."

"There was a heap of Irishmen to work on the railroad; they was paid a dollar a day; there was a good many Americans, too, but mostly they had little carts and mules, and hauled dirt and sich like. They was paid twenty-five or thirty dollars a month and found."

"What did they find them?"

"Oh, blanket and shoes, I expect; they put up kind o' tents like for 'em to sleep in all together."

"What food did they find them?"

"Oh, common food; bacon and meal."

"What do they generally give the niggers on the plantations here?"

"A peck of meal and three pound of bacon is what they call 'lowance, in general, I believe. . . . Ain't niggers all-fired sassy at the North?"

"No, not particularly."

"Ain't they all free, there? I hearn so."

"Yes."

"Well, how do they get along when they's free?"

"I never have seen a great many, to know their circumstances very well. Right about where I live they seem to me to live quite comfortably; more so than the niggers on these big plantations do, I should think."

"O! They have a mighty hard time on the big plantations. I'd ruther be dead than to be a nigger on one of these big plantations."

"Why, I thought they were pretty well taken care of on them."

The man and his wife both looked at me as if surprised, and smiled.

"Why, they are well fed, are they not?"

"Oh, but they work 'em so hard. My God, sir, in pickin' time on these big plantations they start 'em to work 'fore light, and they don't give 'em time to eat."

"I supposed they generally gave them an hour or two at noon."

"No, sir; they just carry a piece of bread and meat in their pockets and they eat it when they can, standin' up. They have a hard life on 't, that's a fact. I reckon you can get along about as well withouten slaves as with 'em, can't you, in New York?"

"In New York there is not nearly so large a proportion of very rich men as here. There are very few people who farm over three hundred acres, and the greater number—nineteen out of twenty, I suppose—work themselves with the hands they employ. Yes, I think it's better than it is here, for all concerned, a great deal. Folks that can't afford to buy niggers get along a great deal better in the free States, I think; and I guess that those who could afford to have niggers get along better without them."

"I no doubt that's so. I wish there warn't no niggers here. They are a great cuss to this country, I expect. But 't wouldn't do to free 'em; that wouldn't do no how!"

Get Rid of the Niggers

"Are there many people here who think slavery a curse to the country?"

"Oh, yes, a great many. I reckon the majority would be right glad if we could get rid of the niggers. But it wouldn't never do to free 'em and leave 'em here. I don't know anybody, hardly, in favor of that. Make 'em free and leave 'em here and they'd steal every thing we made. Nobody couldn't live here then."

These views of slavery seem to be universal among people of this class. They were repeated to me at least a dozen times.

Nigger Panics

"Where I used to live, [Alabama] I remember when I was a boy—must ha' been about twenty years ago—folks was dreadful frightened about the niggers. I remember they built pens in the woods where they could hide, and Christmas time they went and got into the pens, 'fraid the niggers was risin'."

"I remember the same time where we was in South Carolina," said his wife; "we had all our things put up in bags, so we could tote 'em, if we heerd they was comin' our way."

They did not suppose the niggers ever thought of rising now, but could give no better reason for not supposing so than that "everybody said there warn't no danger on 't now."

Hereabouts the plantations were generally small, ten to twenty negroes on each; sometimes thirty or forty. Where he used to live they were big ones—forty or fifty, sometimes a hundred on each. He had lived here ten years. I could not make out why he had not accumulated wealth, so small a family and such an inexpensive style of living as he had. He generally planted twenty to thirty acres, he said; this year he had sixteen in cotton and about ten, he thought, in corn. Decently cultivated, this planting should have produced him five hundred dollars' worth of cotton, besides supplying him with bread and bacon—his chief expense, apparently. I suggested that this was a very large planting for his little family; he would need some help in picking time. He ought to have some now, he said; grass and bushes were all overgrowing him; he had to work just like a nigger; this durnation rain would just make the weeds jump, and he didn't expect he should have any cotton at all. There warn't much use in a man's trying to get along by himself; every thing seemed to set in agin him. He'd been trying to hire somebody, but he couldn't, and his wife was a sickly kind of a woman.

His wife reckoned he might hire some help if he'd look round sharp.

My horse and dog were as well cared for as possible, and a "snack" of bacon and corn-bread was offered me for noon, which has been unusual in Mississippi. When I asked what I should pay, the man hesitated and said he reckoned what I had had, wasn't worth much of any thing; he was sorry he could not have accommodated me better. I offered him a dollar, for which he thanked me warmly. It is the first instance of hesitation in charging for a lodging which I have met with from a stranger at the South.

PART III
Slavery and the Slave

INTRODUCTION

⟨ SLAVES COMPRISED about 35 percent of the southern population in 1860. Obviously, any consideration of the economics of slavery must consider the effects of the system on the Negro slave himself. The first problem is to determine exactly what must be evaluated or measured.

One factor might be his standard of living. Yet even if some measurement of this standard could be established in terms of clothing allowances, housing conditions, medical attention, and the like, the problem of a norm would still exist. Are the living standards of the slave to be measured against those of the free Negro? Or should they be measured against the standards enjoyed by the white population?

Another approach might be in terms of the treatment of the slaves. Abolitionists published lurid descriptions of brutality practiced against slaves. Proslavery writers answered that slaves were well cared for, in fact, even better cared for than the free "wage-slave" in the North, who was forced to work long hours in grimy factories and then was brutally discarded when his productive capacities faltered.

Neither of these approaches to the problem does more than resurrect the old question of the morality of slavery. Although this problem is an important one, it is out of place in a book that deals with the economics of slavery. A more fruitful line of inquiry would be to evaluate the long-term effects of

slavery on the Negro. The problem then becomes not whether or not the slave was treated brutally, but rather how his experiences as a slave affected him as a worker and as a human being.[1]

Stating the question in this way does not automatically lead to a solution, as the readings which follow make clear. It does, however, pose the problem in a meaningful manner and points the way toward a more adequate evaluation of the effects of slavery as an economic system.

In the first section, Albert Taylor Bledsoe, an ante-bellum professor at the University of Virginia and an ardent proslavery advocate, argues that slavery served to transform savages into productive workers; it was a school for an ignorant and barbaric race. Ulrich B. Phillips, writing more than a half century later, echoes these sentiments but qualifies his argument with the assertion that slavery was a school that never graduated its apt students.

Frederick Law Olmsted, in the second section, denies the educational values of slavery. He argues that his experiences in the South proved to him that if slavery was a school, it was a poor one, falling far behind the school of free labor in the North. Frederick Douglass, drawing on his own experiences as a slave in Maryland, maintains that the slave system could not exist if slaves

[1] The effects of slavery on the Negro as a producer and as a consumer are treated separately in Part IV.

were given even the rudiments of an education. A slave who managed to escape in 1838 to become a militant abolitionist, Douglass recalls that his training as a slave laborer was designed to destroy all his independence of spirit and intellect.

Each selection reprinted here relates ultimately to the problem of the effect of slavery on the psychology and character of the Negro slave. In so doing, each deals implicitly or explicitly with the problem of the treatment of the American slave. All assume that life in America was an improvement over life in Africa. Is this a fair assumption? How valid is the picture drawn by Bledsoe of life in Africa? Do modern anthropological studies bear out his description? Another aspect of this question relates to Negro-white relations. What was the nature of the relationship between the whites and the slaves in the ante-bellum South? Did the slave benefit from the relationship? How significant is Phillips' observation that Negroes, trained under slavery, were never released? What effect might this have on the personality of the Negro?

THE READINGS

1] Slavery as a Civilizing Agency

a] TRAINS BARBARIANS

THE ABOLITIONISTS, with the most singular unanimity, perseveringly assert that Southern slavery degrades its subjects "into brutes." This assertion fills us with amazement. If it were possible, we would suppose, in a judgment of charity, that its authors knew nothing of the history of Africa or of the condition of our slaves. But such ignorance is not possible. On the other hand, we find it equally impossible to believe that so many men and women—the very lights of abolitionism—could knowingly utter so palpable a falsehood. Thus we are forced to the conclusion, that the authors of this charge are so completely carried away by a blind hatred of slavery, that they do not care to keep their words within the sacred bounds of eternal truth. This seems to be the simple, melancholy fact. The great question with them seems to be, not what is true or what is false, but what will most speedily effect the destruction of Southern slavery. Any thing that seems to answer this purpose is blindly and furiously wielded by them. The *Edinburgh Review,* in a high-wrought eulogy on an American authoress, says that she assails slavery with arrows "poisoned by truth." Her words, it is true, are lipped in flaming poison; but *that* poison is not truth. The truth is never poison.

The native African could not be degraded. Of the fifty millions of inhabitants of the continent of Africa, it is estimated that forty millions were slaves. The master had the power of life and death over the slave; and, in fact, his slaves were often fed, and killed, and eaten, just as we do with oxen and sheep in this country. Nay, the hind and fore-quarters of men, women, and children, might there be seen hung on the shambles and exposed for sale! Their women were beasts of burden; and, when young, they were regarded as a great delicacy by the palate of their pampered masters. A warrior would sometimes take a score of young females along with him, in order to enrich his feasts and regale his appetite. He delighted in such delicacies. As to his religion, it was even worse than his morals; or rather, his religion was a mass of the most disgusting immoralities. His notion of a God, and the obscene acts by which that notion was worshiped, are too shocking to be mentioned. The vilest slave that ever breathed the air of a Christian land could not begin to conceive the horrid iniquities of such a life. And yet, in the face of all this, we are told—yea, we are perseveringly

FROM Albert Taylor Bledsoe, "Liberty and Slavery: or, Slavery in the Light of Moral and Political Philosophy," in E. N. Elliott, ed., *Cotton Is King and Pro-Slavery Arguments* (Augusta, Ga.: Pritchard, Abbott & Loomis, 1860), pp. 413–17.

and eternally told—that "the African has been degraded into a brute" by American slavery! Indeed, if such creatures ever reach the level of simple brutality at all, is it not evident they must be elevated, and not degraded, to it?

The very persons who make the above charge know better. Their own writings furnish the most incontestable proof that they know better. A writer in the *Edinburgh Review*, for example, has not only asserted that "slavery degrades its subjects into brutes," but he has the audacity to declare, in regard to slavery in the United States, that "we do not believe that such oppression is to be found in any other part of the world, civilized or uncivilized. We do not believe that such oppression ever existed before." Yet even this unprincipled writer has, in the very article containing this declaration, shown that he knows better. He has shown that he knows that the African has been elevated and improved by his servitude in the United States. We shall proceed to convict him out of his own mouth.

"The African slave-trade was frightful," says he; "but its prey were savages, accustomed to suffering and misery, and to endure them with patience almost amounting to apathy. The victims of the American slave-trade have been bred in a highly-cultivated community. Their dispositions have been softened, their intellects sharpened, and their sensibilities excited, by society, by Christianity, and by all the ameliorating but enervating influences of civilization. The savage submits to be enslaved himself, or have his wife or his child carried off by his enemies, as merely a calamity. His misery is not embittered by indignation. He suffers only what—if he could—he would inflict. He cannot imagine a state of society in which there shall not be masters and slaves, kidnapping and man-selling, coffles and slave-traders, or in which any class shall be exempt from misfortunes which appear to him to be incidental to humanity."

Thus, according to this very sagacious, honest, consistent writer, it matters little what you do with the native African: he has no moral sense; he feels no wrong; he suffers only what he would inflict. But when you come to deal with the American slave, or, as this writer calls him, "the civilized Virginian," it is quite another thing! His dispositions have been softened, his intellect sharpened, and his sensibilities roused to a new life, by society and by Christianity! And yet, according to this very writer, this highly civilized Virginian is the man who, by American slavery, has been degraded from the native African into a brute! We dismiss his lawless savage, and his equally lawless pen, from our further consideration.

.   .   .   .

The truth is, the abolitionist can make the slave a brute or a saint, just as it may happen to suit the exigency of his argument. If slavery degrades its subjects into brutes, then one would suppose that slaves are brutes. But the moment you speak of selling a slave, he is no longer a brute,—he is a civilized man, with all the most tender affections, with all the most generous emotions. If the object be to excite indignation against slavery, then it always transforms its subjects into brutes; but if it be to excite indignation against the slaveholder, then he holds, not brutes, but a George Harris—or an Eliza—or an Uncle Tom—in bondage. Any thing, and every thing, except fair and impartial statement, are the materials with which he works.

No fact is plainer than that the blacks have been elevated and improved by their servitude in this country. We cannot possibly conceive, indeed, how Divine Providence could have placed them in a better school of correction. If the abolitionists can conceive a better method for their enlightenment and religious improvement, we should rejoice to see them carry their plan into execution. They need not seek to rend asunder our Union, on account of the three millions of blacks among us, while there are fifty millions of the same race on the continent of Africa, calling aloud for their sympathy, and appealing to their Christian benevolence. Let them look to that continent. Let them rouse the real, active, self-sacrificing benevolence of the whole Christian world in behalf of that most degraded portion of the human family; and, after all, if they will show us on the continent of Africa, or elsewhere, three millions of blacks in as good a condition—physically and morally—as our slaves, then will we most cheerfully admit that all other Christian nations, combined, have accomplished as much for the African race, as has been done by the Southern States of the Union.

b] EDUCATES BACKWARD WORKERS

. . . .

EVERY PLANTATION of the standard Southern type was, in fact, a school constantly training and controlling pupils who were in a backward state of civilization. Slave youths of special promise, or when special purposes were in view, might be bound as apprentices to craftsmen at a distance. Thus James H. Hammond in 1859 apprenticed a fourteen-year-old mulatto boy, named Henderson, for four years to Charles Axt, of Crawfordville, Georgia, that he might be taught vine culture. Axt agreed in the indenture to feed and clothe the boy, pay for any necessary medical attention, teach him his trade, and treat him with proper kindness. Before six months were ended Alexander H. Stephens, who was a neighbor of Axt and a friend of Hammond, wrote the latter that Henderson had run away and that Axt was unfit to have the care of slaves, especially when on hire, and advised Hammond to take the boy home. Soon afterward Stephens reported that Henderson had returned and had been whipped, though not cruelly, by Axt. The further history of this episode is not ascertainable. Enough of it is on record, however, to suggest reasons why for the generality of slaves home training was thought best.

This, rudimentary as it necessarily was, was in fact just what the bulk of the negroes most needed. They were in an alien land, in an essentially slow process of transition from barbarism to civilization. New industrial methods of a simple sort they might learn from precepts and occasional demonstrations; the habits and standards of civilized life they could only

FROM Ulrich B. Phillips, *American Negro Slavery* (New York: D. Appleton and Company, 1918), pp. 342–43.

acquire in the main through examples reinforced with discipline. These the plantation régime supplied. Each white family served very much the function of a modern social settlement, setting patterns of orderly, well bred conduct which the negroes were encouraged to emulate; and the planters furthermore were vested with a coercive power, salutary in the premises, of which settlement workers are deprived. The very aristocratic nature of the system permitted a vigor of discipline which democracy cannot possess. On the whole the plantations were the best schools yet invented for the mass training of that sort of inert and backward people which the bulk of the American negroes represented. The lack of any regular provision for the discharge of pupils upon the completion of their training was, of course, a cardinal shortcoming which the laws of slavery imposed; but even in view of this, the slave plantation régime, after having wrought the initial and irreparable misfortune of causing the negroes to be imported, did at least as much as any system possible in the period could have done toward adapting the bulk of them to life in a civilized community.

2] Slavery as a Demoralizing and Brutalizing Force

a] LIMITS ADEQUATE TRAINING

.   .   .   .

THE BENEFIT to the African which is supposed to be incidental to American slavery, is confessedly proportionate to the degree in which he is forced into intercourse with a superior race and made subject to its example. Before I visited the South, I had believed that the advantages accruing from slavery, in this way, far outweighed the occasional cruelties, and other evils incidental to the system. I found, however, the mental and moral condition of the negroes, even in Virginia, and in those towns and districts containing the largest proportion of whites, much lower than I had anticipated, and as soon as I had an opportunity to examine one of the extensive plantations of the interior, although one inherited by its owner, and the home of a large and virtuous white family, I was satisfied that the advantages arising to the blacks from association with their white masters were very trifling, scarcely appreciable indeed, for the great majority of the field-hands. Even the overseer had barely acquaintance enough with the slaves individually, to call them by name; the owner could not determine with confidence if he were addressing one of his own chattels, by its features. Much less did the slaves have an opportunity to cultivate their minds by intercourse with other white people. Whatever of civilization, and of the forms, customs and shibboleths of Christianity they were acquiring by exam-

FROM Frederick Law Olmsted, *A Journey in the Back Country* (New York: Mason Brothers, 1860), pp. 70–72.

ple, and through police restraints might, it occurred to me, after all, but poorly compensate the effect of the systematic withdrawal from them of all the usual influences which tend to nourish the moral nature and develop the intellectual faculties, in savages as well as in civilized free men.

This doubt, as my northern friends well know, for I had habitually assumed the opposite, in all previous discussions of the slavery question, was unexpected and painful to me. I resisted it long, and it was not till I had been more than twelve months in the South with my attention constantly fixed upon the point that I ceased to suspect that the circumstances which brought me to it were exceptional and deceptive. It grew constantly stronger with every opportunity I had of observing the condition, habits and character of slaves whom I could believe to present fair examples of the working of the system with the majority of those subject to it upon the large plantations.

The laborers we see in towns, at work on railroads and steamboats, about stations and landings; the menials of our houses and hotels, are less respectable, moral and intelligent than the great majority of the whole laboring class of the North. The traveler at the South has to learn that there the reverse is the case to a degree which can hardly be sufficiently estimated. I have been obliged to think that many amiable travelers who have received impressions with regard to the condition of the slaves very different from mine, have failed to make a sufficient allowance for this. The rank-and-file plantation negroes are not to be readily made acquaintance with by chance or through letters of introduction.

. . . .

b] CRUSHES INDEPENDENT INTELLECTUAL DEVELOPMENT

. . . .

THE FREQUENT hearing of my mistress reading the Bible aloud, for she often read aloud when her husband was absent, awakened my curiosity in respect to this *mystery* of reading, and roused in me the desire to learn. Up to this time I had known nothing whatever of this wonderful art, and my ignorance and inexperience of what it could do for me, as well as my confidence in my mistress, emboldened me to ask her to teach me to read. With an unconsciousness and inexperience equal to my own, she readily consented, and in an incredibly short time, by her kind assistance, I had mastered the alphabet and could spell words of three or four letters. My mistress seemed almost as proud of my progress as if I had been her own child, and supposing that her husband would be as well pleased, she made no secret of what she was doing for me. Indeed, she exultingly told him of the aptness of her pupil, and of her intention to persevere in teaching me, as she felt her duty to do, at least to read the

FROM Frederick Douglass, *Life and Times of Frederick Douglass* (Hartford, Conn.: Park Publishing Co., 1882), pp. 69–75, 77–79, 119–21, 187.

Bible. And here arose the first dark cloud over my Baltimore prospects, the precursor of chilling blasts and drenching storms. Master Hugh was astounded beyond measure, and probably for the first time proceeded to unfold to his wife the true philosophy of the slave system, and the peculiar rules necessary in the nature of the case to be observed in the management of human chattels. Of course he forbade her to give me any further instruction, telling her in the first place that to do so was unlawful, as it was also unsafe; "for," said he, "if you give a nigger an inch he will take an ell. Learning will spoil the best nigger in the world. If he learns to read the Bible it will forever unfit him to be a slave. He should know nothing but the will of his master, and learn to obey it. As to himself, learning will do him no good, but a great deal of harm, making him disconsolate and unhappy. If you teach him how to read, he'll want to know how to write, and this accomplished, he'll be running away with himself." Such was the tenor of Master Hugh's oracular exposition; and it must be confessed that he very clearly comprehended the nature and the requirements of the relation of master and slave. His discourse was the first decidedly anti-slavery lecture to which it had been my lot to listen. Mrs. Auld evidently felt the force of what he said, and like an obedient wife, began to shape her course in the direction indicated by him. The effect of his words *on me* was neither slight nor transitory. His iron sentences, cold and harsh, sunk like heavy weights deep into my heart, and stirred up within me a rebellion not soon to be allayed. This was a new and special revelation, dispelling a painful mystery against which my youthful understanding had struggled, and struggled in vain, to wit, the white man's power to perpetuate the enslavement of the black man. "Very well," thought I. "Knowledge unfits a child to be a slave." I instinctively assented to the proposition, and from that moment I understood the direct pathway from slavery to freedom. It was just what I needed, and it came to me at a time and from a source whence I least expected it. Of course I was greatly saddened at the thought of losing the assistance of my kind mistress, but the information so instantly derived to some extent compensated me for the loss I had sustained in this direction. Wise as Mr. Auld was, he underrated my comprehension, and had little idea of the use to which I was capable of putting the impressive lesson he was giving to his wife. He wanted me to be a slave; I had already voted against that on the home plantation of Col. Lloyd. That which he most loved I most hated; and the very determination which he expressed to keep me in ignorance only rendered me the more resolute to seek intelligence. In learning to read, therefore, I am not sure that I do not owe quite as much to the opposition of my master as to the kindly assistance of my amiable mistress. I acknowledged the benefit rendered me by the one, and by the other, believing that but for my mistress I might have grown up in ignorance.

I lived in the family of Mr. Auld, at Baltimore, seven years, during which time, as the almanac makers say of the weather, my condition was variable. The most interesting feature of my history here, was my learning to read and write under somewhat marked disadvantages. In attaining this knowledge I was compelled to resort to indirections by no means congenial to my nature, and which were really humiliating to my sense of candor and uprightness. My mistress, checked in her benevolent designs toward me, not only ceased instructing me herself, but set her face as a flint against my learning to read by any means. . . . In ceasing to instruct me, my mistress had to seek to justify herself *to* herself, and once consenting to take sides in such a debate, she was compelled to hold her position. One needs little knowledge of moral philosophy to see where she inevitably landed. She finally became even more violent in her opposition to my learning to read than was Mr. Auld himself. Nothing now appeared to make her more angry than seeing me, seated in some nook or corner, quietly reading a book or newspaper. She would rush at me with the utmost fury, and snatch the book or paper from my hand, with something of the wrath and consternation which a traitor might be supposed to feel on being discovered in a plot by some dangerous spy. The conviction once thoroughly established in her mind, that education and slavery were incompatible with each other, I was most narrowly watched in all my movements. If I remained in a separate room from the family for any considerable length of time, I was sure to be suspected of having a book, and was at once called to give an account of myself. But this was too late: the first and never-to-be-retraced step had been taken. Teaching me the alphabet had been the "inch" given, I was now waiting only for the opportunity to "take the ell."

Filled with the determination to learn to read at any cost, I hit upon many expedients to accomplish that much desired end. The plan which I mainly adopted, and the one which was the most successful, was that of using my young white playmates, with whom I met on the streets, as teachers. I used to carry almost constantly a copy of Webster's spelling-book in my pocket, and when sent of errands, or when play-time was allowed me, I would step aside with my young friends and take a lesson in spelling. I am greatly indebted to these boys—Gustavus Dorgan, Joseph Bailey, Charles Farity, and William Cosdry.

· · · · · · · · · · ·

When I was about thirteen years old, and had succeeded in learning to read, every increase of knowledge, especially anything respecting the free states, was an additional weight to the almost intolerable burden of my thought—"*I am a slave for life.*" To my bondage I could see no end. It was a terrible reality, and I shall never be able to tell how sadly that thought chafed my young spirit. . . . I was no longer the light-hearted, gleesome boy, full of mirth and play, as when I landed in Baltimore. Light had penetrated the moral dungeon where I had lain, and I saw the bloody whip for my back, and the iron chain for my feet, and my *good kind* master, he was the author of my situation. The revelation haunted me, stung me, and made me gloomy and miserable. As I writhed under the sting and torment of this knowledge I almost envied my fellow slaves their stupid indifference. It opened my eyes to the horrible pit, and revealed the teeth of the frightful dragon that was ready to pounce upon me; but alas, it opened no way for my escape. I wished myself a beast, a bird, anything rather than a slave. I was wretched and gloomy beyond my ability to describe. This everlasting thinking distressed and tormented me; and yet there was no getting rid of this subject of my thoughts. Liberty, as the inestimable birthright of every man, converted every object into an asserter of this right. I heard it in every sound, and saw it in every object. It was ever present to torment me with a sense of my wretchedness. The more beautiful and charming were the smiles of nature, the more horrible and desolate was my condition. I saw nothing without seeing it, and I heard nothing without hearing it. I do not exaggerate when I say it looked at me in every star, it smiled in every calm, breathed in every wind, and moved in every storm. . . . My feelings were not the result of any marked cruelty in the treatment I received; they sprung from the consideration of my being a slave at all. It was *slavery,* not its mere *incidents* I hated. I had been cheated. I saw through the attempt to keep me in ignorance. I saw that slaveholders would have gladly made me believe that they were merely acting under the authority of God in making a slave of me and in making slaves of others, and I felt to them as to robbers and deceivers. The feeding and clothing me well could not atone for taking my liberty from me. The smiles of my mistress could not remove the deep sorrow that dwelt in my young bosom. Indeed, these came in time but to deepen my sorrow. She had changed, and the reader will see that I had changed too. We were both victims to the same overshadowing evil, *she* as mistress, I as slave. I will not censure her harshly.

.   .   .   .

[In 1833, Douglass was sent by Hugh Auld to his brother Thomas, who lived near St. Michaels, Maryland. Thomas, in turn, sent him to a nearby farmer, Edward Covey, "who enjoyed the reputation of being a first rate hand at breaking young negroes."]

If at any one time in my life, more than another, I was made to drink the bitterest dregs of slavery, that time was during the first six months of my stay with this man Covey. We were worked all weathers. It was never too hot, or too cold; it could never rain, blow, snow, or hail too hard for us to work in the field. Work, work, work, was scarcely more the order of the day than of the night. The longest days were too short for him, and the shortest nights were too long for him. I was somewhat unmanageable at the first, but a few months of this discipline tamed me. Mr. Covey succeeded in *breaking* me—in body, soul, and spirit. My natural elasticity was crushed; my intellect languished; the disposition to read departed, the cheerful spark that lingered about my eye died out; the dark night of slavery closed in upon me, and behold a man transformed to a brute!

Sunday was my only leisure time. I spent this in a sort of beast-like stupor, between sleeping and waking, under some large tree. At times I would rise up, a flash of energetic freedom would dart through my soul, accompanied with a faint beam of hope that flickered for a moment, and then vanished. I sank down again, mourning over my wretched condition.

I was sometimes tempted to take my life and that of Covey, but was prevented by a combination of hope and fear. My sufferings, as I remember them now, seem like a dream rather than a stern reality.

. . . .

I shall never be able to narrate half the mental experience through which it was my lot to pass, during my stay at Covey's. I was completely wrecked, changed, and bewildered; goaded almost to madness at one time, and at another, reconciling myself to my wretched condition. All the kindness I had received at Baltimore, all my former hopes and aspirations for usefulness in the world, and even the happy moments spent in the exercises of religion, contrasted with my then present lot, served but to increase my anguish.

I suffered bodily as well as mentally. I had neither sufficient time in which to eat, or to sleep, except on Sundays. The over-work, and the brutal chastisements of which I was the victim, combined with that ever-gnawing and soul-devouring thought—*"I am a slave—a slave for life—a slave with no rational ground to hope for freedom"*—rendered me a living embodiment of mental and physical wretchedness.

. . . .

To make a contented slave, you must make a thoughtless one. It is necessary to darken his moral and mental vision, and, as far as possible, to annihilate his power of reason. He must be able to detect no inconsistencies in slavery. The man who takes his earnings must be able to convince him that he has a perfect right to do so. It must not depend upon mere force: the slave must know no higher law than his master's will. The whole relationship must not only demonstrate to his mind its necessity, but its absolute rightfulness. If there be one crevice through which a single drop can fall, it will certainly rust off the slave's chain.

PART IV
Slavery
and Economic Development

INTRODUCTION

❪ IN 1860, the United States was still an agricultural nation with a primarily rural population. Nevertheless, important changes had already taken place which were ultimately to transform the nation. One such change was a revolution in transportation facilities. Westward expansion had been matched by the expansion of roads, riverboats, canals, and railroads, which linked new areas to old and made possible the development of a national market.[1] Adequate transportation lowered transfer costs and facilitated agricultural specialization and commercial crop production. The shift from self-sufficient to commercial farming, in turn, demanded new services, and a host of middlemen—bankers, merchants, storekeepers, and brokers—arose to meet the needs of internal trade. Old cities in the East expanded and new towns and cities in the West mushroomed as the agricultural produce flowed to areas best able to function as trading and distribution centers.

Industrial changes kept in pace with the revolutions in transportation and agriculture. By 1860, water and steam power were commonplace in the factories and mills producing cotton and woolen textiles, shoes and clothing, machinery and iron, flour and meal, and a multitude of other commodities.

In short, on the eve of the Civil War, the United States was well on its way to becoming a modern industrial power. Limitations on economic growth had been in large part overcome; the growth rate was high and the future promised continued expansion. In W. W. Rostow's words, the United States had made the "take-off into self-sustained growth." [2]

The South, however, did not share fully in these revolutionary changes. The region experienced little of the upsurge in manufacturing in the decades before the Civil War. Measured in terms of the value of the finished product, well over 90 percent of the wool, between 85 and 90 percent of the cotton, and over 75 percent of the flour and meal manufacturing took place in northern plants and mills in 1860, even though the South had about 35 percent of the nation's population. Other statistics of manufacturing development tell the same story: less than 10 percent of the nation's manufacturing capital was invested in the South in 1860; only about 8 percent of the country's manufactured goods (measured by value) came from the South.

Reflecting the changes in the American economy in the decades before the Civil War was the growth of the urban population. Here too, the South lagged. The proportion of its population considered urban (2,500 or more) fell far behind that of New England and the

[1] An important work dealing with the period is George Rogers Taylor's *The Transportation Revolution, 1815–1860* (New York: Holt, Rinehart & Winston, 1951).

[2] See his *The Stages of Economic Growth* (Cambridge, Eng.: The University Press, 1960).

Middle Atlantic States (which were centers of industrial development during this period). But even more significant, for comparative purposes, is the fact that the urbanization of the Middle West exceeded that of the entire South. A list of the fifteen largest cities in the country in 1860 contains only one southern city—New Orleans—and even in that city only 3 percent of the population earned its living in manufacturing. This may be compared with 9.5 percent in New York, 17.5 percent in Philadelphia, and from the West, 18.3 percent in Cincinnati and 4.9 percent in Chicago.

The backward nature of southern manufacturing was matched by the lag in its commerce and transportation. The most important of the nation's exports came from the South, but the shipping, banking, insurance, and other services required for the marketing and financing of the South's staple crops were largely in the hands of northerners. And southern railroad construction fell far behind that of the North, as did telegraphic communication.

Thus, while the rest of the country was experiencing economic growth, the South remained undeveloped or backward economically. Largely self-sufficient agriculture occupied the energies of the majority of its population; commercial production was primarily agricultural and "foreign"-trade oriented, that is, intended mainly for export to other sections of the country or abroad. Rich natural resources remained undeveloped; production techniques were primitive and technological innovation was slight.

Many reasons have been suggested to explain the South's failure to maintain the pace of the nation's growth in the ante-bellum period, but none has been so consistently advanced and debated as that of slavery. Investment in slaves is said to have absorbed capital which otherwise would have been available for investment in manufacturing and trade. Slave labor has been described as inefficient and lacking in adaptability, thereby limiting production and blocking diversification. Moreover, it has been argued, slavery was the heart of a system supporting a political and social order which discouraged innovation and diversification and left control of the section in the hands of a narrow-minded, undemocratic oligarchy which blocked change in order to protect its investment in human beings.

Each of these, and the many other accusations leveled against the South's peculiar institution, have been ardently disputed. The South's economic woes have been traced to causes other than slavery. Contemporaries often blamed the tariff for draining cash from the South to support northern industry. Some have argued that the blessings of nature turned out to be a curse: soil and climate combined to fasten agriculture on the section to the detriment of industrial and commercial development; an extensive river system seemed to make canals and railroads less necessary, and hence the South was denied the economic stimulation arising from the construction and operation of these enterprises. Another argument advanced the thesis that the South chose economic backwardness because its people valued the agrarian over the industrial life.

The readings which follow are designed to illustrate the debate over the effect of slavery on southern economic development. The opinions of both contemporary observers and modern scholars are represented.

Economic historian Robert R. Russel admits that slavery had certain retarding effects, but he argues that, for the most part, the South's economic development lagged for reasons quite apart from slavery. The second selection is from an article by J. D. B. De Bow. The founder (in 1846) and editor of the *Commercial Review of the South and Southwest* (known popularly as *De Bow's Review*), De Bow was an articulate and persistent advocate of southern economic development. In the selection reprinted here, as well as in literally hundreds of other articles, De Bow decries southern economic backwardness, but he finds its cause in the misguided emphasis on agriculture resulting in the neglect of commerce and manufacturing. Slavery, for De Bow, is irrelevant.

In 1855, David Christy published his influential *Cotton Is King*. The title was a slogan for those who felt that the economic well-being of the entire country, indeed, of the western world, rested upon the South's chief staple crop. In the second section, a part of this argument is reprinted. Christy finds slavery to be the single most important stimulus for economic development. He shifts the emphasis, however, from South to North and concludes that northern industrial and commercial prosperity was built and supported by the products of slavery.

Alleged economic disadvantages of slavery are presented in the third section. The first two selections were written by contemporaries, Hinton Rowan Helper, a North Carolina white farmer, and J. E. Cairnes, a Scottish economist. Helper's book, *The Impending Crisis of the South* (1857), was a violent attack on slavery. Coming from the pen of a native southerner, the book had an enormous influence, in part because of the support and publicity given it by the Republican Party. Helper argues that the South lagged behind the North in every conceivable way—including agriculture—and he finds slavery to be the sole cause of this lag. For him, slavery is not simply an economic problem; it is political as well, allowing what he calls a "conceited and tyrannical" minority—the

rich planters—to rule the South. Cairnes' book, *The Slave Power* (1862), was a sharply reasoned attack on slavery from the vantage point of classical economics. Cairnes finds slave labor to be ignorant and inefficient and blames the slave system for what he considers the South's chief economic ills—one-crop production, soil exhaustion, and an unequal distribution of wealth.

The last two selections in the third section are by modern historians of the South. Fabian Linden maintains that the planter class blocked the development of manufacturing in the South because it feared that industrialization would undermine slavery, while Eugene D. Genovese argues that slavery was responsible for a shallow market in the South which prevented the development of large-scale, local production.

In evaluating these essays the reader should be aware of one basic assumption underlying all the points of view presented: the ante-bellum South lagged behind the North in economic development. This, of course, raises the question of the meaning of economic development. What measures of economic development do each of the writers seem to use, and how valid are these measurements?

A number of other questions should also be asked of the readings. Do those authors who claim that slavery retarded economic growth in the South clearly distinguish those elements in the southern economy which existed because of slavery and those which were unrelated to slavery? Or do they assume (or prove) that slavery was of such overwhelming importance that it affected all aspects of the section's economy? On the other hand, do those who find that southern problems arose from other factors prove that slavery had no part in creating or perpetuating these other factors?

THE READINGS

1] Irrelevance of Slavery to Southern Development

a] Problems of an Agricultural Economy

MANY WRITERS have made sweeping generalizations as to the effects, allegedly injurious, of Negro slavery upon the economic progress of the South. It is believed that many time-honored generalizations about the subject are incorrect. The economics of slavery as expounded by the abolitionists, especially the English economist, J. E. Cairnes, seemed to triumph on the battlefield. Such views have subsequently been accepted too implicitly not only in the North but even in the South. It is proposed to examine anew several widely-accepted generalizations.

Slavery is still being blamed for the wasteful and unscientific methods of farming practiced in the South before the Civil War. The authors of two popular college textbooks in the economic history of the United States both quote a table of statistics found in Ezra C. Seaman's *Essays on the Progress of Nations,* published in 1868, which compares the "free" and the "slave" states in respect to number of acres of improved and unimproved land in farms in 1860 and the total value and the average value per acre of farm lands. The comparison shows inferiority of the slave states in all respects; and the writers leave the impression that slavery was the cause. One author says:

> A second condition which made slavery possible and profitable was an abundance of new land. . . . If land anywhere became scarce and dear, slavery tended to disappear. Intensive and scientific methods of farming were seldom possible under the indifferent and wasteful slave system. Consequently, the colonial method was persisted in, of cropping a tract of land until it was exhausted and then moving on to a fresh piece.

As a matter of fact, "skinning" the soil was practiced in all sections of the country. It was as common in most districts of the North as it was in the South. It was at least as common in the small-farm belts of the South as in the plantation districts. The preponderant reason was the same everywhere, namely, the cheapness of land. It was cheaper to acquire and clear a new farm of virgin soil than it was to restore, or even maintain, the fertility of the old. Contributory reasons were inertness and ignorance;

FROM Robert R. Russel, "The General Effects of Slavery upon Southern Economic Progress," *Journal of Southern History,* IV (February, 1938), 34–54. Copyright 1938 by the Southern Historical Association. Reprinted by permission of the Managing Editor.

but the want of initiative and knowledge was not as great among planters as among small farmers. The best farming in the South was done by planters, many of whom took keen interest in agricultural reform and experimental methods and farmed in an intensive manner. In general, however, before the Civil War, it was only in the vicinity of cities, where land became dear by reason of its demand for special purposes, such as dairying and truck gardening, that much attention was given to manuring, fertilizing, and crop rotation. Speaking by and large, Southern soils— except rich bottom lands—wore out more rapidly than Northern. Cotton did not exhaust the soil as rapidly as grain crops; tobacco was hard on the soil. But the land is nearly everywhere rolling or hilly, the soil is generally lighter than in the North, the greater part of the section lacks good native grasses, which would check erosion on lands retired from cultivation, and there are more heavy, dashing rains. Consequently there was much more soil erosion in the South.

There was nothing inherent in slavery that prevented the adoption of more scientific methods of agriculture. A planter could direct his slaves to spread manure, cotton seed, or marl, to plow horizontally on the hill-sides, to avoid shallow tillage, and to pile brush in incipient gullies. The small farmer might do such things himself, but he was less likely to do them than the planter was to have them done.

Slavery may have retarded the adoption of improved agricultural machinery. At any rate, the proposition is true that employers will hesitate to entrust expensive and complicated machinery to careless, irresponsible, and incompetent workmen. On the other hand, large farmers, other things being equal, are abler and more likely to adopt improved machinery than small farmers. The small farmers of the South certainly made no better record in this regard than the planters. Cotton growers were not slow to adopt the cotton gin, one of the most revolutionary pieces of agricultural machinery in our history. Sugar-making machinery was complicated and expensive. Southern planters adopted the various improvements in the plow as the improved plows could be had. They rapidly substituted horses and mules for the slow-moving oxen when they were found to be better adapted to their purposes. In fact, the ox was displaced more slowly in New England than in other sections of the country, including the South.

There is only a modicum of truth in the assertion, which still finds its way into print, that slavery inspired a contempt for physical labor among the white people of the South, and thereby rendered the section a great economic disservice. Slavery, or the presence of Negroes, which was the result of slavery, may properly be credited with responsibility for the idea universally prevalent in districts with considerable black population that whites must not perform *menial* services, that is, such personal services for others as cooking, washing, scrubbing, and attendance as maids or valets. Originally, perhaps, whites shunned the performance of such services simply because of their menial character. Because whites shunned them, they were the more readily assigned to Negroes; and the more blacks were thus employed, the more odious to whites such tasks became. But, although slavery may have excluded whites from menial services, it does not follow that whites were deprived of productive employment on that account.

Slavery and Negroes may also have bred the idea in slaveholding regions that people who could afford to own or hire servants should not perform their own domestic tasks, much as generations of low wages for household servants in England have established the idea that no woman of the middle class or above may do her own housework, at least not without a servant or two about for the sake of appearances. It was indeed true that families in slaveholding regions began to employ domestic servants at a lower income level than was the case in nonslaveholding districts. In so far as slavery was responsible for this, the institution rendered the South an economic disservice to the extent that it caused a greater degree of idleness than existed among similar classes in other sections—provided that such leisure is not to be considered economically desirable. But it should not be overlooked, in this connection, that mistresses on all but the largest plantations had heavy responsibilities in supervising servants in various household manufactures, in looking after the sick, in teaching the children, and in many other concerns.

There was no stigma attached in the South in slavery days to the performance of manual labor, as distinguished from menial, or of any other sort of labor not considered menial. There were *situations,* however, in which whites would not work with slaves, just as now there are situations in which whites will not work with Negroes. White wage earners, except perhaps immigrants who had not yet learned to draw the line, would not labor on a plantation under an overseer. They would, however, work with slaves if there was some evident distinction in tasks or status. A white farmer and his sons had no repugnance to working along with their own or hired slaves at any task required on the farm. White hired men, too, would work with the farmer and his slaves. A farmer's wife and daughters might not work in the fields with slaves, but the women folk of non-slaveholding whites were about as likely to work in the fields as were Northern women similarly circumstanced. In both sections, as in England, women were withdrawn from the fields as standards of living rose. An overseer on a plantation was not supposed to do physical labor, even if so inclined; to do so, it was thought, and no doubt correctly, would be detrimental to discipline. A foreman who had charge of a small group of slaves on a farm or a small plantation—and there were many such—was expected to work along with the slaves. A large planter and his sons might not engage in physical labor; to do so would lower them in the esteem of their neighbors and slaves. It is difficult to say whether slavery was responsible for this pleasing fancy or only made it more possible to humor it. English country gentlemen and their sons likewise eschewed manual labor, and Northern millowners did not as a rule send their sons into the mills as hands. Furthermore, even planters who employed overseers usually had their time well-occupied with the management of their plantations, and their management was economically more productive than wielding the plow or hoe would have been.

The same situation obtained in the cities and towns of the South. In factories, mills, and shops, and about the wharves, white laborers, free Negroes, and slaves, sometimes of both sexes, worked side by side, usually, but not always, with some distinction of tasks. Frequently the whites objected to working with Negroes and sought to have them excluded from certain employments, but never successfully. The opposition arose partly from race prejudice and partly from dislike of Negro competition. In the North, where Negro laborers were relatively few, the opposition of whites to Negro competition was more effective. It would seem unlikely that many whites were deprived of useful employment by their disinclination to work with Negroes or to labor at certain tasks commonly performed by slaves.

Southern people in general were more inclined than those in the East and Northwest to dislike physical labor, especially heavy physical labor, and to seek "white-collar" jobs or to live by their wits. The evidence on this point is overwhelming. But it does not follow that slavery was the cause of this difference. A similar variance in other places and in other times has commonly been explained by differences in temperature, humidity, ease of making a living, eating and drinking habits, general health, cultural antecedents, and social organization. If such explanations are valid for other places and other times, they are equally valid for the United States in slavery times.

A more difficult question with regard to the general economic effects of slavery is whether or not the institution retarded the growth of population of the slaveholding states. If so, it was a grievous fault; for economic history shows that increase in population in a region has been conducive to the development of improved means of transportation, the commercialization of agriculture and manufactures, and the extension of the factory system—developments which, with all their evils, have contributed to economic progress.

At the close of the colonial period the six commonwealths which continued to permit slavery and to colonize new "slave" territory, that is, Delaware, Maryland, Virginia, the two Carolinas, and Georgia, together with Louisiana, Florida, and Texas, had a slightly greater population than the seven states to the north which shortly became "free." In 1860 there were eighteen free and fifteen slave states. According to the census for that year the former had a population of 18,800,527, the latter, 12,315,374. Wherein lies the explanation? We can not now detect any differences in the birth and death rates of the two sections.

For one thing, the number of people of Southern birth who migrated to the North was much greater than the number of people of Northern birth who moved to the South. In 1850 there were 608,626 people of Southern birth living in free states and only 199,672 people born in free states residing in the South. The corresponding numbers for 1860 were 713,527 and 371,421. In 1860 there were, by careful estimate, about 800,000 more people of Southern birth and parentage living in free territory than there were people of Northern stock living in slaveholding regions. This accounts, then, for approximately 1,600,000 of the 6,500,000 disparity in population between sections.

This large net loss to the South in intersectional migration, in turn, is to be explained almost wholly by the circumstances of the westward movement of population during the period and the various conditions and political maneuvers that determined which of the new states beyond the mountains should be free and which slave. The old story of thousands of small farmers from the South fleeing across the Ohio River to escape slavery is almost pure fiction. People from the older states moved west with various motives, the principal one being the acquisition of land. They usually followed the most available routes. Before the railroads were built, great numbers of people from Virginia and Maryland went up the Potomac Valley, crossed over to the Ohio River, using the Cumberland National Road after it had been built, floated down the Ohio, and eventually found homes in Kentucky and the southern parts of Ohio, Indiana, and Illinois, or beyond the Mississippi in Missouri, Arkansas, and Iowa. Many other people from Maryland, Virginia, and North Carolina crossed the Blue Ridge by various routes, picked up the trail in the Great Valley, and followed it down into Tennessee or turned off and went through Cumberland Gap into Kentucky. Thousands of Kentuckians and Tennesseeans in turn, of the first, second, or later generations, moved on west or northwest into southern Indiana, southern Illinois, Missouri, Arkansas, and, in less numbers, into Iowa and southwestern Wisconsin. Only slaveholders who wished to take their slaves with them were debarred from choosing a location north of the Ohio; scores of slaveholders, in fact, did take their slaves into Indiana and Illinois under life or other long-term indentures permitted by the early laws. Of the 608,626 natives of the South living in 1850 in free states, 505,096 resided in the four states of Ohio, Indiana, Illinois, and Iowa, and of the latter number 462,088 had been born in Virginia, Maryland, North Carolina, Kentucky, and Tennessee. The corresponding numbers for 1860 were 713,527, 530,843, and 481,322, respectively.

Many thousands of people from Pennsylvania and, to a less extent, from New York and New Jersey, crossed to the Ohio River, floated down that stream, and eventually settled on the left bank in Kentucky or crossed the Mississippi into Missouri. Other thousands settled first on the right bank of the Ohio, and then later, they or their children moved on into Kentucky or, especially, Missouri. Of the 371,421 people born in free states but living in 1860 in slave states, 208,059 were to be found in Missouri and Kentucky. Northerners certainly did not shun Missouri. In 1860 there were 166,620 people living there who had been born on free soil and 274,572 who had been born in other slave states. There was also a large interchange of population across the line between Pennsylvania and New Jersey on the one side and Virginia, Maryland, and Delaware on the other; 49,827 people born north of the line were living south of it in 1860, and 50,958 born south of it were living on the other side. There was much less exchange of population between New England and the Great Lakes region on the one hand and the Lower South on the other. But such exchange did occur. Thousands of Yankees undeterred by slavery went south to farm, work in mills, run steamboats, buy cotton, sell merchandise, teach school, and fill all manner of other jobs which became available. There were many more Northerners scattered about the Lower South than there were people from the latter region residing in the Upper North. In 1860 there were 12,549 natives of New England living in the seven cotton states and only 2,169 people from the cotton states to be found in New England.

The other important cause of the disparity of population between the North and the South in 1860 was the fact that the former had received much the greater share of the foreign immigration. In 1860 there were 3,582,999 people of foreign birth living in free states and the territories and only 553,176 in the slave states. In 1850 the numbers had been 1,900,325 and 310,514. Why did not the slave states get a larger share of the immigrants? The blame has often been unjustly placed upon slavery.

Most of the immigrants in ante-bellum days, as since, landed at New York City, for that was the principal terminus of the trans-Atlantic packet lines and, after their advent, the steamship lines. Many remained in New York; the majority scattered to various parts of the country. Most numerous among the immigrants after 1845 (about the time the tide of immigration set in strongly) were the Irish. They were poor and sought work for wages. They found it chiefly in the cities and factory towns and in railroad and canal construction. The cities and mill towns were mainly in the East, and the railroads and canals were being built mostly there and in the Northwest. A considerable number of Irishmen found work building Southern railroads and many were employed at the wharves of New Orleans and other Southern towns. They showed no great prejudice against slavery or against Negroes.

Next most numerous among immigrants were Germans. They usually had more means than the Irish, and a larger proportion of them went to the growing Northwest, acquired land, and grew grain and raised livestock. They undoubtedly disliked slavery. But they would have preferred the Northwest even if slavery had not been in the picture. There they could get excellent land at the minimum government price located in districts which were being rapidly opened to markets by the building of railroads. They could practice a type of farming more like that of the old country. And acclimation was less difficult than in the South. Thousands of Germans went to the quasi-slave state of Missouri where land and farming were quite like those of states of the Northwest. And a considerable number were lured to the rich, cheap lands of Texas to grow cotton and grain. Few of them acquired slaves, partly because they disliked slavery and partly because they could not afford to purchase them.

It would seem, then, to be a safe conclusion that neither slavery nor the presence of Negroes was in any direct sense responsible for the failure of the slaveholding states as a whole to grow as rapidly in population as the free states as a whole between 1790 and 1860. No doubt thousands of individuals were deterred from going South by race prejudice, dislike of slavery, or a disinclination to compete with slaves for jobs. But, since so many others were undeterred by such motives and considerations, it is reasonable to suppose that, if economic opportunities had been great enough, people would have come in greater numbers from the North and from Europe to seize upon them.

This conclusion is further justified by events which have occurred since slavery was abolished. The percentage of immigrants locating in the South has been even less than it was in slavery days. For example, in 1890 only 8.3 per cent of the foreign born of this country lived in the South whereas 13.4 per cent had lived there in 1860. Now it is possible that it has been the presence of the Negro, a resultant of slavery, which has repelled. But it is highly probable that it has been the comparative lack of economic opportunities in the South, still suffering from the ravages of war for much of the period. Many whites and blacks have gone North to get jobs, especially during the great boom prior to 1929. Moreover, the presence of Negroes has not kept Northerners out of particular localities or particular occupations in the South where opportunities have called.

The conclusion just stated brings up another question which has caused historians much trouble, namely, to what extent, if at all, was slavery responsible for the comparative dearth of economic opportunities in the South which, in turn, kept the population from growing more rapidly? In agriculture slavery reduced opportunities somewhat for nonslaveholding whites but not for the population as a whole. Because of it the white farm population was probably less than it would otherwise have been, but the total farm population was greater. And, be it noted, when writers say that slavery retarded the growth of the population of the South, they mean total population, not white population only.

The story is briefly this: The staple crops of the South gave the incentive for men of enterprise to engage in large-scale agriculture. Land was plentiful and cheap. The labor problem was more difficult. People of good-enough quality would not work for low-enough wages, in large-enough numbers, and with sufficient regularity in a country where it was so easy to get land and farm independently. The solution was first found in indentured servants, and the earliest plantations were developed with that class of labor. As time passed Negro slaves were preferred, great numbers were imported, they throve and multiplied, and many farmers developed into planters.

Although a time did not arrive when more than about one third of the agricultural population of the South, including the Negroes, lived on plantations as distinguished from small farms, the great bulk of the staple crops came to be produced on plantations—all the sugar and rice, most of the tobacco, and at least three fourths of the cotton. There were several reasons for this. In the production of sugar and rice, which required considerable capital, small farmers could not compete with planters and were crowded out. The competitive advantages of the plantation in the growing of cotton and tobacco were not so great, if, indeed, there were any. But planters held slaves for the primary purpose of producing staples for market; they would not have kept slaves had it not been for this motive. Small farmers, on the contrary, were under no particular urge to engage in commercialized agriculture. They might make a better living by doing general or subsistence farming. Slaves were better adapted to the routine of the plantation than they were to the more varied tasks of general farming with considerable household manufacturing. Also, as a class, the planters were more enterprising and they were better managers than the small farmers; the more ambitious and capable of the small farmers were likely to graduate into the planter class. So planters got the better lands, near enough to transportation facilities to justify staple agriculture, while small farmers had cheaper, but not necessarily poorer, lands more remote from the routes of commerce and followed a more self-sufficing economy or, if they remained in the plantation belts, lived on the poorer lands and practiced a more general agriculture than their planter neighbors.

If slavery had not existed in the South and, consequently, there had been few or no plantations, it is reasonable to presume that the lands which were in fact in plantations would have been held by the more capable small farmers, who would have raised staples although in somewhat smaller quantities than they were actually produced. In that case the white farm population of the South would have been greater than it actually was, but not as great as the actual farm population, both white and black.

But immigrants into the North after 1790 went largely into nonagricultural occupations. To what extent, if at all, was slavery responsible for the backwardness of the South in other lines of economic development than agriculture? Manufacturing may be selected for consideration, since, next to agriculture, it is the most fundamental industry.

Even in colonial times the Southern commonwealths did less manufacturing in proportion to population than did the Northern. In the middle period, as the industrial revolution proceeded, the South did a smaller and smaller percentage of the nation's manufacturing. In 1860 the capital invested in manufacturing in the South was only 9.5 per cent of the capital so invested in the entire country; and the number of hands employed was only 8.4 per cent of the nation's total. Moreover, nearly one half of Southern manufactures consisted of flour and grist, lumber, and turpentine, products of simple operations.

A number of reasons may be advanced to account for the industrial backwardness of the South, few of which have much relevance to slavery. In colonial times in the tidewater region, the continued and anticipated profits of staple agriculture, together with the superior adaptability of slaves thereto, made it unnecessary and unprofitable to do much household and shop manufacturing. In the Northern colonies and the back country of the South, the lack of markets for agricultural products constrained the people to do more manufacturing. A combination of factors—the abundance of white pine, water power near the sea, the demand for ships and boats for the fisheries and the carrying trade, markets for lumber in the same regions where the fish were marketed—caused lumbering and shipbuilding to be concentrated largely along the New England coast. In a similar fashion other special factors caused various other branches of manufacturing to be more or less concentrated in the North.

When the Industrial Revolution reached the United States, population was comparatively sparse in the South, distances were great, and means of transportation poor. The poorer whites afforded little demand for manufactured goods. Neither did the slaves, but the masters, who exploited their labor, presumably compensated for them in this regard. So markets were too dispersed and inadequate to encourage large-scale manufacturing. The population of the East was more compact and, therefore, transportation facilities could be provided at lower cost. The purchasing power of the people was greater.

The streams of the South were less manageable for power than were those of the East. Southern power sites were relatively inaccessible to natural avenues of transportation; in New England, especially, considerable power was available very near the sea.

The principal Southern raw material, cotton, was not at all bulky and would stand transportation to distant markets. The humid atmosphere of the New England seaboard was advantageous to cotton mills. For lumbering the North possessed much the same advantages over the South in the middle period that it had possessed in the colonial. Even before coal came to be used in smelting, parts of Pennsylvania had an advantage over other regions of the country in ironmaking by reason of the juxtaposition of wood, ore, and limestone in localities near navigable rivers or other means of transportation. When coal superseded charcoal the advantage of Pennsylvania was enhanced. To illustrate, in the days of charcoal furnaces a considerable secondary iron industry was developed in Richmond, Virginia, which used pig iron smelted in the back country and brought down the James River. After smelting with anthracite was well developed in eastern Pennsylvania, about 1850, the Richmond iron works procured their pig iron there and the back country furnaces died out. The principal iron ore field of the South, near present Birmingham, Alabama, was in ante-bellum days all but inaccessible. The Pittsburgh field, by way of contrast, lay at the head of a magnificent system of inland waterways transportation. After railroads penetrated northern Georgia, northern Alabama, and eastern Tennessee, during the fifties, numbers of small furnaces and foundries sprang up, but they could not compete with those of Pennsylvania except in the local markets.

In the East, where there had been more household and shop industry, and much manufacturing done under the "putting out" system, there were more laborers to be diverted to mills and factories when they came in. The opening of improved means of communication with the fine farming regions of western New York and the Northwest brought destructive competition to Eastern agriculture, released still more men, women, and children to become mill hands, and supplied them with food and raw materials. In the South the continued profitableness of staple agriculture prevented slaveowners from turning to manufacturing or diverting their slaves thereto. Although slaves were frequently used successfully in mills, factories, and shops, in fact in practically every mechanical pursuit, they were certainly not as well adapted to mechanical employments as to agriculture. It was difficult to transform the small, independent, self-sufficing farmers of the South into urban wage earners.

Capital for industry in the East had come from the profits of merchandising and shipping as well as from the profits of industry. In the South there was no considerable source of capital outside manufacturing itself. The profits of agriculture, such as they were, were absorbed in expanding agriculture and providing facilities for transportation. If the section had offered exceptional opportunities, capital and labor would have been diverted from agriculture or would have flowed in from the outside, but such was not the case. Once the North had gained a good start upon the South in manufacturing, it became harder for the latter to make progress. For then infant industries in the South would have to get started in the face of unrestricted competition from firmly established industries in the North.

Of the various reasons enumerated for the backwardness of the South in manufacturing, only one relates directly to slavery. Slave labor was not so well adapted to manufacturing as to agriculture, and, therefore, other things being equal, slaveowners preferred to keep their slaves engaged in the latter. A second reason for which slavery has frequently been blamed may relate indirectly to the institution, namely, a dearth of capital for investment. It becomes necessary, therefore, to ascertain what effects, if any, slavery had upon saving and investment in the South.

Slavery, as we have seen, made possible the development of large-scale farming. By all the rules of economic history the planters should have saved much for investment in further productive enterprises; it is the people with the larger incomes who do most of the saving for investment. The planters did save. They saved more than their small-farmer neighbors did. They saved enough to keep expanding their agricultural operations. They provided much of the capital for internal improvements and other productive undertakings. But the fact remains that they did not save as much for investment as might logically be expected of them.

Many of the planters, especially those of old families, did not have steady habits and frugal instincts. They often had visions of grandeur inherited from spacious colonial days and reinforced by real or fancied descent from English aristocracy. At any rate, planters who were making money, and often those who were losing it, lived well. They built big houses. Their habitations were literally overrun by domestic servants. They bought luxuries. Those with the largest incomes frequently spent their substance at Northern watering places or in European travel. How slavery could have been responsible for these enlarged views it is impossible to see, except, of course, that it was slavery that made it possible to indulge them.

Again, planters' savings were diminished by the almost universal practice of living and operating not upon the income from the preceding crop but upon the anticipated income from the next crop; that is, they lived largely upon advances received from their factors upon contemplated or growing crops as security. These advances cost dearly. They cost not only interest but also the reduced prices which they occasioned, for the markets were frequently glutted and prices depressed because so many planters were under the necessity of selling their crops as soon as harvested in order to pay their debts. This practice of obtaining advances upon anticipated crops would not have prevented, it might even have facilitated, the accumulation of capital in the South, if the advances had been made by Southern men. But they were not. They were made in last analysis by Northern or British firms. Even if the planter eschewed advances from his cotton factor, the result was much the same, for in that case he bought supplies on long credit from his merchant who in turn had bought them on long credit from Northern jobbers or wholesalers. It would be difficult to name anything more efficacious in preventing the accumulation of capital than eight, ten, or fifteen per cent interest, often compounded.

This system of advances was caused partly by the lack of habits of thrift, already bemoaned. Its principal cause was the speculative character of a commercialized agriculture with distant markets. A farmer who produces for market is always under strong temptation to borrow money, get more land and hands, and put out a larger acreage, because there is always the possibility of raising a bumper crop and selling it at top prices. Nature is not consistent. There is always the prospect in any community of having a big crop while there is a total or partial failure elsewhere, with consequent high prices and big income for those who dwell in the favored community. Farmers gamble on the big year. Such speculation has by no means been confined to slaveowners and cotton growers. It has been as evident in nonslaveholding regions as in slaveholding—the wheat belt for instance. Slavery only made it possible for some farmers to gamble on a bigger scale.

Another thing, closely related to the factor just mentioned, which militated against the accumulation of capital in the South was the occasional overproduction of the staples. Within a few decades after the invention of the gin, the cotton states were producing over three fourths of the cotton sold in the world's markets. A big crop in the South sent the price down, a small crop sent it up. It happened more than once that a smaller crop of cotton at a high price brought in a larger aggregate amount to the growers than a large crop at a low price. But constant pleas to grow less cotton and more corn fell on deaf ears. In the cases of tobacco, sugar, and rice, the American crop was such a small part of the world's total that its quantity had comparatively little effect on world prices, and, therefore, there could be overproduction in the South, considered alone, only in the sense that labor and capital might more profitably have been directed into other channels. A chief reason for the overproduction of staples, when it occurred, was the speculative character of commercialized agriculture just noted. Slavery did not supply the urge to speculate, but it made speculation possible on a larger scale and thus contributed to overproduction. In general, of course, it was to the advantage of the South to produce great crops of cotton and other staples. Occasional overproduction was preferable to consistent underproduction. And without slavery there probably would have been consistent underproduction during the period under consideration.

It has frequently been stated that slavery "absorbed" capital in the South which otherwise might have been used in productive enterprises. Such a statement needs much qualification if it is not to be misleading. While the foreign slave trade lasted, part of the profits of Southern industry went to Yankee skippers, English lords, Dahomey chiefs, etc., in exchange for slaves. Thus capital which might have been used to build sawmills or ships or for other productive purposes in the South was "fixed" in the form of slaves. Capital could not be taken out of the South by the internal or domestic slave trade, however. To illustrate, suppose Mississippi cotton planters, out of the profits of the industry, bought Virginia slaves. The slaves would still be in the South and presumably capable of paying for themselves and providing a reasonable profit on the investment. The savings of the planters would still be in the South also, although in Virginia instead of Mississippi, and, presumably, could be invested in factories, railroads, and other productive enterprises. They in turn might attract labor from the North or from Europe. Suppose, however, the Mississippi planters were able to hire free-born Virginians to come down and work their plantations and, instead of buying slaves, invested their savings in sawmills in their own state, employing workers attracted from the North or from Europe to operate the sawmills. The South as a whole would lose no laborers and no savings in this case, but Virginia would have been to the trouble and expense of rearing workers until they had reached maturity only to see them go away to contribute to the prosperity of another state. Thus slavery did not absorb Southern capital in any direct sense; it affected the distribution of capital within the section. The mere capitalization of the anticipated labor of a particular class did not destroy or diminish any other kind of property.

But in an indirect way slavery may have had the effect of absorbing capital nevertheless. Take the case of the Virginia tobacco planters and the Mississippi cotton planters again. The Virginians probably received considerably more for their slaves than they had invested in rearing them, for the supply of slaves was not adjusted to demand and prices were normally considerably in excess of costs of production. And probably, instead of investing their profits in productive enterprises, the Virginians used them for living expenses, not having produced enough on their worn-out tobacco plantations to maintain their accustomed style of living. Thus as a consequence of slavery the profitable cotton industry of Mississippi might be carrying along the incubus of an unprofitable tobacco industry in Virginia or at least enabling tobacco planters there to live in a style not justified by their earned incomes. Under a free-labor system this would hardly have been possible. But, on the other hand, if it had not been for slavery, cotton growers of Mississippi might not have had any savings to invest.

In conclusion, the importance of Negro slavery as a factor determining the character and extent of the economic development of the South has been greatly overestimated. It brought a racial element into the population which would not otherwise have been represented in any considerable numbers. The importation of slaves and the increase of the Negro population gave the South a larger total population, at any date, than it otherwise would have had, but no doubt retarded the growth of the white population. Slavery made possible the widespread development of the plantation system of farming and, thereby, gave a great impetus to the growing of the various Southern staples. This was beneficial to the South on the whole, although there was occasional overproduction, to which slavery contributed. Slavery may have retarded the diversification of Southern industry. It was conducive to the accumulation of capital on the whole, although it had the serious disadvantage of permitting more productive districts to contribute to the livelihood of the people of less productive regions. But compared with such great economic factors as climate, topography, natural resources, location with respect to the North and to Europe, means of transportation, and character of the white population, Negro slavery was of lesser consequence in determining the general course of Southern economic development.

b] NEGLECT OF COMMERCE AND MANUFACTURING

·   ·   ·   ·   ·   ·   ·   ·   ·   ·   ·   ·   ·

IN LOOKING into the history of the south and southwest since the earliest settlement, we find that the almost entire labor of the country has been applied to agriculture, and that the surplus products have been, up to within a few years past, almost entirely shipped to foreign markets. The country seems to have labored under the impression that wealth could be acquired only by drawing it from other countries. Acting upon this principle, they have gone on from year to year producing cotton, tobacco, and grain for exportation, until their best lands have become exhausted, and they find themselves as poor in all the appliances of comfort as they were many years past. The price of the crops being returned to the country in articles of daily consumption, the proceeds of each year's crop is consumed without leaving any thing to be added to the wealth of the community; and the only increase to be found in the elements or means to procure wealth, consists of the increase of slaves—an increase in no way connected with the exportation of produce, but would have been the same, or in all probability greater, if all the produce had been consumed at home.

If one unacquainted with the present condition of the southwest, were told that the cotton-growing district alone had sold the crop for fifty millions of dollars per annum for the last twenty years, he would naturally conclude that this must be the richest community in the world. He might well imagine that the planters all dwell in palaces, upon estates improved by every device of art, and that their most common utensils were made of the precious metals; that canals, turnpikes, railways, and every other

FROM J. D. B. De Bow, *The Industrial Resources of the Southern and Western States* (New Orleans: De Bow's Review, 1852), II, 113–14.

improvement designed either for use or for ornament, abounded in every part of the land; and that the want of money had never been felt or heard of in its limits. He would conclude that the most splendid edifices dedicated to the purposes of religion and learning were every where to be found, and that all the liberal arts had here found their reward and a home. But what would be his surprise when told, that so far from dwelling in palaces, many of these planters dwell in habitations of the most primitive construction, and these so inartificially built as to be incapable of protecting the inmates from the winds and rains of heaven; that instead of any artistical improvement, this rude dwelling was surrounded by cotton fields, or probably by fields exhausted, washed into gullies, and abandoned; that instead of canals, the navigable streams remain unimproved, to the great detriment of transportation; that the common roads of the country were scarcely passable; that the edifices erected for the accommodation of learning and religion were frequently built of logs, and covered with boards; and that the fine arts were but little encouraged or cared for. Upon receiving this information, he would imagine that this was surely the country of misers—that they had been hoarding up all the money of the world, to the great detriment of the balance of mankind. But his surprise would be greatly increased when informed, that instead of being misers and hoarders of money, these people were generally scarce of it, and many of them embarrassed and bankrupt. Upon what principle could a stranger to the country account for this condition of things? How could he account for the expenditure of the enormous sum of *one billion of dollars* in the short space of twenty years? Indeed, I think it would puzzle the most observing individual in the country to account for so strange a result.

It is true that much has been paid for public lands within this period of twenty years, but the price of two crops would more than cover that account. The purchase of slaves and private lands should not be taken into the account, because the money paid for these should have remained in the country, except that portion paid for the slaves purchased out of the cotton region, which is inconsiderable when compared to the number brought into it by emigrants; and as to the natural increase of the slaves in the cotton region, that has no relation to the subject.

What, then, has become of the other nine hundred millions of dollars? Much of it has been paid to the neighboring states for provisions, mules, horses, and implements of husbandry; much has been paid for clothing and other articles of manufacture, all induced by the system of applying *all*, or nearly all the labor of the country to the production of one staple only, and by neglecting the encouragement of manufactures. No mind can look back upon the history of this region for the last twenty years, and not feel convinced that the labor bestowed in cotton growing during that period has been a total loss to this part of the country. It is true that some of the neighboring states have been benefited to some extent, and it has served to swell the general commerce of the nation; the manufacture of the raw material has given employment to foreign capital and to foreign labor, and has also served to swell the volume of foreign commerce.

But the country of its production has gained nothing, and lost much;— it has lost much because it has not kept its relative position in the rapid march of improvement which marks the progress of other countries; and more than all, in the transportation of its *produce,* it has transported much of the productive and essential principles of the soil, which can never be returned, thereby sapping the very foundation of its wealth.

No country has ever acquired permanent wealth by exporting its unmanufactured products; and if any such case could be found in history, the experience of the southwest would furnish satisfactory testimony that the exportation of the commodities produced here, tends rather to impoverish than enrich the country. With the experience and the lights of the past before them, it would seem to be madness to persevere in a course so detrimental to their interests. If, when the prices of the leading staples were much better than they are likely to be for the future, and when the lands were more fertile and productive than now, this system proved unprofitable and ruinous, what hope is there that the result of the future will be better? Nay, is it not quite certain that each succeeding year will accelerate the progressive deterioration, until a state of irredeemable ruin will ensue?

. . . .

2] Economic Advantage of Slavery: A Source of National Wealth

THE INSTITUTION of slavery, at this moment, gives indications of a vitality that was never anticipated by its friends or foes. Its enemies often supposed it about ready to expire, from the wounds they had inflicted, when in truth it had taken two steps in advance, while they had taken twice the number in an opposite direction. In each successive conflict, its assailants have been weakened, while its dominion has been extended.

This has arisen from causes too generally overlooked. Slavery is not an isolated system, but is so mingled with the business of the world, that it derives facilities from the most innocent transactions. Capital and labor, in Europe and America, are largely employed in the manufacture of cotton. These goods, to a great extent, may be seen freighting every vessel, from Christian nations, that traverses the seas of the globe; and filling the warehouses and shelves of the merchants over two-thirds of the world. By the industry, skill, and enterprise employed in the manufacture of cotton, mankind are better clothed; their comfort better promoted; general industry more highly stimulated; commerce more widely extended; and civilization more rapidly advanced than in any preceding age.

To the superficial observer, all the agencies, based upon the sale and

FROM David Christy, *Cotton Is King,* reprinted in E. N. Elliott, ed., *Cotton Is King, and Pro-Slavery Arguments* (Augusta, Ga.: Pritchard, Abbott & Loomis, 1860), pp. 55-59, 63-66.

manufacture of cotton, seem to be legitimately engaged in promoting human happiness; and he, doubtless, feels like invoking Heaven's choicest blessings upon them. When he sees the stockholders in the cotton corporations receiving their dividends, the operatives their wages, the merchants their profits, and civilized people everywhere clothed comfortably in cottons, he can not refrain from exclaiming: The lines have fallen unto them in pleasant places; yea, they have a goodly heritage!

But turn a moment to the source whence the raw cotton, the basis of these operations, is obtained, and observe the aspect of things in that direction. When the statistics on the subject are examined, it appears that nine-tenths of the cotton consumed in the Christian world is the product of the slave labor of the United States. It is this monopoly that has given to slavery its commercial value; and, while this monopoly is retained, the institution will continue to extend itself wherever it can find room to spread. He who looks for any other result, must expect that nations, which, for centuries, have waged war to extend their commerce, will now abandon that means of aggrandizement, and bankrupt themselves to force the abolition of American slavery!

This is not all. The economical value of slavery, as an agency for supplying the means of extending manufactures and commerce, has long been understood by statesmen. The discovery of the power of steam, and the inventions in machinery, for preparing and manufacturing cotton, revealed the important fact, that a single island, having the monopoly secured to itself, could supply the world with clothing. Great Britain attempted to gain this monopoly; and, to prevent other countries from rivaling her, she long prohibited all emigration of skillful mechanics from the kingdom, as well as all exports of machinery. As country after country was opened to her commerce, the markets for her manufactures were extended, and the demand for the raw material increased. The benefits of this enlarged commerce of the world, were not confined to a single nation, but mutually enjoyed by all. As each had products to sell, peculiar to itself, the advantages often gained by one were no detriment to the others. The principal articles demanded by this increasing commerce have been coffee, sugar, and cotton, in the production of which slave labor has greatly predominated. Since the enlargement of manufactures, cotton has entered more extensively into commerce than coffee and sugar, though the demand for all three has advanced with the greatest rapidity. England could only become a great commercial nation, through the agency of her manufactures. She was the best supplied, of all the nations, with the necessary capital, skill, labor, and fuel, to extend her commerce by this means. But, for the raw material, to supply her manufactories, she was dependent upon other countries. The planters of the United States were the most favorably situated for the cultivation of cotton; and while Great Britain was aiming at monopolizing its manufacture, they attempted to monopolize the markets for that staple. This led to a fusion of interests between them and the British manufacturers; and to the adoption of principles in political economy, which, if rendered effective, would promote the interests of this coalition. With the advantages possessed by the English manufacturers, "Free Trade" would render all other nations subservient to their interests; and, so far as their operations should be increased, just so far would the demand for American cotton be extended. The details of the success of the parties to this combination, and the opposition they have had to encounter, are left to be noticed more fully hereafter. To the cotton planters, the co-partnership has been eminently advantageous.

How far the other agricultural interests of the United States are promoted, by extending the cultivation of cotton, may be inferred from the Census returns of 1850, and the Congressional Reports on Commerce and Navigation, for 1854. Cotton and tobacco, only, are largely exported. The production of sugar does not yet equal our consumption of the article, and we import, chiefly from slave labor countries, 445,445,680 lbs. to make up the deficiency. But of cotton and tobacco, we export more than *two-thirds* of the amount produced; while of other products of the agriculturists, less than the *one forty-sixth* part is exported. Foreign nations, generally, can grow their provisions, but can not grow their tobacco and cotton. Our surplus provisions, not exported, go to the villages, towns, and cities, to feed the mechanics, manufacturers, merchants, professional men, and others; or to the cotton and sugar districts of the South, to feed the planters and their slaves. The increase of mechanics and manufacturers at the North, and the expansion of slavery at the South, therefore, augment the markets for provisions, and promote the prosperity of the farmer. As the mechanical population increases, the implements of industry and articles of furniture are multiplied, so that both farmer and planter can be supplied with them on easier terms. As foreign nations open their markets to cotton fabrics, increased demands for the raw material are made. As new grazing and grain-growing States are developed, and teem with their surplus productions, the mechanic is benefited, and the planter, relieved from food-raising, can employ his slaves more extensively upon cotton. It is thus that our exports are increased; our foreign commerce advanced; the home markets of the mechanic and farmer extended, and the wealth of the nation promoted. It is thus, also, that the free labor of the country finds remunerating markets for its products—though at the expense of serving as an efficient auxiliary in the extension of slavery!

.   .   .   .

Take another view of this subject. To say nothing now of the tobacco, rice, and sugar, which are the products of our slave labor, we exported raw cotton to the value of $109,456,404 in 1853. Its destination was, to Great Britain, 768,596,498 lbs.; to the Continent of Europe, 335,271,434 lbs.; to countries on our own Continent, 7,702,438 lbs.; making the total exports, 1,111,570,370 lbs. The entire crop of that year being 1,305,152,800 lbs., gives, for home consumption, 268,403,600 lbs. Of this, there was manufactured into cotton fabrics to the value of $61,869,274; of which there was retained, for home markets, to the value of $53,100,290. Our imports of cotton fabrics from Europe, in 1853, for consumption, amounted in value to $26,477,950: thus making our cottons, foreign and domestic, for that year, cost us $79,578,240.

In bringing down the results to 1858, it will be seen that the imports of foreign cotton goods have fluctuated at higher and lower amounts than those of 1853; and that an actual decrease of our exports of cotton manufactures has taken place since that date. But in the exports of raw cotton there has been an increase of nearly a hundred millions of pounds over that of 1853—the total exports of 1859 being 1,208,561,200 lbs. The total crop of 1859, in the United States, was 1,606,800,000 lbs., and the amount taken for consumption 371,060,800 lbs.

Thus, while our consumption of foreign cotton goods is not on the increase, the foreign demand for our raw cotton is rapidly augmenting; and thus the American planter is becoming more and more important to the manufactures and commerce of the world.

This, now, is what becomes of our cotton; this is the way in which it so largely constitutes the basis of commerce and trade; and this is the nature of the relations existing between the slavery of the United States and the economical interests of the world.

But have the United States no other great leading interests, except those which are involved in the production of cotton? Certainly, they have. Here is a great field for the growth of provisions. In ordinary years, exclusive of tobacco and cotton, our agricultural property, when added to the domestic animals and their products, amounts in value $1,551,176,490. Of this, there is exported only to the value of $33,809,126; which leaves for home consumption and use, a remainder to the value of $1,517,367,364. The portions of the property represented by this immense sum of money, which pass from the hands of the agriculturists, are distributed throughout the Union, for the support of the day laborers, sailors, mechanics, manufacturers, traders, merchants, professional men, planters, and the slave population. This is what becomes of our provisions.

Besides this annual consumption of provisions, most of which is the product of free labor, the people of the United States use a vast amount of groceries, which are mainly of slave labor origin. Boundless as is the influence of cotton, in stimulating slavery extension, that of the cultivation of groceries falls but little short of it; the chief difference being, that they do not receive such an increased value under the hand of manufacturers. The cultivation of coffee, in Brazil, employs as great a number of slaves as that of cotton in the United States.

But, to comprehend fully our indebtedness to slave labor for groceries, we must descend to particulars. Our imports of coffee, tobacco, sugar, and molasses, for 1853, amounted in value to $38,479,000; of which the hand of the slave, in Brazil and Cuba, mainly, supplied to the value of $34,451,-000. This shows the extent to which we are sustaining foreign slavery, by the consumption of these four products. But this is not our whole indebtedness to slavery for groceries. Of the domestic grown tobacco, valued at $19,975,000, of which we retain nearly one-half, the Slave States produce to the value of $16,787,000; of domestic rice, the product of the South, we consume to the value of $7,092,000; of domestic slave grown sugar and molasses, we take, for home consumption, to the value of $34,779,000; making our grocery account, with domestic slavery, foot up to the sum of

$50,449,000. Our whole indebtedness, then, to slavery, foreign and domestic, for these four commodities, after deducting two millions of re-exports, amounts to $82,607,000.

By adding the value of the foreign and domestic cotton fabrics, consumed annually in the United States, to the yearly cost of the groceries which the country uses, our total indebtedness, for articles of slave labor origin, will be found swelling up to the enormous sum of $162,185,240.

We have now seen the channels through which our cotton passes off into the great sea of commerce, to furnish the world its clothing. We have seen the origin and value of our provisions, and to whom they are sold. We have seen the sources whence our groceries are derived, and the millions of money they cost. To ascertain how far these several interests are sustained by one another, will be to determine how far any one of them becomes an element of expansion to the others. To decide a question of this nature with precision is impracticable. The statistics are not attainable. It may be illustrated, however, in various ways, so as to obtain a conclusion proximately accurate. Suppose, for example, that the supplies of food from the North were cut off, the manufactories left in their present condition, and the planters forced to raise their provisions and draught animals: in such circumstances, the export of cotton must cease, as the lands of these States could not be made to yield more than would subsist their own population, and supply the cotton demanded by the Northern States. Now, if this be true of the agricultural resources of the cotton States—and it is believed to be nearly the full extent of their capacity—then the surplus of cotton, to the value of more than a hundred millions of dollars, now annually sent abroad, stands as the representative of the yearly supplies which the cotton planters receive from the farmers north of the cotton line. This, therefore, as will afterward more fully appear, may be taken as the probable extent to which the supplies from the North serve as an element of slavery expansion in the article of cotton alone.

3] Economic Disadvantages of Slavery

a] STIFLES PROGRESS

IT IS a fact well known to every intelligent Southerner that we are compelled to go to the North for almost every article of utility and adornment, from matches, shoepegs and paintings up to cotton-mills, steamships and statuary; that we have no foreign trade, no princely merchants, nor respectable artists; that, in comparison with the free states, we contribute nothing to the literature, polite arts and inventions of the age; that, for

FROM Hinton Rowan Helper, *The Impending Crisis of the South: How to Meet It* (New York: Burdick Brothers, 1857), pp. 21–25, 33–34, 39–41, 44–45, 65–67.

want of profitable employment at home, large numbers of our native population find themselves necessitated to emigrate to the West, whilst the free states retain not only the larger proportion of those born within their own limits, but induce, annually, hundreds of thousands of foreigners to settle and remain amongst them; that almost everything produced at the North meets with ready sale, while, at the same time, there is no demand, even among our own citizens, for the productions of Southern industry; that, owing to the absence of a proper system of business amongst us, the North becomes, in one way or another, the proprietor and dispenser of all our floating wealth, and that we are dependent on Northern capitalists for the means necessary to build our railroads, canals and other public improvements; that if we want to visit a foreign country, even though it may lie directly South of us, we find no convenient way of getting there except by taking passage through a Northern port; and that nearly all the profits arising from the exchange of commodities, from insurance and shipping offices, and from the thousand and one industrial pursuits of the country, accrue to the North, and are there invested in the erection of those magnificent cities and stupendous works of art which dazzle the eyes of the South, and attest the superiority of free institutions!

The North is the Mecca of our merchants, and to it they must and do make two pilgrimages per annum—one in the spring and one in the fall. All our commercial, mechanical, manufactural, and literary supplies come from there. We want Bibles, brooms, buckets and books, and we go to the North; we want pens, ink, paper, wafers and envelopes, and we go to the North; we want shoes, hats, handkerchiefs, umbrellas and pocket knives, and we go to the North; we want furniture, crockery, glassware and pianos, and we go to the North; we want toys, primers, school books, fashionable apparel, machinery, medicines, tombstones, and a thousand other things, and we go to the North for them all. Instead of keeping our money in circulation at home, by patronizing our own mechanics, manufacturers, and laborers, we send it all away to the North, and there it remains; it never falls into our hands again.

In one way or another we are more or less subservient to the North every day of our lives. In infancy we are swaddled in Northern muslin; in childhood we are humored with Northern gewgaws; in youth we are instructed out of Northern books; at the age of maturity we sow our "wild oats" on Northern soil; in middle-life we exhaust our wealth, energies and talents in the dishonorable vocation of entailing our dependence on our children and on our children's children, and, to the neglect of our own interests and the interests of those around us, in giving aid and succor to every department of Northern power; in the decline of life we remedy our eye-sight with Northern spectacles, and support our infirmities with Northern canes; in old age we are drugged with Northern physic; and, finally, when we die, our inanimate bodies, shrouded in Northern cambric, are stretched upon the bier, borne to the grave in a Northern carriage, entombed with a Northern spade, and memorized with a Northern slab!

But it can hardly be necessary to say more in illustration of this unmanly and unnational dependence, which is so glaring that it cannot fail to be apparent to even the most careless and superficial observer. All the world sees, or ought to see, that in a commercial, mechanical, manufactural, financial, and literary point of view, we are as helpless as babes; that, in comparison with the Free States, our agricultural resources have been greatly exaggerated, misunderstood and mismanaged; and that, instead of cultivating among ourselves a wise policy of mutual assistance and co-operation with respect to individuals, and of self-reliance with respect to the South at large, instead of giving countenance and encouragement to the industrial enterprises projected in our midst, and instead of building up, aggrandizing and beautifying our own States, cities and towns, we have been spending our substance at the North, and are daily augmenting and strengthening the very power which now has us so completely under its thumb.

.   .   .   .

WHY THE NORTH HAS SURPASSED THE SOUTH

AND NOW that we have come to the very heart and soul of our subject, we feel no disposition to mince matters, but mean to speak plainly, and to the point, without any equivocation, mental reservation, or secret evasion whatever. The son of a venerated parent, who, while he lived, was a considerate and merciful slaveholder, a native of the South, born and bred in North Carolina, of a family whose home has been in the valley of the Yadkin for nearly a century and a half, a Southerner by instinct and by all the influences of thought, habits, and kindred, and with the desire and fixed purpose to reside permanently within the limits of the South, and with the expectation of dying there also—we feel that we have the right to express our opinion, however humble or unimportant it may be, on any and every question that affects the public good; and, so help us God, "sink or swim, live or die, survive or perish," we are determined to exercise that right with manly firmness, and without fear, favor or affection.

And now to the point. In our opinion, an opinion which has been formed from data obtained by assiduous researches, and comparisons, from laborious investigation, logical reasoning, and earnest reflection, the causes which have impeded the progress and prosperity of the South, which have dwindled our commerce, and other similar pursuits, into the most contemptible insignificance; sunk a large majority of our people in galling poverty and ignorance, rendered a small minority conceited and tyrannical, and driven the rest away from their homes; entailed upon us a humiliating dependence on the Free States; disgraced us in the recesses of our own souls, and brought us under reproach in the eyes of all civilized and enlightened nations—may all be traced to one common source, and there find solution in the most hateful and horrible word, that was ever incorporated into the vocabulary of human economy—*Slavery!*

.   .   .   .

By taking a sort of inventory of the agricultural products of the free and slave States in 1850, we now propose to correct a most extraordinary and mischievous error into which the people of the South have unconsciously fallen. Agriculture, it is well known, is the sole boast of the South; and, strange to say, many pro-slavery Southerners, who, in our latitude, pass for intelligent men, are so puffed up with the idea of our importance in this respect, that they speak of the North as a sterile region, unfit for cultivation, and quite dependent on the South for the necessaries of life! Such rampant ignorance ought to be knocked in the head! We can prove that the North produces greater quantities of bread-stuffs than the South! Figures shall show the facts. Properly, the South has nothing left to boast of; the North has surpassed her in everything, and is going farther and farther ahead of her every day. We ask the reader's careful attention to the following tables, which we have prepared at no little cost of time and trouble, and which, when duly considered in connection with the foregoing and subsequent portions of our work, will, we believe, carry conviction to the mind that the downward tendency of the South can be arrested only by the abolition of slavery.

[Helper then presents seven tables which give a state-by-state breakdown of agricultural production in 1850 in the free states as compared to that in the slave states. He combines the tables and concludes as follows:]

So much for the boasted agricultural superiority of the South! Mark well the balance in bushels, and the difference in value! Is either in favor of the South? No! Are both in favor of the North? Yes! Here we have un-questionable proof that of all the bushel-measure products of the nation, the free states produce far more than one-half; and it is worthy of particular mention, that *the excess of Northern products is of the most valuable kind.* The account shows a balance against the South, in favor of the North, of *seventeen million four hundred and twenty-three thousand one hundred and fifty-two bushels,* and a difference in value of *forty-four million seven hundred and eighty-two thousand six hundred and thirty-six dollars.* Please

	RECAPITULATION—FREE STATES		
	BUSHELS	DOLLARS	VALUE
Wheat	72,157,486	@ 1.50	$108,236,229
Oats	96,590,371	@ .40	38,636,148
Indian Corn	242,618,650	@ .60	145,571,190
Potatoes (I. & S.)	59,033,170	@ .38	22,432,604
Rye	12,574,623	@ 1.00	12,574,623
Barley	5,002,013	@ .90	4,501,811
Buckwheat	8,550,245	@ .50	4,275,122
Beans & Peas	1,542,295	@ 1.75	2,699,015
Clov. & Grass seeds	762,265	@ 3.00	2,286,795
Flax Seeds	358,923	@ 1.25	448,647
Garden Products			3,714,605
Orchard Products			6,332,914
Total	499,190,041 bushels, valued as above, at $351,709,703		

RECAPITULATION—SLAVE STATES

	BUSHELS	DOLLARS	VALUE
Wheat	27,904,476	@ 1.50	$ 41,856,714
Oats	49,882,799	@ .40	19,953,191
Indian Corn	348,992,282	@ .60	209,395,369
Potatoes (I. & S.)	44,847,420	@ .38	17,042,019
Rye	1,608,240	@ 1.00	1,608,240
Barley	161,907	@ .90	145,716
Buckwheat	405,357	@ .50	202,678
Beans & Peas	7,637,227	@ 1.75	13,365,147
Clov. & Grass seeds	123,517	@ 3.00	370,551
Flax Seeds	203,484	@ 1.25	254,355
Garden Products			1,377,260
Orchard Products			1,355,827
Total	481,766,889 bushels, valued as above, at $306,927,067		

TOTAL DIFFERENCE—BUSHEL-MEASURE PRODUCTS

	BUSHELS		VALUE
Free States	499,190,041		$351,709,703
Slave States	481,766,889		306,927,067
Balance in bushels	17,423,152	Difference in value	$ 44,782,636

bear these facts in mind, for, in order to show positively how the free and slave States do stand upon the great and important subject of rural economy, we intend to take an account of all the other products of the soil, of the live-stock upon farms, of the animals slaughtered, and, in fact, of every item of husbandry of the two sections; and if, in bringing our tabular exercises to a close, we find slavery gaining upon freedom—a thing it has never yet been known to do—we shall, as a matter of course, see that the above amount is transferred to the credit of the side to which it of right belongs.

.   .   .   .

[Helper also presents a number of tables to show the relationship between North and South in products measured in pounds for 1850. He combines these tables and concludes as follows:]

Both quantity and value again in favor of the North! Behold also the enormousness of the difference! In this comparison with the South, neither hundreds, thousands, nor millions, according to the regular method of computation, are sufficient to exhibit the excess of the pound-measure products of the North. Recourse must be had to an almost inconceivable number; billions must be called into play; and there are the figures telling us, with unmistakable emphasis and distinctness, that, in this department of agriculture, as in every other, the North is vastly the superior of the South—

RECAPITULATION—FREE STATES

	POUNDS	CENTS	VALUE
Hay	28,427,799,680	@ ½	$142,138,998
Hemp	443,520	@ 5	22,176
Hops	3,463,176	@ 15	519,476
Flax	3,048,278	@ 10	304,827
Maple Sugar	32,161,799	@ 8	2,572,943
Tobacco	14,752,087	@ 10	1,475,208
Wool	39,647,211	@ 35	13,876,523
Butter & Cheese	349,860,783	@ 15	52,479,117
Beeswax & Honey	6,888,368	@ 15	1,033,255
Total	28,878,064,902 lbs, valued as above,		$214,422,523

RECAPITULATION—SLAVE STATES

	POUNDS	CENTS	VALUE
Hay	2,548,636,160	@ ½	$ 12,743,180
Hemp	77,667,520	@ 5	3,883,376
Hops	33,780	@ 15	5,067
Flax	4,766,198	@ 10	476,619
Maple Sugar	2,088,687	@ 8	167,094
Tobacco	185,023,906	@ 10	18,502,390
Wool	12,797,329	@ 35	4,479,065
Butter & Cheese	68,634,224	@ 15	10,295,133
Beeswax & Honey	7,964,760	@ 15	1,194,714
Cotton	978,311,600	@ 8	78,264,928
Cane Sugar	237,133,000	@ 7	16,599,310
Rice (rough)	215,313,497	@ 4	8,612,539
Total	4,338,370,661 lbs. valued as above, at		$155,223,415

TOTAL DIFFERENCE—POUND-MEASURE PRODUCTS

	POUNDS	VALUE
Free States	28,878,064,902	$214,422,523
Slave States	4,338,370,661	155,223,415
Balance in lbs.	24,539,694,241	Difference in value $ 59,199,108

the figures showing a total balance in favor of the former of *twenty-four billion five hundred and thirty-nine million six hundred and ninety-four thousand two hundred and forty-one pounds,* valued at *fifty-nine million one hundred and ninety-nine thousand one hundred and eight dollars.* And yet, the North is a poor, God-forsaken country, bleak, inhospitable, and unproductive!

· · · · · · · · · · · ·

In making up these tables we have two objects in view; the first is to open the eyes of the non-slaveholders of the South, to the system of deception, that has so long been practiced upon them and the second is to show slaveholders themselves—we have reference only to those who are not too perverse, or ignorant, to perceive naked truths—that free labor is far more respectable, profitable, and productive, than slave labor. In the South, unfortunately, no kind of labor is either free or respectable. Every white man who is under the necessity of earning his bread, by the sweat of his brow, or by manual labor, in any capacity, no matter how unassuming in deportment, or exemplary in morals, is treated as if he was a loathsome beast, and shunned with the utmost disdain. His soul may be the very seat of honor and integrity, yet without slaves—himself a slave—he is accounted as nobody, and would be deemed intolerably presumptuous, if he dared to open his mouth, even so wide as to give faint utterance to a three-lettered monosyllable, like yea or nay, in the presence of an august knight of the whip and the lash.

·   ·   ·   ·   ·   ·   ·   ·   ·   ·   ·   ·   ·

It is expected that the stupid and sequacious masses, the white victims of slavery, will believe, and as a general thing, they do believe, whatever the slaveholders tell them; and thus it is that they are cajoled into the notion that they are the freest, happiest and most intelligent people in the world, and are taught to look with prejudice and disapprobation upon every new principle or progressive movement. Thus it is that the South, woefully inert and inventionless, has lagged behind the North, and is now weltering in the cesspool of ignorance and degradation.

·   ·   ·   ·   ·   ·   ·   ·   ·   ·   ·   ·   ·

b] CREATES AN IGNORANT AND INEFFICIENT LABOR FORCE

·   ·   ·   ·   ·   ·   ·   ·   ·   ·   ·   ·   ·

THE ECONOMIC advantages of slavery are easily stated: they are all comprised in the fact that the employer of slaves has absolute power over his workmen, and enjoys the disposal of the whole fruit of their labours. Slave labour, therefore, admits of the most complete organization, that is to say, it may be combined on an extensive scale, and directed by a controlling mind to a single end, and its cost can never rise above that which is necessary to maintain the slave in health and strength.

On the other hand, the economical defects of slave labour are very serious. They may be summed up under the three following heads:—it is given reluctantly; it is unskilful; it is wanting in versatility.

It is given reluctantly, and consequently the industry of the slave can

FROM J. E. Cairnes, *The Slave Power: Its Character, Career and Probable Designs: Being an Attempt to Explain the Real Issues Involved in the American Contest*, 2nd ed. (London and Cambridge: Macmillan and Co., 1863), pp. 43–47, 53–56, 62–78, 81–85, 87–88, 94–95.

only be depended on so long as he is watched. The moment the master's eye is withdrawn, the slave relaxes his efforts. The cost of slave labour will therefore, in great measure, depend on the degree in which the work to be performed admits of the workmen being employed in close proximity to each other. If the work be such that a large gang can be employed with efficiency within a small space, and be thus brought under the eye of a single overseer, the expense of superintendence will be slight; if, on the other hand, the nature of the work requires that the workmen should be dispersed over an extended area, the number of overseers, and therefore, the cost of the labour which requires this supervision, will be proportionately increased. The cost of slave labour thus varies directly with the degree in which the work to be done requires dispersion of the labourers, and inversely as it admits of their concentration. Further, the work being performed reluctantly, fear is substituted for hope, as the stimulus to exertion. But fear is ill calculated to draw from a labourer all the industry of which he is capable. "Fear," says Bentham, "leads the labourer to hide his powers, rather than to show them; to remain below, rather than to surpass himself. . . . By displaying superior capacity, the slave would only raise the measure of his ordinary duties; by a work of supererogation he would only prepare punishment for himself." He therefore seeks, by concealing his powers, to reduce to the lowest the standard of requisition. "His ambition is the reverse of that of the free man; he seeks to descend in the scale of industry, rather than to ascend."

Secondly, slave labour is unskilful, and this, not only because the slave, having no interest in his work, has no inducement to exert his higher faculties, but because, from the ignorance to which he is of necessity condemned, he is incapable of doing so. In the Slave States of North America, the education of slaves, even in the most rudimentary form, is proscribed by law, and consequently their intelligence is kept uniformly and constantly at the very lowest point. "You can make a nigger work," said an interlocutor in one of Mr. Olmsted's dialogues, "but you cannot make him think." He is therefore unsuited for all branches of industry which require the slightest care, forethought, or dexterity. He cannot be made to cooperate with machinery; he can only be trusted with the coarsest implements; he is incapable of all but the rudest forms of labour.

But further, slave labour is eminently defective in point of versatility. The difficulty of teaching the slave anything is so great, that the only chance of turning his labour to profit is, when he has once learned a lesson, to keep him to that lesson for life. Where slaves, therefore, are employed there can be no variety of production. If tobacco be cultivated, tobacco becomes the sole staple, and tobacco is produced, whatever be the state of the market, and whatever be the condition of the soil. This peculiarity of slave labour, as we shall see, involves some very important consequences.

.   .   .   .

When the soils are not of good quality, cultivation needs to be elaborate; a larger capital is expended; and with the increase of capital the processes become more varied, and the agricultural implements of a finer and more delicate construction. With such implements slaves cannot be trusted, and for such processes they are unfit. It is only, therefore, where the natural fertility of the soil is so great as to compensate for the inferiority of the cultivation, where nature does so much as to leave little for art, and to supersede the necessity of the more difficult contrivances of industry, that slave labour can be turned to profitable account.

Further, slavery, as a permanent system, has need not merely of a fertile soil, but of a practically unlimited extent of it. This arises from the defect of slave labour in point of versatility. As has been already remarked, the difficulty of teaching the slave anything is so great—the result of the compulsory ignorance in which he is kept, combined with want of intelligent interest in his work—that the only chance of rendering his labour profitable is, when he has once learned a lesson, to keep him to that lesson for life. Accordingly where agricultural operations are carried on by slaves, the business of each gang is always restricted to the raising of a single product. . . . Whatever crop may be best suited to the character of the soil and the nature of slave industry, whether cotton, tobacco, sugar, or rice, that crop is cultivated, and that alone. Rotation of crops is thus precluded by the conditions of the case. The soil is tasked again and again to yield the same product, and the inevitable result follows. After a short series of years its fertility is completely exhausted, the planter—"land-killer" he is called in the picturesque nomenclature of the South—abandons the ground which he has rendered worthless, and passes on to seek in new soils for that fertility under which alone the agencies at his disposal can be profitably employed.

·   ·   ·   ·   ·   ·   ·   ·   ·

Slave cultivation, wherever it has been tried in the new world, has issued in the same results. Precluding the conditions of rotation of crops or skilful management, it tends inevitably to exhaust the land of a country, and consequently requires for its permanent success not merely a fertile soil but a practically unlimited extent of it.

To sum up, then, the conclusions at which we have arrived, the successful maintenance of slavery, as a system of industry, requires the following conditions:—1st. Abundance of fertile soil; and, 2nd. a crop the cultivation of which demands combination and organization of labour on an extensive scale, and admits of its concentration. It is owing to the presence of these conditions that slavery has maintained itself in the Southern States of North America, and to their absence that it has disappeared from the Northern States.

The explanation offered in the last chapter of the success and failure of slavery in different portions of North America resolved itself into the proposition, that in certain cases the institution was found to be economically profitable while it proved unprofitable in others. From this position—the profitableness of slavery under given external conditions—the inference is generally made by those who advocate or look with indulgence on the system, that slavery must be regarded as conducive to at least the material well-being of countries in which these conditions exist; and these conditions being admittedly present in the Slave States of North America, it is concluded that the abolition of slavery in those states would necessarily be attended with a diminution of their wealth, and by consequence, owing to the mode in which the interests of all nations are identified through commerce, with a corresponding injury to the material interests of the rest of the world. . . .

In the first place, it must be remarked that the profitableness which has been attributed to slavery is profitableness estimated exclusively from the point of view of the proprietor of slaves. Profitableness *in this sense* is all that is necessary to account for the introduction and maintenance of the system (which was the problem with which alone we were concerned), since it was with the proprietors that the decision rested. But those who are acquainted with the elementary principles which govern the distribution of wealth, know that the profits of capitalists may be increased by the same process by which the gross revenue of a country is diminished, and that therefore the community as a whole may be impoverished through the very same means by which a portion of its number is enriched. The economic success of slavery, therefore, is perfectly consistent with the supposition that it is prejudicial to the material well-being of the country where it is established. The argument, in short, comes to this: the interests of slave-masters—or rather that which slave-masters believe to be their interests—are no more identical with the interests of the general population in slave countries in the matter of wealth, than in that of morals or of politics. That which benefits, or seems to benefit, the one in any of these departments, may injure the other. It follows, therefore, that the economic advantages possessed by slavery, which were the inducement to its original establishment and which cause it still to be upheld, are perfectly compatible with its being an obstacle to the industrial development of the country, and at variance with the best interests, material as well as moral, of its inhabitants.

Further, the profitableness which has been attributed to slavery does not even imply that the system is conducive to the interests (except in the narrowest sense of the word) of the class for whose especial behoof it exists. Individuals and classes may always be assumed to follow their own interests according to their lights and tastes; but that which their lights and tastes point out as their interest will vary with the degree of their intelligence and the character of their civilization. When the intelligence of a class is limited and its civilization low, the view it will take of its interests will be correspondingly narrow and sordid. Extravagant and undue importance will be attached to the mere animal pleasures. A small gain obtained by coarse and obvious methods will be preferred to a great one which requires a recourse to more refined expedients; and the future well-being of the race will be regarded as of less importance than the aggrandisement of the existing generation.

But our admissions in favour of slavery require still further qualification. The establishment of slavery in the Southern States was accounted for by its superiority in an economic point of view over free labour, in the

form in which free labour existed in America at the time when that continent was settled. Now, the superiority of slave over free labour to which
its adoption was originally owing, is by no means to be assumed as still
existing in virtue of the fact that slavery is still maintained. Of two systems one may at a given period be more profitable than the other, and
may on this account be established, but may afterwards cease to be so, and
yet may nevertheless continue to be upheld, either from habit, or from
unwillingness to adopt new methods, or from congeniality with tastes which
had been formed under its influence. It is a difficult and slow process under
all circumstances to alter the industrial system of a country; but the difficulty of exchanging one form of free industry for another is absolutely
inappreciable when compared with that which we encounter when we
attempt to substitute free for servile institutions. . . .

The concession then in favour of slavery, involved in the explanation
given of its definitive establishment in certain portions of North America,
amounts to this, that *under certain conditions of soil and climate, cultivation by slaves may for a time yield a larger net revenue than cultivation
by certain forms of free labour.* This is all that needs to be assumed to
account for the original establishment of slavery. But the maintenance of
the institution at the present day does not imply even this quantum of
advantage in its favour; since, owing to the immense difficulty of getting
rid of it when once established on an extensive scale, the reasons for its
continuance (regarding the question from the point of view of the slaveholders) may, where it has obtained a firm footing, prevail over those for
its abolition, even though it be far inferior as a productive instrument to
free labour. The most, therefore, that can be inferred from the existence
of the system at the present day is that it is self-supporting.

Having now cleared the ground from the several false inferences with
which the economic success of slavery, such as it is, is apt to be surrounded,
I proceed to trace the consequences, economic, social, and political, which
flow from the institution.

.   .   .   .

It was . . . seen that slave labour is, from the nature of the case, unskilled labour; and it is evident that this circumstance at once excludes it
from the field of manufacturing and mechanical industry. Where a workman is kept in compulsory ignorance, and is, at the same time, without
motive for exerting his mental faculties, it is quite impossible that he
should take part with efficiency in the difficult and delicate operations which
most manufacturing and mechanical processes involve. The care and dexterity which the management of machinery requires is not to be obtained
from him, and he would often do more damage in an hour than the produce
of his labour for a year would cover. Nor is it for economic reasons only that
the slave is shut out from this department of industry. A still more potent
reason for his exclusion is to be found in the social and political consequences which would follow his admission to this field. The conduct of
manufacturing industry on a great scale always brings with it the congregation in towns of large masses of workmen. The danger incident to this,

where the workmen are slaves, is too obvious to need being pointed out. Discussion, mutual understanding, combination, secret or open, for the purpose of redressing what is or seems to be amiss, would be the certain consequences. Where, indeed, freedom prevails, such consequences become sources of harmony and strength; but is it to be supposed that slave-masters will consent to encounter the free development of the principle of association among their thralls? The thing is inconceivable. Manufacturing industry, where slavery exists, could only be carried on at the constant risk of insurrection, and this must effectually prevent it in such societies from ever attaining any considerable growth. And no less plain is it that slavery is unsuited to the functions of commerce; for the soul of commerce is the spirit of enterprise, and this is ever found wanting in communities where slavery exists: their prevailing characteristics are subjection to routine and contempt for money-making pursuits. Moreover, the occupations of commerce are absolutely prohibitive of the employment of servile labour. A mercantile marine composed of slaves is a form of industry which the world has not yet seen. Mutinies in mid-ocean and desertions the moment the vessel touched at foreign ports would quickly reduce the force to a cipher. These are obstacles which no natural instinct for commerce is sufficient to overcome. They have proved as fatal to its success in Southern, as in Northern, America, in Brazil as in the Confederate States. In both, notwithstanding the temptation of a vast range of coast line and excellent harbours, the descendants of races who in former ages and elsewhere have shewn a marvellous aptitude for maritime pursuits, have abandoned their natural career, and have permitted the whole external commerce of the country to pass into foreign hands.

Slavery, therefore, excluded by these causes from the field of manufactures and commerce, finds its natural career in agriculture; and, from what has been already established respecting the peculiar qualities of slave labour, we may easily divine the form which agricultural industry will assume under a servile *régime*. The single merit of slave labour as an industrial instrument consists, as we have seen, in its capacity for organization—its susceptibility, that is to say, of being adjusted with precision to the kind of work to be done, and of being directed on a comprehensive plan towards some distinctly conceived end. Now to give scope to this quality, the scale on which industry is carried on must be extensive, and to carry on industry on an extensive scale large capitals are required. Large capitalists will therefore have, in slave communities, a special and peculiar advantage over small capitalists beyond that which they enjoy in countries where labour is free. But there is another circumstance which renders a considerable capital still more an indispensable condition to the successful conduct of industrial operations in slave countries. A capitalist who employs free labour needs for the support of his labour force a sum sufficient to cover the amount of their wages during the interval which elapses from the commencement of their operations until the sale of the produce which results from them. But the capitalist employing slave labour requires not merely this sum—represented in his case by the food, clothing, and shelter provided for his slaves during the corresponding period—but, in addition to this, a sum sufficient to purchase the fee-simple of his entire slave force. For the conduct of a given business, therefore, it is obvious that the employer of slave labour will require a much larger capital than the employer of free labour. The capital of the one will represent merely the current outlay; while the capital of the other will represent, in addition to this, the future capabilities of the productive instrument. The one will represent the interest, the other the principal and interest, of the labour employed. Owing to these causes large capitals are, relatively to small, more profitable, and are, at the same time, absolutely more required in countries of slave, than in countries of free, labour. It happens, however, that capital is in slave countries a particularly scarce commodity, owing partly to the exclusion from such countries of many modes of creating it—manufactures and commerce for example—which are open to free communities, and partly to what is also a consequence of the institution—the unthrifty habits of the upper classes. We arrive therefore at this singular conclusion, that, while large capitals in countries of slave labour enjoy peculiar advantages, and while the aggregate capital needed in them for the conduct of a given amount of industry is greater than in countries where labour is free, capital nevertheless in such countries is exceptionally scarce. From this state of things result two phenomena which may be regarded as typical of industry carried on by slaves—the magnitude of the plantations and the indebtedness of the planters. Wherever negro slavery has prevailed in modern times, these two phenomena will be found to exist. . . . The tendency of things . . . in slave countries is to a very unequal distribution of wealth. The large capitalists, having a steady advantage over their smaller competitors, engross, with the progress of time, a larger and larger proportion of the aggregate wealth of the country, and gradually acquire the control of its collective industry. Meantime, amongst the ascendant class a condition of general indebtedness prevails.

But we may carry our deductions from the economic character of slavery somewhat further. It has been seen that slave cultivation can only maintain itself where the soil is rich, while it produces a steady deterioration of the soils on which it is employed. This being so, it is evident that in countries of average fertility but a small portion of the whole area will be available for this mode of cultivation, and that this portion is ever becoming smaller, since, as the process of deterioration proceeds, more soils are constantly reaching that condition in which servile labour ceases to be profitable. What, then, is to become of the remainder—that large portion of the country which is either naturally too poor for cultivation by slaves, or which has been made so by its continued employment? It will be thought, perhaps, that this may be worked by free labour, and that by a judicious combination of both forms of industry the whole surface of the country may be brought to the highest point of productiveness. But this is a moral impossibility: it is precluded by what, we shall find, is a cardinal feature in the structure of slave societies—their exclusiveness. In free countries industry is the path to independence, to wealth, to social distinction, and is therefore held in honour; in slave countries it is the vocation of the slave, and becomes therefore a badge of degradation. Idleness, which in free countries is regarded as the mother of all vices, becomes in the land of the slave the prerogative of a caste and is transformed into a title of nobility. The free labourer, consequently, who respects his calling and desires to be respected, instinctively shuns a country where industry is discredited, where he cannot engage in those pursuits by which wealth and independence are to be gained without placing himself on a level with the lowest of mankind. Free and slave labour are, therefore, incapable of being blended together in the same system. Where slavery exists it excludes all other forms of industrial life. . . .

Agriculture, therefore, when carried on by slaves, being by a sure law restricted to the most fertile portions of the land, and no other form of systematic industry being possible where slavery is established, it happens that there are in all slave countries vast districts, becoming, under the deteriorating effects of slave industry, constantly larger, which are wholly surrendered to nature, and remain for ever as wilderness. This is a characteristic feature in the political economy of the Slave States of the South, and is attended with social consequences of the most important kind. For the tracts thus left, or made, desolate become in time the resort of a promiscuous horde, who, too poor to keep slaves and too proud to work, prefer a vagrant and precarious life spent in the desert to engaging in occupations which would associate them with the slaves whom they despise. In the Southern States no less than four millions of human beings are now said to exist in this manner in a condition little removed from savage life, eking out a wretched subsistence by hunting, by fishing, by hiring themselves out for occasional jobs, by plunder. Combining the restlessness and contempt for regular industry peculiar to the savage with the vices of the *prolétaire* of civilized communities, these people make up a class at once degraded and dangerous, and, constantly reinforced as they are by all that is idle, worthless, and lawless among the population of the neighboring states, form an inexhaustible preserve of ruffianism, ready at hand for all the worst purposes of Southern ambition. The planters complain of these people for their idleness, for corrupting their slaves, for their thievish propensities; but they cannot dispense with them; for, in truth, they perform an indispensable function in the economy of slave societies, of which they are at once the victims and the principal supports. It is from their ranks that those filibustering expeditions are recruited which have been found so effective an instrument in extending the domain of the Slave Power; they furnish the Border Ruffians who in the colonization struggle with the Northern States contend with Freesoilers on the Territories; and it is to their antipathy to the negroes that the planters securely trust for repressing every attempt at servile insurrection. Such are the "mean whites" or "white trash" of the Southern States. They comprise several local subdivisions, the "crackers," the "sand-hillers," the "clay-eaters," and many more. The class is not peculiar to any one locality, but is the invariable outgrowth of negro slavery wherever it has raised its head in modern times. It may be seen in the new state of Texas as well as in the old settled districts of Virginia, the Carolinas, and Georgia; in the West India Islands no less than on the Continent. In the States of the Confederacy it comprises, as I have said, four millions of human beings—about seven-tenths of the whole white population.

The industry of the Slave States, we have seen, is exclusively agricultural; and the mode of agriculture pursued in them has been represented as partial, perfunctory, and exhaustive. It must, however, be admitted that, to a certain extent, this description is applicable to the industrial condition of all new countries, and will find illustrations in the western regions of the Free States; and it may therefore occur to the reader that the economical conditions which I have described are rather the consequence of the recent settlement of the societies where they prevail than specific results of the system of slavery. But it is easy to show that this view of the case is fallacious, and proceeds from confounding what is essential in slave industry with an accidental and temporary feature in the industrial career of free communities. The settlers in new countries, whether they be slaveholders or free peasants, naturally fix in the first instance on the richest and most conveniently situated soils, and find it more profitable to cultivate these lightly, availing themselves to the utmost of the resources which nature offers, than to force cultivation on inferior soils after the manner of high farming in old countries. So far the cases are similar. But here lies the difference. The labour of free peasants, though of course more productive on rich than on inferior soils, is not necessarily confined to the former; whereas this is the case with the labour of slaves. Accordingly, therefore, as free peasants multiply, after the best soils have been appropriated, the second best are taken into cultivation; and as they multiply still more, cultivation becomes still more general, until ultimately all the cultivable portions of the country are brought within the domain of industry. This has been the course of industrial progress throughout the settled portions of the Northern States, but it has been otherwise in the South. As slaves multiply, their masters cannot have recourse to inferior soils: they must find for them new soils: the mass of the country, therefore, remains uncultivated, and the population increases only by dispersion. Again, although the mode of cultivation pursued by free peasants in new lands is generally far from what would be approved of by the scientific farmers of old countries, still it does not exhaust the soil in the same manner as cultivation carried on by slaves. . . . The superficial and careless mode of agriculture pursued by free peasants in new countries is, in short, accidental and temporary, the result of the exceptional circumstances in which they are placed, and gives place to a better system as population increases and inferior soils are brought under the plough; but the superficiality and exhaustiveness of agriculture carried on by slaves are essential and unalterable qualities, rendering all cultivation impossible but that which is carried on upon the richest soils, and not to be remedied by the growth of population, since to this they are an effectual bar.

My position is, that in slave communities agriculture is substantially the sole occupation, while this single pursuit is prematurely arrested in its development, never reaching those soils of secondary quality which, under a system of free industry would, with the growth of society, be brought under cultivation; and of this statement the industrial history of the Free and Slave States forms one continued illustration. . . .

The reader is now in a position to understand the kind of economic success which slavery has achieved. It consists in the rapid extraction from the soil of a country of the most easily obtained portion of its wealth by a process which exhausts the soil, and consigns to waste all the other resources of the country where it is practised. To state the case with more particularity—by proscribing manufactures and commerce, and confining agriculture within narrow bounds; by rendering impossible the rise of a free peasantry; by checking the growth of population—in a word, by blasting every germ from which national well-being and general civilization may spring—at this cost, with the further condition of encroaching, through a reckless system of culture, on the stores designed by Providence for future generations, slavery may undoubtedly for a time be made conducive to the pecuniary gain of the class who keep slaves. Such is the net result of advantage which slavery, as an economic system, is capable of yielding. To the full credit of all that is involved in this admission the institution is fairly entitled. . . .

c] DISCOURAGES THE DEVELOPMENT OF MANUFACTURING

THE MOVEMENT for a "home industry" in the Old South was another expression of the sectional conflict that was to culminate in civil war. The growing aggressiveness of the industrial North exposed the inadequacies of the cotton economy. Each new crisis in the South brought forth attendant panaceas, of which the movement for manufacturing gained widest support, for its proponents held that only a "diversified economy" could make the South truly independent.

But, as will be seen, the movement was sown on barren ground. The economic and social measures necessary for its success conflicted with the interests of the planters, and this challenge aroused a determined opposition. But, perhaps more important, the institutions engendered by a slave economy denied Southern industry the very conditions essential to its growth.

The agitation for manufacturing, latent since the 1820's, emerged with renewed vigor during the agricultural depression of the 1840's. In that decade the price of cotton hit an all-time low. While the average price for the period sank to approximately 8 cents a pound, cotton sold in 1844 for 5.6 cents and at times yielded as little as 2 or 3 cents. This was in contrast to the 12.3 cents of the preceding decade. As a consequence profit on capital in agriculture during the '40's was seldom higher than four per cent and was often as low as two per cent. With the ever increasing cotton production of the Southwest, little hope could be held out for an immediate up-

FROM Fabian Linden, "Repercussions of Manufacturing in the Ante-Bellum South," *North Carolina Historical Review*, XVII (October, 1940), 313–14, 318–24, 326–31.

turn. On the contrary, predictions of utter impoverishment and systematic breakdown of the slave system were rife.

Manufacturing, on the other hand, was enjoying a relative prosperity. In the depth of the depression, cotton mills were reporting large profits. The DeKalb mill claimed to yield dividends from 10 to 15 per cent, while factories near Augusta, Georgia, were paying as high as 20 to 30 per cent on investments. And even the warning of William Gregg, the leading advocate of diversification, to prospective investors "not to look for more than 10 per cent, 12 per cent or 14 per cent on investments" represented a bountiful return in contrast to the prevalent levels of agricultural profits. Thus the primary contention of the pro-manufacturing elements was that industry promised better returns on dollars invested. And, indeed, successes of enterprises like the DeKalb, Graniteville, and Prattsville mills constituted a most convincing argument.

.   .   .   .

[The diversificationists added other arguments to support their cause. Textile manufacturing in the South would enjoy the advantage of being close to raw materials; the South had rich deposits of coal and other minerals and an abundant supply of cheap labor. Failure to take advantage of these assets would put the South far behind the North.]

It was therefore from pure self-interest that plantation owners were urged into widespread manufacturing. For, it was argued, with the slaves engaged in agriculture and the whites in the factory, every freeman would, as a matter of class preservation, become a "firm and uncompromising" supporter of the slave system. Even those who doubted the imminence of open revolt could not fail to perceive the value of converting a non-productive group into a productive one. Thus industry was held to be a bulwark at once against internal and external enemies.

Convincing and justified as the arguments in behalf of "home industry" were, there was nevertheless launched against it a bitter opposition. Plantation owners clearly recognized in this movement a formidable threat to their interests. Diversificationists, however, realized that without the support of the plantocracy their plans to bring the spindle to the cotton would collapse, and hence put forward every effort to enlist their sympathy. They passionately urged the planters to take cognizance of a crisis in their own economy, and pointed out that their interests were inseparable from those of the entire section. Thus it was contended that with industry increasing the demand for slaves, the value of both Negroes and cotton would be "enhanced." Further, as Southern capital flowed away from the plantation into the mill, the restriction of cotton production would also result in the rise of prices. And, conversely, since the demand for cotton fabrics was held to be unlimited, an increase in the number of factories would lead inevitably to a higher price for cotton. Finally, increased land values were promised on the basis of the predicted growth of industrial towns. In brief, manufacturing would stabilize rather than destroy the plantation economy.

Increasingly it was accepted that political independence could be achieved only through economic emancipation. Early in 1861, when sectional animosity was near the breaking point, Gregg wrote, "We trust that it has been manifest to the people of the South that a prosperous state of commerce and manufacture is . . . absolutely necessary to render us politically independent." Others, however, believing open conflict inevitable, foresaw the weakness of an agrarian economy in time of war and urged the immediate establishment of factories as an absolutely essential military precaution.

Thus the agitation for industrialization sought, in the most practical terms, to win adherents from among the people of the South and, most particularly, the plantations.

The slaveholders, on the contrary, relentlessly hostile to the rising "menace," fought determinedly to block the establishment of factories. William Gregg, James H. Taylor, Richard F. Reynolds, A. H. Brisbane, all leading figures in the movement for manufacturing, complained bitterly of the opposition they met at "every turn." "Surely there is nothing in cotton spinning," sardonically commented *De Bow's Review,* "that can poison the atmosphere of South Carolina."

The hostility was encountered on all sides. The state legislatures erected effective legal barriers to fledgling industries. Charters of incorporation, so vital to the development of large-scale projects, were frequently denied, and those finally passed contained provisions that hampered their effectiveness. In 1837 the *Greenville Mountaineer* denounced as "an act of legalized fraud" a bill before the North Carolina legislature which authorized limited partnerships. Gregg, in chartering his Graniteville mill, applied circumspectly to both the Georgia and South Carolina legislatures, and while the latter reluctantly legalized his venture, Georgia gave him an outright refusal.

In the current journals the planters' views had powerful exponents, blending argument with vituperation in abundant measure. The Southern climate and the lack of skilled labor, as well as the essentially "rural character" of the people, were deemed unsuitable for so "complicated" a pursuit as manufacturing. Hostility to the North was turned effectively against industry as a "Northern Corruption." Politicians branded manufacturing, bearing with it the vice, poverty, and ignorance of the cities, as incompatible with Southern culture and liberty. George Fitzhugh, author of *Sociology for the South,* vilified "the filthy, crowded, licentious factories . . . of the North."

Such agitation had for decades succeeded in massing popular sentiment against industry. During a South Carolina political compaign the *Free Press and Hive* "exposed" candidate William Preston by revealing that his brother had invested in a manufacturing enterprise. Even so remote a connection with the hated pursuit, it was believed, would decrease Preston's chances for victory. Thus the political and social fashion was determined largely by the views and interests of slaveholders.

Their position, however, was clearly defensive, for essentially they saw in manufacturing a threat to their interests. Professor Beard has suggested that the planter's hostility to industry be attributed to his "rural habits of life" and his "tribesman's instinctive dislike for unaccustomed ways." But beneath "rural habits" and tribesman's instincts lay a more fundamental desire to protect vested wealth and power, which acknowledged in industry a formidable rival. Allowed to develop unchallenged, it might engulf the whole of Southern economy. Thus manufacturing was seen as a Trojan horse, and Graniteville, Prattsville, DeKalb, Vancluse, and Salude were the invading columns of the enemy.

A social change was believed inevitable. The *Southern Quarterly Review* warned that once industry established itself firmly on Southern soil, the agricultural class would perforce lose its position. It was precisely this, it was pointed out, that had taken place in the North which now, with tolerant patronage, could refer to its "honest" and "sturdy" farmers. The *Review* urged resistance against "the efforts of those who, dazzled by the splendors of Northern civilization, would endeavor to imitate it," which, it held, could be done "only by the destruction of the planter."

An immediate threat was seen in the proposals of industrialists to introduce immigrant workers as a source of skilled labor. Planters stood squarely against it. Foreigners, bringing with them European anti-slave traditions, were susceptible to abolition agitation. Moreover, those immigrants that ventured South were rarely able to buy themselves into the slaveholding class, but immediately became laborers, and as such resisted slave competition. The *Morehouse Advocate,* a Louisiana newspaper, stated the case simply: "The great mass of foreigners who come to our shores are laborers, and consequently come into competition with slave labor. It is to their interest to abolish slavery; and we know full well the disposition of man to promote all things which advance his own interests."

Immigration, moreover, tended to strengthen as a class the non-slaveholding whites, a situation which the planters viewed apprehensively. Already indications of a developing "class consciousness" were beginning to appear among the white factory workers. As early as 1824 signs of industrial organizations in the large cities had made themselves felt. Baltimore, Charleston, New Orleans, Richmond, Savannah, and Wilmington had labor organizations. Later, in the 1830's, strikes for higher wages and shorter hours had become a common occurrence. Even Graniteville, the pride of Gregg and his followers, felt the tremors of labor difficulties when, in 1857, the workers made formal demands for increased pay, and probably "quit work in an effort to get it."

Slaveholders recognized the danger in labor's organization; it had, in fact, already come into conflict with their interests. In North Carolina the Raleigh Workingmen's Association challenged an old revenue law which taxed mechanics' tools more heavily than slave property. More fundamentally, organized labor, fearing a reduction in its wage standards, was demanding that Negroes be kept out of mechanical pursuits. Indications of strife between the groups were not wanting. A farm building in North Carolina built by colored labor was destroyed, and suspicion was focused on a white organization for the elimination of Negro competition. In 1845 the Georgia legislature made the employment of a Negro mechanic or mason illegal, and similar legislation was being considered in other states. So strong had grown the popular feeling against Negro labor in industry that C. G. Memminger, a leader in Southern affairs, predicted, in a letter to Hammond, that "ere long we will have a formidable party on the subject."

In this situation slaveholders faced a dilemma. On the one hand, legislative limitation on the use of slaves restricted not only their powers but an immediate source of profit, for planters had turned in the crisis to industry to hire out their idle Negroes. More significantly, however, a victory for organized white labor set an ominous precedent, which, if left unchallenged, would lead only to more restrictive demands on the part of the new-fledged class. Slaveholders feared lest, with Negroes out of industry, the cities fall into the hands of native and foreign whites who would legislate for their own interests and perhaps become an abolitionist bulwark. L. W. Spratt, editor of the *Charleston Standard,* expressed this apprehension when he wrote that "they will question the right of masters to employ their slaves in any works that they may wish for; . . . they may acquire the power to determine municipal elections; . . . thus the town of Charleston, at the heart of slavery, may become a fortress of democratic power against it."

On the other hand, many believed that even greater danger was to be apprehended from the employment of slaves in the factories. It was feared that a slave, made mechanic, was more than half freed. Moreover, an absorption of slaves from the plantation to the factories meant essentially a contraction of the plantations, for the blacks used in industry were needed in the agricultural expansion movement of the 1840's and 1850's.

Thus, in essence, the rise of manufacturing forced upon the plantocracy the choice of paths leading to its eventual engulfment. To join in keeping the slaves out of industry meant actually to support and strengthen the rising industrial classes which were by nature set in opposition to the slaveholder. To allow, on the other hand, the slave to become a member of an industrial society was tantamount to giving him the weapon with which to gain his own freedom. Moreover, it would serve as an immediate springboard for the organization of the white worker. In either case the forces for manufacturing stood ultimately to gain at the expense of the slaveholding economy.

A more immediate threat to planters' interests, however, was a high national tariff. Thus resentment against the loom was intensified by the popular Southern belief that manufacturing implied the acceptance of a protectionist policy. Apprehension was felt that Southern industrialists would inevitably join forces with the North in its demand for a high tariff.

.   .   .   .

The fears of the slaveholders that the manufacturing element would go the whole hog in their demand for protection were not far-fetched. While Gregg gave assurances in 1850 that he would never join the "clamor for protection" we find him a decade later writing uncompromisingly in favor of the tariff. His about-face was typical, for more and more Southern newspapers were turning to an outright advocacy of protection. Wrote one paper, the *Jackson Southerner:* "The people of the South and West, who until recently were opposed to protection are retracing their steps almost unanimously."

Thus the planters found ample justification for the conviction that "home industry" was at bottom the Yankee foe attacking from within.

A far more formidable obstacle than planter opposition, however, was the slave system; for the impracticability of manufacturing lay within the character and institutions of the plantation economy. Slavery denied industry its fundamental needs: skilled labor, liquid capital, and a receptive market.

The use of slaves in industry, which had held great promise to the new manufacturers in the early 1840's, proved unfeasible in actual practice. Slaves transplanted from the plantations to the factories failed to make productive mill hands, for, since they were hired out for the period between planting and picking, the constant alternation between the land and loom prevented even a gradual accumulation of industrial skill.

This could be obviated by the outright purchase of slaves, but that in turn entailed even greater difficulties. First, buying slaves meant a larger immediate outlay of capital. It was estimated that the initial investment would have to be increased by as much as 50 per cent, and that in the face of a constant insufficiency of funds. Secondly, bought labor was precisely the factor industry could not endure. The ownership of slave labor would freeze Southern industry at the start, denying it the capacity to expand and contract with relative ease. While an increase in production would demand a much larger outlay for the purchase of additional slaves, any slight depression, on the other hand, would bring relatively greater losses. Slaves, unlike free labor, could not be "fired" and thrown onto the open market; on the contrary their maintenance persisted, independent of profit or loss. Moreover, the forced sale of Negroes in a depressed market, like that of any other superfluous commodity, would entail great losses. Conversely, during prosperous periods, the competitive demands of manufacturers and planters would serve to inflate the price of slaves, perhaps even beyond their productive value.

Manufacturers had no choice but to turn to the whites for a labor source. (The free Negroes were too negligible a group to supply completely even the early needs of industry.) But the "poor whites," having for generations been unable to find a progressive place in the Southern system, had degenerated into a backward, sickly people, unskilled in any craft and difficult to train, while the non-slaveholding independent farmers, who were no less unskilled in industry, were reluctant to give up independence to sink to the level of "hired" help.

Hence an immediate solution was sought in the importation of skilled foreign and Northern workers. Such an experienced group would at least partially answer the technical needs of industry, and at the same time serve to train the native whites. Here, too, however, the economic and social conditions engendered by a slave economy proved an almost insurmountable barrier. The standard of living set for the slave influenced the level for all Southern labor, and this was below that established in an industrial society. Yet even if higher wages were paid, none of the facilities making for a higher standard of living in manufacturing centers were available in the South. Further, where slaves did the manual labor a social stigma attached itself to all physical work. But foreigners, seeking improvement in their social as well as economic status, were as reluctant to accept social degradation in a backward system as they were to accept a standard of living set for slaves. Olmsted noted that New England factory girls, lured by high wages offered in Georgia mills, found conditions so unpleasant that they soon returned to the free states.

Side by side with a shortage of trained labor, Southern manufacturers were faced by a shortage of capital. For the wealth of the section was fixed in the expensive agrarian economy. Planters, rather than look to new and precarious forms of investment, turned instinctively to the improvement and expansion of their plantations. Moreover, industry was unwelcome in the South and hence there was a psychological reluctance to support it. Encouraged by the increasing world demand for cotton and the ever-present promise of higher prices, planters reinvested profits in land and labor. Nor did Eastern business men show an enthusiasm to invest in the dubious and untried South while the North and West were expanding sections offering relatively sure opportunities for profitable investment.

The character of Southern industry during this period was determined largely by its dependence for financial backing almost solely upon the small investments of some few slaveholders and upon the initiative of scattered individuals. Both the scarcity of capital and the agrarian character of investors are aptly illustrated by the Nesbit Company of South Carolina, where no less than $34,000 of the capital stock was paid for in the form of slaves. Not infrequently individuals embarking in industry had to set up independent mills, for, unlike the North, the South had but a small middle class to which to sell its stock. Hence the size, as well as the number of industrial enterprises, was limited by the scarcity of investors' capital. As the following table demonstrates, Southern cotton mills were at all times substantially smaller than similar New England establishments.

The scattered and unconcentrated quality of Southern industry handicapped it badly in competition with the North. To each establishment it meant concretely a relative increase in the cost of production. As J. H.

SECTION	YEAR	NO. OF PLANTS	CAPITAL INVESTED	CAPITALIZATION OF AVG. PLANT
New England	1840	675	$34,931,000	$ 52,000
	1850	564	53,832,000	95,000
	1860	570	69,260,000	122,000
South	1840	248	4,331,000	17,000
	1850	166	7,256,000	44,000
	1860	159	9,596,000	60,000

Taylor, the treasurer of Graniteville, pointed out, a superintendent who received a salary of $12,000 to $15,000 a year could manage a mill of 12,000 spindles as efficiently as one of 3,000. And this was equally true for the fireman, machinist, overseer, and engineer. Consequently, New England mills, which were by 1860 more than twice the size of Southern factories, could produce cheaply enough to compete effectively with the cotton states in the home market.

While, on the one hand, the plantation system denied Southern industry adequate capital, the system required it, on the other, to maintain a large liquid reserve. Planters bought on credit in anticipation of the profit on their growing crops, and unless a company could gear itself to the "advance system" it could not hope to sell in the Southern market. Naturally, New England mills, in virtue of their superior reserve, could meet this requirement more readily than could Southern mills. While Lowell sold cloth to the South on a six-to-ten-month credit basis, "home industry" allowed little more than sixty days.

Constant lack of reserves, moreover, prevented the pioneer manufacturers from purchasing raw materials cheaply in depressed markets. On the contrary, becoming increasingly mortgaged to Northern banks, from which they sought loans in times of crisis, they were forced to dump goods, frequently at a substantial loss, in order to meet maturing obligations.

Adding to the difficulties of Southern industrialists was the inadequacy of the home market. Traditionally, the North was the manufacturing section, and as such was believed to produce superior and more fashionable goods. Consequently, while there was a "rage" for the "Yankee-made," Southern products gathered dust on the shelves. And despite a widespread campaign in behalf of home patronage, the prejudice persisted. But quite apart from this psychological attitude, the slave system failed to produce a significant buying public. The consumption of the slaves was kept at a minimum, and the whites were similarly geared to a low standard of living. Hence, since the middle and industrial classes, which constitute the largest spending groups in a manufacturing society, were still undeveloped, the burden of buying fell on the planters. But they, unfortunately, preferred the "Yankee-made."

The movement to bring industry to the early South can thus be seen as an attempt to impose a "foreign system" upon a preponderantly agrarian economy. As such it challenged the *status quo,* arousing the adamant opposition of the dominant interests. Materially, moreover, it attempted to build where there was but slight foundation, for, as we have seen, the inherent nature of the prevailing economy denied it the elements essential to its growth.

It was only after the abolition of slavery that home industry was able to dig its roots into Southern soil. Not until 1880 did the South, politically and economically free, witness its first unhampered spurt of industrial growth. While in 1880 there was as little as seventeen millions invested in cotton mills, ten years later the capitalization had grown to over fifty-three millions. This phenomenal increase is all the more remarkable in contrast to the increases of two or three million for the pre-war decades. Undoubtedly many factors were responsible for the tremendous acceleration in the rate of growth, but fundamental among these influences was abolition.

.   .   .   .

d] RETARDS THE DEVELOPMENT OF A HOME MARKET

HISTORIANS ARE no longer sure that plantation slavery was responsible for the economic woes of the Old South. The revisionist doubts rest on two propositions of dubious relevance. The first is that slave labor could have been applied successfully to pursuits other than the raising of plantation staples; the second is that slave agriculture was possibly as profitable as were alternative industries and can not be held responsible for the unwillingness of Southerners to use their profits more wisely. The first confuses slave labor and its direct effects with the slave system and its total effects; it is the latter that is at issue, and the versatility of slave labor is a secondary consideration. The second rests on the assumption that the master-slave relationship was purely economic and not essentially different from an employer-worker relationship. Yet, when confronted with the issue direct, who could deny that slavery gave rise to a distinct politics, ideology, and pattern of social behavior and that these had immense economic consequences?

We need not examine at the moment the precise relationship between slavery and the plantation. Certainly, plantation economies presuppose considerable compulsion, if only of the *de facto* type now prevalent in Latin America. The historical fact of an ante bellum plantation-based slave economy is our immediate concern, although, undoubtedly, post bellum developments preserved some of the retardative effects of ante bellum slavery.

Those retardative effects were too many even to be summarized here. A low level of capital accumulation, the planters' high propensity to consume luxuries, the shortage of liquid capital aggravated by the steady drain of funds out of the region, the low productivity of slave labor, the need to concentrate on a few staples, the anti-industrial, antiurban ideology of the dominant planters, the reduction of Southern banking, industry, and commerce to the position of auxiliaries of the plantation economy— all these are familiar and yet need restudy in the light of the important work being done on the economics of underdeveloped countries. For the present let us focus on another factor, which in itself provides an adequate explanation of the slave South's inability to industrialize: the retardation of the home market for both industrial and agricultural commodities.

Thirty years ago Elizabeth W. Gilboy complained that economic historians studying the process of industrialization were too much concerned with supply and insufficiently concerned with demand. Her complaint was justified despite brilliant work on the problem of markets by a few

FROM Eugene D. Genovese, "The Significance of the Slave Plantation for Southern Economic Development," *Journal of Southern History*, XXVIII (November, 1962), 422–37.

outstanding men from Karl Marx to R. H. Tawney and Paul Mantoux. Since then, demand has received much more attention, although possibly not so much as it deserves. Important essays by Maurice Dobb, Simon Kuznets, H. J. Habakkuk, and Gunnar Myrdal, among others, have helped to correct the imbalance, as has new research on European industrialization and the economics of underdeveloped countries. If there is one lesson to be learned from the experience of both developed and underdeveloped countries it is that industrialization is unthinkable without an agrarian revolution which shatters the old regime of the countryside. While the peasantry is tied to the land, burdened with debt, and limited to minimal purchasing power, the labor recruitment and market pre-conditions for extensive manufacturing are missing. "Land reform"—*i.e.* an agrarian revolution—is the essential first step in the creation of an urban working class, the reorganization of agriculture to feed growing cities, and the development of a home market.

There are several ways in which agricultural reorganization can provide markets for manufactures; for our immediate purposes we may consider two. First, when the laborers are separated from the land, as they were during the English enclosures, they necessarily increase the demand for clothing and other essentials formerly produced at home. Paradoxically, this expansion of the market is compatible with a marked reduction in the laborers' standard of living. Second, the farmers left on the countryside to produce for growing urban markets provide an increased demand for textiles, agricultural equipment, and so forth.

The rapid extension of the rural market was the way of the North, but the slave plantations dominated the South until such time as reorganization was imposed from without by a predatory foe interested primarily in a new system of rural exploitation. An adequate home market could not arise in the ante bellum South and has only evolved slowly and painfully during the last century.

In 1860 about seventy-five per cent of the Southern cotton crop was exported; during no ante bellum year did the grain exports of the United States exceed five per cent of the grain crop. No doubt, cotton profits were an important element in the financing of America's economic growth. The question is, were the profits syphoned off to build up the Northern economy? We know that the credit mechanisms alone, to a considerable extent, did just that. The South's dependence on the export trade, in contradistinction to the North's primary reliance on its home market, indicates not merely a social division of labor but the economic exploitation of the exporting South.

Robert G. Albion, in his excellent examination of the colonial bondage of the South to the North, concludes that the South's lack of direct trade with Europe constituted an irrational arrangement secured by the impudence of New York's aggressive entrepreneurs. We can agree that, had the South imported from abroad as much as the North and West, there could have been no sensible reason to route through New York either the South's cotton or its share of European goods; but Albion's assumption of a rough equality of imports, an assumption shared by contemporaries like

George McDuffie and T. P. Kettell, can not be substantiated. The slave South's total market for manufactured goods was small relative to that of the free states; and even though the South depended upon Europe as well as the North for manufactured goods, its imports from Europe were smaller in value than imports into the North and West and smaller in bulk than the staples it exported. If the ships carrying cotton had sailed from Southern ports direct to Europe and back, they would have had to return in ballast, New York's domination of the South's export trade was, therefore, not accidental. Furthermore, if the South's share in American imports had been as Albion suggests, and if the coastal trade had been as large as he implies, the greater part of the goods sent from New Orleans to the plantation areas would have originated in Europe and been reshipped through New York rather than being—as is known—of Western origin.

Albion's acceptance of the assumption of nearly equal imports is the more surprising in view of the evidence of restricted Southern demand. The Southern cotton, iron, paper, wool, and railroad industries—to mention a few—struggled with indifferent results against a low level of Southern patronage. Antislavery leaders like Henry Ruffner and Cassius M. Clay made slavery's effects on the home market a cardinal point in their indictment. Thoughtful proslavery Southerners also commented frequently on the market problem. The opinion of the editor of the *Southern Agriculturalist* in 1828 that the South lacked sufficient customers to sustain a high level of manufacturing was echoed throughout the ante bellum period. The speech of Col. Andrew P. Calhoun to the Pendleton, South Carolina, Farmers' Society in 1855, for example, was strikingly similar in tone and content. On the other side, someone like Beverley Tucker would occasionally argue that Northerners would never risk a war "which, while it lasted, would shut them out from the best market in the world." It is difficult to imagine that many, even those who adopted such arguments for political purposes, took seriously a proposition so palpably false.

Alfred Glaze Smith, Jr., and Douglass C. North have traced the low level of Southern demand, in part, to plantation self-sufficiency. This view is not borne out by the data in the manuscript census returns from the cotton belt, which reveal only trivial amounts of home manufactures on even the largest plantations and which bear out the judgments of Rolla M. Tryon and Mary Elizabeth Massey on the weakness of Southern house-hold industry. In De Soto and Marshall counties, Mississippi, the big planters (those with thirty-one or more slaves) averaged only seventy-six dollars worth of home manufactures in 1860, and farmers and small planters averaged much less. In Dougherty and Thomas counties, Georgia, the small planters (those with from twenty-one to thirty slaves) led other groups of slaveholders with one hundred and twenty-seven dollars, and the big planters produced only about half as much. Most of the plant-ers in both clusters of counties recorded no home manufactures at all.[1]

---

[1] From the five Mississippi and the five Georgia cotton belt counties regarded as typical by Lewis C. Gray in his *History of Agriculture in the Southern United States to 1860* (2 vols., Washington, 1933), I, 334–35, II, 918–21, I have analyzed for each state the two that come closest to the mode in the only variable for which there is clear

Sample studies from Virginia's tobacco area, wheat area, and tidewater reveal the same situation. Plantation manuscripts show surprisingly frequent, and often quite large, expenditures for artisans' services and suggest that plantations were much less self-sufficient and exhibited much less division of labor than is generally appreciated. The root of the insufficient demand must be sought in the poverty of the rural majority composed of slaves, subsistence farmers, and poor whites.

In nineteenth-century America as a whole both capital and labor were in short supply. Industrial development was spurred by farmers who provided a large market for goods and tools, and manufacturing arose on the foundation of this immense rural demand. Eastern manufacturers gradually awoke to their dependence on this rural market and by 1854 were supporting homestead legislation not only to gain support for higher tariffs and for purposes of speculation but to expand the market for their goods. Farmers in New England saw their futures linked with industrial development, and their hostility toward commercial middlemen was not usually transferred to the manufacturers. The same was true in the West. As the shrewd Achille Murat noted in the 1830's, the manufacturing interest of the West "is not constituted by the manufactories which exist, but those which they look forward to in prospective." An agrarianism uncompromisingly hostile to industry and urbanization—to what was called "manufacturing as a system"—existed only in the South and can not be separated from the ideological leadership of the slaveholding planters. Even there, those seriously interested in economic progress saw the link between agricultural reform and industrialization and tried to work out proposals for increased manufactures that would be palatable to their fellow slaveholders.

The West was able to import capital because Eastern manufacturers and European creditors were confident of her growth and prosperity. Outside credits at that time had to be accumulated by the importation of commodities and the maintenance of an unfavorable trade balance. The immense internal market guaranteed the West an import surplus until

---

evidence, the size of slaveholdings. A review of the economic and natural conditions of the South reveals nothing to suggest that the four counties so chosen are not roughly typical of the cotton belt. I have used the four counties primarily for an investigation of purchasing power—to gain clues to the general structure of the market—and the insignificant expenditures recorded indicate that even with due allowance for the possibility of a wide, say 50%, deviation in other counties and for incorrect reporting in the census returns, the results could not conceivably be substantially different.

As a random sample, I selected the first ten names on each page of U.S. Census, 1860, Georgia, Schedule 4, Productions of Agriculture, Dougherty and Thomas counties (Library, Duke University, Durham, North Carolina) and U.S. Census, 1860, Mississippi, Schedule 4, De Soto and Marshall counties (Mississippi State Archives, Jackson). From the U.S. Census, 1860, Georgia, Schedule 2, Slave Inhabitants, Dougherty and Thomas counties, and U.S. Census, 1860, Mississippi, Schedule 2, De Soto and Marshall counties (National Archives, Washington), I determined the number of slaves held by each agriculturist in my sample. Where Schedule 4 gave the amount of produce but not its monetary value, I used a specially prepared price schedule in order to translate the amounts into dollar values. See Eugene D. Genovese, The Limits of Agrarian Reform in the Slave South (unpublished Ph.D. thesis, Columbia University, 1959), appendixes.

1850. Its insatiable demand for manufactured articles contributed to the unfavorable trade balance of the United States, but on the whole this was not a serious problem for the country because American importers were strong enough to obtain long-term credits on relatively easy terms; and, during the 1850's, profits from shipping and other invisible gains largely restored the balance. Thus, on the one hand, the national economy was sufficiently strong to overcome the worst effects of a trade deficit, and, on the other hand, the agrarian West was able to obtain the credits required for industrial development. The South did not benefit from this arrangement. It provided an exportable surplus, which, although of great help to the national economy in offsetting the large quantity of imports, was exploited by Northern capital. The invisible gains that were so important to national growth were made partly at the expense of the South.

The population statistics for 1860 offer a clue to the structure of the market. If we exclude Maryland, in which slavery was declining, and Delaware, which was a slave state in name only, the median population per square mile in the slave states was 18, and Kentucky was high with 31. In comparison, Massachusetts had a population of 158 per square mile; Rhode Island, 138; Connecticut, 98; New York, 84; New Jersey, 81; and so forth. In the West, Ohio had 59; Indiana, 40; and Illinois, 31.

These figures do not tell the important part of the story. A country that is sparsely settled, in absolute terms, may have a high population density, in economic terms, if its system of transportation and commodity production are well developed and integrated. For example, the Northern states in 1860 had a much higher population density—from an economic point of view—than the thickly populated countries of Asia. When we consider the superiority of Northern transportation and economic integration, relative to those of the South, we must conclude that the difference in the magnitude of the market greatly exceeded that suggested by the population figures.

Historians have long appreciated—at least since the pioneer researches of U. B. Phillips—that the Southern transportation system tied the staple-producing areas to the ports and that this was the best possible arrangement for the planters. The planters controlled the state legislatures in an era in which state participation was decisive in railroad construction and generally refused to assume the tax burden necessary to open the back country and thereby encourage and strengthen politically suspect farmers. Without a fully developed railroad network tying the South into an economic unit, the absorption of nonstaple producers into the market economy, except in a peripheral way, was impossible. Poor transportation was, for example, one important factor in the retardation of the Southern cotton textile industry.

With good reason alert Southerners spoke of the connection among railroads, markets, diversified agriculture, and manufacturing. James Robb pointedly described improved transportation and greater industry as necessary ingredients in the process of unifying the South. Oscar M. Lieber noted that without an adequate transportation system South Carolina farmers were prevented from entering the market as corn producers. John Bell warmly supported federal land grants to railroads to strengthen the bonds of commodity production. Within the South these men could, at best, expect to be received with an impatient silence. Where their message was sometimes listened to attentively was in the upper South, as for example in what came to be West Virginia; the subsequent construction of road and railroad links to existing markets generally bound parts of the upper South to the free states and helped remove them from the slaveholders' domain.

In the slave South the home market consisted primarily of the plantations, which bought foodstuffs from the West and manufactured goods from the East. The planters needed increased Southern manufacturing but only for certain purposes. They needed cheap slave clothing, cotton gins and a few crude agricultural implements, rope for cotton bagging, and so forth. This narrow market could not compare with the tremendous Western demand for industrial commodities of all kinds, especially for agricultural implements and machinery on the more capital-intensive Western farms. The Northeast had the capital and skilled labor for fairly large-scale production and had established its control over existing markets in the North and West. Southern manufacturers could not hope to compete with Northern outside the South, and the same conditions that brought about Northern control of the Northern market made possible Northern penetration of the Southern market despite the costs of transportation.

The South was caught in a contradiction similar to that facing many underdeveloped countries today. On the one hand, it provided a market for outside industry. On the other hand, that very market was too small to sustain industry on a scale large enough to compete with outsiders who could draw upon wider markets. Only one fifth of the manufacturing establishments of the United States were in the South, and their average capitalization was well below that of the manufacturing establishments of the free states. Consider the situation in two industries of special importance to the South—cotton textiles and agricultural implements. New England had almost three times as many cotton factories as the entire South in 1860, and yet the average capitalization was almost twice as great. The concentration in this industry had proceeded so far by 1850 that of the more than 1,000 cotton factories in the United States only forty-one had one half the total capital investment. As for the agricultural implement and machinery industry, New York, Pennsylvania, Ohio, and Illinois each had a greater total capital investment than did the entire South, and in three of these the average capitalization was between two and two and a half times as great as the average in the South.[2] This Northern advantage led

[2] U.S. Census Office, *Manufactures of the United States in 1860* . . . (Washington 1865), xxi, ccxvii, lxxiii, 729–30; Evelyn H. Knowlton, *Pepperell's Progress; History of a Cotton Textile Company, 1844–1945* (Cambridge, Mass., 1948), 32. The average capitalization of manufacturing establishments was in 1850 more than 25% higher in the free states and territories than in the slave states, and the gap widened in the 1850's when the increase in average capital investment was 68% in the free states and territories and only 51% in the slave states. The lower South (North Carolina, South Carolina, Georgia, Florida, Alabama, Mississippi, Louisiana, and Texas) fell even further behind. The average capitalization here, 38% less than in the free states in 1850, was 47% less by 1860. Furthermore, the rate of increase in the number of establishments during this decade was appreciably greater in the North than in the South.

Edmund Ruffin and T. L. Clingman, among others, to look forward to a Southern confederacy protected by high tariffs against Northern goods.

In view of the nature of the plantation market it is not surprising that data on the cotton textile industry almost invariably reveal that Southern producers concentrated upon the production of the cheapest and coarsest kind of cloth to be used in the making of slave clothing. Even so, local industrialists had to compete for this market with Northerners who sometimes shipped direct and sometimes established Southern branches and who had facilities for the collection and processing of second-hand clothing. Just as New England supplied much of the South's "Negro cloth," so it supplied much of the boots and shoes. Firms like Batchellor Brothers of Brookfield produced cheap shoes especially for the Southern market and as early as 1837 opened a branch at Mobile to consolidate its Southern market.

Producers of better cotton goods had little hope of making a living in the South. Occasionally, a William Gregg could penetrate Northern markets successfully, but Southern demand for such goods was too small to have much effect on the industry generally. Northern firms like the Pepperell Manufacturing Company or A. A. Lawrence Company did little business in the South. On the other hand a rising demand for textiles in the agrarian West had greatly influenced the New England cotton industry since 1814.

The Southern iron industry, hampered as it was by the restricted railroad development in the slave states, also had a poor time of it. American iron producers generally were handicapped because much of the country's railroad iron was being imported. The small scale of operations and resultant cost schedule, which hurt the industry nationally, hit the Southern manufacturers especially hard. Dependent upon a weak local market, Southern iron manufacturers had great difficulty holding their own even during the prosperous 1850's.

No wonder the Augusta, Georgia, Commercial Convention added to its demand that Southerners buy Southern goods the qualification, "unless you can get Northern cheaper." And no wonder the proposal was ridiculed as amounting to "Never kiss the maid if you can kiss the mistress, unless you like the maid better."

We can not measure precisely the extent of the Southern market nor even make a reliable, general, quantitative comparison between the Southern and Western rural markets, but we can glean from various sources some notion of the immense difference. For example, Phelps, Dodge & Co., a prominent cotton shipping firm that also distributed metals, tools, machinery, clothing, and an assortment of other items, reported at the beginning of the Civil War that only five per cent of its sales were to the South and that those were primarily to the noncotton states. We do not know the extent of the firm's participation in the cotton export trade, but it was considerable. Phelps, Dodge & Co. was in an excellent position to exchange industrial goods for cotton, but the Southern demand for imported goods could not compare in bulk or value with the supply of cotton. In the West, on the other hand, farmers and townsmen provided a growing and lucrative market, and the firm had more customers in Ohio than in any state except New York.

An examination of the 1860 manuscript census returns and other primary sources pertaining to two representative cotton counties in Mississippi and to two in Georgia permits us to judge roughly the extent of the market in the cotton belt by estimating the expenditures made by planters and farmers in these counties. (See above, note 1.) The estimates are the most generous possible and exaggerate the extent of the Southern rural market in relation to the Western in two ways: There were far more rural poor with little or no purchasing power in the cotton belt than in the West, and the concentration of landholdings in the South resulted in fewer landowners than could be found in a Western area of comparable size. Thus, even if the estimate of the expenditures made by these Southern planters and farmers had been larger than the expenditures of a similar group of individual proprietors in the West—which was by no means true—the total purchased in each county would still have been far less than in a comparable Western area. Furthermore, as food was a major item in the expenditures of the Southerners, the market for industrial commodities was much smaller than might appear.

The concentration of landholding and slaveholding in the Mississippi counties meant that six per cent of the landowners commanded one third of the gross income and probably a much higher percentage of the net. That is, the majority of landowners were faced with a disproportionately small portion of the total income accruing to the cotton economy as a whole.

Only the largest planters—ten per cent of the landowners—spent more than $1,000 a year for food and supplies, and they rarely spent more. These expenditures include the total purchases for the slaves. The slaveholding farms and plantations in Mississippi annually spent about thirty or thirty-five dollars per person for food and supplies; nonslaveholders spent about twenty-five dollars per person. In Georgia slaveholding farms and plantations spent about twenty-five dollars per person, and nonslaveholders were just about self sufficient. In contrast, Philip Foner reports that contemporary newspapers and other sources indicate that the small farmers who made up the great majority of the rural population of the West accumulated store bills of from one hundred to six hundred dollars. Even if we allow for considerable exaggeration and assume that the accounts were generally closer to the lower estimate, these figures, which are exclusive of cash purchases, mail orders, payments to drummers, and so forth, are at least a clue to the impressive purchasing power of the Western countryside.

However imprecise the estimates for the South may be, they indicate the lack of purchasing power among the rural population of the cotton belt and demonstrate how greatly the situation there differed from that in the West. With such a home market the slave economy could not sustain more than the lowest level of commodity production apart from that of a few staples. The success of William Gregg as a textile manufacturer in South Carolina and the data produced by Professor John Hebron Moore showing that a cotton textile industry could and did exist in ante bellum Mississippi would seem to contradict this conclusion; but Gregg, who was aware of the modest proportions of the home market, warned Southerners against trying to produce for local needs and suggested that they focus on the wholesale market. His own company at Graniteville, South Carolina, produced fine cotton goods that sold much better in New York than in the South. Gregg's success in the Northern market could not easily be duplicated by others, and when he discussed the Southern market, he felt compelled, as did Benjamin L. C. Wailes and other astute observers, to advocate production of cheap cotton goods for the plantations. Moore's conclusion that his data prove the adaptability of manufacturing to the lower South requires for substantiation more than evidence of particular successes, no matter how impressive; it requires evidence that Southern producers were strong enough to drive out Northern competition and, more important, that the market was large enough to sustain more than a few firms.

The plantation system did have its small compensations for industry. The planters' taste for luxuries, for example, proved a boon to the Petersburg iron industry, which supplied plantations with cast-iron fences, lawn ornaments, balconies, fancy gates, and other decorative articles. A silk industry emerged briefly but was destroyed by climatic conditions as well as by a shortage of capital. The hemp industry, which supplied rope for cotton baling, depended heavily on the plantation market.

Some Southern industrialists, especially those in the border states, did good business in the North. Louisville tobacco and hemp manufacturers sold much of their output in Ohio. Botts and Burfoot of Richmond, Virginia, reported the sale of $1,000-worth of straw cutters in the North during a six-month period. The more successful Southern iron producers were those of the upper South, who were able to sell outside the slave states. Smith and Perkins of Alexandria, Virginia, began production of locomotives and railroad cars in the 1850's and obtained a good many orders from the North; but the company failed because shipping costs made consolidation of its Northern market difficult and because only a few orders were forthcoming from the South. Similarly, the paper industry in South Carolina did well until the 1850's, when Northern orders dropped and no Southern orders appeared. The political dangers of these links with the free states were widely appreciated. The Virginia Commercial Convention, for example, reported that West Virginia was being cut off from the South in this way. During the Civil War, William Henry Holcombe, a thoughtful doctor from Natchez, listed in his diary various reasons for the adherence of the border states to the Union and placed close commercial ties high on the list. One suspects that there was more than hindsight here, for politically sophisticated Southerners were alert to the danger well before 1861. But what could they have done about it?

The inability of the slave South to generate an adequate rural market inhibited industrialization and urbanization, which in turn limited the market for agricultural produce and undermined attempts at diversification. With the exception of New Orleans and Baltimore, the slave states had no large cities, and few reached the size of 15,000. The urban population of the South could not compare with that of the Northeast, as is generally appreciated; but, more to the point, it could not compare with that of the agrarian West either. The urban population of the lower South in 1860 was only seven per cent of the total population, and in the western part of the lower South, embracing most of the cotton belt, there was a relative decline during the preceding twenty years. In New England, the percentage was thirty-seven; in the Middle Atlantic states, including Ohio, thirty-five; and perhaps most significantly, in Indiana, Illinois, Michigan, and Wisconsin, fourteen.

The urban market in the South was even less developed than these figures suggest. If we except New Orleans, which was a special case, three cities of the lower South had a population of 15,000 or more: Mobile, Charleston, and Savannah, with a combined population of 92,000. Of this number, thirty-seven per cent were slaves and free Negroes, who may be assumed to have represented only minimal purchasing power. In the 1850's American families certainly did not spend less than forty per cent of their incomes on food, and the importance of a large urban market for foodstuffs may be judged accordingly.

Eugene W. Hilgard, state geologist of Mississippi, explained his state's failure to develop a cattle industry largely by the absence of a local market. Similarly, Oscar M. Lieber, state geologist of South Carolina, warned farmers in a state that was never comfortably self-sufficient in corn not to produce more corn than they could consume, for there was no place to market the surplus. Charles Yancey of Buckingham County, Virginia, wrote that planters and farmers would not grow oats because the only possibility of disposing of them lay in person to person barter.

The weakness of the market for agricultural produce had many detrimental consequences for the South, of which we may mention only two. First, those sections of the border states which found markets in the Northern cities were increasingly drawn into the political-economic orbit of the free states at the very moment when the slave states required maximum solidarity to preserve their system. Second, the weakness of the market doomed the hopes of agricultural reformers and transformed their cry for diversification into a cry for a backward step toward natural economy.

When that great antislavery Kentuckian, Cassius M. Clay, finally receives from historians the honor and attention that he deserves, he will surely be recognized as one of the most penetrating commentators on the economics of slavery. Consider his remarks on the problem of markets, with which we are presently concerned:

> Lawyers, merchants, mechanics, laborers, who are your consumers; Robert Wickliffe's two hundred slaves? How many clients do you find, how many goods do you sell, how many hats, coats, saddles, and trunks do you make for these two hundred slaves? Does Mr. Wickliffe lay out as much for himself and his two hundred slaves as two hundred freemen do? . . . All our towns dwindle, and our farmers lose, in consequence, all home markets. Every farmer bought out by the slave system send off the consumers of the manufacturers

of the town: when the consumers are gone, the mechanic must go also. . . . A home market cannot exist in a slave state.

Plantation slavery, then, so limited the purchasing power of the South that it could not sustain much industry. That industry which could be raised usually lacked a home market of sufficient scope to permit large-scale operation; the resultant cost of production was often too high for success in competition with Northern firms drawing on much wider markets. Without sufficient industry to support urbanization, a general and extensive diversification of agriculture was unthinkable. Whatever other factors need to be considered in a complete analysis, the low level of demand in this plantation-based slave society was sufficient to retard the economic development of the South.

PART V

Legacy of Slavery: The Economy Since the Civil War

INTRODUCTION

⟨ PROFESSOR C. Vann Woodward has noted that one of the distinctive features of southern life has been "a long and quite un-American experience with poverty." [1] We have already seen how southern economic growth did not keep pace with northern development before the Civil War. The same trend continued after the war, despite the efforts of Henry Grady and others in the New South movement to bring industry and progress to the section. The Populist revolt of the 1890's drew national attention to the South's plight and produced a rash of articles, books, and official investigations attempting to describe, explain, and solve the problems the South faced. Yet, forty years later, little had changed: "The South," wrote President Franklin D. Roosevelt in 1938, "presents right now the nation's No. 1 economic problem."

Technological changes—some of them already under way when F. D. R. wrote —and large-scale government spending, as well as the movement of industry into the South, have, in recent years, begun to alter the southern economy.[2] Never-

theless, the South still has not caught up to the rest of the nation. In 1963, no southern state came within ten percentage points of the average national per capita income, and some—Mississippi, Alabama, Georgia, South Carolina, and Arkansas—were 25 percent or more below the national average.

Many efforts have been made to account for the South's economic problems since the Civil War. Some students have suggested that the destruction of war and the dislocation of reconstruction have been the chief cause; others have blamed the postwar credit mechanisms, pointing an accusing finger at the furnishing merchant who is said to have forced a one-crop agriculture on a helpless people. Some explanations have been frankly racist: the Negro was racially inferior and consequently was an inefficient farmer. Others have blamed whites as well as Negroes for being lazy— unwilling to work to get out of debt, stand on their own feet, and promote sectional progress.

Not all explanations focus on the post-Civil War period. Often commentators look back to the ante-bellum era to discover the roots of southern economic woes. Inevitably, some of these explanations deal with the lasting effects of slavery on the South.

In the selections which follow, the reader is introduced to a number of explanations for the lack of postwar economic progress in the South. Ulrich B. Phillips, in the first selection, argues

[1] C. Vann Woodward, *The Burden of Southern History* (Baton Rouge: Louisiana State University Press, 1960), p. 17.

[2] Thomas D. Clark, in *The Emerging South* (New York: Oxford University Press, 1961), traces these changes. He concludes that "much of the course of the South into the future is already charted, and that course gives every evidence of leading the region away from many of the old and familiar ways of the past," pp. 285–86.

that the plantation system—but not necessarily slavery—was needed to organize Negro labor before the Civil War and continued to be required after slavery was abolished. In the second selection, economist Douglas F. Dowd compares the economic development of the West with that of the South. His emphasis is on the post-Civil War period, but he finds that a "core of institutions," all of them dating from the ante-bellum period—slavery, cash-crop monoculture, and the plantation system—are the cause of the South's failure to equal the economic development of the West. Another economist, William H. Nicholls,

contends that southern traditions stemming from the ante-bellum period have consistently barred progress. The influence of the slave system in creating and promoting these traditions is evident in his analysis.

The questions raised here are, of course, of great significance. If the problems facing the South today stem from an institutional legacy of slavery, their solution requires a major change in the southern way of life. The current civil rights movement, then, should be the first step toward revolutionary change in the South.

THE READINGS

1] Need for Plantation Organization

SINCE THE end of the civil war there has been in the South a tendency toward the multiplication of small holdings of land, which has been thought to promise the disappearance of all the plantations. But a more careful study of the general problem will show that the tendencies in the unsettled periods of reconstruction and later were probably of temporary character, and that something like the old plantation will be established as the predominant type of agricultural organization in the South for the future.

The plantation was evolved in early colonial Virginia as the most efficient system for growing tobacco. That was before African slaves were imported in any appreciable numbers. The negroes were soon found to fit in admirably with the plantation arrangements. A similar system was established in the Carolina districts producing rice and indigo, and in the sugar-cane fields of Louisiana. Finally the invention of the cotton-gin and the extension of cotton culture into the uplands carried the plantation into the whole of the staple-producing South. Wherever the land was adapted to tobacco, rice, indigo, sugar, or cotton, the plantation won the victory over the small farm. It was the survival of the fittest. The involuntary servitude of the laborers was merely an incident. There is no essential reason why the freedom of the slaves should destroy the plantations.

The conditions of the problem in Southern agriculture were and remain as follows: 1. Abundance of land; 2. Money crops, with uncertain money returns; 3. Ignorant and unenterprising labor; and 4. A large number of efficient managers of agricultural labor, who are usually also the owners of the soil and of such capital as exists. The problem is how to organize this labor under the existing conditions to secure the best returns. In former times the plantation system was developed as the most efficient for the purpose, and today it is not at all clear that the usefulness of that system has departed.

The plantation system was the application of manufacturing or capitalistic methods to agricultural production. The planter was a captain of industry. He owned the land, he planned the work of the year, and he saw to it that the work was done. His problem was to lay out the fields for the best return, to keep his laborers profitably at work in all seasons, to guard against the overworking of his laborers or his mules, and to watch receipts and expenditures with an eye for economy. If the planter failed in any of these requirements, he lost his wages of superintendence.

FROM Ulrich B. Phillips, "The Economics of the Plantation," *South Atlantic Quarterly,* II (July, 1903), 231–36.

If he allowed expenditures to exceed receipts, he lost first his profits, then his rent, and finally his capital. By overworking his land, his mules, or his laborers, to their injury, he might secure a greater return for one year, but was sure to be the loser in the long run.

In a normal period the small farm could not compete with a well managed plantation in the production of the staples. A man who is able to manage a small farm to advantage is usually able also to superintend the labor of others in his line of work. Wages of efficient superintendence are always much higher than the wages of mere labor. The tendency, then, in the staple regions where additional labor was to be had, was for the successful farmer to establish himself as a planter. When an independent artisan becomes a foreman in a factory, or advances further to the owner-ship and superintendence of a mill, he does no wrong to the other artisans or to the factory operatives. By his efficient work on the larger scale he serves the whole world better than before. The advance of a ploughman into efficient plantation management and ownership causes a net increase in production, with a lowering of cost, and usually also means a betterment for the laborers under him.

The plantation system in the South can be no hardship for the negro. If his wages are low and the wages of superintendence high, it is because the laborer is careless and slovenly, and the risk of loss is great. The capable mulatto, and even the exceptional negro under present conditions, may hope to advance by thrift from the status of a hired ploughman or an independent farmer to become an overseer or the owner and manager of a plantation.

In the reconstruction period, there was a complete upheaval in the system of Southern industry. With the manager dead in battle, with labor disorganized, and with capital vanished from the land, some new arrange-ment had to be devised. As a rule the negroes became tenants, either on the basis of giving a share of the crop for the use of the land and stock, or on the basis of a rental in money or in cotton. By industry and economy, a number of the negroes have been able to buy land and mules of their own, but the great majority remain renters, or croppers, today. A large number even of those who own their farms are in a chronic state of debt to the merchants who furnish their supplies. These merchants require this class of debtors to plant a given amount of land in a money crop, and they often employ inspectors to see to it that the crops are kept in adequate cultivation. Thus they make sure that the debtor will be able to settle his account in full or in part when the crop is sold. In good years the farmer is able to pay off his current debts and perhaps has a surplus left on hand. But when crops are bad or prices are low, a mortgage must usually be made in order to secure the advance of supplies for another year. A second year of failure may establish the merchant as an unwilling landholder, and the debtor as his tenant.

The present system of renting, or cropping, can be but temporary. Under it the negro is superintended in but a half-hearted way. Whenever he fails to raise a good crop and to sell it at a good price, he involves his landlord and his creditor with himself in a common embarrassment. Furthermore, the average negro cannot maintain himself as an independent farmer, because his ignorance, indolence, and instability prevent him from managing his own labor in an efficient way.

The most promising solution for the problem is the re-establishment of the old plantation system, with some form of hired labor instead of slave labor. The whole tendency of American industry is toward organization for more efficient management. It is a dead loss for a good manager to have no managing to do. It is also a dead loss for a laborer who needs management to have no management. The most successful grain farms in the West are really plantations, where great gangs of men and machines work under a single direction. A system of small farms in the South would be an unprofitable reaction from a better system in the past. It would be a lessening of the net output in the staples and in grain, meat, and dairy products. It is necessary to bring Southern industry in agriculture as well as in manufacturing to a modern progressive basis; and the plantation system seems to be the most efficient for the purpose.

For the last thirty-five years the most progressive men in the country districts of the South have been moving to near-by towns or to the Northern cities. This is disastrous to agriculture, and a reverse tendency should be set at work. Under the present regime, a hundred schools of agriculture and dairying would do little good, for the farmer boy now goes to college only in order to leave the farm for good. Efficient managers can be attracted back to the soil only by some arrangement which will offer promising opportunities for management. A new plantation system must offer profitable and attractive careers to well-equipped men, or the pine thicket and the sedge field will continue to be conspicuous features of the landscape in the cotton belt, wasteful methods will continue in use, and the Southern farmers and Southern merchants will ever lag behind those of the North and the West. The colleges of agriculture in Wisconsin, Nebraska, and California have demands always pouring in for twice or thrice as many men as they can equip to fill the attractive positions which are offered upon the large farms in need of managers. In Georgia the college of agriculture has for decades been without students, because the system of renters and croppers and small farmers has prevented the rise of any demand for agricultural managers.

Yet there already exists a tendency for betterment in the South. There are several colleges of agriculture, like that of Tennessee, which are drawing a fair number of students; and the prosperity of these schools indicates that the soil is efficiently demanding a number of trained managers. Model plantations are to be found here and there, which are most attractive as patterns. There are planters in the Georgia cotton belt, for instance, who have withstood the disintegrating tendencies, and who at this day conduct large plantations upon the old system of management, but with hired labor. The Georgia Convict Farm serves as an example in its community. The managers are the most capable men to be had. They adopt the most approved methods, and they conduct experiments in draining, terracing, ploughing, fertilizing and rotating crops, which lead to surprisingly good returns. It is easy to see that the same managers with hired labor instead of convicts might win equal success. This has been done in fact in numerous recent instances by men who have had no special training, but who possess natural or inherited fitness for plantation management.

I am acquainted with a gentleman, born and reared upon a cotton plantation in Troup county, Georgia, who moved to Atlanta, upon reaching manhood, and established himself in business. He achieved moderate success, but always felt that yearning for the soil which is felt by so many Southerners away from the plantation. At length he resolved to return to the country and apply, with hired labor, the methods of cotton raising which his father had applied in ante-bellum days. He bought a tract of land in the Alabama cotton belt, built comfortable cabins, hired several negro families, selected the best of modern implements and fertilizers, and by good management made such a success that capitalists have offered to buy an unlimited amount of land for him if he will undertake to organize upon it a modern plantation system. A number of other men have received instruction from his example, and his whole community is tending to change from the renting and cropping system to the system of the plantation. This is not an isolated case; but seems to be an earnest of a general movement. The great new peach orchards of middle Georgia further illustrate the recent tendency toward the plantation system and its adaptation to a variety of crops.

When the plantation comes to be re-established predominantly in the fertile parts of the South, it will bring order out of the existing chaos. By introducing system in place of haphazard work, it will lower the cost of production, increase the output, and enable the South to produce a greater amount of its food and other needed supplies. It will infuse a spirit of thrift into the Southern community, for the competition of plantation managers for the market will not permit of indolence.

The plantation system offers to the South the best means of offsetting the ignorance and laziness of the negro laborers. It offers profitable work for blacksmiths, engineers, millers, carpenters, and other artisans. As in a factory or a great business concern, the system, when thoroughly developed, will put a premium upon ability and enterprise. Capable men will be promoted to responsible positions. And yet it need not involve any hardship upon the ordinary laborer, further than the requirement of regular hours of work. Under present conditions the average negro cropper, or renter, lives from hand to mouth with an extremely low standard of living. Money wages would be much better. Savings facilities could well be established, and perhaps also a profit-sharing system. The unenterprising whites would be drawn off to the factories, or they would continue as small farmers, learning improved methods from the neighboring plantations.

The great fault of the ante-bellum system of plantations lay in its exclusive devotion to the staple crops, and in its discouragement of manufacturing and other forms of industry. But the experience of latter years has destroyed the belief in the omnipotence of raw cotton. The planter of today and tomorrow must accept his place as only one of many captains of industry, without expecting to become the autocratic master of production or of politics in the country.

Any modern system must take a tone from the active, pushing, world of to-day; but in essentials the plantations of old could again look with hope to the system which produced the fine type of the Southern gentlemen of the old regime. The present heterogeneous conditions can only be transitional. The prevalence of small farms would be the prevalence of mediocrity and stagnation. The hope of the South is in the application of the principle of the division of labor to agricultural production.

2] Comparative Economic Development of the West and the South

I

IN 1930, the West—for present purposes, Kansas, Nebraska, the Dakotas, Montana, Idaho, Wyoming, Utah, and Colorado—had a level of per capita income payments that stood at 79 per cent of the national figure. In that same year, the figure for the South—Kentucky, Tennessee, Virginia, the Carolinas, Georgia, Florida, Alabama, Mississippi, Louisiana, and Arkansas —was 51 per cent.

This West was part of what used to be called the Great American Desert. The South, physically, has been thought of since the beginning as "the garden spot of America." Although it is not true that the West is a desert, nor the South a garden spot, the South has the better resources—in the combined terms of soils, waterways, climate, terrain, minerals, timber— and, of course, a much more abundant labor supply. And yet, the economic development of the West surpassed that of the South, using almost any criteria of economic development.

Because of the divergent characteristics of past economic developments in the West and the South, using the time period 1865–1930, their comparative treatment may enable us to tighten up our notion of the meaning of "underdevelopment," and extend our understanding of the process of development by illuminating those aspects of the developmental process that are fundamental and those that are incidental, either as obstacles or stimuli. There will be no pretense here of uncovering new data; rather, I shall attempt to reorganize what is well known.

Unintentionally, a by-product of this analysis will appear as a repudiation of the theme of these meetings. For, taking the development of the West at any time, and through time, it is difficult to conceive of it as being, in any acceptable sense, an underdeveloped region. Up until 1930, at least, quite the contrary is true of the South.

FROM Douglas F. Dowd, "A Comparative Analysis of Economic Development in the American West and South," *Journal of Economic History*, XVI (December, 1956), 558–74.

The argument here will be a familiar one, which nonetheless requires continuous reiteration, and which certainly can stand further substantiation: namely, that the core of the developmental problem is institutional. This is not to overlook the obvious fact that resources, natural and human, must be obtainable if things are to be produced. But the mere presence of a "good" resource base does not insure economic development, as witness the difference between Russia and the Soviet Union; and the presence of a relatively "poor" resource base does not preclude substantial achievements in production, per capita income, health, education, and the whole run of other advantages associated with development, as witness, say, Japan. This is merely another way of saying that the nature and the extent of resources are of course meaningless apart from the social context within which they exist. And it is differences in social context that so strikingly set apart the West from the South.

The social context, in the West, was such that its resources were exploited rapidly and successfully (ignoring conservation criteria), and apparently close to their potential, given time and circumstance. The South, with a markedly better and more diversified resource base, lagged miserably, not only behind the nation as a whole, but also well behind the West. The basic reason for these disparate, and on resource grounds unintelligible, developments is that western development was *ancillary* to that taking place to the east of it; that the physical differences between West and East were, Webb's "institutional fault" to the contrary notwithstanding, unmatched so far as key institutions *affecting development* were concerned. In the last analysis, the economic development of the West cannot be looked upon as a regional development; it is the physical extension of dynamic developments taking place to the east and overseas.

The South, on the other hand, was *not* an extension, or, in an important sense, even a part of an industrializing America. The South was one of America's colonies; it was, as Cash has put it, "another land, sharply differentiated from the rest of the American nation, and exhibiting within itself a remarkable homogeneity." It is the component parts of that "homogeneity" that deserve extended treatment, for they were antithetical to healthy, sustained economic development. If, as seems to be true, the South is currently engaged in a process of rapid economic growth, it is precisely because its "homogeneity" is crumbling, largely under the combined impact of two world wars, a major depression and a long world-wide boom.

II

Out of the hubbub over underdeveloped areas that has sounded for the last decade or two, we should be in a position to state simply the major defining characteristics of such areas, in terms of quantity, quality, and process. Quantitatively, underdevelopment is expressible in terms of per capita income, the degree of surplus (savings and investment), levels and patterns of consumption and investment, and productivity; in measures of health, education, etc., where the bias is heavily toward lowness and inadequacy. Qualitatively, the underdeveloped society exhibits a structure of production, ownership, and control which, taken together with thin and shallow markets, and an absence of adequate financial institutions and the factors making for external economies, combines to keep the quantitative achievements of the society at a low level. Often there is an associated population problem that holds back growth and wipes out gains. In terms of process, the underdeveloped society is one that is spinning its wheels in the mud; which, to use the more common metaphor, is revolving slowly and helplessly within a series of intertwined vicious circles.

Did the American West fit this definition? Of course not. We may note that the productive structure of the West has been dominated by primary production; that much of the ownership (particularly in railroads, mining, cattle, and timber) was nonwestern; that Westerners were faced with unfavorable terms of trade in their dealings with the more powerful East; that the per capita income of Westerners throughout our period and to this date is lower than that of those to the east of them above the Mason and Dixon line, and lower than those in the Far West. These and other particular characteristics often associated with underdevelopment may be found in the West. What *cannot* be found is the over-all quality of underdevelopment: the matrix of inhibiting institutional relationships is almost totally absent. The West, from its inception as a settled area, was possessed of vitality; it continually changed and expanded.

The West was settled and exploited in a series of *booms:* railroad booms, cattle booms, farming booms, mining and timber booms. These booms were in time followed by the rise of commercial and financial nuclei, and by the growth of secondary industries. That much of the profitability of the booms may have drained out to eastern (and some foreign) owners is true, but because the West was an integral part of the society to which the largest part of it went, the drain did not have a long-run negative impact on development possibilities, although it did affect the distribution of income as between West and East.

In its critical period of development, the thirty years or so following the Civil War, the West was of course subjected to falling prices for its goods—as was the rest of the nation, and the rest of the world. As is well known, price drops were a consequence of newly opened food lands, and a connected rapid improvement in technology, transportation, and communications. Western resources were exploited ruthlessly and often stupidly, as were western miners, farm workers, and loggers; and many western farmers sank into tenancy or were pushed out of farming. But through it all western production and productivity grew, so much so as to provide simultaneously a rising level and improving quality of life for Westerners, cheap food and raw materials for the rest of the country, and a surplus of foodstuffs that played a crucial role in our balance of payments.

In brief, the West was never a region faced with a development *problem.* It developed as an outcome of the needs of the rest of the nation, and out of its inherent possibilities as an area empty of people (except the easily brushed-aside Indians), and relatively well equipped with natural resources. Extravagant and some not so extravagant hopes pulled people and capital out of the regions of the East and from Europe—both on the make, the people ambitious and relatively flexible, the capital speculative and always forthcoming; albeit at high rates.

The story of the impact of technology on western farming has been told frequently and well. The point of it, for present purposes, is that the West was quick to adopt relevant new techniques on a general scale. If settlement was to take place in the West, it had to take place with a more capital-intensive agriculture than had existed in the regions to the east and south. Fencing and barbed wire, deep wells and windmills, seeds and agricultural science; all had to be experimented with if the Plains were to be cultivated. Given the climate and soils, a labor-extensive agriculture had to be practiced, and cultivation had to be mechanized. The needs were faced, the technical problems were solved, and settlement rapidly followed the solutions. What is true of agriculture—the necessity of adopting new techniques —is true of cattle raising, of mining, and of timber exploitation, though fewer people and therefore less drama were involved. This was an area that innovated quickly and extensively, held back only briefly by preconceived notions, driven on by a "boomer" optimism and a materialistic social philosophy.

Puritanism in Kansas and Mormonism in Utah, to mention the most striking cases, combined religion and economics to promote rapid development. For the region as a whole, it is clear that the social outlook of the people was completely in harmony with sustained economic growth, particularly with the prodding of an East and a world hungry for raw materials and food. Though we may deplore wheat cultivation in lands better suited to grazing, though many "busted" in Kansas and points west and north, though we may muse on the ultimate meaning of wasted mineral and timber resources, we cannot argue, at this point in our history, that economic growth was sickly, or its results unfortunate, in the West.

Perhaps it was the relatively lower levels of income in the West that led to the notion that it was underdeveloped. Perhaps it is the still wide-open spaces. But if underdevelopment is to have any serious meaning, that meaning must lie in the realm of comparing actual with potential. Looking back at the West, it is hard to imagine how, given the technology and markets of the period 1865–1930, much more could have been made of the area.

III

The West remained empty until its resources could fit the needs of the vigorous East. As such, vested interests and inhibiting forms of economic and social organization were absent. There were no significant institutional obstacles to the maximum development of western resources. And when settled, the West was thinly settled, by people whose eyes were fixed on the main chance.

The South, of course, stands in sharp contrast. As the southern region moved through time, it developed a set of institutions and accompanying attitudes which, intensified by the shock and chaos flowing from the Civil War, produced a formidable barrier to the achievement of rational economic organization. At the terminal year of this study, 1930, the South presented an almost classic picture of an underdeveloped society.

Per capita income in the South in 1929 was $365, the lowest of any region in the nation—about 60 per cent of the West's, and about 39 per cent of the Far West's. Illiteracy rates for the eleven southern states were among the highest fourteen in the country (the other three were in the Southwest); the nine western states (with the exception of Colorado) ranked among the twelve lowest in illiteracy. Estimated tangible wealth per capita in the South did not rise above $2,000 for any state in 1930; no state in the West fell below $3,000. Value added per wage earner in the South in 1929 was 60 per cent of that in the West. With 40 percent of the nation's farms in 1930, the South had 56 per cent of the nation's tenants. With a sixth of all the nation's croplands, in 1929, the eroded lands of the South used two thirds of the fertilizer used in the nation; with a fifth of the agricultural income, the South paid three fifths of the nation's fertilizer bill. The South ranked lowest in terms of health, with a particularly high incidence of diseases associated with malnutrition and poverty, such as pellagra and tuberculosis. Malaria alone was estimated as late as 1938 to have reduced the industrial output of the South by one third. And so on, with other measures of underdevelopment. These were the "fruits" of the southern industrialization process up to 1930.

"The nation's No. 1 economic problem," as Roosevelt called the South in 1938, was also the nation's No. 1 political problem, and, of course, the nation's No. 1 social problem. All grew from the same core of institutions; and these, in combination, retarded and stultified southern development. What was that core?

It consisted of three elements: cash crop monoculture, the plantation system, and Negro slavery. All these elements were present in some degree in the colonial period, when the major crops were tobacco, rice, and indigo. But during the colonial period, and for a generation or so after independence, the South possessed a relatively diversified economy. Its peak in diversification—in agriculture and industry—was probably reached between 1810 and 1820. With the cotton gin, cotton could not but become king. King Cotton brought about the decay of small manufactures and what diversification there had been in agriculture, and ineluctably eliminated meaningful protests against slavery.

Negro slavery and the plantation became simultaneously the roots from which stemmed the economic, social, and political life of the South. The planter naturally took over the best lands, whether for cotton, rice, sugarcane, or tobacco, and the small farmer was squeezed into the pine barrens, the hills, or out of the South. If he stayed in the South, the onetime small farmer might become a planter's overseer, or he might, rarely, become a planter himself. Most likely, he added to the ever-growing poor white group. There was no place else to go for most whites but down, or out.

As the American version of the *latifundia*, plantations were the ganglia of the southern economy. The plantation did its own marketing and buying (operating through the factor, the commercial and financial representative of nonsouthern interests), often produced, and always distributed the goods needed for all people and functions on the plantation. The growth of a middle class was thus stunted. There was, of course, no wage system on the plantation. Nor was there much work to be had for those off the plantation. The Negro did the agricultural work on the plantation, and he was also the skilled and unskilled artisan on and off the plantation.

As is well known, the plantation was only formally disrupted by the southern defeat in the war. Large-scale ownership remained the dominant characteristic; what changed was the identity of the owner. Increasingly, after the Civil War, the owner was absentee in location, northern in origin, and a commission house or banker in function. But the abolition of slavery required that a new means of getting the work done be found.

The attempt was made, in the first two years or so following the War, to utilize the freedmen on a free, wage-labor basis, but it miscarried. The freedmen, logically enough, could not be counted on to be around at the critical harvest time, voluntarily. Neither they, nor their poor white brethren, possessed land or tools or seed, and the planters wanted a guaranteed labor force. By 1867 the sharecropping and tenancy system began to spread rapidly throughout the South, as a natural and easy outgrowth of the combined needs of the propertied and propertyless. "Guarantees" for labor were provided by the commercial and financial system that grew up simultaneously with cropping and tenancy: the furnishing and supply system, and the crop lien. Once begun, there was no turning back, for cropper, tenant, planter, merchant, or creditor (where the latter three were often two, and sometimes one).

The differences between the plantation-cum-slavery system of the antebellum South and the system just described were that the Negroes were now debt slaves, or peons, rather than chattel slaves, and probably lived less well, the growing class of poor whites, who had at least not been enslaved before the War, now joined the Negroes, and in numbers ultimately outstripped them. Of the approximately 1,800,000 tenants (including croppers) in the cotton belt in 1930, over 1 million were white, slightly under 700,000 were colored.

The furnishing and supply system extended credit to cropper, tenant, and planter, for guano, food, and, for those who could afford them, clothes and other articles. Money rarely changed hands, and indebtedness was permanent and growing. Foreclosures, which were frequent (and unpublicized), changed the form but not the functioning or the results of the system, which was highly exploitative. Illiterate and ignorant Negroes and poor whites had neither the information nor the power to recognize or demand honest bookkeeping. Even with honesty—and there appears to have been some—the risks for the lender were high, and interest rates were accordingly oppressive, often running between 40 and 80 per cent per annum. With poor techniques, low productivity, mined soil, and high fertilizer costs, with continually fluctuating and secularly falling prices for their crops, the agriculturalists in the South (often including the planter) fell ever more hopelessly into a vicious downward spiral: deadening commitment to the cash crop, rising costs, falling prices, increasing indebtedness, poverty and, for most, peonage. The movement toward the deconcentration of land ownership after the Civil War was reversed. By 1930, it is estimated that 30 per cent of cotton lands were owned by insurance companies and banks.

Apart from the legal commitment to the cash crop required in the crop-lien contract, the Southerner was in any event unable to diversify. Away from the rivers, the road system, if the lack of roads may be called a system, prevented the marketing of anything but the cash crop, which did not perish with time and heat. And had there been roads, there were no marketing arrangements. Add to it all the lack of substantial opportunities in secondary and tertiary industry even during the "industrial revolution in the South," and the highest rate of population growth in the nation, the South found itself in the familiar pattern of overcrowding on the land, fragmentation, increasing pressures, and rural idleness. By the 1880's the social situation in the South had become explosive.

IV

Railroads, mines, and mills had of course existed in the South before the 1880's and they had been profitable. But around 1880 there began a rapid expansion of all three, at a rate that was unprecedented for the South. The "industrial revolution" in the South was given its impetus by many factors, including eager capital from the North and from England, and the favorable location of raw materials and power sources, but the most important were the tinderbox social situation and a large, unused labor pool. The latter made it possible for wages to be kept low and hours long, and the former made it imperative that some outlets for the labor of impoverished poor whites be found. The two were of course but different sides of the same coin.

Railroad mileage more than doubled in the South in the 1880's. The public lands were thrown open for sale for a decade or so after 1877, and were swallowed up almost completely in vast tracts by predominantly non-southern railroad and timber interests. Pig iron production in the Birmingham area rose by seventeen times in the space of twenty-five years, and coal mining expanded in rhythm. Tobacco processing and cigarette manufacturing became a big business, particularly in North Carolina, and, of course, it was in the 1880's that the southern cotton mills began their spectacular rise.

In 1870 there were 151 cotton mills in the South, in 1880 there were 161, in 1890 there were 239, and by 1900 there were 401 mills. In that period, capital invested had risen from $11.1 millions to $124.6 millions; the cotton processed had risen from about 34 million pounds to about 708 million pounds, and the number of factory operatives had risen from a little over 10 thousand to almost 98 thousand. By 1930 there were 280,000 cotton-mill workers, and the South had over half the active spindles in the country. The associated cottonseed oil industry also grew rapidly, immediately stimulated by the great need for fertilizers in the area; ultimately to be used for oleomargarine and other products. As time went on, the South's great forest resources were to be turned to furniture-making and paper products, and its phosphates, zinc, and bauxite were to be actively exploited.

Surely this growth defies the notion that the South remained under-developed throughout the period under examination? Not at all. For the quality of the development, the control over it, and its consequences cannot be said to have benefited or affected the majority of the people, nor to have furnished a basis for a sustained process of expansion. In 1930 only 19.6 per cent of Southern employment was in manufacturing and mechanical occupations, and one third of this was in the cotton mills.

Listen to Cash, a Southerner, as he tells us of the benefits to the mill worker of his new-found job:

> By 1900 the cotton-mill worker was a pretty distinct physical type in the South; a type in some respects perhaps inferior to even that of the old poor white, which in general had been his to begin with. A dead-white skin, a sunken chest, and stooping shoulders were the earmarks of the breed. Chinless faces, microcephalic foreheads, rabbit teeth, goggling dead-fish eyes, rickety limbs, and stunted bodies abounded—over and beyond the limit of their prevalence in the countryside. The women were characteristically stringy-haired and limp of breast at twenty, and shrunken hags at thirty or forty. And the incidence of tuberculosis, of insanity and epilepsy, and, above all, of pellagra, the curious vitamin-deficiency disease which is nearly peculiar to the South, was increasing.

We may doubt that the cephalic index or the shape of the Southerner's chin had changed within a few generations, but the general picture was still valid as late as the 1930's in and around the mill towns.

Of all the industrial workers the southern cotton-mill workers were perhaps the worst off, and the source of the greatest profits to southern and northern owners. It can scarcely be argued that the New England mill worker was well off; but it was the even greater exploitation of the mill worker in the South that acted as the most important justification of the new location of cotton textile mills. And this may be expressed in terms of lower wages and longer working days, and the extensive use of child labor.

In 1900 the average wages of cotton-mill workers in the South were about half of those in New England; in 1927, average weekly earnings in the five leading New England states were still 47.8 per cent higher than those in the five leading southern states. In 1900 the work week in the South was sixty-eight to seventy-two hours; in New England, it was fifty-six to fifty-eight. Children labored for from twelve to fourteen hours a day, and in the poor-white family all able-bodied children worked. Without the work of the entire family, wages were insufficient for subsistence. And, if it be thought that the cost of living was lower in the South than in New England, and this seems to be the generally accepted notion, it is at least startling to read that a National Industrial Conference Board study of the cost of living in 1919 and 1920 found that the higher cost of food, clothing, and sundries in the South offset the lower cost of shelter, so that it cost a southern family anywhere from one to three hundred dollars more a year to live, in the towns studied (Fall River and Lawrence, Mass., and Green-ville and Pelzer, South Carolina and Charlotte, North Carolina). Perhaps these figures are deceptive, because of the years or the manner in which they were gathered, but at worst they argue against any clear-cut lower cost of living in the South.

How was the poor white held in the thralldom of low wages, long hours, miserable health, illiteracy, and the gamut of conditions that led him to be called "trash"? By several factors: the always great abundance of labor; the fact that he had been lifted from the brink of starvation to a position perhaps an inch or two removed; the fact that life in the mill town was in its basic essentials a continuation of plantation life, with not only the exploitation but the paternalism thereby implied; and by the "race issue." The conditions of the mill worker were matched by those of his farming counterpart, and by a comparable situation for the entire South, which was an economic colony of the North.

Some have been tempted to compare the "industrial revolution" in the South with the industrial revolution in England. The differences are so great, however, that it is doubtful that the term can be applied sensibly to what took place in the South. The process in England was dynamic and pervasive, ultimately bringing forth an economy widely diversified in its production. Industrial England had arisen from a previously advanced commercial, financial, and efficient agricultural nation.

Compare the South. There a transition was made from a virtually one-crop agrarian economy to a virtually one-product industry embedded in a still heavily agrarian, backward society. Cotton textile production in England was but one step, and not the first step, in a long series, the upshot of which was to make England the industrial, political, financial, and military leader of the world. The South's industrial development was as lopsided as its agrarian development. The South did not become less, but more heavily dependent on outside capital. It did not develop a modern political system, but continued, even worsened, the nature and structure of political control of the ante-bellum period—minus whatever dignity might have been found in the earlier period. The South did not develop an empire on the basis of new-found strength; it became even more a colony of the North than it had been before the Civil War. Apart from its internal politics, the political position of the South in the nation was down, not up, from the earlier period. And so on.

How can all this be explained? I have already argued that the three elements of the southern past that were decisive in its development after the Civil War were cotton monoculture, the plantation, and Negro slavery. Here I believe it is necessary to bring the role of the Negro in the South more sharply into focus. For after all else is said, it was the treatment of the Negro, and his numbers, that led all in the South—whether powerful or weak—to behave in such a fashion that the South could not emerge from its economically desperate situation—until sucked out of its isolation by unprecedentedly powerful national and international developments.

V

What has been the role of the Negro in the South? Simply this: he was the basis of the southern labor system before the Civil War; he was, taken together with the land he worked, the wealth of that same South; owning him was the basis of the social prestige of the southern aristocracy; and the Negro's existence, last but by no means least, enabled the poor

white to feel somehow elevated. The Negro slave was the depth below
the depth. After the Civil War, the freeman remained the rock on which
the white's respectability was based. But the Negro was also part of the
enormous agricultural and industrial labor pool in the South. As such,
the economic competition of Negro and white kept both impoverished, and
ate away at the poor white's illusions of respectability—thereby intensifying
the race issue.

The Emancipation Proclamation transformed the legal status of the
Negro, without bringing in its wake a lasting change in the substantive
economic, political, and social life of the overwhelming majority of the
Negroes. Indeed, it has been the attempts of whites to prevent such
substantive changes that have given the Negro question its importance in
southern life, and have been so important in conditioning the entire
quality of southern development.

The profits of southern industry were dependent upon cheap and
abundant labor. The self-respect of the mass of southern whites was
dependent, to a critical degree, upon the existence of the underprivileged
and oppressed position of the Negro. The power of southern business and
political leaders rested on the creation and maintenance of the one-party
system, a post-bellum development in the South. The maintenance of the
South as an economic preserve of the North was dependent to an important
degree on the continued political sterility of the South in national affairs.
All these, of course, were interconnected.

The basic nature of the southern economy owes its origins to cash
cropping and the plantation system, with consequent weaknesses, stresses,
and backwardness. But the *prolongation* of this situation, in an area
contiguous to, and presumably part of, a nation that in the same period
outstripped the world in its economic development, rested on the dominance
of southern economic, political, and social affairs by the "race question."
Let me elaborate.

When, in the late 1880's and early 1890's American labor and farmers
heated to the boil that ultimately became Populism, they were joined by
workers and farmers in the South, where, indeed, the demands were
greater, the shouting more strident—for a while. Unions and farmers'
political groups would have been weak in the South in any event, given
the general surplus position of people in the South, and their isolation
and ignorance. But in the South, the shapers of public opinion—newspapers
and political leaders—had one weapon not available in the North: for the
underprivileged in the South to achieve success, white and Negro had to
combine forces. And when, for a short time, they did so, all the forces
of the southern race mythology were brought to bear. Protest dissolved,
and its place was taken by increased race violence, and continuing mass
impoverishment.

That impoverishment was itself another potent obstacle to the development of southern industry, of course, and one that needs no elaboration
here. Southern industrial and farm workers were a market for only the
barest of necessities, symbolized in the three M's: meat (i.e., sowbelly),
meal, and molasses. On the farm and in the town, the plantation tradition

dominated all, in the sense that a genuine money economy existed neither in the ante-bellum nor the post-bellum South. The planter had provided all; the landowner, or the supply merchant, and the mill owner provided all. And the "all" in neither period constituted a market sufficient to justify the growth of industry in the South.

What of the upper crust in the South? The middle class was stunted both before and after the Civil War, but that does not mean there was none. Rather, the *size* of the middle class necessary to provide the South with the enterprise and capital needed for balanced development was lacking. But a middle class existed, and it was its members who held both economic and political power. It was this group, made up of bankers, merchants, landowners, lawyers, speculators, and publicists, that fought for southern political autonomy and won it in the Compromise of 1877. It was this group that gave, as a *quid pro quo,* easy access to the natural riches of the South to those on the outside, a process that greatly furthered the economic domination of the South by the North. And it was this group whose political power was ultimately dependent upon the continuation of the one-party system. That meant the continuation of the Democratic Party as the white man's party: i.e., the single-minded focusing upon the race issue as the dominant and persistent issue in southern politics.

The North's role in this power play was to sacrifice what had remained of abolitionist idealism for the right to plunder the South, and to look the other way in the long decades after 1877 when the common principles of American government were violated.

The South got its railroads after 1877—one of its goals in the Compromise —but the price it paid was ownership and control by the North, and rates that fostered northern and inhibited southern development. The South, with the best natural location for a steel industry in the nation, saw its developed capacity in Birmingham brought up and restricted by U.S. Steel, in 1907, with the connivance of trust-buster Roosevelt.

The North gave up political control of the South; the South gave up political interference in the affairs of the nation, to keep political control of itself. For North and South alike this meant stability, for a genuinely democratic, represented South would dull the Gilded Age, and free the Negro and the poor whites.

VI

This paper began with the hope that a comparative treatment of West and South would enable us to shed some light on the manner in which institutions affect economic development. After one has pointed to the initial "emptiness" of the West, and the long history of cash crop monoculture in the South, there seem to be at least three general remarks worth making.

First, it may be noted that both West and South were short of capital, and thus had to rely on outsiders if investment was to take place. Both areas became, in some sense of the word, economic colonies. It is the difference in the "sense" as between West and South which is fundamental, however. For the West, "colonial" status meant that some of the cream was skimmed off; that is, had ownership and control been indigenous to the area, more of the income generated would have stayed in the area. For the South, "colonial" status meant that the cream was skimmed off, too; but it also meant that development there was seriously unbalanced.

The explanation for this difference leads to a second point. The West was exploited primarily because of the abundance of its physical resources. The South was exploited because of the abundance of its physical and its *human* resources. The individual and national advantages to be gained from exploiting the potentialities of the West—in cattle, timber, minerals, and grains—did not require a superabundant pool of labor. Moreover, those who went to the West—from further east, or Europe—were geared to social mobility and, obviously, geographic mobility. When times worsened for Westerners, some fell into tenancy, but more left for the Far West, returned to the East, or became migratory, i.e., hobo labor. There was no such geographical mobility of the abundant labor in the South. Not until World War I, the depression of the 1930's, and, particularly until World War II, does substantial geographic migration of Southerners take place. The poverty and indebtedness of whites and Negroes is one explanation for their immobility. But certainly of equal importance is the uniqueness that white Southerners attached to themselves—to leave the South would be to leave for another and an enemy country.

It seems to be undisputed that the major factor that attracted industry to the South was its cheap labor (which is not to overlook favorable resource factors). Cheap labor as a stimulus to industrial location may be counted as a favorable factor in the early stages of industrialization. But when cheapness takes on the overwhelming proportions it did in the South, it appears to act as a decisive obstacle to *balanced* development. For, under such conditions, the ability to attract industry becomes geared to the maintenance of general impoverishment.

There was, of course, a "crusade"—and so it was called—to attract capital in the South, particularly from the 1890's on. The crusade, from that day to this, self-consciously stressed the docility of southern workers, whether white or Negro. That docility can be explained in part by the abundance of the people, but a full explanation requires that the "race issue" be given its due. Terrorism must be added to explain the "docility" of Negroes; the doctrine of white supremacy and the associated lack of sustained focus on economic issues must be added to explain the economic docility of the whites.

Finally, one further difference between West and South may be drawn. Politically, the West was part of the nation; the South was not. The West was never a powerful political region in our history, but it has been listened to, and it has been part of the mainstream of American economic and social advancement. The West had no reason to become or remain a separate region; it had every reason to catch up with, to become *like* the rest of the nation, and to fight legislatively toward that end.

The South chose, both before and after the Civil War, to remain "another land." The South's participation in the political affairs of the nation has been more in the nature of keeping it apart from than of drawing it closer to the rest of the country—that is, the cardinal issue in the South, the issue that has absorbed its energies, its emotions, and its intellect, has been the negative one of maintaining a color caste society. But the ultimate price paid for the second-class citizenship of Negroes was the second-class status of the South in the nation. There is no reason to believe that the "price" will decline in the future; there is, however, some reason for believing that the willingness to pay the price is decreasing.

3] Stultifying Effects of Tradition

TRADITION AS A BARRIER TO PROGRESS: A SUMMARY

IN ITS recent advertisements, The Southern Company has declared: "The march has just begun! The last half of the twentieth century belongs to the South!" Whether or not such extravagant claims are possible of fulfillment is still unsettled. To the extent that the South still belongs to the nineteenth century, it must fail to make its full and wholly realizable claim to the twentieth. Let me attempt to summarize briefly here my previous analysis of those elements in the Southern tradition which have seriously impeded its economic progress.

In Chapter 2, I noted the effects of the dominant agrarian values in the Southern heritage. Early American tradition combined the philosophy of agrarianism with a strong spirit of progress. The South embraced agrarianism but, with its burgeoning system of slavery and plantation, lost interest in progress even with reference to agriculture. Increasingly, in ante-bellum days the South's dominant agrarianism took the form of a positive antagonism toward industrial-urban development as an inferior way of life. With defeat and Reconstruction, the South's agrarian philosophy first came into serious question, but the region's frenzied efforts to industrialize produced only modest results, so that the traditional agrarian values were ultimately reinforced and largely restored to a position of dominance. As a consequence, agrarianism impeded balanced and broadly based regional economic progress in the following ways: (1) It created an agrarian-oriented scale of social prestige, which has directed a disproportionate share of the South's indigenous capital into agricultural rather than business assets and too much of its superior human talent into nonbusiness fields. (2) It insulated the large planter from competing economic forces, which otherwise might have weakened his excessive social, political, and economic hold upon his local community. (3) It perpetuated a strong love of the land and outdoor life, which has discouraged human mobility and created a belief that Southerners are unsuited for the discipline of the factory system. (4) It made a tradition of leisure, which has discouraged economic enterprise on the part of the wealthy class and has produced, and even

FROM William H. Nicholls, *Southern Tradition and Regional Progress* (Chapel Hill: University of North Carolina Press, 1960), pp. 157–63.

given sanction to, laziness and lassitude on the part of poor whites and Negroes.

In Chapter 3, I considered at length the effects of the South's rigid social structure. The Revolution largely ended the tendency in America to take over the British system of large landholdings and a socio-politically dominant landed aristocracy. However, the British pattern, already firmly established in the Southern Tidewater in colonial days, became the model for a new planter aristocracy which waxed fat on the rich new combination of cotton, slavery, and plantation after 1800. The consequence was an environment unusually favorable to the perpetuation of a carefully stratified rural society in which first the Negro, and later the typical white, had his place. Whereas the rest of the United States largely rejected the aristocratic ideal derived from England, the South took it over as a major element in its value system. As in England, the new Southern aristocracy at its best accepted *noblesse oblige,* which made the social system sufficiently attractive to win rather general acceptance by the masses of yeoman farmers and poor whites.

The net effects of this rural social structure on regional economic progress were distinctly unfavorable for the following reasons: (1) The aristocratic ideal was seriously corrupted through its association with the positive defense of slavery before the Civil War and with white supremacy after the war. (2) The spirit of extreme individualism became increasingly dominant over *noblesse oblige,* so that the aristocrat increasingly held that his less fortunate neighbors were wholly responsible for themselves rather than being either his responsibility or a product of the social system. (3) There was an abnormal subordination of the Southern rural middle class, which was unable to contribute nearly as much to the democratization and economic development of its region as did its counterpart in the other American regions. (4) The South took on a backward-looking, pessimistic, and static outlook which was the natural product of its status society as the region emerged from the ordeal of military defeat. (5) The South's upper classes came to accept as normal and inevitable socio-economic arrangements based on a disproportionate number of low-income people, arrangements made tolerable to lower-income rural whites by a social structure which at least clearly supported their claims to superiority over the Negro race. (6) The relatively rigid, rural social substructure gave little ground to the development of Southern cities which, despite their more fluid social substructures and their growing urban middle classes, were handicapped by inadequate growth rates and a discriminatory political structure.

In Chapter 4, I emphasized the effects of the South's undemocratic political structure. We saw there how early interregional conflicts of economic interests over the tariff and slavery formed the political basis for the South's sectionalism and ultimately for the Civil War. During this period a relatively small minority of large slaveholders not only were able to persuade most of their white neighbors to take up arms in defense of slavery but also succeeded in defeating the threat of post-bellum agrarian radicalism by raising the battle-cry of white supremacy. The consequence was a monolithic political structure, based on the overriding end of maintaining white supremacy whatever the cost, which has seriously impeded regional economic progress in the following ways: (1) It embodied a blind sectionalism which has encouraged the trend toward coercive federalism instead of toward a healthy federalism under which the nation's resources might be used to promote greater regional balance in economic development. (2) It embraced a negative and defensive States' Rights doctrine which, too narrowly based on considerations of race, has offered a serious political impediment to much-needed federal grants-in-aid to the low-income South. (3) It was based upon a narrow electorate, reflecting not only restrictions on the suffrage of most Negroes and many whites but also low voter-participation rates attributable to a one-party system and the generally low educational and income status of much of the citizenry. (4) Consequently, it gave a disproportionate political influence to Black Belt whites relative to Negroes and low-income rural whites. (5) It insulated rural political leaders from the political counterforces of Southern industrial-urban development, because of the general failure of legislatures to reapportion legislative districts in response to radical rural-urban population shifts. (6) It perpetuated political control by a coalition of economic conservatives and racial extremists who continue to use racial antagonism as a means of maintaining the status quo against the liberalizing influences of the new social forces abroad in the South.

In Chapter 5, I examined the effects of the weakness of social responsibility in the Southern tradition, particularly as reflected in inadequate support for public-school education. Even before the Civil War, the development of public-school systems in the South was severely handicapped by the preference of the dominant planter class for private schools and the general view that public schools were "schools for paupers." Although Reconstruction brought a partial social revolution which for the first time established a sound basis for the public financing of common-school systems in the South, the indifference or even antagonism of the dominant socioeconomic class seriously inhibited the general advancement of public education. At the same time, the dominant class has allowed its self-interest in perpetuating a cheap labor supply to override any feeling of general social responsibility for the economic development of the local community.

This weakness of social responsibility on the part of the South's traditional socio-political leadership has been a formidable barrier to regional economic progress in several ways: (1) It has kept the masses of Southern people, white and Negro, in relative ignorance in a world in which knowledge and skills are increasingly the key to both personal and social betterment. (2) It has led responsible political leaders to propose abolition of public schools as a solution to the school-integration controversy, without regard for the educational needs of the vast majority of their people or for the effects on concurrent industrialization campaigns. (3) It has caused large planters and the managers of local low-wage industries to oppose measures to facilitate outmigration and local industrialization, despite the general community interests in such developments. (4) It has encouraged a continued belief that the South's low-income people are poor because they are innately inferior, rationalizing a policy of inaction toward the improvement of schools and other public services and the attainment of a more efficient and equitable social and economic organization. (5) It has resulted in a too-easy approval of the recent high outmigration rates by Southern Negroes, which, while undoubtedly contributing to an easing of racial tensions, must increasingly represent a substantial social loss—in terms of potential industrial labor force and prior public educational investments—to the states from which they migrate.

Finally, in Chapter 6, I discussed the intellectually debilitating effects of the Southern tradition of conformity of thought and behavior. The South's extreme cultural and ethnic homogeneity was transformed into strait-jacket conformity and intolerance of dissent, first by intersectional rivalry before the Civil War and later by solidification against the vindictive forces of the Reconstruction period. In rejecting Yankee thought and the Yankee mind, Southerners closed their minds on every other important social doctrine as well. The results were a general intolerance of intellectualism, an acceptance of violence as an ultimate weapon against nonconformity and dissent, and a corruption of higher education as it too increasingly repudiated innovation and novelty in thought and behavior. In all these respects, the Southern tradition of conformity has been a serious handicap to regional economic progress. (1) It created an environment hostile to the use of intellectual processes as a means to technological and social innovation and advancement, with consequent intellectual stagnation and the draining off of the South's best intellectual and industrial talent into other regions. (2) It gave public acceptance of, and often official sanction to, the use of violence as a means of enforcing conformity, even though an atmosphere of law and order is a fundamental condition for attracting industrial plants from other regions. (3) It seriously threatened both the academic freedom and the public-school base which are so vital to the development of great Southern universities and without which the South cannot attract and hold superior faculties, develop its own indigenous industrial and intellectual leaders, or provide the research and training facilities which are a prerequisite for sound and broadly based industrialization of the South.

. . . The South must choose between tradition and progress. It must choose because, as the above summation makes abundantly clear, Southern tradition has essential elements—its value system, social and political structure, weakness of social responsibility, intolerance of nonconformity and the intellectual process—which are irreconcilably at war with regional economic progress.

CONCLUSION

FOR MORE than one hundred years, men have argued about the economic impact of slavery. The reader who has followed the controversy through the pages of this book might be ready at this point to conclude that the problem defies solution. He will find little solace in knowing that he has only been introduced to the question and that the bibliography which follows will merely add to the controversy.

Yet, if definitive answers have not been found, it should be apparent that progress has been made in analyzing the problem. The first step toward a clearer understanding is to achieve precision of definition. Recognition that an investigation of the profitability of slavery must involve more than a consideration of slavery as a business enterprise is an indication that the first step has been taken.

This understanding should make it clear that slavery cannot be treated simply in economic terms. The sophisticated analytical tools available to the modern economist can teach us much about slavery—as they can about many other problems in economic history. But they cannot do the whole job. Slavery was an economic system influencing planters (both as investors and as masters), slaves, and nonslaveholders. Understanding the extent of this influence and the way in which it manifested itself requires more than the quantitative analyses of the economist. Only the historian, aided by the tools developed through related disciplines in the social sciences, can make the qualitative judgments required for a solution to the problem.

That historians continue to disagree among themselves is no sign that the search for an answer will be fruitless. Hopefully, each new investigation will provide new insights and, hence, a deeper knowledge. With this knowledge, students will be better able to evaluate and understand the economic impact of slavery on the South.

SUGGESTED READINGS

(Books and articles from which selections have been reprinted in this volume are not listed below.)

BUCK, PAUL H., "The Poor Whites of the Ante-Bellum South," *American Historical Review*, XXXI (October, 1925), 41–54.

CLARK, THOMAS D., *The Emerging South*. New York, 1961.

COLES, HARRY L., JR., "Some Notes on Slaveownership in Louisiana, 1850–1860," *Journal of Southern History*, IX (August, 1943), 381–94.

DAVIS, CHARLES F., *The Cotton Kingdom in Alabama*. Montgomery, 1939.

DOWD, DOUGLAS F., "The Economics of Slavery in the Ante Bellum South: A Comment," *Journal of Political Economy*, LXVI (October, 1958), 440–42.

ELKINS, STANLEY M., *Slavery*. Chicago, 1959.

EVANS, ROBERT, JR., "The Economics of American Negro Slavery, 1830–1860," Universities-National Bureau Committee for Economic Research, *Aspects of Labor Economics*, pp. 185–256, Princeton, N.J., 1962.

FITZHUGH, GEORGE, *Cannibals All! or, Slaves Without Masters*. Richmond, 1857.

FLANDERS, RALPH BETTS, *Plantation Slavery in Georgia*. Chapel Hill, 1933.

GENOVESE, EUGENE D., *The Political Economy of Slavery*. New York, 1965.

HILL, JAMES D., "Some Economic Aspects of Slavery, 1850–1860," *South Atlantic Quarterly*, XXVI (April, 1927), 161–77.

KETTELL, THOMAS PRENTICE, *Southern Wealth and Northern Profits*. New York, 1860.

MILLER, WILLIAM L., "A Note on the Importance of the Interstate Slave Trade of the Ante Bellum South," *Journal of Political Economy*, LXXIII (April, 1965), 181–87.

———, "J. E. Cairnes on the Economics of American Negro Slavery," *Southern Economic Journal*, XXX (April, 1964), 333–41.

———, "Slavery and the Population of the South," *Southern Economic Journal*, XXVIII (July, 1961), 46–54.

MOES, JOHN E., "The Absorption of Capital in Slave Labor in the Ante-Bellum South and Economic Growth," *American Journal of Economics and Sociology*, XX (October, 1961), 535–41.

OWSLEY, FRANK LAWRENCE, *Plain Folk of the Old South*. Baton Rouge, 1949.

PHILLIPS, ULRICH B., "The Decadence of the Plantation System," *Annals of the American Academy of Political and Social Science,* XXXV (January, 1910), 37–41.

———, "The Origin and Growth of the Southern Black Belts," *American Historical Review,* XI (July, 1906), 798–816.

———, "Plantations with Slave Labor and Free," *American Historical Review,* XXX (July, 1925), 738–53.

RUSSEL, ROBERT R., "The Economic History of Negro Slavery in the United States," *Agricultural History,* XI (October, 1937), 308–21.

SARAYDAR, EDWARD, "A Note on the Profitability of Ante Bellum Slavery," *Southern Economic Journal,* XXX (April, 1964), 325–32.

SMITH, ROBERT WORTHINGTON, "Was Slavery Unprofitable in the Ante-Bellum South?" *Agricultural History,* XX (January, 1946), 62–64.

STAMPP, KENNETH M., *The Peculiar Institution.* New York, 1956, Chapter ix, especially.

STONE, ALFRED HOLT, "The Negro and Agricultural Development," *Annals of the American Academy of Political and Social Science,* XXXV (January, 1910), 8–15.

———, "Some Problems of Southern Economic History," *American Historical Review,* XIII (July, 1908), 779–97.

STREET, JAMES H., *The New Revolution in the Cotton Economy.* Chapel Hill, 1957.

SUTCH, RICHARD, "The Profitability of Ante Bellum Slavery—Revisited," *Southern Economic Journal,* XXXI (April, 1965), 365–77. (See "Reply" by Edward Saraydar, *ibid.,* 377–83.)

TAYLOR, ROSER HOWARD, *Slaveholding in North Carolina: An Economic View.* Chapel Hill, 1926.

WEAVER, HERBERT, *Mississippi Farmers, 1850–1860.* Nashville, 1945.

WOODMAN, HAROLD D., "The Profitability of Slavery: A Historical Perennial," *Journal of Southern History,* XXIX (August, 1963), 303–25.